ALSO BY IRAD MALKIN

AUTHOR

Religion and Colonization in Ancient Greece. 1987.
Myth and Territory in the Spartan Mediterranean. 1994.

EDITOR

Mediterranean Cities: Historical Perspectives (with R. L. Hohlfelder). 1988.
La France et la Méditerranée. 1990.
Leaders and Leadership in Jewish and World History (with Zeev Tzahor). 1992.
Leaders and Masses in the Roman World: Studies in Honor of Zvi Yavetz (with Z. W. Rubinsohn). *Mnemosyne Supplementum* 139. 1995.
Ancient Perceptions of Greek Ethnicity (forthcoming).

The Returns of Odysseus

The Returns
of Odysseus

Colonization and Ethnicity

Irad Malkin

UNIVERSITY OF CALIFORNIA PRESS

Berkeley   Los Angeles   London

The publisher gratefully acknowledges the contributions provided by the Joan Palevsky Endowment in Classical Literature.

University of California Press
Berkeley and Los Angeles, California

University of California Press, Ltd.
London, England

Malkin, Irad.
    The returns of Odysseus : colonization and ethnicity / Irad
Malkin.
      p. cm.
    Includes bibliographical references (p. 275) and index.
    ISBN 0-520-21185-5 (cloth : alk. paper)
    1. Homer. Odyssey. 2. Odysseus (Greek mythology) in literature.
3. Epic poetry, Greek—History and criticism. 4. Trojan War—
Literature and the war. 5. Literature and society—Greece.
6. Greece—Social conditions. 7. Ethnicity in literature.
8. Colonies in literature. 9. Civilization, Homeric. 10. Heroes in
literature. I. Title
PA4167.M34 1998
883′01—DC21   98-4955
                                                CIP

Printed in the United States of America
9 8 7 6 5 4 3 2 1

For Tali and Noga

CONTENTS

MAPS

PREFACE

The question addressed in this book is how myths, especially what we know as Greek myths of the returns of Odysseus and other heroes, were used to mediate encounters and conceptualize ethnicity and group identity in the Archaic and Classical periods. The issue relates less to a binary model of Greeks and Others than to the intricate, sometimes hybrid, mutually reflecting world of exploration, contacts, colonization, and coexistence involving various Greeks and native populations. It concerns the historical function of such collective representations and traces the changing roles of mythic articulations through a whole spectrum of protocolonial perceptions, friendly mediating contacts, justification of expansion and annexation, and failure and decolonization. Odysseus of the *Odyssey* and Odysseus of its various alternatives looms large, first as a protocolonial, exploratory hero and then, along with other heroes returning from the Trojan War (Nostoi), in the world of Greek settlements in the Ionian, Adriatic, and Tyrrhenian Seas (roughly, northwestern Greece, Albania, and Italy). The Nostoi appear both in their various Greek functions and perspectives, and as the internalized and integrated heroes of others, such as Epirotes, Etruscans, and Romans, with the lines of articulating identities crisscrossing cultures.

This book is a third contribution to the study of the relationship between religion, myth, and society. As in my previous works the perspective belongs to the world of colonization, although the term itself has now been expanded beyond both the foundation of cities and the Greek perspective. This book builds on as well as departs from my earlier studies. In the past I have concentrated on the role of religion (Delphi, divination, foundation rites, sanctuaries, and the cult of the founder) and of myth in articulating attitudes to territory, especially in the world of Spartan colonization. From foundation acts and founders' cults and territorial myths I now turn to the mediation of encounters and ethnicity.

The introduction to this book presents both argument and methodology. Since the arguments of particular chapters can sometimes become rather intricate, at the risk of some repetition I have opted for identifying the main points in the introduction and restating them in the chapters' conclusions. This approach may be compared to the provision of both small- and large-scale maps. Before starting a journey through either the book or a particular chapter one may want to know its general contours and itineraries; to find one's way the more detailed maps will be needed. The first chapter presents some of my thoughts on how to understand the existence of myths "in the heads" of Greeks and others and therefore contains some observations on orality and iconography. Several Homeric questions have been relegated to an appendix.

I try to be consistent in transliterating Greek words and names, preferring Greek forms (Hekataios rather than Hecataeus, Metapontion rather than Metapontum). However, since so many of the myths connected with the Trojan Cycle have entered the Western literature and since the language of this book is English, I do turn to conventional usages for the sake of clarity (Corinth rather than Korinthos, Circe rather than Kirke). The English translations from the *Odyssey* are by Richmond Lattimore, with some adaptations when needed. Bibliographical references appear in the notes in an abbreviated form; except for items in lexica and encyclopedias and some epigraphical publications, the full references can be found in the bibliography at the end of the book. Abbreviations follow *L'année philologique*.

During the work on this book I have benefited from the help, criticism, and advice of many friends and colleagues. John Graham and David Asheri have given freely of their time to read all of the first draft. I owe special thanks to Catherine Morgan, who commented in great detail on chapters 2 through 4 and steered me away from some pitfalls. Conversation, correspondence, and readings of selected parts by other colleagues have proven to be of enormous help. I wish to acknowledge, in alphabetical order, the following: Bruno d'Agostino, Walter Donlan, Margalit Finkelberg, Aharon Frimerman, Erich Gruen, Jonathan Hall, François Hartog, Emily Kearns, François Lissarrague, Oswyn Murray, William Murray, Martin Ostwald, François de Polignac, Claude Rolley, Ronald Stroud, Benjamin Sass, Christianne Sourvinou-Inwood, Pierre Vidal-Naquet, and Froma Zeitlin. I owe special thanks to the Press's no-longer-anonymous readers, Carol Thomas and Ian Morris, whose comments were invaluable. I have lectured on matters related to this book on the University of California's campuses at Berkeley, Irvine, and Los Angeles and at the University of Pennsylvania, Princeton University, Stanford University, Washington University, and Tel Aviv University. I have also spoken of related matters in conferences in Ithaca, Naples, and Liège. I am grateful to those who invited me and to the participants who contributed to the discussion.

I thank especially Erich Gruen and the Graduate Group in Ancient History and Mediterranean Archaeology at the University of California at Berkeley, who extended their hospitality to me as a visiting scholar during the academic year of 1994–95. I thank also Maurice Aymard of the Maison de Sciences de l'Homme in Paris for sponsoring a stay in Paris during February 1996 as a guest scholar. Pierre Vidal-Naquet was so kind as to include me in his Seminar at the Ecole des Hautes Etudes en Sciences Sociales and to extend to me, as he has done several times in the past, the hospitality of the Centre Louis Gernet, of which he is the director. Members of the Centre, especially Catherine Darbo Peschanski, François Hartog, François Lissarague, François de Polignac, John Scheid, Pauline Schmitt Pantel, and Jaspar Svenbro, have been particularly helpful with their comments. Finally, I owe warm thanks to Marcel Detienne, for his advice and for arranging my participation in his seminar as a visiting professor at the Ecole Pratique des Hautes Etudes during February 1997. Finally, I thank Barbara Metzger for her perceptive and careful editing.

The research for this book was first supported by the Basic Research Foundation, administered by the Israeli Academy of Sciences and Humanities. During my stay in the United States I enjoyed the research support of the National Endowment for the Humanities, for which I am very grateful.

INTRODUCTION

Leaving behind the wondrous and terrible lands of the Beyond, unknown and unsought, a Nostos—a returning hero—came home to a familiar reality on the island of Ithaca. The return of Odysseus must have been on the minds of historical Greeks when they were sailing beyond Ithaca, past the point where the good Phaiakians landed the returning hero. From the ninth century B.C. on, Greeks sailed, explored, established guest-friendship (*xenia*) relations, raided, traded, and colonized on the coasts beyond Ithaca. These were real people, doing concrete things, observing coasts and populations in the Ionian, Adriatic, and Tyrrhenian Seas, but they perceived the reality that they encountered there through screens woven of both experience and myth. Myths, especially about the Nostoi—the returning heroes from the Trojan War—were projected onto new lands, articulating landscapes, genealogies, and ethnicities. Nostos myths provided cultural and ethnic mediation with non-Greeks and, once integrated, often came to provide the terms of self-perception for native populations.

Among the Nostoi Odysseus, perceived as someone who had once lived on this earth but who had also transcended it as a traveler *malgré lui,* held a special fascination for these explorers, traders, and colonists. Probably evoking primal fears of travel and exploration, Odysseus's transcendent travels were positioned in a clear dissonance: the practical destination of historical Greeks was not the terrible places Odysseus had been to. However, once past Ithaca, en route to Corcyra (Corfu), Epirus, or Italy, they probably perceived the direction of their sailing as precisely the reverse of Odysseus's return. Greeks were sailing in imagined space as well as, in the words of Michel de Certeau, *espace comme lieu pratiqué.*[1]

Odysseus was meaningful as a protocolonial hero to exploring Greeks as early as the ninth and the first half of the eighth century. The resourceful, persevering, self-made man was the appropriate hero for people who sailed away *and* expected to return. He was particularly evocative for individual traders or aristocrats, who took their chances and hoped for divine guidance and protection such as Athena gave Odysseus. Sailing experiences, the image of the traveling/returning hero, and Ithaca converged to create a powerful focus for articulating the protocolonial experience. After the mid-eighth century the coasts and islands of the Ionian, Adriatic, and Tyrrhenian Seas became areas of Greek colonization, and here special types of myths became "useful." The figures the Archaic Greeks used for site orientation and articulations of ethnicities, genealogies, and identities and often of cult were predominantly Nostoi. Their choice was not cynical and perhaps not even self-conscious, but it was a clear and consistent choice all the same, privileging a type of myth and a category of heroes for application to these areas of modern northwestern Greece, Albania, and southern Italy.

The pattern of Nostos identifications and articulations of genealogies and ethnicities in these areas overlaps with the historical record of Greek navigation and colonization in the Geometric and Archaic periods. Here, in contrast to the rest of the world of Greek exploration and colonization from the Black Sea to Africa and Spain, we see rather less of the ubiquitous culture hero Herakles or the Argonauts. Herakles, for example, was thought to have traversed Italy with a sacred herd of oxen; he became prominently associated as founder with Kroton, and his cult flourished at Taras. But this was a phenomenon not of the Archaic (roughly the eighth, seventh, and sixth centuries) but of the Classical period (the fifth century B.C.). In later centuries, particularly in the Hellenistic era (following the third century), a mishmash of erudite guesses and constructions drawn from the whole spectrum of Greek mythology was being grafted onto the countries of the west. In the Archaic period, however, it was the Nostoi who were used by both Greeks and local populations in an intricate web of cultic and cultural mediations and articulations.[2] The word *nostos,* possibly expressing at once a spatial dimension and the human undertakings, occurs already in the *Odyssey* itself, where it signifies both the action of returning and the hero who re-

---

1. De Certeau 1990: 170–91.

2. The Nostoi, of course, were not unique to the west: in Libya, for example, Menelaos served as an "opening hero," giving his name to the first port of landing of the Theran colonists in the middle of the seventh century. But Cyrene's explicit charter myth, that of the clod of Libyan soil given to the ancestor of the colony's founder, was associated rather with the Argonauts. See Malkin 1994a: chaps. 2, 6.

turns (hereafter the Nostos) and the story or song about him (henceforth italicized, *nostos*).[3]

The fifth-century Greek perception of the beginning of history, probably drawing on a long tradition of employing Nostoi as explanations of "origins," gave the Nostoi a special role. History began with the returns from Troy. Whereas the Trojan War itself was often regarded in ancient historiography as the inception of the human dimension of history (*spatium historicum*),[4] the war was perceived by Greeks as an exceptional, isolated, convergent pan-Hellenic action. But since there was no "Greece" in antiquity but only hundreds of discrete political communities, a particularized origin explanation was needed for each. The Nostoi were capable of particularizing history in a manner truer to the realities of Greek existence. The returns, as Thucydides's introduction illustrates, created revolutions, migrations, and foundings of new cities.

Aside from the function they sometimes shared with mythical progenitors who might explain the "birth" of peoples, the Nostoi also explained why peoples moved about. Thus they provided both for a "Greek" perspective (e.g., how Greeks came to Cyprus) and for the existence of distant, non-Greek peoples. Many Nostoi had to leave home altogether and migrate elsewhere, siring royal genealogies, establishing new settlements, and so on. The entire ethnography of the Mediterranean could be explained as originating from the Big Bang of the Trojan War and the consequent Nostos diffusion. In short, with the Nostoi things started moving.

The Nostoi provided an ethnographic model that must be distinguished from another kind of Greek ethnographic construct: that of the mass migrations in the age before the Trojan War. For example, such migration ethnography traced the origins of the Italian peoples to the migrations of Pelasgians, Arkadians, or Cretans. These mass migrations have no great Greek heroes at their heads; by contrast, the post-Troy foundations are prominently heroic and individual. The construct of the pre-Troy mass migrations seems to have been a relatively late development (not before the sixth century), explaining a situation existing before the arrival of Greeks in the west; by contrast, the post-Troy framework of the Nostoi was rather early.

ODYSSEUS AS A PROTOCOLONIAL HERO

The *Odyssey*'s characterization of Odysseus as *polytropos*, "of many turns," is apt for the varied roles played by this most prominent Nostos in the Archaic

3. This double meaning, as Gregory Nagy rightly observes, is current in Homer, signifying awareness of the genre of this kind of poetry. Nagy 1979: 97 n. 2; cf. 35–36.

4. Cf. Drews 1973: chap. 1. Ephoros (*FGrH* 70 T 1 T 8), for example, begins it with the return of the Herakleidai; the preoccupation with starting points may have begun with Hekataios (Fornara 1983: 6–7, 9).

and Classical periods. His myths, cults, and historical functions varied with the regions and peoples with which he was associated. Sometimes he was regarded as a progenitor of royal houses or entire peoples or as a city founder. For Ithaca he became the national hero, and Greeks sailing to (or past) Ithaca dedicated tripods at his seaside shrine. Because of who he was and where he came from, however, he seems to have been particularly evocative for the earlier (ninth- to mid-eighth-century) Greek protocolonists and thus may have been responsible for the dissemination of the pattern of *nostoi* to the west.

The return of Odysseus to Ithaca must be seen as markedly distinct from most return stories, and this difference will prove significant for the way in which the various Odysseus myths articulated exploration, contact with non-Greeks, ethnic definitions, trade, and colonization. Unlike other Nostoi, Odysseus had wandered in a fantastic geography. Other Nostoi founded cities and never returned home; such were the Nostoi of colonization. By contrast, the countries in the "stories told to Alkinoös" are vague and frightening and are set in the lands of the Beyond. Odysseus reached not the places that people wanted to know about but those that were better left Out There; meeting Scylla, Charybdis, the Sirens, and Circe was no one's ambition. What Odysseus reflects is the ambivalence implied in exploration and protocolonization: hope of discovering a magnificently rich land mixed with fear that its inhabitants might be Cyclopes.

Comparison with another type of protocolonial hero, Herakles, brings certain features specific to Odysseus into sharper relief. Both sometimes operate as civilizing heroes, opening new paths for men to follow. Herakles conquers Antaios in Libya, for example, and makes this rich country, till then inaccessible because of the visitor-slaying monster, finally suitable for human habitation. Most of Herakles's monster-slaying stories provide no political charter for colonization, since they specify no particular colonists, but in exceptional cases they may do that as well: when Herakles vanquishes Eryx in western Sicily, the land is placed in the hands of the inhabitants for safekeeping until one of his descendants comes to claim it (and the Spartan Dorieus, for example, does so).[5] Odysseus too opens new paths and rids humanity of dangers: in sailing where no one has sailed before he has silenced the Sirens (who, in late accounts, are said to have hurled themselves into the Tyrrhenian Sea). Again, the Phaiakians, having brought Odysseus safely to Ithaca, are punished by Poseidon; their ship is turned into a rock and their homeland shrouded in impenetrable mist. From "now on" no Greek colonist can expect to be saved by them. Human exploration and colonization begin when the Phaiakian option disappears.

5. On the Herakleid charter myth, see Malkin 1994a.

In contrast to Herakles, Odysseus fails miserably every time he encounters enemies on land; he succeeds only in saving his own skin, losing all his ships and every one of his men. He muses about the advisability of settling on the *empty* island (accessible only by ship) facing the Cyclopes, where he has no enemies, but when he encounters the Cyclops on the mainland he merely succeeds in getting away, blinding—but not killing—Polyphemos. With Herakles the story would have ended differently. In short, whereas Herakles opens up the land for settlement and sometimes provides a charter of legitimation, Odysseus opens up the sea. It is his perspective, from ship to land, that is the salient characteristic of the protocolonial hero.

THE QUESTION: MYTH AND HISTORY

The question raised in this book is how myths of Odysseus and other Nostoi were used to mediate encounters and conceptualize ethnicity and group identity and how such conceptualizations functioned historically, especially in the Archaic period. What matters here is the "active" role of myth in filtering, shaping, and mediating cultural and ethnic encounters. This role applies not only to Greeks projecting their images onto new lands but also to non-Greeks adopting Nostoi and sometimes internalizing and projecting back Greek concepts of their own identity. The question thus comprehends Greek views of non-Greeks, Greek views of other Greeks, and perceptions of native populations with regard to both themselves and Greeks. The discussion lies at the intersection of several paths of investigation, including the history and archaeology of Greek exploration and colonization, literary sources (including the *Odyssey* and fragments of the various sequels and other *nostos*-related material), iconography, sources relating to various aspects of religion and myth, and discussions of ethnicity.

We are concerned here with the function of myth in history. Rather than searching for the history behind the myth or examining the role of myth in ancient historiography, I treat myth as a mediating function resulting from and influencing encounters and colonization. "Representations," says Stephen Greenblatt, "are not only products but producers, capable of decisively altering the very forces that brought them into being."[6] The encounter between colonists and native populations creates what Richard White calls a "Middle Ground," an area in which both play roles according to what each side perceives to be the other's perception of itself. In time this role playing, the result of a kind of double mirror reflection, creates a civilization that is neither purely native nor entirely colonial-imported. According to changing circumstances each side will also come to emphasize certain

6. Greenblatt 1991: 6.

aspects of the image constructed of the other, either for the sake of mediation and coexistence or as justification of hostilities.[7]

The *nostoi* will be seen as mediators of cultural and ethnic encounters. In
some sense myth may be regarded as a desirable commodity. In trade the
success of commodities is not a simple matter of supply and demand, since
the desirability of objects can be culturally conditioned. In the early thirties,
for example, diamond magnates paid Hollywood to show young men giving
their beloveds diamond engagement rings, which quickly developed into a
status symbol and a "tradition." In antiquity something similar has been observed, for example, in the case of wine as a social drink implying all the associated symposiac and status-oriented paraphernalia. Asking himself what
the Greeks had to offer the peoples of the west, David Ridgway suggests
myth.[8] The one thing the latter did not have was the Trojan Cycle, adaptable
to an aristocratic heroic code and sufficiently flexible to articulate and ac-
commodate local genealogical and group identities. This approach should
be taken seriously; like other objects of trade, myths can be made desirable.

It will also be observed that the carriers of the Greek myths were not necessarily only Greek. To return to the analogy, when discussing items of trade
such as wine amphorae archaeologists invariably ask who their bearers were.
Corinthian or Athenian pottery, for example, was not necessarily exported
by Corinthians or Athenians. We will have occasion to observe others carrying Greek myths and perhaps influencing Greek perceptions of these myths.
In addition, internalized and integrated myths, probably including both genealogical notions and topographical identifications of Nostos itineraries,
may have been reflected back and picked up later by Greek erudites. At the
same time, not all myths carried by the Greeks themselves were necessarily
the result of colonization or some other organized activity. The role of individuals, both in forming guest-friendships with various elites and in settling among local populations (as farmers, potters, traders, and so on, called
katoikoi in some sources) will prove important, especially in the frontier regions of trade and settlement. In short, both Greek individuals and organized Greek political communities (whether mother cities or colonies) were
disseminating *nostoi,* projecting these onto new lands. Nostos articulations
should be seen as mutual, reflexive, and continuous.

In a general intellectual climate of nonessentialism and antipositivism
it may seem superfluous to defend an investigation based on the premise
that the Nostoi—mythic figures—functioned *in* history. However, since not
everyone shares this approach and since many of those who do share it confuse nonessentialism with disregard of hard facts instead of looking for the

7. White 1991.
8. Ridgway 1992: 138.

dynamism between that which "happens" (e.g., a shot fired in battle) and that which is continuously influenced by observation (who won the war), I wish to reiterate my way of approaching myth in history. I have little interest in myth as containing some kernel of truth, for example, considering whether the *nostoi* reflect actual Greek settlement. I am not saying that such questions lack value, but they usually apply to periods other than the ones that interest me. Instead, I would like to know, for example, what the concept of Odysseus meant to the Greek protocolonists and colonists or to the Etruscans who adopted Odysseus/Utuze, how the myth functioned, whether it was modified in the process, whether it was translated into cult, and, if so, whether the cult changed in significance over the centuries.

Nostoi were "historical myths." Today one is perhaps more accustomed to historical myths of a different sort—actual occurrences, such as Bastille Day or the Boston Tea Party, that for some reason are elevated to mythic stature. In contrast, preexisting Greek myths were often brought down to earth to function as historical ones. Their main figures were heroes living long ago in never-never land, but with exploration, contact, and settlement they came to be superimposed onto ethnic identities and territories. The reality of sailing experiences, trade, guest-friendships, raids, and colonization influenced the selection of and emphasis on evocative themes and myths. The *nostoi* and other myths functioning in history are not to be relegated to *histoire de mentalité* as distinguished from *histoire événementielle*. *Faits de mentalité* cannot be separated from faits accomplis; perceptions, concepts, and mythic images affect both intention and interpretation.

The *nostoi* mediated and informed cultural, ethnic, and political encounters among Greeks, in relation to non-Greeks, and in the relations of non-Greeks to Greeks. A historian of myth may wish to take such encounters into consideration, since mythic representations were informed by them; conversely, historians of events and hard facts will see that myth is more important than more conventional data precisely in their domain. I do not think I am being particularly original here; however, the persistent calls—for example, by Robert Parker, a prominent historian of Greek religion—for bringing history into religion and vice versa[9] highlight an existing gap.

VIABLE ARTICULATIONS

Translating mythical geography into concrete topography has always been an attractive occupation. By the sixth century, erudites such as the idiosyncratic Hekataios were providing "analytical" identifications for Greek myths as well

9. Parker 1996: introduction.

as laying the basis for some far-fetched modern generalizations about what the Greeks thought. However, erudite guesses such as those of Hekataios or the Hellenistic poets and scholars and early poetic impressions should not be lumped with functional cult sites of Nostoi and identifications probably stemming from non-Greeks who had internalized *nostoi.*

Ancient scholarly or even popular itinerary geography of the *Odyssey* will therefore not be a major concern in this book unless it can be shown that such identification became meaningful. One suspects that identifications of certain sites observed from a ship, such as Monte Circeo (Circe) or Corcyra = Phaiakia, began rather early. It is no accident, perhaps, that the *Odyssey*'s localizations of this type, mentioned in Hesiod, are in Campania, possibly the earliest area of Greek western contacts. However, Oswyn Murray has convincingly shown that Homer was not used in antiquity as the basis of the geographic knowledge of the west. The various site identifications (distinct from ethnicity articulations) belong, he argues, to a postfoundation era. Colonies started living their own histories and developed particular needs to familiarize points in the hinterland and render them somehow "Greek." By contrast, Murray suggests, the centers were, as it were, secure and needed less mythological articulation. Colonies had real founders who received cults after their deaths. Only later (not before the fifth century) did they acquire a taste for heroic figures and add heroic founders, such as Herakles Ktistes at Kroton (distinct from Myskellos, its human founder).[10] I shall disagree with this view to the extent that the term "identification" itself obscures composite and diachronic developments. Some identifications do, in fact, appear to have originated rather early, not in fact to serve geographical knowledge but to function in a context of coexistence and cultural mediation.

Genealogy may serve as an example of the relation between poetic or erudite identification and living reality. Quite early, probably by about 700 B.C., a Greek poet applied Nostos genealogy to peoples in Italy. The notion of Odysseus as the progenitor of rulers of the Etruscans would normally not be taken too seriously as reflecting commonly held opinions; it is basically no different from the claim that India was colonized by Herakles and Dionysos.[11] Unsubstantiated as these free-floating poetic or erudite articulations may at first appear, however, they sometimes acquire historical force, and when they do the "imagined community" of the ethnos or nation can be of far greater significance for self-definition and relations with others than any

10. Murray 1989. On the cult of the founder, see Malkin 1987a: pt. 2; on envy of the antiquity of the Greek mother cities as the cause for later invention of heroic founders, see Malkin 1994a: chap. 4.

11. Diod. 2.28–39; Strabo 3.171; Arrian *Indica* 5.8–9; 7.5; 8.4.

"objective" definition of race or primordial ethnicity.[12] Certain Greek stories of origins, notably the Trojan origins of nations, have been known to acquire the force of constitutive national identities and must therefore not be
dismissed as "merely" poetic. There is nothing inherent in the Greek story
of the Trojan Aeneas that would render it a story of the Trojan origins of
Rome, although by the time of Augustus it had certainly become precisely
that. This is a familiar example of the adoption of an element of someone
else's myth as one's own constitutive identity. In the Roman case the idea
caught on; in the Indian, Egyptian, or Persian cases it did not.

WHY "RETURNS"?

Both the *Odyssey* and its sequels are about the returns (in the plural) of Odysseus. The term "returns" will be justified here not only from the literary
point of view but also in terms of the function of the Nostoi in the world of
Greek exploration and colonization as heroes articulating and mediating
cultural and ethnic encounters. With some ambivalence, and perhaps because of it, the *returns* of the heroes came to articulate the consequences of
Greeks' *setting out* for the coasts of the west. The Nostos Odysseus never
stops returning, and the *Odyssey* echoes return stories of all kinds. Moreover, the alternative realities in the *Odyssey* conventionally known as the
"lying tales" tell not only of dissimulated identities but also of alternative
returns of Odysseus himself. Notably, instead of reaching an other-worldly
Phaiakia he reaches a very concrete one, where he declines the offer of Alkinoös and chooses to go to Epirote Thesprotia on his own to enrich himself
by collecting gifts. Phaiakia here loses its meta dimension and becomes simply a stop on the way to familiar Thesprotia.

   This alternative return may be important for those who want to recon-
struct an "original" *Odyssey,* and whether the protocolonial experience also
informed the composition of the *Odyssey* is a question that may be of interest to Homeric scholars. But this is not the point here. The issue is rather
the correspondence of such realistic itineraries to the Greek protocolonial
experience. Whether or not the *Odyssey* reflected this historical experience
(it probably did), I argue that it articulated it in poetic fashion to make
(Homeric) Odysseus at once a realistic protocolonial hero with contacts in
Epirus and a traveler to a frightening Beyond. By contrast, the non-Homeric
Odysseus of the sequels and most of the other Nostoi do not go to the Beyond
but overlap precisely with Odysseus's image in the reality-oriented lying
tales. Just as the other Nostoi will serve both Greek and native colonial functions, so will Odysseus: in Epirus and in Italy he sires royal lines and entire

12. Anderson 1983 and see below on ethnicity.

peoples; like other Greek Nostoi (such as Menelaos and Philoktetes) he is accompanied by a Trojan Nostos (Aeneas) and implicated in the foundation of a non-Greek city (Rome); and, like other Nostoi, he is integrated into non-Greek (e.g., Etruscan) myths in an independent role. In short, Odysseus should be viewed not in isolation but in conjunction with other Nostoi. Almost singularly a hero of protocolonization, together with other Nostoi he becomes also a hero of Greek settlement and non-Greek reception.

COLONIZATION AND PROTOCOLONIZATION

The book is concerned with a time span of about six centuries, from the ninth through the fourth century B.C., with emphasis on the Archaic period (especially from the second half of the eighth century to the sixth). Its geographic focus is defined from the maritime perspective that is the immediate context of both the protocolonial or exploratory period (ninth to mid-eighth century) and the colonization movement of Greeks in the west. In other words, the globe is rotated to place the Greek northwest and Italy in the center (map 1). Too many textbook and historical school maps divide the Mediterranean in two: from Greece to the east, from Italy to the west.[13] This book looks at them together.

Between the eleventh and the eighth century Greeks migrated and established settlements in the eastern Aegean and Asia Minor; between the second half of the eighth century and the sixth, they founded cities in what we know as mainland Greece (map 2), along the coasts of the Black Sea, and almost throughout the Mediterranean; colonization continued in the Classical period and intensified in the Hellenistic, reaching the east. Its causes, political character, and organization and the makeup of the bodies of settlers changed in the course of the centuries, but it seems to have remained a constant option for at least a thousand years.

Greek colonization in the west began with the foundation by the Euboians of Pithekoussai (ca. 750 or possibly 770), across from Campania in the Bay of Naples. It probably also began, as is suggested in this book (chap. 2), with that of Eretrian Corcyra (ca. 750) across from Epirus and, farther north, of Orikos on the Bay of Valona. From a Greek perspective it is somewhat difficult to characterize the preceding period under discussion, since the conventional terms are either too neutral (Geometric) or too loose (Dark Age). Terminology is especially important because I am arguing that Odysseus began as a hero of *proto*colonization and this term may seem improperly teleological—suggesting that Greeks who sailed to the west, say, in the last

---

13. I have done so myself (Malkin 1987a). The difficulty is not just technical (admittedly, it is hard to produce a book-size map of the entire Mediterranean at a useful scale) but also conceptual.

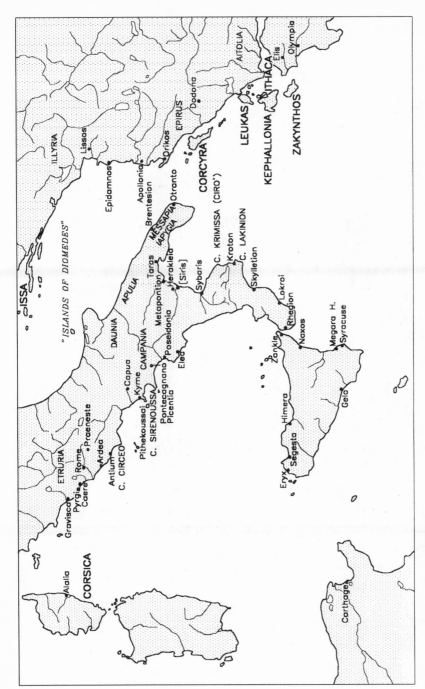

Map 1. Western Greece and Italy.

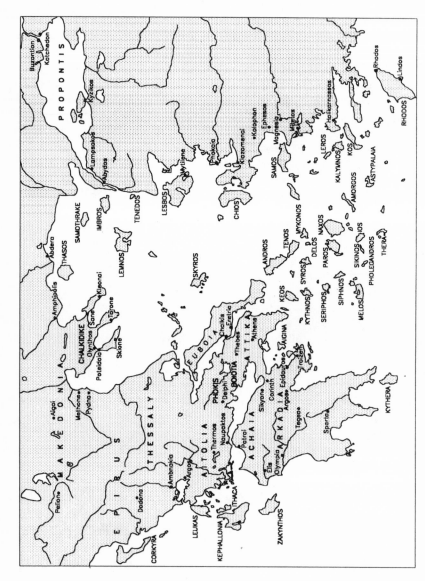

Map 2. The Greek mainland and the Aegean.

quarter of the ninth century knew that eventually they would also colonize it. (In fact, this is why I avoid the term "precolonization," which has come under criticism in international and local colloquia in Italy and France in particular). The term "exploration," which I occasionally use, may seem more convenient, since it can imply both geographical and human contacts, but it remains too broad to be generally useful.

Since much of the historian's work consists in shifting facts from a category of *post hoc* to one of *propter hoc* and vice versa, perhaps we may remind ourselves that in the case of "protocolonization" the hint of sequence and causality is not so self-evidently fallacious. Exploratory contacts may well have led Greeks to recognize the potential for colonization, just as the Age of Exploration in the late fifteenth and sixteenth centuries A.D. was closely connected with the colonization of the New World.

A more historically oriented consideration has to do with deconstructing the term "colonization" itself. The term is conventionally applied to the foundation of poleis (hence not earlier than the eighth century) resulting from the organized activity of a mother city (*metropolis*) under the leadership of an official founder (*oikistēs*). Thus it contrasts, for example, with the earlier Ionian migration resulting in the settlements in the eastern Aegean and Asia Minor; these were supposedly the results of a mass exodus and only gradually acquired the character of poleis. However, the distinction between post-eighth-century colonization in the west and earlier settlements is not as sharp as one might wish. First, Greek writers in later periods made no such distinction, using the terminology of colonization for the earlier periods. Second, it appears that the Greek settlements in the eastern Aegean were the result not of a single sweep but of a gradual process extending right down to the eighth century and consisting of both "internal" movements (e.g., within islands) and new overseas foundations.[14] Third, the polis nature of colonies after the mid-eighth century is not always clear; some would prefer to regard Pithekoussai, for example, as an emporium. Moreover, not all mother cities were poleis, and colonization may sometimes have been responsible for the consolidation of the political community of the city of origin; because of their *ex novo* character colonies provided models of more sophisticated political and social organization to be emulated in the older world.[15] Finally, the sites of the "migration" settlements in the eastern Aegean and those of the "colonial" world are of the same type. In both the sites were chosen from a maritime perspective (sea-to-shore): offshore islands, capes, and promontories defensible from the sea and facing a boundless hinterland.

14. Vanschoowinkel 1991.
15. Malkin 1994b.

Thucydides observes that the Greek cities that he considers of great antiquity were all situated inland for fear of raids from the sea; by contrast, the newer cities were settled from the sea, along the coast. Here he could be referring both to cities in Ionia (ca. 1000 B.C.) and to colonization from the mid-eighth century on (he makes no distinction between the two).[16] Somehow, Greeks were no longer afraid of the sea; they were sailing it themselves. There is a Homeric implication in all this. Sea raids are often mentioned in both the *Iliad* and the *Odyssey,* and historical sea raids are known independently: Ionians were raiding the coasts of the Levant in the seventh century, as the Assyrian texts testify.[17] Except for Phaiakia, most of the Greek cities in the *Iliad* and the *Odyssey* are inland ones, conforming to Thucydides's model. In fact, the foundation story (*ktisis*) of Phaiakia corresponds more closely to Ionian stories of mass exodus and relocation (pressure from the Cyclopes) than to that of Archaic colonization, in which mother cities were the norm. If this is not another case of deliberate "distancing" (always a possibility), the reality reflected in the *Odyssey* seems to be that of a world in which sea raids are still commonplace, most Greek cities are inland, and colonization has not yet taken place. Accordingly, Phaiakia is indeed modeled on Ionian sites in the eastern Mediterranean, but the realities of navigation in the west are those of the protocolonial period. The protocolonial aspect of the *Odyssey* evokes a situation of sailing *and returning* rather than sailing in order to settle overseas.

Therefore, in terms of practice and the nature of the sites chosen, if we disregard for the moment both the possibility of even earlier Mycenaean colonization and the polis issue, it would be wrong to dissociate the option of settlement from the minds of Greeks of the ninth and the first half of the eighth century, since settlement in that type of coastal and island site had been taking place in a world familiar to Greeks at least since the end of the eleventh. My point here is not to rewrite the history of Greek colonization but rather to justify the term "protocolonization": the possibility of finding a "land good to settle" (as Odysseus calls the offshore island facing the land of the hostile Cyclopes) had been a realistic option in the minds of protocolonial sailors throughout the Dark Age.

PERIPHERIES

It is from a protocolonial and "peripheral"[18] perspective that Ithaca may be regarded as the first concrete place to have been functionally identified

16. Thuc. 1.7.

17. Saggs 1963: 76–80 ("The people of the land Iauna have come. They made an attack on the city. . . ."). Cf. Brinkman 1989; Haider 1996.

18. The term is familiar, especially from contemporary "postcolonial" literary discourse (see the discussion in Ashcroft, Griffiths, and Tiffin 1995). Since "colonization"

with the *Odyssey*—that is, linked in the minds of Greeks sailing past it and in ritual with Odysseus. The *Odyssey*'s Ithaca is the limit, or periphery, of Homeric geography. "You yourselves, though you live apart (νόσφιν ἐόντες), have heard of Atreides," says Nestor to Telemachos,[19] and Athena says that Ithaca is "very far from any Achaian country."[20] "Above" Ithaca lies the great Beyond, whence the Phaiakians bring Odysseus back home. In the *Odyssey* it is the transition from Phaiakia to Ithaca that marks the return to the real world. Ithaca, apparently a prosperous and independently active community during the protocolonial period, was also precisely at the geographical point where departure or return could have been perceived as sailing in the wake of Odysseus. Greeks in the ninth and eighth centuries were sailing to a humanly explorable "beyond," opposed to the fantastic one of the *Odyssey*. Since Ithaca had always been identified in antiquity with Homeric Ithaca, it was the double role of the people of Ithaca themselves and those who stopped at Ithaca en route that made the identification viable.

Another intriguing fringe category that should emerge from this study concerns a rather consistent pattern of "peripheral" superimposition of myth onto peoples and territories. As a protocolonial hero Odysseus is particularly linked with articulations of ethnicity. It is indicative, for example, that in a passage at the end of the *Theogony* (chaps. 5 and 6) he appears as a progenitor of peoples (the Latins and the Wild Men) not identified with sites of direct contact—those facing Pithekoussai and Kyme in Campania (where the Euboians first settled)—but residing beyond the immediate Campanian horizons. The peripheral colonial perspective, distinguishable from the protocolonial one, concerns more direct links with the topography of the land. For example, Nestor, Philoktetes, Epeios, and Diomedes (chaps. 7 and 8) were almost never placed in the centers of Greek colonies; their localizations were frontier-related and peripheral. They will be seen as having functioned initially as mediators between Greek colonies and non-Greek populations and among some Greek cities.

The peripheral Nostoi do not for the most part seem to have justified or legitimated a priori the foundation of a colony as, for example, the foundation oracle of Herakleia Pontike, founded in the mid-sixth century, stipulated that the city be established around the tomb of the Argonaut Idmon. Instead, their peripheral sitings may have originated in a Greek wish to approach non-Greeks in ways that might flatter them (White's hybrid Middle

---

has become almost a technical term in the study of Greek settlements and since it has already caused enough confusion because of its similarity to "colonialism," I am afraid that using "postcolonial" terminology will confuse the issue even more. I do, however, share some of the concerns that have made "hybridity" a central issue.

19. *Od.* 3.193.
20. *Od.* 13.249: τήν περ τηλοῦ φασὶν Ἀχαιίδος ἔμμεναι αἴης.

Ground again); they may also have been the consequence of individual Greeks' moving or settling among non-Greeks in the frontier regions of colonies and establishing for themselves a Nostos cult. Independent relations with peripheral or hinterland peoples were especially important in view of the limited territories of the early colonies,[21] and the *nostoi* may have been an important cultural device of mediation. At the same time, these same sitings and Nostos cults would later (in the late sixth century) come to serve precisely as justifications for expansion, war, and annexation.

The peripheral Nostoi of colonization evoke for me the image of the robe of Nessos. Pierced by Herakles's arrow, the Centaur Nessos tells Deianeira to soak a robe in his blood and hide it from the rays of the sun. If she ever suspects Herakles of falling out of love with her she is to give him the robe and be assured of his devotion. When the day comes and Herakles arrives home from Euboia with the beautiful Iole, Deianeira presents him with the robe. Exposed to the light of day, it clings to Herakles's flesh and devours him. The *nostoi* too sometimes functioned as gifts of acculturation and mediation, but when exposed to the rays of expansionist ambitions these Nostoi robes would burn their wearers.

ANALOGIES AND DICHOTOMIES

Observing new worlds and new lands is a subject that is happily gaining popularity, especially with regard to the New World in the sixteenth century and the European discovery and colonization of Australia. Comparisons between ancient Greek colonization and the European exploration and settlement of the New World are not new. John Finley, for example, compares the *Odyssey*'s perception with that of Shakespeare's *Tempest*,[22] reflecting dim awareness of the New World with no interest in geographic precision. Combined with a general interest in the New World and a changing evaluation of it is the above-mentioned growing preoccupation with the image of the Other, applied to antiquity, for example, in the seminal study by François Hartog, *The Mirror of Herodotus*, or Edith Hall's *Inventing the Barbarians*. To what extent are these approaches and interests, relying especially on analogy, helpful in understanding the articulation through myth of Greek attitudes to the west?

At first glance analogies with the European discovery of the New World seem inviting; both Greek and European voyages and colonization involved encounters with foreign peoples, usually perceived through the filters of

21. See Whitehouse and Wilkins 1989 with Dench 1995: 31.
22. Finley 1978: 50.

the colonizer's mentality. In both cases alien lands and ethnographies were articulated in terms of the frame of reference of the beholder. The natives of the New World, some argue, seemed to the Spaniards "absolute others," and the world encountered was "new." However, the differences between the Greek and the Spanish situation are significant. First, there are important differences in point of departure.[23] Europeans observed the New World from a culture of the "center," setting out in new directions confident of their unquestionable superiority and—most significant—their monopoly over religious truth. Ancient Greek religion was totally unlike the revealed religion, monotheistic and exclusionary, professed by the Spanish. Its polytheistic and especially its polyheroic nature allowed instead for a comprehensive perception of humanity contradictory to the idea of an absolute other. As far as we know, Greeks assumed alien gods to have been the same as Greek ones, albeit with different names, rites, and representations. Unlike the Christian encounter with "heathens," Greek religion was a universal *langue,* the local names of the deities the distinctive *parole.* Thus, as we shall see, it was equally easy to attribute Greek heroic genealogy to Indians, Persians, Aiginetans, or Molossians, because what we call "Greek heroes" were not Greek but simply heroes.[24]

The notion of a superior center from which the world of colonization is viewed was almost certainly absent in the Archaic period. Long before Herodotus said so in the fifth century, Greeks were familiar with the highly developed and more ancient cultures of the east. Their own position was on the periphery. Their starting point was thus not a European center but a place between two worlds—the politically advanced Near East and the more backward Mediterranean and Black Sea areas. In the west and the north Greeks found populations either somewhat similar to them (Etruscans) or less developed technologically and politically. The Greek starting point of "place" was one of diffusion, not concentration. Not only were the Greeks not the most advanced civilization in the world, as the Spaniards seem to have felt they themselves were, and not only did they not have God and truth on their side but they did not come from the same place. The Greek place in the Archaic period consisted of difference. Aside from occupying ourselves with the observation of differences between "others" that seems to be the focus of so much intellectual discourse, we should look for a more sophisticated difference within a "same." For Greeks such observation would have come naturally, since, in contrast with the idea of Europe, which had already emerged by the Middle Ages,[25] the idea of "Greece" as a place did not exist in the Archaic period.

23. Cf. Greenblatt 1991: 123 on the decentered worldview of Herodotus.
24. Drews 1973: chap. 1.
25. Barnavi 1995.

Greeks were also very different among themselves in terms of the places they inhabited. The particular places from which Greeks set out to colonize—the "country" (not a polis) of Achaia or the individual mother city of Chalkis or Corinth—valued local rather than ethnic characteristics. Thus, for example, when mixed colonies (such as Sicilian Himera) had to decide on their *nomima* (calendar, social division, magistracies, rituals, and so on), the terms of their decision were not ethnic but city-oriented (such as "Chalkidian").[26]

Nor was there in the Archaic period a unified ethnic Greek image through the prism of which the ethnicities of others were articulated. As Jonathan Hall observes, before the fifth century the character of Greek ethnicity was "aggregate" rather than "oppositional"—the latter implying a unified entity demarcated against "others/barbarians." The easy-to-grasp dichotomy between self and other, Greek and barbarian, that has been so popular in the scholarship of the past twenty years becomes quite misleading when applied to the Archaic period. It belongs more properly to the fifth century, when, following the Persian Wars in the east and the wars with the Carthaginians, Etruscans, and various Italic populations in the west, a stronger sense of a victorious pan-Hellenism under siege emerged to encourage the identification of mythical Trojans as barbarians and historical "Greeks" as "not others." By contrast, in the Archaic period we will find no Greeks in the sense of self contrasted with non-Greeks as absolute others.[27] What we have instead is much more complex, mutually influential, socially stratified, poetically powerful and reality-shaping images and perceptions.

Aside from the place one departed from, the Greeks and the sixteenth-century Spaniards also differed in their conceptions of the place one reached. Greek colonization, especially after the second half of the eighth century, did not involve entire "worlds" as the papal bulls implied with regard to the division of the New World between Spain and Portugal. Colonization was conducted more in terms of points of settlement than in terms of a priori claims to vast and potentially bounded territorial spaces. Where such claims are manifest, as in the case of the seventh-century Cyrenaeans, who clearly saw all of "Libya" as their promised domain,[28] they have to do with an undefined potential beginning from a coastal demarcation.

Looking at the world not from a central, superior culture (itself imaginary though real to its perceivers) but from a multiplicity of points of observation and reference, one explored and colonized a world that seemed not absolutely other but probably more of the same. No one can even be sure

26. Thuc. 6.1–5.   28. Malkin 1994a: 169–74.
27. Cf. Dench 1995: 22.

to what extent (or whether) the populations in the northwest and in Italy were perceived in terms of contrast, as non-Greeks. They may have been regarded as *xenoi* (foreigners), as the Spartans continued to call the barbarians in the time of Herodotus.[29] The famous case of the "Scythians," whose staggering distance could make them useful for Herodotus to portray as absolutely other,[30] was exceptional and late (fifth-century). The nearer (some of them contiguous) lands reached by Greeks ("Greeks" is our term) in the ninth and eighth centuries were neither Scythia nor America. Distances, although relative to the technology of travel, still did not imply the complete unawareness and novelty of Columbus's time. Even if Mycenaean contacts with Italy had been forgotten by the ninth century, protocolonization involved not crossing unknown oceans but sailing farther along the same coasts (Epirus) or crossing to lands observable with the naked eye (Otranto). Some awareness of the existence of these lands and perhaps even a certain familiarity with the identity of their inhabitants surely existed.

We see, then, that to the extent that at some point in time Greeks perceived themselves in Homeric terms (there is no general Greek appellation in the *Iliad* and *Odyssey*), the term "foreign" may be misguided, since "difference" may not have been regarded at all in ethnic terms. Just as in "Greece," for example, there were autochthonous Arkadians (Greeks but outside the genealogy of the eponymous Hellen), "pre-Greek" Pelasgians (e.g., at Lemnos), and a mixture of Eteo- and Dorian Cretans, so too in the Greek colonial "new world" there were individual royal descendants of Odysseus (Epirus) and even entire descendant nations (Etruscans). I propose that, just as Greek ethnicity itself was aggregative, so too was that of the peoples encountered during the protocolonizing and colonizing periods. Perhaps the colonial situation accelerated oppositional developments, but it does not seem to have resulted in an overall Greek-barbarian opposition. In time, especially during the fifth century, when coalitions of Greeks fought Phoenicians and Etruscans in Sicily and Italy and Persians in Greece, the oppositional ethnic model took over.

Greenblatt wryly remarks that the conquistadors were enraged at the natives' lack of readiness to believe in their suffering god of love and saw it as a justification for killing them. By contrast, Greeks converted no one,[31] but readily promoted their heroes as the progenitors of the entire world. A Persian probably shrugged off an eponymous Perseus as his ancestor, but some of the Nostoi were so accepted in Epirus and Italy. By the sixth century, how-

29. Hdt. 9.11.2; cf. 9.55.2 with Hall 1989: 10.

30. Hartog 1988; cf. Cartledge 1993.

31. With the interesting exception of the cult of Artemis Ephesia, propagated by Massalia (see Malkin 1990d).

ever, the acceptance of Greek heroes could serve as the cause for war, proof that what Kroton, for example, was conquering was "Greek." The Spaniards fought the natives because supposedly they were not Christians like themselves; the Greeks might fight natives because they had become "Greek."

MYTH AS CHARTER

If historical analogies are false friends, the historian's Zeitgeist might be considered an enemy. Living in a country in which justification is part and parcel of one's identity, one comes to pay particular attention to arguments of legitimation, historical (a return to a national homeland), religious (God's "Promised Land"), socialist (building a new society), and national (preserving the nation and enabling it to fulfill its potential). I have always wondered to what extent Greek religion and mythology served as charters for colonization, but I have tried to confront my Zeitgeist as the background to my questions rather than the sum total of my answers. In general, I find that writers on antiquity use the term "justification" too loosely, applying it to almost any use of myth in the context of colonization. It is perfectly legitimate to claim that myths and cults were "used" as justification of either territorial appropriations or political domination as long as such uses are explicit. There is a world of difference between the explicit charter myth, such as the one Dorieus used for his claims in western Sicily (Herakles left there a city for his descendants, Dorieus being one of them) or that of Alexander the Molossian (a descendant of the Nostos Neoptolemos, claiming the legacy of Diomedes in Italy), and the "implied" justifications a modern scholar may claim for this or that historical context. In such cases, even if the implication seems reasonable, one will still need to fine-tune the definition of "justification" in order to employ it responsibly. Implied justification is a question, not an answer.

Not every use of myth in a political situation is irredentist, propagandistic, or cynical. François Jouan, for example, chooses as an epigraph for a paper read at a conference on myth and politics[32] a quotation from George Bernard Shaw's *The Man of Destiny* in which the playwright sums up British imperialism: "When he [the Englishman] wants a new market for his adulterated Manchester goods, he sends a missionary to teach the natives the Gospel of Peace. The natives kill the missionary; he flies to arms in defense of Christianity; fights for it; conquers for it; and takes the market as a reward from heaven." This seems to be the basic approach that underlies, for example, Lorenzo Braccesi's interesting thesis (chap. 8) that the *nostos* of Diomedes was used to justify Greek expansion in the Adriatic in a relatively late

---

32. Jouan 1990.

period. Since its initial role should be seen (I argue) rather in terms of proto-colonization, I shall have to disagree, unless what is meant by the term is some very general connection. Similarly, not every localization of an *Odyssey* scene is to be explained in terms of a territorial charter myth.

It is a mistake in my opinion to assume that most Greek colonies used myths for a priori justification of their foundation. The world of Spartan colonization, where this was indeed the case, was exceptional.[33] Religion, especially the Delphic oracle, did function a priori, providing a blanket sanction for colonization and the colony itself as the gift of Apollo; but Delphi's prophecies were contextualized, ad hoc oracles, not myths. Nor do the extant prophecies with some claim to authenticity mention mythic justifications.[34] The adaptation of myth (and sometimes of the cult of mythic figures) to the land was a more gradual and particularized process.

The offhand remarks that one finds about the role of the *Odyssey* in the "discourse" of colonization[35] can be quite misleading. Nothing that Odysseus does in the *Odyssey* even remotely resembles the foundation of a colony. All his travels are the exact opposite of a foundation story, and Homer is kind enough to provide us with a few of these (which modern historians may construe as echoes of actual colonization). Still, there are those who think, for example, that the *Iliad* and the *Odyssey* "legitimate" colonization[36] without asking how, when, for whom, and what is meant by legitimation. Does the blinding of Polyphemos constitute a justification for vanquishing and expelling natives? Possibly; but one would have to argue the case and to do so facing an inherent contradiction. It may appear counterintuitive, but it must be stated categorically that no Greek foundation story, a "collective representation" recounting the foundation of a *political* community, had ever done so in terms of vanquishing a monster.

COLLECTIVE REPRESENTATIONS AND MODERN SCHOLARSHIP

Too often the sources are silent, but the images of Odysseus, Diomedes, and others open the door to the thoughts and collective representations of those who are (for us) inarticulate explorers/settlers. Moreover, by showing that indigenous populations were receptive of the same Greek heroes they may give us insight into the attitudes of those peoples. But what are the terms of access to these collective representations?

Greek collective representations have been studied in the past generation especially in France, by scholars associated with Jean-Pierre Vernant, the

33. See Malkin 1994a.
34. Malkin 1987a: chap. 1.
35. Hall 1989: 47–50; cf. Dion 1977: 15 and Dench 1995: 37.
36. Hall 1989: 48.

founder of the Centre Louis Gernet (later under the directorship of Pierre Vidal-Naquet). From a different angle Stephen Greenblatt's New Historicism is now having increasing impact on the study of "cultural poetics" in ancient Greece. In my own work on Greek colonization I have always studied "representations" not as essentialist entities but in terms of their contextualized historical function and impact. The whole point of my work has been to combine positivistic history and the study of religion, myth, and cult, tracing their mutual influences as ongoing processes. For this approach to be valid, the implicit methodology requires assessment, at each point, of what its historical context was. Thus, for example, in my *Myth and Territory in the Spartan Mediterranean,* the charter myth of the return of the Herakleidai is studied at one point in terms of continuous validation of the Spartan royal houses, at another in terms of its impact on and use for legitimating the attempts of the Spartan Dorieus to settle in western Sicily at the end of the sixth century, at a third point in terms of its relationship to the religious festival of the Karneia, and at a fourth in relation to the Dorian invasion. Each historical context relativizes the overall assessment of the myth as a collective representation. The representation remains "collective," but its functions and appearances are multivalent and multiform. Representations are therefore to be viewed through a prism, allowing the same multiplane lens to observe several collective representations in different contexts.

Martin Nilsson, in *Cults, Myths, Oracles, and Politics in Ancient Greece,* comes close in some of his questions to mine, although he never meant to write more than a general essay without much attention to the colonial world and his concept of "politics" is, in my view, too narrowly intentionalist. The most impressive work on myth in the colonial world, comprehensively treating a relatively major area of Greek colonization (Italy and Sicily), is that of Jean Bérard. But Bérard (perhaps following his father, the Homerist Victor Bérard) adopts the "myth as history" approach, which explains cults identified with Greek heroes as necessarily originating in prehistorical (e.g., Mycenaean) contacts. As I have said, my approach may be considered "myth as history" only after having turned Bérard's on its head: I study myths as an integral part of the history of the period in which they were told. Studies of foundation stories such as those of Schmid, Gierth, and Prinz express a thematic concern that is sometimes quite useful for what I am attempting here. Other works on Greek religion will be discussed ad hoc; none, however, seems to devote comprehensive study to the function of religion and mythology as mediators between communities and lands.

There is one significant and welcome exception. The focus of Carol Dougherty's *The Poetics of Colonization: From City to Text in Ancient Greece* approaches some of my own interests. The book examines certain Greek representations of colonization mainly from a literary angle, in terms of their "emplotment" as "colonial narrative," which is "one of the ways the Greeks (as a culture) authorize their common past."[37] Dougherty's method involves creating a rather essentialist abstraction of "Greek culture" and making her points by freely drawing from sources from the Archaic, Classical, and Hellenistic periods as representing Greek cultural poetics. My own inclination is to contextualize explicit claims in the sources and only then to judge the validity of generalization. This is not just a question of the difference between a "literary" and a "historical" approach. If a *nostos* could serve a conciliatory and mediating function at one period and at another become a justification for conquest and annihilation, these are not the same "representation" even though the "myth" is the same. For example, to make a general point about "Greek" representations of founders of colonies as murderers (a point for which there is in fact a very small corpus), Dougherty adds "exiles" as a "variant" of murderers (although this equivalence requires special argumentation).[38] To add Battos, Cyrene's founder, to the list (Cyrene's foundation story is one of the best-attested and hence important to her case) she skips over the heads of Pindar, Herodotus, the text of the inscribed foundation decree of Cyrene, and even Callimachus, all of whom provide rich and detailed foundation stories that have nothing to do with either exile or murder. She chooses rather to adopt the version of Menekles of Barke, a second-century Hellenistic erudite, who by his own account merely guesses that Battos had to leave home because of civil strife. Dougherty is obviously right to claim that for Menekles that was indeed the relevant representation, but to treat this claim as a *collective,* Greek-cultural representation is questionable.

"Representation," in my view, is not a transparent concept, and what constitutes representation and what the relation is between explicit representations and implied ones need to be established. There are questions that need addressing, especially the interdependence of representations and historical contexts.[39] Representations change throughout the centuries. This also seems to be Greenblatt's view: representations are "engaged," "relational," "local," and "historically contingent." Only by examining this interdependence, asking perhaps also about the input of native populations, may one arrive at a sophisticated and multileveled approach.

I am uncomfortable with the modern scholar's predilection (Dougherty is not alone here) for inferring "representations" while disregarding well-attested explicit ones. It is curious, for example, that the explicit, often attested Greek choice to represent colonization as the result of Apollo's initiative is pushed aside in favor of inferences concerning "colonial ideology."

37. Dougherty 1993: 6.
38. Dougherty 1993: 35.

39. Greenblatt 1991: 12.

Terms such as "colonial ideology" need to be either attested in the sources or elicited from argued implications in a well-controlled context.

Finally, condensing various categories of myths runs the risk of generalizing about "ideology" when it is rather the difference between those categories that seems to matter. For example, to support Dougherty's claim that the myth of Apollo and the nymph Cyrene stands for the dominance of Greek culture over native culture[40] would require, first, showing that the concepts of "dominance" of "Greek culture" (or even just of "culture") and "native cultures" are valid in the context under discussion[41] and, second, demonstrating that the myth even belongs to a colonial discourse and, if so, to what aspect of that discourse. By contrast, Dougherty's approach becomes more sophisticated and convincing when she analyzes the work of specific authors, especially Pindar, or applies elements of folklore to what she describes as colonial discourse in order to elucidate its metaphors.

In sum, the major differences between Dougherty's cultural poetics and mine consist in my preference for historical (as well as archaeological and iconographical) contextualization from multiple perspectives and my rejection of essentialist abstractions.

CONTENT AND CONTOURS

Following a discussion of categories of myth, orality, and ethnicity (chap. 1), the context for the presence of Odysseus as a protocolonial hero is set in the second chapter by analyzing the sailing up, down, and around of Greeks in the Ionian Sea and part of the Adriatic. Ithaca figures both in the maritime routes of other Greeks and as an independent player. Archaeologically, as Catherine Morgan in particular has shown, Ithaca was not just on the way for others (the earliest Greek *xenia* inscription, for example, comes from its main sanctuary of Aetos) but precisely like the type of site that Greeks were colonizing in the west from the second half of the eighth century on. It was, in relation to the mainland, an offshore island, a point that the *Odyssey* too makes time and again. The pattern that emerges for Ithaca in the *Odyssey*

40. Apollo does not establish the nymph Cyrene as foundress as Dougherty claims— a point that is not carried by the meaning of *archepolis*.

41. The problem has been argued at length in several well-known and well-published conferences on Greek colonization. Dougherty has not confronted the work of the generation of scholars (writing mostly in French) on the question of *penser la cité* ("imagining the city"), which address the heart of the question of collective representations in ancient Greece. Similarly, her treatment of the research published in German on some of her issues (notably Schmid 1947; Gierth 1971; Prinz 1979) is cursory; nor does she confront the second part of Jean Bérard's work on Greek colonization (Bérard 1957), which deals exclusively with myth.

is familiar from other offshore situations: contacts, often hostile, with the mainland directly opposite and friendlier relations with the more distant (again, "peripheral") mainlands: Elis to the south and Thesprotia (Epirus), whose people were allies of the Ithacans, to the north. By the mid-eighth century actual colonization begins, and I offer a reconstructed history for Eretrian (Euboian) colonization on Corcyra (later identified by Greeks as Phaiakia, where a cult to Alkinoös was instituted) and much farther up the Epirote coast at Orikos on the Bay of Valona, facing Otranto in Italy, where significant finds have rewritten the story of Greek presence and contacts (Euboian and Corinthian) in these regions. The Greeks were not alone, and the Illyrians too seem to have been crisscrossing the straits, opening the possibility for others to have disseminated *nostoi*. The Euboians of Corcyra and Orikos (as well as the Corinthians) were contemporary with the Euboian settlers of Pithekoussai (in the Bay of Naples) who drank from the "Nestor cup," thus implying some awareness of the Trojan Cycle (chap. 5).

The first indication of the reception of Odysseus by Ithacans and others will appear to us (chap. 3) in a characteristic sailing site on the island of Ithaca, also perceived as the liminal point of Homeric geography. Sailing to the northwest, historical Greeks (not epic heroes) would have passed by the island and probably stopped at one significant place. In practical maritime terms this place was the only available harbor in the Ithaca-Kephallonia channel. It is a small, beautiful deep-water bay on Ithaca, Polis Bay, made famous by the discovery there of a seaside cave shrine in which magnificent bronze tripods were dedicated during the ninth and eighth centuries. This is also where local Ithacans and other Greeks worshiped Odysseus, and there are good reasons to believe that the dedication of the tripods emulated the hero's landing, familiar to us from the *Odyssey*.

In the Classical era Odysseus was undoubtedly Ithaca's "national" hero, appearing on its coins and explicitly as the object of cult. The evidence concerning this will prove important in the assessment of a Hellenistic inscription expressly identifying the cult of Odysseus at the cave of the tripods. I shall be arguing that the process of relating to Odysseus on a community level had started much earlier. But the Ithacan cult was not independent of an "international" dimension, and the context for the presence of expensive dedications at peripheral Polis Bay is to be explained in relation to maritime traffic. However, once the sailing routes through the Leukas channel had been politically secured, the Ithaca-Kephallonia channel was much less frequented, and people would no longer have found it necessary to stop at Polis Bay. No tripods seem to have been dedicated there after the seventh century. Ithaca illustrates, in sum, that the ninth and eighth centuries were a time of *convergence* of myth and history: exploration, protocolonization, the independent role and implied identity of the community of Ithaca, and the salient qualities of Odysseus both as a "local" Ithacan hero and as a proto-colonial, pan-Hellenic type.

The tripods themselves, combined with archaeological evidence of Greek contacts farther up the coast of Epirus (including modern Albania) and at Italian Otranto, imply a cult whose participants transcended locality. Euboians and Corinthians, either directly or through *xenia* relations with Ithacans, were also involved. Their participation seems to point to one of the earliest known cults to involve Greeks from abroad and of diverse "ethnic" lines (Corinthians were Dorians, the Euboians Ionians). Their dedications were made to a hero whose own story was pan-Hellenic: Odysseus was both an Ithacan and an Achaian. The cult community was therefore proto-pan-Hellenic.

In Epirus (chap. 4) it is the lying *tales* of Odysseus and the sequels to the *Odyssey* that matter. Odysseus's salient characteristic is neither protocolonial nor any longer that of the fantastic traveler. The superimposition of *nostoi* was a gradual process, beginning with the articulation of royal genealogies and implied ethnicities. Here neither the *Odyssey* nor its sequels provided charters of colonization. Rather, the "charters" were genealogical ones (especially for the Thesprotians, Molossians, and Chaones). The *Odyssey* itself artfully proposes alternative Thesprotian itineraries, and the prophecy of Tiresias opens the way for its sequels. Examining these against the yardstick of Tiresias's prophecy, it may be possible to determine which belong to a relatively early period and how they came to matter for the articulation of Epirote genealogies and ethnicity. The *Odyssey* reflects contacts and familiarity with Thesprotia, perhaps alluding to episodes of oral poetry relating specifically to the Greek northwest. These aspects may have made local aristocracies particularly receptive to *nostoi* and Nostos genealogies. The conspicuous absence in Epirus of Herakles, the archetypical progenitor, seems to indicate a historical situation of a particular adoption of Odysseus. In his Thesprotian, non-*Odyssey* story, Odysseus founds a city and an oracle, fights wars with the barbarian Brygi, helps the local king, and sires a royal line. Independent, Epirote traditions are apparent here.

Historical Ithaca, properly belonging to the region, may have been responsible for the appeal of Odysseus in Epirus (either directly or through contacts with other Greeks who stopped in Ithaca). The Epirotes themselves were probably drawn to Odysseus because of his Homeric status, associated with a nearby island (but not a too-familiar close neighbor), and translated his stories in human, genealogical, and political terms. Epirote rivalries too may have been partly responsible: Thesprotians, Molossians, and Chaones competed among themselves in claiming Nostos ancestry. The purpose of Epirote royal houses was probably not to Hellenize the ethnic origins of their peoples but to heroize those of their dynasties, and it will prove an interesting question to what degree such notions were extended in terms of ethnicity. Epirus, whose "Greekness" was debated in antiquity, could also claim a share in Hellenism through the Nostoi. When "objective" Epirote ethnicity, dependent, for example, on criteria of "language," "way of life," religion, and "lineage," is juxtaposed to the Nostos articulations of Epirote ethnicity, what emerges is ambiguities resulting not from some objective, primordial reality of ethnicity but from changing group definitions from the royal/ heroic to the comprehensive political.

As elsewhere, it is the fifth century that sees the emergence of "oppositional" definition of Hellenism. The people of Apollonia expressed this new attitude in a dedication at Olympia articulating their new conquests in Epirus in terms of Greek heroes fighting barbarian Trojans. It should be emphasized that the Greek-barbarian antithesis appears in connection not with Apollonia's foundation but with its subsequent, "peripheral" expansion at the expense of others. A pattern of challenge and response emerges: the greater the challenge of territorial expansion, the more explicit the charter myth.[42] This change in the "chemistry" of the myth, expressed from the perspective of the colonial newcomer, was not, however, mutually exclusive. The great Epirote houses continued to be proud of a double Nostos ancestry. For example, more than a century later, the mother of Alexander the Great, the Molossian princess Olympias, was happy to be a descendant of both Greek Neoptolemos and the Trojan Helenos.

After several generations the robe of Nessos is exposed to a different light. For Greeks sailing to Epirus, the *nostoi* begin by mediating perceptions and contacts with both the land and its inhabitants. They are adopted by its royal and aristocratic houses; the landscape itself becomes punctuated with sites associated with Odysseus's travels: a city is founded, an oracle established. With time (and with more recent Greek colonists) myth as justification emerges. It functions not a priori, with the inception of exploration and colonization, but at the end of the process, when territories have become "full" and any expansion means war.

Turning to the Tyrrhenian Sea, the Bay of Naples, and Campania (chaps. 5 and 6), I discuss the implications of the "Nestor cup" from Euboian Pithekoussai—a cup bearing a hexameter inscription from the last third of the eighth century that seems to allude either to a textual Homer or to a more general awareness of Trojan Cycle traditions. From this and other considerations I conclude that these Euboian Greeks had Homer (though not necessarily a textual Homer as we know it) "in their heads," a fact of far-reaching implications for contemporary Greek-Etruscan encounters in Italy.

Etruscans too, in time, adopted Odysseus in various roles. The process of *nostos* adaptation was neither Hellenocentrist nor one-sided, but the terms

---

42. This is a general claim I make in Malkin 1994a.

of the mythic discourse were Greek. Although not exclusive (Phoenicians too influenced Etruscans), Greek influence on the evolving Etruscan civilization was widely felt from the eighth century on. Acculturation took place mainly in Campania, where both were newcomers as either traders, settlers, or colonists. It was there that things such as the alphabet, symposiac lifestyle, and myth were probably transmitted. The Greeks involved were primarily the Euboians of Pithekoussai and Kyme, compatriots of the Euboians who were sailing past Ithaca to the Ionian and Adriatic Seas and contemporaries of Hesiod, who sang in Chalkis, one of the two Euboian mother cities. Odysseus was probably introduced to the Etruscans very early; it was a Euboian alphabet and a Euboian form of the name of Odysseus that were transmitted, and the imagery of the blinding of the Cyclops was current in seventh-century vase painting. Greek images and myths spread also through individual immigration of artisans and aristocrats.

In later centuries Odysseus was associated with particular Etruscan cities and received a founder's cult at Cortona. Sometimes he was cast as the reverse of Neleus, leader of the Ionian migration to Asia Minor: Odysseus leads the Etruscans from Lydia to the west. These too were Greek terms of reference, following the general pattern of Greek foundation stories and founder cults.

What was there in the framework of the Greek *nostoi* that made the peoples of the western Mediterranean particularly open to accepting them as "ethnic explanations" of their identity? The Trojan War and especially its aftermath reverberate in the western Mediterranean beyond the Middle Ages, when even invading peoples, assimilating to the civilization of the Mediterranean basin, took care to connect themselves with either Greek or Trojan Nostoi. Around A.D. 632 the Frankish king Dagobert proclaimed himself a descendant of Priam, the Homeric king of Troy.[43] Rome will have been responsible for much of that, but Rome, with its own Trojan origins, simply begs the question (chap. 6).

There is a danger, in a context of a modern, postcolonial academic discourse, of judging Greek myths of ethnic origins as cultural imperialism. Aside from the anachronism of the terms involved, what is "Greek" about Greek myths of ethnicity is in itself questionable. I have already remarked that Greek polytheism signified the gods and heroes could never be exclusively Greek. When, especially in the sixth century, worldwide genealogical schemes were developed connecting Greek heroic progenitors with most known civilizations and peoples, something fundamental was happening.

43. This has become a commonplace in histories of the Franks, notably those by Gregory of Tours and Fredegar; see *Monumenta Germaniae Historiae ii: Scriptores rerum Merovingicarum* (Hannover, 1888) 42.20; 45.15; 93.1; 94.25; 195–99; 241.20; 244.

If Persians, Indians, Epirotes, Iapygians, and many others could be descendants of the great progenitors of Greek mythology, then what was un-Greek about them? Greekness, often a modern construct rather than a viable concept in the pre-Classical period, becomes very much diluted: if everyone is Greek, then no one is.

In the Classical and Hellenistic eras, claims Elias Bickerman,[44] it was a sense of superiority of knowledge, the result of research, that allowed Greeks to disregard local claims about the origins of nations. Thucydides, for example, knew the "truth as it is found to be": the Sikans in Sicily had migrated from Iberia, even though they themselves claimed autochthony. What natives had to say about themselves mattered little; everyone had myths, but the Greeks succeeded in convincing others that their version was, as it were, scientific.

Perhaps responding to the same reflex of acquiescence that makes snobbery—that underrated historical force—so successful, peoples often accept the other's view of themselves. Arjun Appadurai suggests that it is particularly significant when one party convinces the other that to be valid and credible that other's past must be interdependent with its own. I suggest that it was the *nostos* frame of reference (with its flexible genealogies and widely applied heroic ethos) that provided such interdependence in the western Mediterranean. Powerful and beautiful, aristocratic and heroic, the Trojan Cycle and the Homeric epics afforded others a "full past."

Greek perceptions of Roman links with the Nostoi began, in my view, rather earlier than is commonly thought. Greeks were aware of Rome at the latest by the end of the sixth century, and they were also interested in foundation stories of other, non-Greek cities in Italy. The coupling of a Greek (Odysseus) and a Trojan (Aeneas) in the foundation of Rome has so troubled historians as to cause them to question the authenticity of the fifth-century source, Hellanikos, that reports it. However, this coupling actually provides the Odysseus-Aeneas foundation myth with a pre-fifth-century, "aggregative" aspect. Before the rise of the antithetical identification of Trojans as barbarians, the coupling of Greeks and Trojans was rather a consistent pattern: Menelaos and Antenor, Neoptolemos and Helenos, Philoktetes and Aigesthes, and others were supposed to have roamed the Mediterranean and founded cities. Eventually, when Romans came to articulate Rome's origins, they defined them in Greek terms (the Trojan Cycle) while distancing themselves from the Greek side as Trojans (a notion that was itself a fifth-century Greek emphasis). "Difference" (Greek/Roman) is yet again seen to be articulated within a "same" Greek mythological discourse.

44. Bickerman 1952.

Not only Rome but Greek cities too could be regarded as having Trojan origins. "Trojan" Siris, according to my reconstruction (chap. 7), affords us a fascinating glimpse of a Greek complex of ethnicity articulations that seem to have nothing to do with the identification of Trojans as non-Greeks. A colony of Kolophon in Asia Minor, Siris was violently founded apparently at the expense of a mixed Greek-native population. The violence is portrayed in the sources in terms similar to the destruction of Troy: in both cities the goddess averted her gaze. Siris's foundation involved sacrilege, a rare articulation of the foundation act in the world of Greek colonization; perhaps Mimnermos's characterization of Kolophon's own foundation as hubris was replicated in Siris, its Italian colony. Specifically, the fact that the native population probably included Greeks perhaps contributed to the sense of sacrilege and evoked the need for an articulation of "ethnic" difference *within* a "same," "Greek" population. The locals were Trojans, claiming to be far more ancient than the Ionian newcomers from Kolophon, but they were also different.

The Nostoi of colonization (chaps. 7 and 8) were perceived in terms of permanent settlement rather than of preliminary and exploratory contacts. Their stories seem to have developed not a priori but subsequent and consequent to settlement and colonization. But the Nostos articulations did not begin late: in certain cases they may have started within one to three generations after the establishment of Greek cities. The pattern was never simple and involved both Greeks and non-Greeks, major cities and frontier zones. For example, before reaching his home in Pylos Nestor was swept to the heel of Italy, and his Pylian followers became, in turn, the founders of Etruscan Pisa and of Greek Metapontion.

Originating probably with settlements in the frontier regions by small groups or individuals, the Nostos identifications apparently started as myths of cultural mediation, as well as posing some antiquity challenge to the new Greek colonies. The new colonies may indeed have welcomed such mediation. Proud of their recent history and their founders' cults, Greek colonies in the west only in the sixth or fifth centuries began to create for themselves a past as ancient as that of the old cities in Greece "proper." Thus the *nostoi* appear to have answered, simultaneously, the needs of Greek settlers in frontier regions, non-Greek populations, and the politically organized Greek colonies.

Finally, Diomedes (chap. 8) encapsulates every conceivable function of Nostoi, from the Greek protocolonial to non-Greek colonization, spanning the Archaic through the Roman period. No synoptic map pointing out sites "connected with" Diomedes in Italy can do him (or any other Nostos) justice, since each place came to have a Nostos attachment independently and in a different period. Hence I shall be arguing against a tendency to ascribe the attachments of myth and cult to a single appropriate circumstance, as if

Diomedes's exceptional presence in the Adriatic needed one sweeping explanation. Here is a hero whose *nostos* flatly contradicts the *Odyssey:* fleeing Argos, he sets off to Italy and quite early appears in a protocolonial, maritime, "offshore island" context; various traditions tell of the metamorphosis of his companions into birds; late traditions, probably belonging to the era of decolonization of the Greeks in Italy, make these birds hostile to barbarians and friendly to Greeks. In the north of the Adriatic, around river deltas (Timavo) and other points of inland and maritime convergence, his cult flourished. But Diomedes also represents powerless, ineffective colonization: cheated by the local king Daunos, Diomedes curses the land with sterility and the stones from the walls of Troy that he has used to mark the boundaries of his lost territories fly back of their own accord whenever the traitors move them. When Alexander the Molossian came to Italy in the fourth century, like Dorieus before him, he was claiming a legacy of Diomedes. However, these are fantasies of colonial frustration: curses, happy metamorphosis into birds of dead colonists, and a territorial charter fixed for eternity but with no one to realize its possession.

ONE

Contexts and Concepts

Much of this book will rest on the assumption that Greeks had the *nostoi* in their heads. I should try to explain what I mean by this, in what time-frames and contexts it is legitimate to infer this, and, especially, how I relate the spectrum of *nostos* imagery existing in texts (Homer and the sequels) and sometimes in pictures (iconography) to the *histoire de mentalité* of both Greeks and non-Greeks in the time span covered by this book.

Nostos mythology was shared by Greek society throughout the Archaic and Classical periods. It was a "generative" mythology, giving rise to stories, images, rituals, historiographical interpretation, and ethnic articulations. The *nostoi* were not just "stories"; they were "ideas" in the Greek sense, in which image and thought are condensed. Understanding myth involves, among other things, abandoning the idea of the monopoly of narrative and instead regarding myth, in the words of John Scheid and Jasper Svenbro, as a *concaténation des catégories*.[1] Thus, for example, the *myth* of Odysseus engendered not only the epic narrative of the *Odyssey* but also alternative versions and "sequels," pictorial images that remain available to us mostly through vase paintings and coins, and forms of cult expressed in dedications, annual offerings, and even games at historic Ithaca.[2] The categories (mostly) of story, image, and rite are surely interconnected but not necessarily in the form of a genealogical tree. Sometimes one can point to a direct cause-and-effect relationship, but often a parallel development can be traced. The myth

1. Scheid and Svenbro 1994: 10–11.
2. In later centuries we find other expressions of the great narrative themes in different kinds of poetry, such as that of Stesichoros (Burkert 1987: 50–52), Pindar (Nagy 1990), and the Dramatists.

of Odysseus was in the heads of poets and audiences, artists and viewers, explorers and colonizers, and members of the political community of Ithaca. The stability of the framework of the *nostoi* is remarkable. It operated from Archaic through Roman times, with different societies sharing, repeating, and adapting it. To the extent that myth, as an idea shared both synchronically and diachronically, serves as a filter through which societies explore and organize reality, the *nostoi* can be said to have generated articulations of cultural and ethnic encounters as well as the constitutive and foundational narratives of Greek cities.

This perspective is particularly important for appreciating the various expressions of the simultaneity of the *nostoi* while resisting the temptation to force them into some kind of hierarchic or chronological order. Homer's *Odyssey* and its alternative return myths—whether about Odysseus, Diomedes, Nestor, or any other Nostos—imply and presuppose each other in a way that provides insight into their effect upon the history of the Greeks in the period of exploration, trade, and colonization.

FLOATING RETURNS: WORDS AND IMAGES

The issue is the modes of coexistence of the various returns as well as the means of their dissemination, their relationship to the *Iliad* and *Odyssey*, with their implications and allusions, and their effect upon history. We can be relatively certain that by the seventh century the *Odyssey*, some of its alternative narratives,[3] and other *nostoi* already coexisted. The so-called Trojan Cycle preserves story patterns, motifs, and type-scenes that are "as Archaic as the material in the Homeric poems, to which they are related collaterally, rather than by descent," and its narratives "offer invaluable mutual perspective on the recombination of elements deriving from a common source in myth."[4] The extent to which this coexistence goes back to the ninth and eighth centuries (the earliest time frame of this study) will be discussed later. At this point I confine myself to a general statement that, if not the text as we know it, at least the *story* of the *Odyssey* and probably some of the *nostoi*, too, were already familiar by then, probably through a variety of media including tales and oral poems.[5]

Orality is important here in order to comprehend the modes of parallel existence and mutual implication of a whole range of *nostoi*, which repre-

3. Cf. Griffin 1987: 26–32.
4. Slatkin 1991: 14. Homer and the Cycle drew from a common stock; see Edwards 1990.
5. Ford (1992: 60) remarks that *kleos* (glory, renown) implies that "stories of heroes have descended through time in an oral tradition . . . but fame or tradition may also be handed down in other ways."

sent only one segment of a body of myths that were "in the air." The Homeric epics themselves indicate the familiarity to the audience of myths such as those of the *Argonautica* and the *Thebaïs*.[6] The eleventh book of the *Odyssey* alone expressly refers to the myths of Tyro and Poseidon, Antiope, Alkmene and Amphitryon, Oedipus, Herakles, Theseus, and others. The *Odyssey* also indicates awareness of its own alternatives: its sequels or alternative returns are either alluded to or expressly attested. By "allusion" I mean not specific verse allusions—a contested question among Homerists—but the more basic plot elements. For example, just as the bards Phemios and Demodokos refer to episodes outside the *Odyssey*, such as the Trojan horse or the return of the Achaians, the scene in the Underworld in which Tiresias prophesies to Odysseus about his further wanderings after his return to Ithaca alludes to a sequel story, also outside the *Odyssey*. In other words, the allusions are to episodes that from a narrative perspective either precede, coexist with, or follow the *Odyssey*. The sequels, of course, must not be regarded a priori as *neoteroi* (newer, late, or inferior)[7] merely because they follow in narrative time the story told in the *Odyssey*, just as the story of the Trojan horse (sung by Demodokos in the *Odyssey*) was not composed earlier than the *Odyssey* or the epos (presumably) of the *Argonautica* before either of these.

The implicit reliance of oral poems on previous knowledge of other stories further clarifies that certain narrative themes known to us only from sequels, such as the death of Odysseus, must have been contemporary with the *Odyssey*. Can one seriously believe that the *Odyssey* or episodes of it were sung to an audience completely indifferent to or ignorant of some version relating also the death of Odysseus? We know, for example, of a poem called *Telegony* (which recounts his death), composed by Eugammon of Cyrene in the middle of the sixth century; however, this does not mean that up to that point there was no epic song whose subject was the death of Odysseus. (Eugammon, incidentally, was said to have plagiarized a seventh-century poem [see chap. 4].) The *Telegony* was probably one more epic rendition of an earlier epos, following ancient story patterns, that in its turn also chose its theme from a broad spectrum of epic themes.

The example concerning the death of Odysseus highlights a further distinction about the coexistence of myths. This is a distinction between the articulated narrative and the coexisting untold one.[8] Unlike readers of a modern novel, audiences listening to the epics in the eighth century responded

6. Edwards 1990: 315.

7. For discussion of this term, developed by Aristarchos, see Severyns 1928: 31–61, 83–92.

8. This is a point restated and well developed by Slatkin 1991.

not only to what came from the lips of the bard but also to what he was silent about. The words of the poet echoed against what was known outside the framework of the particular poem he was singing. This commonplace observation is of the utmost significance for the appreciation of the Cycle. For example, when Demodokos "sings the Trojan horse" or Phemios "sings the sad return of the Achaians," the episodes resonate against the whole framework of Trojan and Nostos associations of the audiences in Phaiakia and Ithaca. They also resonate for the real-life audience listening to the bard singing about those bards' singing.[9]

The poetics of oral poetry, involving an interplay between the articulated and the untold with every scene reverberating against what remains in the background, not only reveals an interdependence of choice and exclusion but underlines the existence of that background of concurrently floating stories. Aristarchos in antiquity and some of the analysts of modern times, bent on dissecting before-and-after relationships of derivation, seem misguided with respect to this essential feature. There is, of course, no denying the existence of late creations and derivative influences, but this should not obscure the fact that ancient audiences knew various stories and their various alternatives. A bard must have been appreciated partly for his ability to justify his choice of theme—his selection from the spectrum. Would he sing Odysseus's further travels? Would he sing his death? Where would he begin and/or end the (already well-known) story? The audience must have been in suspense until the moment of the performance.

The audiences of the oral poets and bards studied by Parry and Lord in Yugoslavia cannot always tell where the bard will turn, what he will expand or condense, what elements he will include or exclude. On the one hand, since the basic narrative of the stories is usually known, whatever the bard says at any point foreshadows what comes next. On the other hand, because improvisation plays such a significant role in oral poetry, what Michael André Bernstein calls "sideshadowing" is of equal importance. Bernstein argues, in a different context, against an aesthetic of foregone conclusions in literature[10] and in favor of one in which all the options of narrative seem to be open at the same time. In spite of the traditional aspect of the epic narrative, the singer can choose at any given moment either to pick up another strand of the story or to incorporate another stock scene or—and here is the crux— to take the hero elsewhere.[11] For example, he can end the story at Ithaca, or

9. Cf. Doherty 1991; Ford 1992: 101–10.

10. Bernstein 1994.

11. Cf. Peradotto 1990: 59–93 on the "ends of the *Odyssey*," a mapping of the various "proximate" endings implicit in the text. Tiresias's prophecy, for example, is equivalent to the narrator's "grid of possibilities" (67). See also Katz 1991 (on aspects of indeterminacy in the *Odyssey* and esp. 12–19).

he can start it there and take the hero to Troy or Thesprotia or Crete or even Italy.[12] Although I shall later stress the singularity of the *Iliad* and the *Odyssey* in relation to other oral poems, it is important to note at this stage that to the extent that episodic oral poetry was performed (and it most probably was), sideshadowing and awareness of alternatives and sequels were essential features of its poetics.

Some of these issues of coexistence, mutual implication, and overlap are also apparent with vase painting. Although seemingly an oxymoron, the discussion of Greek paintings of epic scenes well illustrates the oral nature of the dissemination of Trojan themes. This is because one can point to a parallelism between the ways in which spoken narrative and painted images were received within a familiar frame of reference of both context and episodic detail.

Specialists in oral poetry often distinguish between a stock theme such as hero mounting a chariot and saying goodbye to wife/companions and a narrative-specific one. The bard may freely, it is claimed, fill in a stock scene with different heroic identities according to the needs of the poem he is composing. Thus Hektor mounting a chariot and saying goodbye to Andromache is a narrative-specific scene that uses the framework of the stock departure scene.

Similarly, historians of Greek art have classified painted scenes as either generic (or "general heroic") or narrative-specific (*Lebensbild* versus *Sagenbild*);[13] for example, a painting depicting a man holding the wrist of a woman and boarding a ship may represent a generic image of loving farewell, forceful kidnapping, or taking a female captive on board; conversely, it may be specifically Odysseus saying goodbye to Penelope, Theseus and Ariadne, or Paris taking Helen to Troy.[14] Without an inscription identifying the scene, its classification remains open-ended unless its salient features are beyond doubt, as in the case of the Trojan horse. Instead of this rigid classification, some art historians have emphasized the independence with which Greek artists worked.[15] Kannicht sensibly argues for an overlap, emphasizing the "reception" of the figurative scene: whereas the artist might have intended a generic scene, buyers of the piece might have perceived it as illustrating some

12. Cf. Ford 1992: 83: "The very form of epic poetry lends itself to infinite continuation . . . The sublime Muses in Homer intervene on a moment of stoppage."

13. See Kannicht 1982 for a convenient summary. Kannicht clarifies the implications of this distinction, although he is still thinking in terms of stemmata of derivation, an approach against which I shall be arguing.

14. Cf. Fittschen 1969: 51–60.

15. Stansbury-O'Donnell 1995.

specific narrative; conversely, although the artist had had something specific in mind, such as the capsizing of Odysseus's ship, his painting might have been perceived as depicting a generic drowning at sea.[16] In other words, the same (uninscribed) scene could have been interpreted as either narrative-specific or generic. The scenes drew upon a body of stock images shared by audiences, poets, and painters alike. Another approach introduces a category intermediate between the specific and the generic, essentially arguing for a narrative structure with such elements as a "succession of moments, action and consequences" and "indications of setting, progression of time, series of oppositions or contrasts in actions, a potential for interpolation."[17] Thus Snodgrass has developed the concept of the "generalized heroic" and Stansbury-O'Donnell that of "generic narrative." However, since many of the generic scenes (whether life-generic or narrative-generic) seem equivalent in content to the stock themes of oral poetry (funeral, farewell, ship capsizing, etc.), for my purposes here the difference between the two kinds of generic scenes is unimportant.

The significance of this equivalence for the question of orality and the Trojan Cycle is substantial. The paintings, as we have seen, depict either stock scenes (shipwreck, farewell, etc.) or very similar scenes that also have narrative-specific value. In addition, there are paintings, such as the Trojan horse, that even without inscriptions undoubtedly belong to the Trojan narrative. If we forget for the moment the insistence on derivation, we note a striking feature common to iconography and oral poetry: the stock *narrative theme,* coexisting with the 'stock theme' of the oralists. As we shall see, the importance of *themes* in oral poetry has been recognized since the investigations of Parry and Lord. However, oralists usually mean something less narrative-specific when they speak of themes. The assembly, the hero's farewell, the ambush, etc., are stock themes, often expressed poetically in stock scenes transferable from one narrative to another to which audiences are conditioned and responsive. The generic scenes of vase paintings may be regarded as the counterpart in iconography of oral poetry's stock themes. The narrative-specific pictures, in turn, may be seen as equivalent to the narrative-specific themes of oral poetry, such as the Trojan horse. This parallelism is highly significant for the appreciation of the Trojan Cycle, including, specifically, the *Odyssey,* its internally implied alternatives, its external sequels and alternatives, and myths about other Nostoi aside from Odysseus.

16. Kannicht 1982; cf. Isler 1973.

17. Stansbury-O'Donnell 1995: 324, 330, relying on Snodgrass (esp. 1987: 153, "a narrative content of some kind"); cf. Coldstream 1991.

The description of the Shield of Achilles in the *Iliad* is a good example:[18] on the Shield is depicted a raid; no name is attached to either the raiders or the site raided. The image of the raid (oral poetry's stock theme) is somehow floating in the mental frame of reference of the audience listening to the bard singing about the *picture* on the Shield (narrative-specific). The audience is expected to envision a generic scene: city and countryside are being raided. At the same time the audience is also identifying, specifically, the "vehicle": the shield of none other than Achilles, made by the god Hephaistos. Thus the generic theme (raid) and the narrative-specific (Shield of Achilles) coexist and overlap. The raid theme is repeated elsewhere in the epos, either potentially (Odysseus plans to compensate himself by raiding for the damage the suitors have inflicted on him) or as reported events: Odysseus raids the Kikones, Herakles raids Pylos, the Cretan Odysseus raids Egypt, and so on. The details of the description are similar to what we see on the shield, the impression equally pathetic and horrifying. In sum, the epos itself illustrates the acceptable overlap between the generic and the specific, between its expression in words or in pictures, and in relation to the frame of reference of an audience.

The majority of the identifiable, narrative-specific scenes on Greek vases illustrate subjects not from the *Iliad* and *Odyssey* but from the Trojan Cycle. Pictures on Archaic Greek vases depict themes related to Odysseus in particular and to the Trojan War and its aftermath in general.[19] It has often been observed that the specific subject matter of the *Iliad* and the *Odyssey* is not predominant, although the whole Trojan Cycle seems to stand out in relation to other myth cycles that Greeks in the early Archaic period chose to represent through paintings. Some pictures relate to "Trojan" stories that, although completely unknown to us, were obviously expected to be familiar. It is as if, at least from the mid-seventh century on, all the images, whether stock or narrative-specific, whether taken from the *Iliad* and *Odyssey* or from other Trojan poems, were floating together. What was expressed in art need not have been the direct result of an "influence" of a text of Homer;[20] instead it might have arisen from "a more variegated complex of Trojan themes"[21] transmitted in a variety of ways, including, possibly, bedtime stories for children (Plato's "lesser myths").[22] Both stock images and narrative-

18. So much has been said about the shield that one risks triggering a host of associations that may be beside the simple point raised here. Cf. Stansbury-O'Donnell 1995.

19. See bibliography in Touchefeu-Meynier, *LIMC*, s.v. "Odysseus." I thank François Lissarrague for help on questions of iconography.

20. Webster 1955.

21. Burkert 1987: 46.

22. Plato *Resp.* 377c with Graf 1993: 4; see Snodgrass 1979.

specific ones may be seen not in any *post hoc/propter hoc* relationship to any fixed text but in a parallel one, variously expressed in words, pictures, or both. This interrelation between Trojan themes and *nostoi* needs to be approached laterally rather than in the vein of Aristarchos. Once we accept the probability that major parts of the "Cycle" (itself a late misnomer) are not necessarily "younger" than the *Iliad* and the *Odyssey*,[23] the parallelism becomes meaningful. This general claim is still a long way from determining where particular stories circulated and when, but this issue will have to be addressed later with regard to particular episodes.

We note a wide-ranging variability that should be appreciated in itself rather than serving as an indication for or against the existence of certain fixed texts. Painters chose their subjects according to criteria not always comprehensible to us. There is much in the *Iliad,* the *Odyssey,* and what we know of the Cycle[24] that is never represented in paintings either in the Archaic or in the Classical period; perhaps more surprising, many motifs appear in iconography but not in any text. According to Fittschen's highly critical selection,[25] out of some ninety identifiable scenes in Late Geometric and early Archaic representations, about fifty relate to the Trojan myths. Of these only about nine are directly identifiable as illustrations of *Iliad* themes and some ten[26] as Cyclops-related (*Odyssey*) scenes. F. Brommer observes[27] that none of the eighteen persons killed by Odysseus in the *Iliad* is ever represented, nor are such major adventures in the *Odyssey* as the Lotophagoi, Charybdis, the Planktai, and the second visit to Circe. Also missing are what must have been famous scenes of the Cycle such as the killing of Palamedes by Odysseus and Diomedes (*Aithiopis*), the killing of Astyanax (*Ilioupersis*), and anything at all from the *Telegony.* By contrast, we find Diomedes killing someone whom Odysseus kills in the *Iliad.*

With regard to the *Odyssey,* the tables prepared by Touchefeu-Meynier and Brommer indicate a certain chronological pattern of popularity of themes. I repeat it somewhat hesitantly, since the corpus is rather small: a late-eighth-century oinochoe from Ithaca shows a male and a female each holding a curious plant; some have interpreted it as Odysseus and Circe holding the mysterious moly.[28] If acceptable (although the identification seems highly uncertain), this would be the earliest known narrative-specific *Odyssey-*

23. Edwards 1990.

24. Allen 1924: 42–50; Severyns 1928; Pfeiffer 1968: 73; cf. Schoeck 1961.

25. Fittschen 1969.

26. To the nine usually mentioned can now be added the beautiful mid-seventh-century pithos. *A passion for antiquities* 1994: 182–86. I thank Oliver Taplin for drawing my attention to this.

27. Brommer 1983.

28. Brommer 1983: 70–71, fig. 28 (Robertson 1948: 42 no. 163).

related scene. It may be particularly significant that it was found in Ithaca, belonging to a time when Greeks (mostly Euboians and, by this time, especially Corinthians) were sailing via Ithaca to the areas of commerce and colonization in the northwest and Italy. It also belongs to the time of one of the earliest hexameter inscriptions, also found in Ithaca, celebrating *xenia*,[29] and to that of some of the bronze tripods deposited in the cave of the nymphs at Polis Bay. However, except for this somewhat borderline identification, the Cyclops is the only *Odyssey* scene known from seventh-century painted vases.

Cyclops-related scenes, sometimes compressing various elements of the story, appear between 670 and 650, the Sirens ca. 600, Circe (aside from the moly vase) ca. 560. All the other motifs (the massacre of the suitors, Odysseus and Penelope, Nausikaa, Nekya, Eurikleia) belong to the fifth century. The case of Odysseus blinding the Cyclops is particularly telling.[30] Walter Burkert, among others, finds its identification with the Cyclopea of the ninth book of the *Odyssey* problematic: since it has been shown that the Cyclops is a common folk motif, its appearance on ten vases does not have to be linked with the *Odyssey*.[31] However, in my view the point is misguided: the generic blinding of *a* Cyclops (a folk motif) and the blinding of *the Cyclops Polyphemos* apparently coalesced at some point. A Greek of the mid-seventh century observing the Eleusis amphora or the Aristonothos krater (to refer to Burkert's examples) would have to have been particularly blinkered not to recognize them as depicting the narrative-specific *Odyssey* scene.[32] One can (and perhaps should) claim that the *Odyssey* too drew on the folk motif; however, whether both the *Odyssey*'s Cyclops scene and the vase paintings have their origins in folk motifs is beside the point. What matters is the seventh-century association that the painting evoked. That it did not evoke Polyphemos requires some very special pleading.[33]

29. Robb 1994: 49–52. See also chaps. 2 and 3.

30. Cf. Courbin 1955.

31. Burkert 1987; cf. Hackman 1904; Glen 1981; Calame 1977; Mondi 1983.

32. On the Aristonothos krater at Caere, see Ahlberg-Cornell 1992: 94–95; Shapiro 1994: 49–54; on the Euboian letters on the krater, see Jeffrey 1990: 239. See also chaps. 5 and 6.

33. See Snodgrass 1987: 140–41; cf. Shapiro 1994: 49–55. Even without inscriptions we can decide the matter by looking for unambiguous attributes of the *Odyssey*. The Eleusis amphora (ca. 670) shows Polyphemos with some interesting features: the Cyclops is sitting rather than lying down, the stake is driven into his eye horizontally rather than from the top, and he is holding in his hand the wine cup that Odysseus had offered him (earlier, in the *Odyssey*). The identifying features, especially the wine cup, are "textual details." The painter condenses the action and "quotes" the wine cup. On a Lakonian vase of the sixth century a third element is added: the wine cup is shown, and Polyphemos holds in each hand a leg of one of Odysseus's companions. At the same time the stake is also being driven into his eye(s).

Taste relating to subjects of pictures was probably different from that pertaining to oral poems, and this may explain the range of early representations. At the same time, it seems likely that when painters chose subjects unknown to us from extant poetry they expected viewers not to be ignorant of those subjects. An Odysseus riding a turtle must have corresponded to some tale of which we are ignorant. The painting did not *tell* a story, but it did remind observers of one. Whether one proceeded to tell it is another matter. Such images may be compared with icons on a computer screen: it is up to the user to decide whether to click on the icon and enter the story or let it remain there simply representing the myth. The image, then, appears as an *idea* of a story (in the sense of myth = idea mentioned above); its verbalization may but need not follow. Our problem is that when we click on Odysseus riding the turtle, our files are empty—but it is *our* problem, not that of the ancient observers. The familiar warning against arguments from silence may be reiterated: aside from the *Iliad* and the *Odyssey* all we have are brief summaries, late mythographies, and a handful of fragments. No other epics have survived, and one should be cautious in making general pronouncements about what we have as opposed to what we assume existed or did not exist in texts.

The iconographic familiarity with Trojan themes has been used to argue for—or against—the implication of the textuality of the Homeric epics. Those favoring the existence of actual texts of the *Iliad* and the *Odyssey* by 700 find comfort in the appearance of motifs "derived" from these poems; those arguing against it emphasize the paintings' independent origins, their variability, and the dangers of confusing generic pictures with narrative-specific ones. But variability in and of itself cannot be used to argue against fixity. By the fifth century, for example, there undoubtedly existed texts of Homer, but then too the written texts did not cause alternative stories and scenes to disappear. The phenomenon has similarly been observed for illustrations of Greek drama, although the issue of theater, itself a visual medium, is more complicated.[34] This variability indicates, first, the coexistence of floating images that I have been discussing and, second, that it is dubious methodology to argue for or against the existence of texts from pictures.

For my purposes the point of interest is that the *variability* of iconography, consistent from the Late Geometric through Roman times, indicates that fixed texts, improvised songs, and a wide spectrum of painted scenes could coexist even long after the so-called fixation of the epics. Therefore, no argument for the existence or nonexistence of fixed texts can rely on the evidence of variability. Just as orality persisted side by side with literacy, so did a variety of modes of expression of the Trojan themes. A second con-

34. Cf. Shapiro 1994: 124–82; Green 1994: 16–48; March 1989: 33–65.

clusion is that the notion of stemmata is misleading. Not everything is "derived" in an evolutionary sense: although in some cases there were surely derivative influences, we must not assume a priori relationships of before and after, cause and effect. One may picture a sky filled with balloon-ideas of the Trojan War from which artists—poets or painters—could pull whatever string struck their fancy, sometimes compressing, sometimes expanding stories and scenes.

To what extent may we still speak of oral poetry as responsible for creating a frame of reference within which both poets and painters operated? A study by Anthony Snodgrass comes close to an approach that places the representation of epic tradition in words and in pictures on much the same basis, although without taking the further step of integrating the implications of oral theory; in fact, he finds it necessary to exclude oral performances from the world of the painter.[35] This is an extreme position, but the main thrust of the argument is convincing: Snodgrass argues that we must rid ourselves of the notion of stemmata—the idea that the appearance of Trojan themes on Greek vases must have had epic poetry as its source. He advances the concept of "a great web of vernacular, orally-transmitted mythology . . . known to everyone of whatever level of education and which did not need to depend at all on epic poetry." Trojan themes could have been transmitted in the form of tales, even as bedtime stories for children, as well as in full-blown hexameter poetry. They were simply in the air. This clearheaded proposal makes perfect sense; however, it fails to account for the particular popularity of the Trojan themes in comparison with other well-known myths.

If, as most oralists will agree, bards would more often than not sing episodes rather than long epic poems, it is conceivable that they created a climate of response to certain popular scenes, such as the suicide of Ajax (not in the *Iliad* and only briefly mentioned in the *Odyssey*). Vase painters need not have heard a poet perform a poem about Ajax's suicide to know that this was a popular subject. But the question is not only how a painter *knew* of the stories; Snodgrass's idea of "vernacular mythology" is sufficient explanation for that. The question is also why painters considered that these *Trojan* stories would elicit a particular response from viewers or buyers of their vases. It was that response that was probably conditioned by and depended on the

35. Snodgrass 1980. In a later work (1987) Snodgrass insists on mutual exclusiveness, arguing that the assumption of "parallels between the painter and the epic poet, not just at the level of their general mentalities, but in terms of their interest in identical narrative subjects" is an approach that "must be judged to have failed." I cannot see what fault is to be found in "general mentalities" (specific narrative is something to be judged ad hoc).

deeper impression created by oral poems. In short, painters did not have to listen to bards; it was enough that they knew that others did.

The presence of the Trojan subject matter among pictorial representations of Greek myths is illustrated by the *Odyssey*'s bard Demodokos, who says in the eighth book of the *Odyssey* that "the fame of this song (οἴμη) at that time had reached broad heaven."[36] Moreover, these themes coexisted not just in vernacular mythology (which included Bellerophontes, Meleager, Jason, Herakles, and others) but also, as we have seen, in the form of episodic oral poetry related specifically to the Trojan Cycle. "Post-*Iliad*" events were popular as oral poems. This coexistence, as well as Homeric awareness of both post-*Iliad* and post-*Odyssey* developments, eventually led to the belief that it was "Homer" who was the author of all Troy-related epics.[37]

To sum up: Whether one starts with the texts and turns to iconography or vice versa, the general impression remains the same: the frame of reference of eighth- and seventh-century Greeks was informed by a world of images articulated in verse, story, or painting. These images should be understood as ideas in the sense suggested above: condensed, "icon" myths, as it were, expanded into narrative myth (epics), image myth (iconography), or even ritual myth (such as cults to Homeric heroes). This coincidence in itself is the major point to be noted. I emphasize it not in order to answer grand questions such as the origins of Greek narrative art or the existence of the *Iliad* and the *Odyssey* before a certain date. Rather, precisely because we are faced not with representations of the *Iliad* and the *Odyssey* but with a whole spectrum of Homeric scenes ("Homeric" in the sense understood by Greeks in the fifth century, including the so-called Trojan Cycle), we can be more confident of the availability of *nostoi* for the articulation of contemporary cultural and ethnic encounters. These brief comments open the way for questions such as what the various *nostoi* meant to Greeks sailing northwest from Ithaca to Epirus and Italy, how they could have influenced the cultural and ethnic rencontres implied in exploratory and trade contacts and, later, colonization, and to what extent we can identify them as early as the ninth and eighth centuries.

To answer such questions I should also confront some of the points raised in the flourishing discourse on orality and poetry. Again, my purpose is limited, as this is not a study of Homer, but some of the points concerning the reception of the *nostoi* may be relevant here. Orality is also directly relevant to the existence, dissemination, transmission, and historical function of

36. *Od.* 8.74, quoted by Kannicht 1982: 77 to make this particular point.
37. Cf. Burkert 1987: 45–48.

nostoi and to the understanding of the notion of alternative myths. It is also important for understanding a claim made later in this book (chap. 3) that the particular details of the climactic landing scene from the *Odyssey* (as we know it) was what prompted Greeks to dedicate tripods to Odysseus at Ithaca.

To begin with the latter: need one assume the existence of a textual Homer in order to claim that the details of landing scene (described in the thirteenth book of the *Odyssey*) were articulated in the dedications of the tripods at Ithaca? This is a moment of justifiable trepidation for any scholar of Greek antiquity, and the number of ingenious ways modern scholars have found to avoid pronouncing on the date of Homer is itself impressive. I therefore draw immediately two lines in the sand: the first is the proposition that the *Odyssey*, as we know it, existed in the ninth century. The second and more modest claim is that even if there was no monumental *Odyssey* so early, there was enough of its specific *story* to make its framework and some of its particular episodes meaningful to Greeks of that time. The role of Ithaca (the real, historical Ithaca) and that of the Greeks who landed there en route to the northwest and back will be better understood if particular, salient features of the *Odyssey* were at play. Both propositions concern not just the *Odyssey* but also its implied spectrum of other *nostoi*. The second proposition is, of course, safer, especially with regard to the commonly held view that the *Iliad* and the *Odyssey* were composed not before the mid-eighth century,[38] and for my purposes it should be sufficient. Oral poets, as we will see immediately, had specific stories (not just themes) in their heads. These must have included significant, detailed episodes—such as the climactic landing of Odysseus after twenty years of absence in Ithaca. Ultimately, we will never be certain; however, some of the elements of the discussion of orality and of the social world implied in the *Odyssey* will help us clarify the context in which *nostoi* functioned. However, since this is a book neither about Homer nor about "Homeric society," I will limit myself to several points raised in modern scholarship with direct implications for the (co)-existence and dissemination of the *nostoi*, including the alternatives and sequels of the *Odyssey*.

There is ample reason to accept the general claim of the oral character of the ancient epics, whether those attributed to Homer or the poems of the Cycle. Transmission, however, remains problematic, and the argument seems to concentrate on two issues: implications of literacy and the likelihood of the transmission of epic stories such as the particular story of the return of

38. And note the more current trend to place Homer in the seventh century (e.g., West 1995).

Odysseus to Ithaca relatively unchanged. The extent to which specific stories with particular attributes were in the heads of Greeks also depends on these questions.

With the general acknowledgment of the oral character of the Homeric poems the pendulum that, since the beginning of the Historical Age, has been swinging between notions of change and continuity, flux and fixity, started skipping erratically. For the literal- and textual-minded, the discovery of fluid improvisation and "composition-in-performance" was striking. Despite claims to the contrary by modern bards, oral transmission of "the same songs" has been shown almost never to preserve verbatim accuracy. Not only do bards not repeat older poems verbatim but they may change them to a significant degree while insisting that they are, in fact, singing the same traditional poems. Comparative studies extending to other kinds of oral transmission, such as memorized genealogies, seem to confirm the fluid aspect of orality. The principle of fluidity observed by the researcher but unacknowledged by the bard had been stated by Radlov long before Parry and Lord conducted their investigations in Yugoslavia: "Every capable singer always improvises his song for the presentation of the moment, so that he is never in the situation of reciting a song in precisely the same way twice. They do not believe that this improvisation constitutes an actual new composition."[39] Milman Parry and, in particular, Albert Lord have extended the principle of improvisation and fluidity to the extreme, regarding fixity, whether in the form of memorization or of writing, as virtually stifling orality. Herakleitos has won out yet again over Parmenides and for many still seems to have the upper hand.

In his numerous writings, especially in the seminal *Singer of Tales,* Lord has always been careful to remind his readers that the relationship between the Serbo-Croat bards and Homer is one of analogy. In his novel *Dossier H,* the modern Albanian writer Ismaïl Kadare plays with this warning: a provincial Albanian bureaucrat is charged with the task of assisting two foreign scholars who have come to his region to record bards and, recognizing an opportunity to rise above the obscurity of his situation, prompts the replacement of the analogy with a positivistic claim: dossier H (= Homer) is transformed into evidence that ancient Homer was, in fact, an Albanian.

A key issue of oral theory is that of theme, since it directly bears on the question of how much of the specific stories of the *Odyssey* and other *nostoi* Greeks could have known in the ninth and eighth centuries. In Lord's earlier writings, especially in *The Singer of Tales,* the emphasis is on the high degree of variation—creation and re-creation—and fixity is generally treated as a matter of form: the traditional medium provides for the exercise of cre-

39. Quoted by Foley 1988: 11 from Radlov 1885: xvi.

ative and original imagination within the limits of conventional narrative structure.[40] What is "traditional" and "conventional," therefore, is not primarily the story content or plot. At the same time, it is not claimed that an entirely new story is invented in every performance; on the contrary, bards often insist that they have learned their poems from their own masters. Thus the question of what is being transmitted becomes crucial for any attempt to regard oral poetry as a vehicle for transmitting myths and stories through the Dark Ages. This is where oral theory can sometimes become too vague for comfort: the question remains how close we can get to the idea of a particular content of a story as an element of fixity and continuity in oral poetry.

Of the three basic categories formulated by Ruth Finnegan for discussing oral poetry—communication, composition, and transmission[41]—the third is the most significant for claims regarding knowledge of the particular story of the *Odyssey* as early as the ninth century. The emphasis of both Parry and Lord on composition-in-performance and improvisation has tended to overshadow the narrative content of transmission. The material of oral poetry was essentially stock formulae, set themes, and traditional language; the channels of transmission have been regarded as formal, more emphasis being placed on traditional and conventional narrative structures and themes and on generic narrative images than on specific stories.

The term "theme," which usually connotes content rather than form, is used somewhat differently by Lord. In 1951 Lord defined theme rather vaguely as "a recurring element of narration or description in traditional oral poetry."[42] In the fourth chapter of *The Singer of Tales* "themes" appear as an element of "narrative grammar." Themes are characterized by groupings of ideas rather than words, a structure that allows compression, digression, or enrichment. Examples of themes, as noted above, are assembly, arming of the warrior, storming of a city, and so on. For Lord a theme is an "idea" (his term), not a "story." "Idea," with Lord, seems to function close to its semantic meaning of an image or picture, and if contemporary oralists prefer the term "type-scene" to Lord's "theme," it may be because the latter seems too close to the signification of "content."[43]

Themes thus join formulae and traditional language as elements of fixity. But what about the story contents? Do these have no fixity in transmission? In an article entitled "Memory, Fixity, and Genre in Oral Traditional Poetries," published almost twenty years after *The Singer of Tales,* Lord maintains that the bard neither memorizes his lines nor freely improvises but instead

40. See Lord 1953.
41. Finnegan 1977: 16–24; cf. Jensen 1980: 26.
42. Lord 1951: 73.
43. For a balanced discussion of type-scenes and their significance, see Reece 1993.

remembers "the essential 'ideas' rather than the exact verbal expression . . . then renders the song in the special language of the tradition." So far this is vintage Lord. But he then goes on to claim that the result is that versions of the same idea have a distinct verbal correspondence that identifies them as "the same" even if a line or a scene is not repeated verbatim. "This, then, is the kind of fixity one would be led to expect in poetry composed in the traditional style."[44] In this late article Lord seems to take a long step away from the original meaning of "idea." Its meaning is now much closer to an actual story or, perhaps, to what I have suggested in the beginning.[45] If not only the narrative structure but also a variation of verbal correspondence around the theme sung is fixed, how different is this from a "story"? In other words, if the notion of flux is to be maintained, a theme must be not narrative itself but only a grammatical unit, a type-scene, within a narrative structure. But we have just seen that in addition to the generic theme (as with the type-scenes in vase painting) there is also the basic framework of stories of the great myths. Lord too does not believe that stories and myths were invented out of whole cloth in each composition-in-performance. The stories were myths, traditional tales, collectively familiar.[46] A singer would probably be asked to "sing the return of Odysseus." According to the oralists he probably improvised and changed; according to others he may have been more loyal to an idea of repetition, following memorized poems or great passages.

The rather vague term "tradition" seems to mediate in oral theory between fluidity and consistency, since it seems to function as another vehicle of narrative fixity. Lord comes close to saying this when he argues, for example, that "the term of greater significance is *traditional*. Oral tells us 'how,' but traditional tells us 'what,' and even more, 'of what kind' and 'of what force.'[47] When we know how a song is built, we also know that its building blocks *must* be of great age. For it is of the *necessary* nature of tradition that it seeks to maintain stability, that it preserve itself." Lord is speaking here not only about the conventions of telling but also about content. But if narrative—specific narrative—is also traditional, then the fluid stream of com-

44. Quoted by Foley 1988: 52.

45. See above, following Scheid and Svenbro 1994; cf. Nagy 1992: 27 regarding themes as "basic units of contents."

46. Lord is of course aware of this: "We must distinguish, then, two concepts of song in oral poetry. One is the general idea of a story, which we use when we speak in larger terms, for example, of the wedding of Smailagic Meho, which actually includes all singing of it. The other concept of song is that of a particular performance or text, such as Avdo Mededovic's song, 'The Wedding of Smailagic Meho,' dictated during the month of July, 1935." Lord 1960: 100.

47. Lord 1960: 220.

position-in-performance should be perceived as conveying logs of fixed, "stable" narrative units.

For the purpose of this book these narrative building blocks are what matters. Once their existence is accepted, without yet a commitment to a finished, fixed text, then at least one of the two propositions mentioned above seems justified: the returns of Odysseus and other *nostoi* may be regarded as coexisting, floating down the river of oral poetry to the Archaic period.

It must be made clear that I have no argument with the notion of the generic type-scene in oral poetry (or in iconography). Rather, I wish to emphasize that type cannot freely replace content (a point not always considered obvious). What matters for the purpose of this argument is that it would have been the *story* of Odysseus—not just any Nostos returning to any home but Odysseus coming home to Ithaca—that was repeated. Troy and Mycenae are not interchangeable: it must always be Troy that is destroyed and Hektor dying, not just any city and its prince. Priam cannot be replaced by Agamemnon or Odysseus by Achilles. Without Odysseus and Ithaca there is no *Odyssey*. Hence the narrative content of the theme is part and parcel of what is being transmitted orally. Homer too, monumentally transcending other bards, must have been restricted in his choice of narrative episodes to a limited range of frameworks. The poet could choose, perhaps, to make the wrath of Achilles the central, organizing theme of the *Iliad*,[48] but his selection had to be made not just from any range of stock themes but from the narrative-specific episodes around the war at Troy.

The cloudy terms "tradition" and "traditional"[49] too often obscure rather than reveal. Tradition seems to make it possible for the extremism of fluidity and that of fixity to appear together without creating useful categories. My own inclination is to consider tradition as narrative-oriented, perhaps in line with the famous Nilsson thesis that, I think, has not yet been refuted. The origins of Greek mythology, claims Nilsson, are Mycenaean, because the geographical centers of that mythology themselves were particularly significant during the Mycenaean era whereas some, such as Mycenae itself, sank into obscurity in the Archaic and Classical periods. The school of Emily Vermeule[50] basically follows Nilsson, sometimes going farther in time into the ancient Bronze Age Aegean. Again, I shall not argue this here, as this is not the issue at hand. Rather, I mention the continuity thesis in order to enlarge the context of appreciation of the narrative context within which bards gave expression to their creative individuality, singing episodes of the returns

48. See Ford 1992: 60.   50. See Carter and Morris 1995.
49. See Lenclud 1994.

and, in the case of one of them, monumentally transcending all others and creating the *Odyssey*.

The tension between fixity and fluidity, between transmission and improvisation, problematizes the lines in the sand mentioned above: that there was enough narrative detail of the *Odyssey* to have been evoked and articulated by Greeks in the ninth century. At least the second line may be redrawn with a firmer hand following a recent argument developed by Margalit Finkelberg[51] involving a distinction between two types of knowledge. The Serbo-Croat bard claims to know everything through training and to repeat it (although in fact every oral performance involves unique improvisation). By contrast, the Homeric bard professes two kinds of knowledge. He knows how to play the lyre[52] and, like the bard Phemios, he knows many epic subjects.[53] But he also knows what the muse inspires him with for the ad hoc performance.[54] What is true of Greek myth in general is also relevant here. "A myth is not a specific poetic text," says Fritz Graf. "It is the subject matter, a plot fixed in broad outline and with characters no less fixed, which an individual poet is free to alter only within limits."[55] Comparably, the "ethos" of reception of the epos is that of a "past."[56] If the poem is about Odysseus, the hero must come to Ithaca and nowhere else. Finkelberg emphasizes that the way in which Odysseus *retells* Penelope the plot of *Odyssey*, organized succinctly in a systematic and linear manner (unlike the *Odyssey*'s own structure), illustrates the existence of that outline.[57] It is a kind of "historical truth" that the audience also knows. To this example of Finkelberg's may be added Demodokos's Trojan songs, which are presented as summary paraphrases, not poems: "and then he told how . . ." is the recurring formula. The paraphrase, incidentally, is not too dissimilar to Proclus's summaries of the Cycle: "Next they sail as far as Tenedos. . . . Then the Greeks try to land at Ilium. . . . Achilles then kills Kyknos. . . . After this Achilles," etc.

Finkelberg warns against confusing "facts" (what the audience knows) with themes. "The sphere of the poet's competence is connected with the epic subject (= *oimē*) he sings about. It is *oimē* which in the *Odyssey* is the ob-

51. Finkelberg 1990 and n.d.

52. *Od.* 11.406–9.

53. *Od.* 1.337–38.

54. The muse is thus also responsible for selection from the vast subject matter (Ford 1992: 79). Ford (chap. 2), however, sees the muses as standing for the symbolic "tradition" (1992: 59). See n. 61 and the appendix.

55. Graf 1993: 2.

56. Ford 1992: 30, 47, and passim.

57. *Od.* 23.310–41.

ject of teaching."[58] By contrast, claims Finkelberg, the gift of the muse to the poet is *aoidē* (the "lay" or "song").[59] Thus the muse, for example, is responsible for the point where the bard chooses to begin the narrative.[60] The tension between the fixity of the story and the relative freedom of its expansion is equivalent to the tension between what the poet (in contrast to the Serbo-Croat bard) knows a priori and what the muse inspires him with. It amounts in effect to the tension between the poet's commitment to preserve his tradition and his creative freedom.[61]

The distinction developed by Finkelberg may be carried over methodologically to the lines I have drawn in the sand. That Odysseus landed in Ithaca, met Athena, and hid the treasure in a cave are all "facts." The poet's telling of what Odysseus said to himself or what Athena said to him would probably have been considered ad hoc inspiration and thus more prone to change.[62] However, what I shall consider as significant pieces of evidence, such as the tripods dedicated at Ithaca or the Nestor cup at Pithekoussai, relate to a world of "fact" that the audience at large knows a priori and are therefore less prone to transformation by individual bards. Of course, even poetic facts are numerous, and the poet's individual ability must have included choosing among them. But this consideration is less relevant to the proverbial mighty cup, the immensely popular blinding of the Cyclops, or the climactic landing at Ithaca.

It is well-known that although Homer refers to his bards as singers of discrete episodes,[63] the *Odyssey* itself is the opposite of such singing, integrating much of their own alternative material. It seems to pride itself on its uniqueness, but it also evidences the existence of episodic singing as the norm for epic poetry. In one sense, Phemios and Demodokos, episode singers, are a bard's "fantasy bards," singing at the time when the world was younger, in the age of heroes, when the events sung about had sometimes yet to hap-

58. *Od.* 8.481.

59. *Od.* 8.44, 64, 498. "This means that the *oimē* in which the poet is competent cannot be more than the basic knowledge of the principal events constituting the story and of the order of their succession."

60. *Od.* 8.499–503.

61. "Thus what the Homeric poet sees himself as competent in is the range of epic subjects at his disposal and their basic plots (techne), and what he sees himself as ignorant of is the way in which he expands these subjects by elaborating on them within these basic plots, and the point within the epic saga at which his narrative would start (improvisation)." Cf. Murray (1989: 10), who distinguishes between the permanent gift of the muses and their temporary inspiration. See also Jensen 1980: 68.

62. See Arist. *Poet.* 24, which may indicate that other Cycle poems contained little speech.

63. Even Achilles sings *klea andrōn* (the glorious deeds of men) to himself (*Iliad* 9: 186 ff).

pen.[64] To the extent that they fitted the image of real bards this aspect may have belonged to the poet's enhancement. Perhaps some bards were famous precisely for their originality. Yet originality must not be judged in modern terms; the poet works within the framework of the *known* stories. Phemios does not invent the "actual" return of the Achaians, but he seems to be credited with the song about the return. Conversely, when Demodokos "sings the Trojan horse" Odysseus seems to be asking to hear a familiar piece.[65]

What this means for the composition of the *Odyssey* is not the issue here; however, the awareness of episodic, narratively discrete singing indicates something about the dissemination of oral poetry. I can certainly envisage the landing of Odysseus in Ithaca and the placing of the treasure in the cave (in the thirteenth book) as being such an episode. In the fifth century we have evidence that episodes *from Homer* were also sung separately. Herodotus, for example, refers to the exploits of Diomedes, Thucydides to the catalogue of ships, Plato to the battle for the wall, and so on.[66] I draw particular encouragement from this. In assuming *Odyssey*-related episodes from outside the *Odyssey*, one may envisage them as, say, an Epirote episode, per-

64. See Jensen 1980: 71–72. The Sirens are the supreme singers, knowing everything that happened to the Argives and the Trojans.

65. Unlike Demodokos's song about Ares and Aphrodite, his Trojan poems lack any pretense to verisimilitude. They contain no dialogue or speeches. Verisimilitude is achieved rather through the response of Odysseus, who praises precisely that quality of Demodokos's singing that he would have if he had actually been there. It is remarkable how the poet of the *Odyssey* both tells us of other poems and distinguishes them as unique without *singing* them. Point by characteristic point, Phemios and Demodokos seem different from the bards of Parry and Lord. They are both singers and musicians, sometimes playing (apparently without song) for the dancers alone (*Od.* 8.266; cf. 1.152). They are both original and traditional poets. The subject—the Trojan War and the Nostoi—is new; it has all just happened. Penelope charges Phemios with preferring the new: "You know many other actions of mortals and gods, which can charm men's hearts and which the singers celebrate," says Penelope, asking him to avoid the "return of the Achaians." Telemachos asks her not to interfere: "There is nothing wrong in his singing the sad return of the Danaans. People surely always give more applause to that song which is the *newest* to circulate among the listeners" (*Od.* 8.337–52; Lattimore 1962 translates as "latest" ἥ τις ἀκουόντεσσι νεωτάτη ἀμφιπέληται). Again, Demodokos is praised by Odysseus for his accuracy in singing of the Trojan horse, as if he had been there (Jensen 1980: 70; cf. Hainsworth 1970: 96 with Kirk 1976: 107 with regard to *Od.* 8. 489–90). Again, the novelty and personal involvement of the heroes is marked. The novelty is also expressed, time and again, in the motif of heroes' consciously acting in such a way as to be worthy of *kleos* and song. "We shall be poetry," says Helen to Telemachos, implying songs not yet composed (*Od.* 6.356 ff). Alkinoös says that the gods destroyed the heroes at Troy "for the singing of men hereafter" (*Od.* 8.579–80), and Agamemnon says that the fame of Penelope's virtue will not die "for the gods will make a song for mortals" (*Od.* 24. 196–98).

66. Hdt. 2.116; Thuc. 1.10; Pl. *Ion.* 539b.

haps popular among Epirote or Ithacan aristocrats, sung by the bards on request much as Phemios—appropriately enough for a community (Ithaca) that has lost most of its sons in the war at Troy—sings the sad return of the Achaians. Just as in vase paintings we have Odysseus running on vases floating in the sea and blown forward by Boreas or riding a turtle—both completely unknown stories—so too one may accept the Epirote or Italiote "episode-*Odysseys*" as early, coexistent poems; some are implied, as we shall see, in the *Odyssey* itself, and some are mentioned in relatively late sources.[67] This not quite original explanation also provides us with a plausible link between the *Odyssey* and its sequels as well as emphasizing their contemporaneity. At least it can be said to indicate the range of possibilities for simultaneous diffusion of Odysseus-related stories.

Thus the claim that Greeks in the ninth and eighth centuries had the *nostoi* in their heads does not absolutely necessitate the existence of full epics. However, as previously remarked, stories could be and probably were also transmitted simply as tales. The existence of such tales seems very likely, but it does not explain the particular, sustained, and forceful impact of the tales of Troy in particular. Since I shall argue that specific *nostoi* as well as the narrative details of particular scenes (not stock themes) also had a powerful impact, I cannot make do with the notion of "tales." Full episodes and significant details and characteristics (if not whole epics) need to have been transmitted and diffused. Those who reject the possibility that *Odyssey* episodes were sung (or memorized) [68] as early as this may also reject some of my arguments concerning the dedications to Odysseus at Ithaca. Most of the other expressions of the *nostoi* that I shall be discussing belong, somewhat more safely, to later periods.

A recent influential theory developed by Gregory Nagy seeks to explain the fixation of the Homeric texts through a process of pan-Hellenic diffusion. Although not without its problems, his approach contains some attractive arguments, since he emphasizes, on the one hand, the contextual interdependence of the *Iliad,* the *Odyssey,* and other epics and, on the other, the evolutionary process of selection by which the *Iliad* and the *Odyssey* in particular became, so to speak, canonized.[69] He also accepts the idea of "performance segments," popular until the Panathenaic performances in the sixth century.[70] Nagy's perspective may help us see how other *nostoi* could have been regarded by Greeks experiencing sailing in the new regions of

67. See Phillips 1953: 66–67.
68. See appendix on orality and memorization.
69. Nagy 1992: 37.
70. Nagy 1992: 39–40; cf. Shapiro (1993: 103), who thinks that bards sang highlights, discrete episodes, such as the funeral games of Patroklos. Around 580 the Athenian painter Sophilos used this as the title for a picture.

the northwest (Epirus, the Strait of Otranto, and southern Italy) as particularly applicable—but in a peculiar interplay between the localized and the pan-Hellenic. Thus the literary Ithaca, the island connecting the *Odyssey* and its alternatives and sequels with the real Ithaca and the real sailing experiences of Ithacans, Euboians, and Corinthians, probably functioned as a proto-pan-Hellenic focus for evoking a whole range of Odysseus and other *nostoi*. In contrast, Epirote episodes, for example, may be interpreted on the more regional level of dissemination.

The *Odyssey*, organized around the *nostos* of Odysseus, presents us with a rich treasure house of *nostoi*. It is sung, thematically, in comparison with the *nostoi* of others, such as Agamemnon, Nestor, Diomedes, and Menelaos,[71] but it also includes some alternative "Odysseys" of its own hero. The poet of the *Odyssey* is a true master when it comes to alluding to other myths, such as the *Argonautica*,[72] or to Troy-related episodes not covered in the *Iliad* such as the struggle for the arms of Ajax or the wooden horse. He does not recount such episodes in detail but certainly implies their independent "contemporary" existence. The genre of *nostoi* is, as we have seen, expressly mentioned in the *Odyssey* (the sad return of the Achaians), and the word *nostos* itself signifies both the actual return and the song about it.[73] The *Odyssey* in particular seems to have integrated its own alternatives. It does not simply bring its hero to a crossroads and have him choose a course; rather, it picks up the crossroads and takes it along with the poem. Perhaps the lying tales of Odysseus are Homer's special contribution to narrative oral traditions. For example, we shall see how Odysseus in the thirteenth book is transported by the Phaiakians to Ithaca; yet in one of the lying tales that is the closest to what "really happened" he declines the offer of the Phaiakians and chooses instead to go to Thesprotia—a story that neatly connects, I shall claim, with a well-attested sequel, an "independent" Odysseus *nostos* in Thesprotia.

Outside the *Odyssey*, alternative Odysseus myths are attested as early as Hesiod, although most of our detailed knowledge about Greek *nostoi* comes from late summaries of the so-called Trojan Cycle. The situation is both frustrating and familiar: whenever a fragment, an allusion, or even a detailed

71. Katz 1991: 7.

72. The *Argo, Od.* 12.70; Circe, sister of Aietes, *Od.* 10.137–39; the fountain Artakie (near Kyzikos), *Od.* 10.108 (a probability). Jason visits Lemnos, where his son by Hypsipile was born; this son gave the Achaians wine before the war (*Il.* 7.467–69) and ransomed a Trojan captive (*Il.* 23.747–48). On Jason see *Il.* 7.468–69; 21.41; 23.747. See also chap. 4.

73. Nagy 1979: 97 n. 2; cf. 35–36.

nostos summary appears—and, as we shall see, this recurs consistently from the Archaic period through the Hellenistic—it always seems self-evidently to imply a wide-ranging familiarity with *nostoi*. This is a familiarity that we often cannot share, and the methodology often involves arguing backward from a late source, trying to find a controlling anchor in an earlier period. In any case, in arguing for a whole matrix of *nostoi* poems, stories, and images, coexisting and floating, cloudlike, in the mental skies of the Archaic period, our purpose is to see when such clouds touched land and people and how they colored their perceptions.

CATEGORIES OF ETHNICITY

Ethnicity, a term coined in 1942,[74] has been the focus of discussion by anthropologists, sociologists, historians (and ethnohistorians), and veterans of cultural studies.[75] Whereas nationalism (sometimes ideologically based on ethnicity) is arguably a modern phenomenon,[76] ethnicity and ethnic feelings are not, since we find primordialist group notions of ties of kinship, language, religion, race, shared experience, and territory already in antiquity.[77] Current discussion seems to have gone beyond the essentialist or "natural" ethnicity of the myths of nation building originating in the late nineteenth century. Such myths portray nations as perennial and natural, waiting for the political moment to awaken. Current discussion also seems to have transcended the race-oriented and phenotypical definitions of group identity that were in vogue before World War II. These focused on "objective," natural, and inherited (mostly biological) traits. By contrast, ethnicity (or ethnic identity) is now debated mainly in conceptual terms. There seems to be a general inclination to examine the ethnicity of "peoples" (to be distinguished from that of immigrants within modern states) while emphasizing its constructedness or "invention."

One definition, comfortable yet limited, considers ethnicity "the conscious expression of group identity" or "the way in which social groups consciously choose to assert their identity and to define and constitute themselves in relation to others in any given set of circumstances."[78] The comfort consists in the role of consciousness; the severe limitation is the emphasis on *self*-definition. More often than not, as Benedict Anderson among others

74. Banks 1996: 4, 9–10 (replacing Glazer and Moynihan's [1975: 1] "1953" with Hall 1997: 34).

75. Cf. Shils 1957; Geertz 1963; Isajiw 1974.

76. Gellner 1983; Hobsbawm 1992. Anderson 1991, while correctly stressing the role of conceptualization as the key, still sees it as a modern phenomenon. Cf. Banks 1996: 52.

77. Alty 1982.

78. Morgan 1991: 131, 133.

has shown,[79] group definitions are the result of outsiders' articulations that become internalized and accepted.

There is a basic distinction in current discussion that at a first glance may seem confusing. The older distinction between essentialist and primordial (= perennial, natural, racial, etc.), on the one hand, and context-oriented or "circumstantial," on the other, has been replaced by similar terms that signify a completely different approach. Within a *mentalité* of denial of most kinds of essentialisms, we find the terminology of "primordial" versus "circumstantial" operating differently. The circumstantialists emphasize the creation of ethnicity (ethnogenesis) in relation to fluctuating historical situations. The primordialists mostly no longer look for hard, objective existence of ethnic groups but rather look for the primordial perceptions and boundaries such groups employ; they examine whether and to what extent such notions, in and of themselves, operate over long periods. To the extent that they do, and therefore function historically, primordialist notions acquire their force of authentic, even "objective," existence.

Generally one finds that even in cases of identifiable ethnogenesis ethnic identity is represented as traditional with a predominantly past time orientation, "embedded in the cultural heritage . . . of the group."[80] The point is borne out also by anthropologists, who may be less interested in the operation of primordial notions over long periods of time. In some anthropological discussions we find the terms "etic" (the anthropologist's point of view) versus "emic" (how the group defines itself), with the latter inclining toward a primordialist discourse.[81] Thus, when discussing "primordial identity," such as the association of a group with common ancestors and/or an ancient homeland, that view too is regarded as a historically and socially conditioned phenomenon, even though the emic view may represent such traits as unchanging and "old as the moon."[82] The difference between the primordial and the circumstantial relies heavily, therefore, on point of view, whether that of the observer or that of the group, and on the identifiable chronology and circumstances of the creation of ethnic identity (or ethnogenesis). Judith Nagata defines the "circumstantial" as "interests and issues that create, activate, sustain, and perpetuate the loyalties and sentiments that are

79. Anderson 1983.

80. Shils 1957: 20.

81. On etic/emic, see Nagata 1981: 96; cf. LeVine and Campbell 1972: 13, claiming that many isolated homogeneous tribes/ethnic units are largely the creation of colonialism, missionaries, or ethnographers who wanted them to be identifiable on a map.

82. Hdt. 8.73.1; cf. 1.146; Xen. *Hell.* 7.1.23; Dem. *De fals. leg.* 261; Paus. 8.1.4–5; Strabo 338 (on Arkadian autochthony). Ap. Rhod. 4.264; Lucian *De astr.* 26; Schol. ad Aristoph. *Nub.* 397 (on the moon theme).

subsequently rationalized by a primordial charter." She emphasizes that the status of cultural characteristics as primordial or nonprimordial may vary for the same people in different situations. Thus Malays, for example, by invoking a place of origin divide into Javanese and Minangkabau; conversely, by using religion (Islam) as a primordial charter, both Indian Muslims and Arabs can be incorporated into the category of "Malay."[83] Similarly, in 1947 religion was the salient distinguishing mark between "Pakistan" and India; by contrast, in 1972, when claiming its independence, Muslim Bangladesh stressed its language.[84]

Anthony Smith correctly observes that the "core" of ethnicity (whether or not it has come to serve modern nationalism) resides in "myths, memories, values, and symbols," often relating to mythic elements of beginning in time (usually through an eponymous ancestor), place of origin, destination of migration, and a triad of Golden Age, decline/oppression/exile, and liberation/rebirth. By adding to ethnicity the dimension of myths, memories, values, and symbols we may also understand why ethnic groups "are both mutable and durable" and ethnicity appears as "both fluctuating and recurrent."[85] The mythic, "imagined," or discursive[86] aspects of ethnicity are thus emphasized as the salient aspects of one's approach to ethnic considerations and perspectives.

One controlled example of ethnogenesis may clarify the conditioning of primordial ideas within identifiable historical circumstances. Roosen has demonstrated how, in the case of the contemporary Canadian Hurons, "within 20 years (1948–1968) a self-conscious people was created, starting from a very few cultural relics of an Indian past . . . and fully accepted as a nation by Canadian leaders."[87] The Hurons, numbering in 1968 some 1,500 (979 on the reservation, 471 outside), are phenotypically not different from other Canadians, and their language is French. Yet they became the leaders of the Association des Indiens de Québec. A Jesuit dictionary was used to revive the language, and counterfeit cultural traits—moccasins, hair styles, parade costumes, canoes, music, etc.—were created. The Hurons, claims Roosen, have introduced a difference between themselves and other Canadians, conforming to a Canadian stereotype of what Indians are supposed to be.[88] In terms of self-portrayal the Hurons consider their culture basically from the outside, from the French point of view.[89]

Huron ethnogenesis is thus clearly circumstantialist, created in the face of utter disappearance (and some opportune political moments). "We are

83. Nagata 1981: 94–95.
84. Hall 1997: 23.
85. Smith 1986: 192, 211.
86. Anderson 1983; Hall 1997: 34–66.

87. Roosen 1989: 20.
88. Roosen 1989: chap. 3.
89. Roosen 1989: 152.

probably never so aware of phenomena and objects as when we are about to gain or lose them."[90] But it also illustrates the genesis of the primordialist myth as "invented" within the limits of some known past: Hurons were an ancient people, decimated by both French and Iroquois, with their own language, an original homeland from which they were displaced, and a distinct culture. The fact that these salient characteristics had to be rediscovered (or invented) only stresses the need for primordialism as the constitutive communal myth. Yet these rediscoveries and inventions also have their limits.

It is perhaps too easy to unmask "inventions" of ethnicity. In modern times such inventions have been a distinct preoccupation of intellectual circles. Thus in Israel, for example, a group of Jewish immigrant intellectuals consolidated in the forties around the idea of a "Canaanite identity." Having immigrated to the Land of Israel (Palestine), it was claimed, one ought to abandon Jewish identity and mingle in the "Semite region," whose ethnic substrate is commonly Canaanite. A recognition of this substrate by both Jews and Arabs would resolve all conflicts provided that each side give up its separate ethnic identity. Not many, it seems, were convinced, and the idea remained the domain of certain prominent poets and journalists. In terms of its effect it was not very different from the Phoenician identity invented by Lebanese-Maronite intellectuals or the Pharaonic identity advocated by some intellectual circles in Egypt. These failures conform to Anthony Smith's suggestion that nationalism does not write its history as it pleases. The past is "full" and intellectualist inventions must "cohere with" what is already there—inherited mythologies and symbolisms.[91] Thus, whereas the Canaanite ethnic myth has failed, that of the Jewish "Return" has succeeded in its Zionist form, drawing on an ancient and persistent ("full") tradition of a primordial homeland.

Conversely, on the Arab-Palestinian side, another idea that has been circulating in intellectual circles since the thirties has now caught on as a constituent myth of nation building. Palestinians are autochthonous, it is claimed, direct descendants of the Canaanite peoples who were conquered by Joshua. Jews were invaders then as well as now. The same Canaanite myth is now being used not for the sake of integrating Jews and Arabs into a single nation but rather to create a distinction from a too similar "Other." Paradoxically, the oppositional Palestinian ethnic myth uses the discourse adopted from the Hebrew "myth of the other" (as expressed in the Old Testament—the only source on which modern Palestinians can draw). We shall observe a similar phenomenon with the Roman use of the Trojan (= Greek)

90. Smith 1986: 7.
91. Smith 1986: 178, 206. Here lies the main difference between Smith's approach and that of Anderson 1983. I find the works of these two scholars complementary.

myth of origins. The point here, however, is that an idea that may have a rather limited life among intellectuals and erudites can suddenly take root and spread into the national (in this case Palestinian) curriculum of education in the 1990s. According to Smith, when communities simply know too little about their pasts "the fuller *ethnie* set the pace for the empty ones. . . ." For example, says Smith, to define the contours of their ethnicity Slovak historians were busy disentangling their myths from the Bohemian Moravian ones.[92]

Modern Greece may serve as an example of ethnogenesis in Smith's sense of a "full" past. As Robert Just observes, in Greece there is a marked historical tension between state/nation (*kratos*) and people/nation (*ethnos*). Whereas in the Ottoman empire "Greek" (Rum) was a religious appellation, modern Greek state-ethnicity implies territorial irredentism, "to expand the *kratos* to encompass the *ethnos*,"[93] especially, as John Kolettis said in 1844, since "a Greek is not only a man who lives within this kingdom but also one who lives . . . in any land associated with Greek history or the Greek race."[94] This irredentism failed in the Catastrophe of 1922–23, when Greece attempted the conquest of Asia Minor. In contrast to expressing Greek ethnicity through territorial expansion, Greek past-oriented primordiality and essentialism were (re)created through particular attention to a unified Greek language and culture expressed in a rigorous system of education.[95] A process of selection from the past has been under way in Greece, but it is a selection from a "full" past rather than an invention out of whole cloth. There is, of course, one major difference: whereas Greek ethnicity today is clearly bound up with the idea of a national Greek state, in antiquity there never was a "Greece," and ancient Greek ethnicity, while sometimes dependent on what we may regard as shared cultural traits, was not state-oriented.

The most recent study of ancient Greek ethnicity, by Jonathan Hall, sensibly argues for two distinct phases in the formation of Hellenic ethnicity. The first, up to the Persian Wars, he calls "aggregative"[96] ethnicity, "based on similarity with peer groups and achieved by attaching ethnic eponyms to one another within the single overarching genealogy (of Helenos) that is recorded in the *Catalogue of Women*." Hall pays particular attention to this genealogical construct of the eponym Helenos, claiming that systematization took place and was widely accepted around the mid-sixth century. He

92. Smith 1986: On "full" pasts, see Appadurai 1981, mentioned above.
93. Just 1989: 79; cf. Smith 1986: 203.
94. Quoted by Clogg 1986: 76.
95. Herzfeld 1982.
96. Hall 1997; cf. Nagata 1981: 103: "The category of Malay has been built up by a gradual series of *aggregations* [my emphasis] from a variety of other peoples who still sometimes assert their separate identity."

argues against the viability of the linguistic criterion among ancient Greeks, demonstrating the degree of its variability; language was important but not definitional.[97]

A good illustration of the aggregative nature of ethnicity in a "colonial" context is the sanctuary common to various Greek communities in Naukratis in Egypt ca. 570. It was called the Hellenion, and its officers were the Hellenotamiai. These names, perhaps forced into being by an oppositional situation in relation to the Egyptian king, who closely supervised the Greek emporium, clearly signify a common Greek awareness that transcended Greek-ethnic divisions (such as Dorians and Ionians). Hall, who argues that the aggregative construction of Greek ethnicity was still in force in the sixth century, notes that this construction was "expressed materially outside of Greece proper."[98] But the Hellenion, because of its context, was something more than an aggregative concept; I prefer to consider it as a precursor to the full-blown oppositional model of the fifth century both because of the peculiar situation in Egypt[99] and because it involved a convergence of various Greeks in one spot.

The cult to Odysseus at Ithaca, to be discussed as another point of convergence, may have anticipated certain aspects of the Hellenion, being contextualized in circumstances of sailing away from one's country to and from the alien Beyond. Also, long before the Hellenion in Egypt we find the altar to Apollo Archegetes in Sicilian Naxos, the earliest Greek colony in Sicily (734). The altar was common to all Greek colonists (whether they were of Dorian or Euboian-Ionian origin), and all religious expeditions leaving Sicily would first stop there.[100]

As Frederik Barth notes, an oppositional model is very useful for group definition; specifically he claims that there is no "core ethnicity" and one should look instead for the conceptual boundaries that an ethnic group creates against others.[101] Hall takes up this observation and applies it to the period following the Persian Wars, which sharpened a pan-Hellenic oppositional model between Greeks and barbarians. The oppositional model came to replace the aggregative one and too often has colored our view of ancient perceptions of Greek ethnicity. "Greek ethnicity was not created then [in the fifth century] but shifted the mechanism of the construction of its self-identity."[102] In general terms, Hall is of course right in emphasizing the

97. And see Hall 1995, arguing against restatements of the view that Greekness consisted in language difference.

98. Hall 1997: 50.

99. See Austin 1970.

100. Thuc. 6.3.1 with Malkin 1986.

101. Barth 1969: 9–39.

102. Hall 1995: 91.

significant change in Greek *mentalité* that took place in the fifth century. However, the case for "proto-pan-Hellenism" in the preceding centuries is more nuanced in the colonial world, as we have seen in the cases of the cult to Odysseus, the altar of Apollo Archegetes, and the Hellenion in Egypt.

Finally, a point about genealogy as a construct of ethnicity: more than any other mode of articulation, genealogy played an important role. The modern Greek characteristic of *elleniko ema,* Greek blood,[103] is paralleled by Herodotus's criterion of Greek common blood, *homaimon (ὅμαιμόν).*[104] This is the primordialist definition of ethnicity as kinship. In antiquity, however, it was mostly heroic genealogy that could explain shared descent. Genealogy can be an uncertain device for articulating ethnicity because it is open to free manipulation and conflicting claims. It is capable, moreover, of differentiating and relating nations at the same time. The biblical genealogy of the sons of Noah (Shem, Ham, and Yaphet) is a case in point. However, because of its open-endedness ("Greek" heroes had sons with women from all over the world) genealogy cannot be sufficient for exclusive or oppositional ethnicity. Again, Hellenic exclusivity could be claimed *within* a particular genealogical line (Hellen's), but that too involved too many Greek exceptions (e.g., the Arkadians). In some respects genealogy may function ethnically in that it "provides a structure in which life and loyalty are mutually determining, and are granted by members of one generation to members of the next."[105] However, the case is far from clear. It depends on the function of the genealogy, whether it is accepted and by whom, and whether it remains the exercise of an erudite, disregarded by those to whom it is supposed to apply (e.g., the Greek genealogy for the Persians) or accepted and used to substantiate claims (e.g., the Makedonian Herakleid genealogy). It will be interesting to note under what circumstances Greek articulations of ethnicity through Nostoi (mostly genealogical ethnicity) were integrated and adopted. Was this another case in which "the fuller *ethnie* set the pace for the empty ones"? Was a Greek "full" past superimposed on the "empty" past of indigenous populations?

103. Just 1989: 77.   105. Davis 1989: 110; cf. Henige 1984 (1974).
104. Hdt. 8.144.2.

TWO

Sailing and Colonizing
in the Sea of Returns

A new history needs to be written, reconstructing a context for the presence of Odysseus in the minds of Greeks as early as the later ninth century in regions that link the real and the unreal geographies of the *Odyssey*—Ithaca and the sea to its north. I suggest that it is now possible to write some of that history, if only in outline form. The archaeology of presence and contact, both of Greeks and of non-Greeks, opens a new direction for reassessing the role of Ithaca itself during this period and the movement of Greeks up, down, and around the Ionian and Adriatic Seas along the coasts of Epirus and Italy. We need to identify the temporal and geographical context of Odysseus's entry into the real geography of western colonization. We need to know which Greeks could have been responsible for this exportation of Odysseus and for his adoption by some of the native populations of ancient Epirus and Italy. We will also need to abandon certain a priori arguments about what was possible or likely for the ninth-, eighth-, and seventh-century Greeks.

The position of Odysseus's island, Ithaca, is an important key, opening two interlocking gates. The first belongs to the *Odyssey,* in which the island constitutes the inclusive limit of human geography. Beyond Ithaca exist the mythical Phaiakia and various lands of monstrous beings and dangerous goddesses. Like Alice reentering her living room through the looking glass, Odysseus returns to the real world when the dreamlike ship of the Phaiakians finally transports him home. Ithaca's position connects it with the second gate, that of historical Ithacans and other Greeks sailing to and past Ithaca in the opposite direction of the return of Odysseus, beginning with the ninth and eighth centuries. Their dedications to Odysseus in the cave of the nymphs at Polis Bay in Ithaca, which belong to this period, will be shown to express a superimposition of Homer's geographical threshold, approximately coterminous with the geography of Greece in the Dark Age, on new and actual maritime itineraries. Thus Odysseus will have been a hero first of protocolonization (ninth to mid-eighth century) and later of colonization. This aspect of the Ithaca Odysseus was particularly significant, I will argue, for Greeks observing themselves sailing beyond Ithaca and returning to their homes (notably Euboia and Corinth) via the island. It was also important for observing other peoples, articulating genealogies and ethnic origins in Epirus (northwestern Greece, Albania), across the Strait of Otranto in Italy, and even in Campania and Etruria. Ithaca itself and its own historical role (not merely as a way station for other Greeks) in relation both to Epirus and to Odysseus as its own "national" hero is also in urgent need of reassessment. But before discussing the intriguing cult to Odysseus (chap. 3) and before confronting the various articulations of ethnicity dependent on the hero and the sequels to the *Odyssey*, Ithaca and its "beyond" need to be observed with fresh eyes.

Reassessment began for me with a personal observation. In the summer of 1992 some friends and I chartered a yacht in Corfu and sailed to Ithaca via the Leukas channel. Aside from taking in impressions of the beautiful Ionian islands, I wished to empathize with previous "searchers for Odysseus," whether ancient, such as Strabo, or modern, such as Victor Bérard, Ernle Bradford, and Tim Severin.[1] I did not consider questions such as "Where, in fact, is the island of Calypso?" of any scientific value, preferring Eratosthenes's view that anyone who really wanted to trace the itinerary of Odysseus had better first look for the cobbler who had made him the bag of winds.[2] The poet of the *Odyssey* is beautifully clear about Odysseus's itinerary, which he traces in two different dimensions. Once he had rounded Cape Malea, Odysseus entered a world apart. The device is well known in various types of "other-dimension" tales; in the language of Tolkien, Odysseus entered the land of Faerie, where witches might change one into a pig. Phaiakia, where Odysseus tells his story and whence he returns to Ithaca, is the *Odyssey*'s looking glass, through which the hero reenters the dimension of a concrete and topographical world. The sailing trip did, however, help me to visualize the geographical and maritime position of Ithaca and Corfu in relation to the Ionian and the Adriatic Seas, to Epirus, Albania/Illyria, and Italy. Depending on weather conditions and visibility, everything is practically within sight and even swimming distance. We were warned, for example, to be on the lookout for Albanians who take to the sea in inflated tires, seeking a passage to Italy or Greece. In Vathi, the modern port of Ithaca, we were told that Ithacans too were told to beware of Albanians arriving in small

1. Bérard 1927–29; Bradford 1963; Severin 1987.
2. Strabo 1.24.

craft and that some had in fact reached there. Accessibility in the eighth century B.C. could not have been much different.

ITHACA

Ithaca island looks as if someone had squeezed some modeling clay and twisted it, nearly breaking it in the middle. Some twenty-two kilometers long and six kilometers wide, narrowing to some five hundred meters at its middle (the Gulf of Molo), it is full of astonishingly beautiful coves and bays and rises steeply from the water. Although it is small, sailing around it can take some time because of its numerous inlets. To sail today in a forty-foot yacht from Polis Bay to Vathi takes at least four to five hours, often with the motor running, in a calm sea. Since the geography of Ithaca and wind patterns have not changed since antiquity,[3] we may regard the sailing conditions as a constant. This may prove important with regard to the Greeks who sailed to Ithaca and beyond and deposited their dedications at the shrine on Polis Bay. In fact, the clearest map for the appreciation of the position of Polis Bay in relation to sailing routes may be found in Rod Heikell's *Greek Waters Pilot*. Polis Bay is situated on Ithaca's northwestern coast, facing Kephallonia, and is the recommended stop for most yachts chartered in Corfu (ancient Corcyra) to sail "down" toward the Corinthian Gulf (see map 3).

The point about sailing down from Corfu or up toward it is highly relevant. Today, sailing "up" to Corfu via the Leukas channel (see map 4), one would not necessarily wish to get on the "wrong side" of Ithaca, where Polis Bay is situated. In fact, the better and more numerous anchorage bays are on the eastern side of the island (from south to north, Ayias Andreas, Parapigadi, Sarakiniko, Vathi, Kioni, and Frikes). Before the Corinthians cut the Leukas channel in the mid-seventh century, however, it was more convenient to sail toward Corcyra through the Ithaca-Kephallonia channel, where Polis Bay is the *only* available port on the Ithaca side[4] (on the Kephallonia side one could conveniently stop at Pronos, Samos Bay, Ayias Eifemia, Kato Limene, Kakogito, Deskalio, and Fiskardo). The information about the cutting of the Leukas channel is derived from Strabo, and I see no reason to question it. Even if Strabo was wrong, however, and some sort of (natural?) channel existed in the eighth century, it could not have been safely navigable without political control of the sort that the Corinthians exercised later. Even today, with the aid of a motor, the trip through the long, narrow, shallow channel is very slow going (although the modern risk of hitting shoals was

3. Murray 1987.

4. The point, incidentally, may be of importance to those concerned with localizing the suitors' attack (at Kephallonia) on the returning Telemachos. He would not have been expected to go to Polis unless his home were in that area.

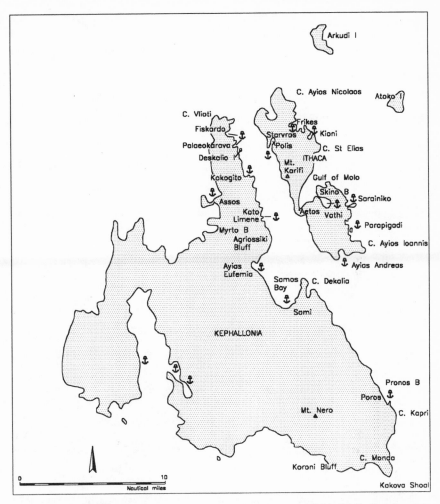

Map 3. Ithaca and Kephallonia: main sites and anchorages (after Heikell 1982: 51).

probably less in the Archaic period, when boats did not have deep keels). A boat is extremely vulnerable to human attack in such a situation, and with the slightest uncertainty regarding the situation on the mainland an eighth-century Leukas channel (even if one were to believe in one) would almost certainly have been avoided.[5] In other words, whether sailing up toward Cor-

5. Strabo 10.451–52. In antiquity towboats (*paktones*) were apparently used. These are mentioned in a grammatical excerpt of C. Julius Hyginus (Keil, *Gramm. Lat.* 1.134). Channels markers too were employed (Arr. *Ind.* 42.2). Murray 1982: 243–54, 260–65.

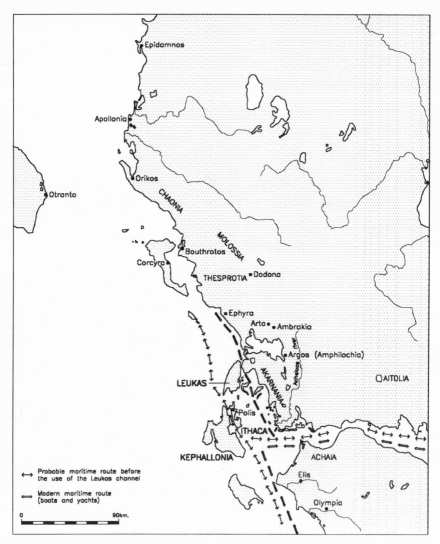

Map 4. Epirus and maritime routes.

cyra or down, Polis Bay was an inviting site. It certainly makes excellent sense (as it does today, even with the Leukas channel) for Polis Bay to have been frequented by Greeks sailing down from Corcyra, making it their first stop in Ithaca. This should not be understood as denying Vathi the role of Ithaca's main port; for people whose destination is Ithaca itself, as well as for the people of the island, Vathi is obviously superior. However, for those needing a port of call on the route north or, more significant, for those returning from the northwest, Polis is the better.[6]

Most scholars who pay attention to Ithaca's geographical and maritime position remark that Ithaca lies on the route to the north—Corcyra, the Adriatic, and the crossover to Italy. However, once started, maritime traffic is usually two-way. During the half-century of intensive protocolonial contacts (the first half of the eighth century), when both Euboians and Corinthians were trading up to the Strait of Otranto and perhaps beyond it and Ithaca itself was active in this trade as well as in its regional network, the way back was perhaps just as important as the way up; moreover, I shall argue that in religious terms the way back was even more meaningful. It was obviously important not only during protocolonization but also during the colonization period. Traffic went both ways, and failed colonists sometimes returned home; Archias, for example, the Corinthian founder of Syracuse (733 B.C.), is said to have picked up such a group.[7]

The island known today as Ithaki was identified with the Homeric Ithaca from the Classical era on. This identification (unlike that of other sites associated with Homer) was never disputed in antiquity.[8] Scholarly attempts to localize the "real" Homeric Ithaca elsewhere may have their appeal but have nothing to do with the realities of cult in the Archaic and Classical periods. Schliemann's assistant, Dörpfeld, produced long and involved arguments[9] for regarding Leukas, and not Ithaki, as the ancient Ithaca. Although the thesis engendered hot disputes, it seems to have created more difficulties than it resolved.[10] In order to combat the identification of Ithaki = Ithaca that seems so consistent since antiquity, Dörpfeld had to postulate a change of Ithaca's name by migrants from the "original" Ithaca (= Leukas), who had been uprooted by the Dorian invasion. We know now, however, that there was apparently no break in Ithaca's own settlement. Following the excavations at Nichoria and Kaphirio in Messenia and the ensuing refinement of the pottery sequences,[11] Coulson concludes that, at least in the Po-

6. Cf. Symeonoglou (1984: 109), who thus understands *Od.* 9.21–28 but without the implication for Polis Bay. "Homer had in mind the location of Ithaca relative to the route followed by the mariners of his time: departing from Kyllene in Elis they traveled in a northwesterly direction towards Kephallenia and continued along its eastern coast."

7. Strabo 6.270; Ps.-Scymn. 277–78. We should remember, however, that once Corinth took control over the Leukas channel maritime traffic along Ithaca's western coast probably declined.

8. *PW* 9.2 col. 2289–90 (Bürchner). Stubbings (Wace and Stubbings 1962: 399–421) sums up the ancient and modern discussion of the subject. Cf. Heubeck in Heubeck and Hoekstra 1989 on 9.21–27; Sieberber 1990.

9. Summed up in Dörpfeld 1927.

10. Stubbings in Wace and Stubbings 1962: 398–421; cf. Sieberber 1990: 159–162.

11. Coulson 1991; cf. Coldstream 1977: 182–84.

lis Bay cave, there was continuity from the late second millennium (Late Helladic III C) though the Dark Age down to Middle Geometric II (ca. 800). In short, says Coulson, whereas before one could rely on Benton's notion of a break just before the beginning of Protogeometric in order to insert Dörpfeld's hypothetical migrants, this is no longer possible.[12]

Today Dörpfeld himself is "heroized" at Leukas: his villa, which he received as a gift from the Kaiser, and a commemorative obelisk are perched on one of the Scorpion Islands in the Bay of Nidri, across from Leukas itself (Dörpfeld kept his mingling to a minimum). Machine-guns mounted on guard boats ward off yachts venturing too close (the Scorpions belong to the rich). From its secluded position Dörpfeld's villa overlooks the modest houses of Leukas, covered with pastel corrugated iron (against earthquakes), and its main street—named after the European archaeologist who had come to donate an ancient Hellenic hero to the modern, mostly poverty-stricken Lefkadians. Even ardent followers of Dörpfeld such as some modern Lefkadians would have to admit that according to his own calculations Ithaca's identification with Homeric Ithaca and its hero Odysseus began long before the ninth century, the period that concerns us here. In modern Ithaca too Odysseus plays a prominent role, somewhat overlapping with the one he played in the Archaic period, as a focus of communal heroic identity. One may sit today at the foot of Odysseus's bronze bust, modeled after the figure of Odysseus on Ithaca's coinage, and share the hero's view of the beautiful Polis Bay below. The inscription on the column is a quotation from an incised inscription on a terra-cotta female mask discovered in the Polis Bay cave and reads εὐχὴν ’Οδύσσει, "a prayer (or votive offering) to Odysseus."[13]

An interesting feature of early Ithacan history is its apparent individuality. The two relatively well-excavated sanctuary sites of Aetos and Polis indicate a continuity of use that may mean that the settlement on the island had not been seriously disturbed from the Mycenaean period[14] to the Geomet-

---

12. Coulson 1941: 43 referring to Benton 1934–5a: 52 (Benton, however, does not use the term "break").

13. Benton 1934–35a: 53–56. In another direction, Benton translates [ὁ δεῖνα ἀνέθ]η[κε]ν, "Votive offerings to Odysseus, so and so dedicated it." εὐχὴν ’Οδύσσει is also the title of the recent publication of the Center for Odyssey Studies at Ithaca (see *Euchen Odyssei* 1995).

14. The sanctuary at Aetos yields evidence of use not before the Protogeometric and seems to take off only in the Geometric; however, Mycenaean pottery was found both in the sanctuary area and in the settlement area to the northwest (mostly Late Helladic III C, some III B), which seems to indicate settlement, although no houses have yet been discovered. Excavation work is being conducted by Sarantis and Nancy Symeonoglou; I am very grateful to the latter for keeping me up to date on this and related Ithacan

ric period and beyond.[15] This probable continuity not only underlines Ithaca's individuality but also may tell us something about its attitude toward Odysseus. Whereas we can fairly safely assume that when the Spartans set up the cult to Menelaos ca. 700 they were relating to a Homeric, "pre-Dorian" past, bridging the gap between themselves as recent arrivals and the famous lord of Sparta in the *Iliad*,[16] at Ithaca Odysseus must have meant something different. He probably came to signify at some point an unbroken, "autochthonous" notion of identity.

Ithaca's position is best appraised the way meteorologists view microclimatic regions. Such regions have their own rules and local behavior but at the same time are part of wider climatic zones. Coulson claims that the pottery from the regions around Ithaca shows that in the Dark Age it belonged to a western Greek *koinē* (a shared ceramic tradition). One may discern a regional network, he claims, involving western Messenia, Achaia, Elis, Akarnania, Ithaca, and Epirus (Phokis and Aitolia may also be included) that had been active during the Protogeometric and Geometric periods.[17] The *Odyssey* may also reflect this.[18] Once the Euboians and Corinthians began sailing up to Otranto, Ithaca became part of the wider Greek scene. In this period of protocolonization, (the ninth and the first half of the eighth century) Ithaca should therefore be considered an independent entity. To what extent, however, should we consider it as a port of call for other Greeks?

The appearance of Middle Geometric II pottery that is of Euboian or (more often) Corinthian origin after 800 need not be seen strictly in terms of a port en route to Italy or as a prelude to colonization.[19] Perhaps western colonization should not be the first thing to spring to mind, given that we have no evidence for it before the mid-eighth century, but hindsight may be helpful in a geopolitical sense. Ithaca's own geographical position is "colonial": an offshore island tapping the resources and trade routes of the main-

issues. See reports in *Praktika* 1984: 109–21; 1985: 201–15; 1986: 234–40; 1989: 292–95; 1990: 271–78.

15. Snodgrass 1971: 84–85; Desborough 1972: 243; Coldstream 1977: 182–84; Coulson 1991.

16. Malkin 1994a: chap. 2.

17. Snodgrass 1971: 339; Coldstream 1977: 187; Coulson 1991: 44.

18. *Od.* 14.334–35. Coulson's Messenia material is being reexamined by Brigitta Eder of the Austrian Institute in Athens. Some questions may arise with regard to the western Greek pottery *koinē* (cf. Morgan 1990: 104), but even if regional diversity proves considerable and the shared elements turn out to be confined to Late Helladic III C, this does not preclude the coming and going among the islands, Elis and Messenia, that is reasonable in itself and explicit in the *Odyssey*.

19. Dehl 1984: 147; Salmon 1984: 89 with Coldstream 1977: 182–84.

land (literally, "Epeiros"). This position constitutes a recurring pattern for preliminary or permanent site selection by maritime colonization in general (e.g., Hong Kong) and in the Greek world in particular (e.g., Ortygia versus Syracuse, Thasos versus its Thracian mainland).[20] In spite of its small size (much smaller than neighboring Kephallonia), Ithaca appears to have been in a particularly independent and prosperous position at the time of protocolonial contacts with the northwest and Iapygia. Its small size may encourage us to view certain aspects of its sanctuary evidence as relevant to the island as a whole, although settlement data from the island for this period are still limited. Its central sanctuary at Aetos had known prosperity after ca. 800, with evidence for imports from Corinth as well as for contacts with at least two Epirote sites, Arta and Vitsa.[21] The island was a port of call on the way not only to Italy but also to the Epirote coasts and islands and possibly farther north. When colonization began after the mid-eighth century, Ithaca probably continued to be a port of call both on the way to and on the way back from the western colonies.[22]

The history of Ithaca during the eighth century and the beginning of the seventh may be of the utmost importance for an understanding of the cult at Polis and of the *Odyssey*'s migration to the west. Ithaca's independent position in relation to the trade with Epirus had been brought to the foreground by Catherine Morgan, who emphasizes its position both en route north and south and in relation to the mainland. The island came under some Corinthian influence, although its independent history should not be regarded solely through a Corinthian prism. Before the mid-eighth century, probably around 780 or even earlier, it seems evident from the number of Corinthian (or Corinthianizing?) dedications in Aetos that it was frequented by Corinthians. This was either because the Corinthians were en route north or (a possibility rarely considered)[23] because Ithaca itself was sometimes their destination, being expected to mediate contacts with Epirus and the Ionian Sea. A more common suggestion, however, is that Corinthians es-

20. Graham 1971.

21. An Ithacan juglet at Vitsa, no. 52238 from Tomb 161 in Vokotopoulou 1984: 94, fig. 22; Vokotopoulou 1986: 205–6, fig. 67.b with pl. 323a (Vokotopoulou notes parallels with Ithaca but suggests that the juglet is Corinthian); note also (following Nancy Symeonoglou) the kantharos from Tomb 173 (no. 5412), fig. 67xc; cf. Morgan 1988: 323; 1995.

22. Morgan 1988: 323; cf. D'Andria 1982; 1985. Morgan (1995: n. 48) corrects her error in 1988, where, she says, she did not sufficiently appreciate the quantity of Corinthian imports and the extent of variation between Epirote sites. I still consider the fluctuations indicated by her studies relevant to Ithaca's own position. Morgan (1995) also joins the call for further investigation of Ithaca's role.

23. With the exception of Morgan 1988.

tablished some kind of a staging area[24] or even an actual settlement on Ithaca[25]—in other words, that Ithaca perhaps became Corinthian *tout court.*

According to this proposition we would need to read Ithaca as a chapter of Corinthian history, but there are very good reasons for rejecting it out of hand. Ancient evidence, relatively plentiful for Corinthian colonization in northwestern Greece, is absent for such colonization in Ithaca. This small island's alphabet is not Corinthian, as might be expected if there had been a Corinthian settlement on it during the first half of the eighth century. A very early inscribed vase from Ithaca, dated to about 700, shows Euboian influence; it includes a Chalkidian lambda and an exaggerated iota, and the alphabet in general is more closely related to the Achaian.[26] Another case of Euboian influence is pointed out on an Ithacan kantharos with a peculiar design that "must have been copied from an Euboian original."[27] If we were to assume Corinthian settlement wherever great quantities of Corinthian pottery are found we might also make Amphissa and Delphi Corinthian, which is obviously not the case.[28] Moreover, it is probable that much of the pottery in Ithaca identified as Corinthian was locally produced.[29] Throughout the Protogeometric and Geometric periods, Ithaca's pottery retained its independence and affinities with other northwestern pottery. Local, "Corinthianizing" imitations of Corinthian pottery are evident, but Ithaca's pottery does not lose its individuality.[30] Rather than seeing the island as a passive port of call, one should look for signs of its independent, active role. It is possible that Ithaca enjoyed direct relations with Achaia independent of Corinth.[31] Finds of Ithaca-style kantharoi both in the Bay of Naples and in Corinthian Isthmia strengthen this impression of a mediating role between Corinth and Italy.[32] Ithaca seems to have had connections

24. Coldstream 1977: 187; cf. Snodgrass 1971: 339, 416.

25. Robertson 1948: 123–24; cf. Hammond 1967: 414; Waterhouse 1996: 313.

26. Jeffrey 1990: 230.

27. Coldstream 1977: 188.

28. Snodgrass 1971: 339. However, at p. 416 Snodgrass seems to accept some kind of Corinthian settlement at Ithaca.

29. Nancy Symeonoglou claims that the fabric is consistent with "local" pottery as well as certain shapes that are common in Ithaca but rare in Corinth.

30. Coulson 1991; cf. Coldstream 1968: 221–23; 1977: 183–84.

31. Coldstream 1977: 323–29.

32. Dominant Ithacan shapes such as the black-glazed kantharos (e.g., Coldstream 1968: 197 n. 9) may indicate influence on Corinth or even imports from Ithaca. Lo Porto (in *Not. Scavi.* 1964: 228–29, fig. 48) talks about imports from Ithaca (cf. Benton 1953: 292 n. 773, fig. 11, with Melissano 1990: 41–42). See, however, Dehl 1984: 258 (on Corinthian or "Corinthianizing"). Morgan (1995) notes that pottery from Isthmia shows close connections with that from Ithaca's main sanctuary at Aetos, adopting Ithacan forms (the kantharos) and plates (rare in Corinthia). Nancy Symeonoglou currently identifies

with and knowledge of southern Italy as early as the Protogeometric period. It was possibly from Ithaca that "the very, very few Protogeometric sherds found in southern Italy (specifically, the region of Taras) came."[33] Otranto and Messapia reveal a network of material culture (pottery and bronzes) linking Ithaca, Corinth, and Euboia.[34]

Ithaca's position becomes particularly meaningful for its history during the eighth century in view of the studies of Julia Vokotopoulou and Catherine Morgan of Epirote Arta (the Corinthian Ambrakia of the Kypselid era) and Vitsa. It has been shown that throughout the eighth century—even in its later part, when Corinth seems to have neglected its interests in Epirus and concentrated on Corcyra and Sicilian Syracuse—Ithaca kept up its contacts with these sites.[35] This is analogous, perhaps, to its contact with the *Odyssey*'s Ephyra[36] and Thesprotia (see chap. 4), which seem to have had routine maritime connections with Ithaca. Ithaca itself may have been channeling Corinthian goods already in the first half of the eighth century; we may assume that not all Corinthian material was carried by Corinthians.[37] The small dedications at Aetos also seem to evidence Ithaca's varied contacts: amber (probably reaching the island via Italy and the Adriatic), miniature bronze amulets in the shape of vessels, similar to Makedonian ones, scarab-like seals made of stone from Cilicia, and a gold ornament from Crete.[38] Some of the dedications, such as the ivory seals, may have been made by Corinthians, but there is no reason to suppose that Aetos itself was therefore a Corinthian staging area.[39]

Possible connections with Italy seem to be implied in the figure of Mentes in the *Odyssey*.[40] Mentes, prince of the Taphians and a metal specialist, is

---

Ithacan potters' marks in Perachora: a juglet and a fragment of a cup with crosses in orange paint, comparable to a juglet found in Vitsa (Vokotopoulou 1986: 205–6, fig. 67.b and pl. 323), and some forty vases in Ithaca itself (*Praktika* 1989: 293–94). Robertson 1948 was the first to insist on the local aspects of Ithacan pottery.

33. Snodgrass 1971: 85–86 with Benton 1953: 327 n. 491 = Taylour 1958: 118, no. 165. Dehl 1984: pl. 3a (cat. no. 3) illustrates what he believes is a Corinthian pyxis from Francavilla Maritima. On the basis of parallels of shape and poor preservation of paint (probably due to firing at a lower temperature, a characteristic of the Ithacan Late Geometric), Nancy Symeonoglou concludes that the pyxis was Ithacan (as well as a kantharos fragment in Dehl 1984: pl. 7d [cat. no. 1]), a conclusion that fits well with Catherine Morgan's warning (1995) against confusing "Corinthianizing" with Corinthian.

34. Melissano 1990: 41–42.

35. Vokotopoulou 1984; cf. Morgan 1988: 332.

36. *Od.* 1.259; 2.326–28; cf. Huxley 1969: 61–62; Papadopoulos 1990: 364–66.

37. Morgan 1988: 323 (the point about Ephyra is not hers).

38. Coldstream 1977: 184.

39. Ibid.

40. Introduced in *Od.* 1.105.

represented as visiting Ithaca while on his way to Temesa to exchange iron for copper. A possibility known to Strabo that seems to find favor today identifies Temesa with Tamassos in Cyprus, well-known for its copper.[41] However, it could have been, as Strabo was convinced it was, in Bruttium, in southern Italy, where he knew of abandoned copper mines near Bruttian Temesa.[42] This would make excellent sense in the context of maritime connections up from Ithaca (Cypriote Tamassos, Politiko, is not a port). The Bruttian Temesa is said to have been a failed colony of the Aitolians (another northwestern connection), who were expelled by the natives; the place was resettled by Epizephyrian Lokrians[43] and later came under the influence of Kroton.[44] According to Solinus,[45] Odysseus founded a temple to Athena there, and this perhaps strengthens the impression that in antiquity it was identified with the *Odyssey*'s Temesa. Another point in favor of this identification is that Mentes's own home was apparently in Meganisi, near Leukas,[46] which provides a western orientation for Bruttium.

Some have raised the question of whether Mentes was a Greek. Because he does not seem interested in the Trojan War, it has been claimed that he was not.[47] The issue seems somewhat irrelevant, since it is certainly not a Homeric concern in this case. Rather, what seems to matter in the *Odyssey*'s introduction to Ithaca is the image of Ithaca as a crossroads of aristocratic traders, probably like the early Euboians or Corinthians, with their own, personal networks of guest-friendship connections. Mentes perhaps illustrates a preexisting commercial context, mentioned above, into which Greeks from farther away entered during the period of protocolonization. It is to such a context of coming and going to—and via—Ithaca that one of the earliest inscriptions in Greek belongs. It is a guest-friendship (*xenia*) inscription on a wine jug discovered in Ithaca's main sanctuary of Aetos.[48]

In sum, an independent Ithaca stood at a particular crossroads: a maritime one, on the route to the Albanian coast and to Italy (the Strait of Otranto), and an inland one, on the route through Arta into Epirus and to Albania via Vitsa and southern Zagora to northern Greece.[49] It seems that Corinthians were active both alongside of and through the mediation of

41. Heubeck, West, and Hainsworth 1988 on *Od.* 1.184.
42. Strabo 6.255–56; Philipp (*PW* 5 A 459–60) curiously denies the existence of these mines.
43. Strabo 6.255.
44. See Graham 1982: 181.
45. Solinus 2.8.
46. Strabo 6.255 mentions Taphious as a place-name there.
47. Heubeck, West, and Hainsworth 1988 on *Od.* 1.105.
48. Robb 1994: 49–52 with chap. 1, n. 49 and chap. 3, n. 100.
49. Morgan 1988: 330.

Ithacans. With the beginning of colonization its position was probably strengthened: the Euboians from the 750s, the Corinthians from the 730s, and the Achaians from ca. 700 all colonized Italy, and all must have passed through Ithaca. As we shall see, some, at least, probably stopped at the island and made expensive dedications to Odysseus.

PROTOCOLONIZATION AND COLONIZATION: EUBOIANS AND CORINTHIANS IN THE NORTHWEST

Before reaching Italy we must first look at Corcyra, the island that was identified in antiquity, with no serious rivalry, as the country of the Phaiakians who transported Odysseus on his final sea voyage home. When trading and sailing resumed in the (late?) ninth century via Ithaca toward Corcyra, the Strait of Otranto, and southern Italy, this was in the opposite direction of Odysseus's final voyage in the *Odyssey*. The poetical metaphor of transition from mythical geography into the real world was reversed and made concrete. This, I shall argue, is the context of the cult to Odysseus in Ithaca, discernible since the ninth century. Among the Greeks confronting the metaphor were Corinthians (and probably Ithacans), but the first explicitly reported to have settled in Corcyra are the Euboians.

The Euboians are often represented as the Greeks who, from the tenth and, especially, the eighth century, linked east and west. Although it now seems clear that they probably did not have a Near Eastern colony at Syrian Al Mina and that the role of the Phoenicians as traders and carriers was probably greater than previously admitted,[50] the Euboian maritime achievement between the tenth and the eighth century is impressive. Tenth-century Lefkandi (on Euboia itself) and the diffusion of Euboian pottery in the Aegean indicate a rich, reciprocal maritime culture. Moreover, Euboians now seem to have been colonizing earlier than had been thought possible. Their most famous western colony at Pithekoussai in the Bay of Naples was clearly established by 750, and the excavators argue for an even earlier date (770). The Euboian story has been written by others and is not the main concern here.[51] I may mention, however, that it now seems that Chalkidike

50. On Al Mina, see Graham 1986 contra Boardman 1990. Kearsley 1996 (esp. 67–75) concludes that the earliest pottery does not go beyond ca. 750; although she accepts Boardman's observation that the Greek pottery at Al Mina is relatively abundant and belongs to the "foundation level," she considers it too isolated (no tombs, no architecture, etc.) to support the idea that Al Mina was a Greek settlement. On the Phoenicians, see Coldstream 1982; Niemeyer 1982; 1984; 1990; cf. Negbi 1992; papers in Kopcke and Tokumaru 1992; and Popham 1994.

51. See Ridgway (1992: 11–42) for a recent survey and references and especially Crielaard 1996 with Crielaard 1994; Lemos 1997.

too (Torone, Mende, Koukos) may have been settled by Euboians as early as the time of the Ionian migrations, with possibly a second wave arriving in the eighth century.[52] A Euboian Protogeometric sherd discovered at Tell Hadar by the Sea of Galilee in Israel not only is the earliest Euboian find so far to the east but also may push the chronology of the entire class of such pottery farther back (with all the chronological implications for similar material found elsewhere).[53]

Euboian maritime activity around the middle of the eighth century in the areas of Corcyra and Italian Messapia seems to have involved both trade and colonization. Several statements in our sources indicate Euboian colonization of Corcyra and Orikos (in the Bay of Valona). The evidence for Euboian colonization of Corcyra comes from a passage in Plutarch recounting that Eretrian colonists were expelled by Corinthians intent on colonizing the island themselves. The Eretrians tried to return home and were repelled with slings. They proceeded to the Gulf of Therma (northeastern Greece), where they founded Methone.[54] The story, which has some of the elements of an aition, not only contains explicit data beyond what we usually find in colonial aitia but can be understood in the general context of colonists' right to return to the mother city. This right, which I have discussed in detail elsewhere,[55] is particularly relevant for the years immediately after the beginning of the colonial venture and, as the case of Thera indicates, basically concerns the success or failure of the establishment of the colonial landfall. In the case of Thera we have the explicit information that colonists had to stay five years before they could declare the colonization a failure and return home.[56] Strabo speaks of the expulsion of Libur-

52. Cf. Kontoleon 1963. Vokotopoulou (forthcoming) claims that "it is most probable that a second wave of immigrants followed their [= twelfth-century immigrants of the Euboian *ethnos*] step, but no 'foundation' of colonies took place, since there already existed Euboian communities. During this recent phase, it seems that the Eretrians were directed towards Pallene, while the Chalkidians towards Sithonia." See also Lemos 1992; Snodgrass 1994b. Papadopoulos (1996) has recently argued that Chalkidike's name is not derived from Euboian Chalkis, that some of the characteristic Euboian wares may not be Euboian in the early phases, that eastern Greek connections have been underestimated, that Euboian imports are a mere fraction of the total and, in general, that "the more one tries to focus archaeologically on Euboians in the north Aegean, the hazier they become" (p. 165). One awaits responses to these arguments.

53. The sherd is being published by Günther Kopcke. I thank him for showing it to me and explaining its significance.

54. Plut. *Quaest. Graec.* 11 with Graham 1983: 110.

55. Malkin 1994b.

56. Some interpret the relevant passage to mean that the colonists could return only within the first five years. Graham 1983: 53; contra Malkin 1994b: 5 n. 28.

nians from Corcyra by Corinthian colonists.[57] This time what is being contextualized is the Corinthian type of colonial action, which seems to correspond to what they did to the Euboians—a point that indirectly supports
Plutarch's story.

All this seems to indicate that the chances of finding evidence for an Eretrian settlement on Corcyra are rather slim. Few would go so far as to deny
the historicity of Eretria's colonization of Corcyra, although there is nothing to support it archaeologically; for some, the lateness of the source and
the lack of archaeological evidence from Corcyra cast doubt on Plutarch's
story. Again we are faced with the frustrating situation of confronting positivistic arguments from lack of finds. My own approach, before dismissing
detailed and contextualized evidence in an ancient source, is to see whether
there might be good reason for our not having found archaeological corroboration for it. There is. First, precolonial contacts apparently concerned
the mainland, not Corcyra itself; in fact, the site of ancient Corcyra, at Palaiopolis, is located with reference to Butrint on the mainland.[58] One may
therefore not expect to find too much on the island itself. Second, the archaeological situation is rather different from, for example, the rich deposits
in the cemeteries of Pithekoussai, which promise more finds in the future.
Work on Corcyra has been marked by salvage operations on several building sites in Palaiopolis (graves and settlement deposits are reported) and
work in the area of the Roman baths that extends below the modern water
table.[59] It is true that not a single Middle Geometric Euboian sherd has been
found in these operations and that one would expect to find some even if
no Euboian had ever settled on the island.[60] I would be very hesitant, however, to draw any conclusion from this negative evidence. Third, salvage work
is not the same as systematic excavation and/or surface surveys. A survey of
the relevant archaeological publications on Corcyra since the 1960s illustrates the scattered nature of these excavations. Even the better sites, such
as the cemeteries of Garitsa or Kanoni, reveal no evidence before the seventh
century (somewhat late even for Corinthians).[61] Without systematic excavations and surface surveys we cannot seriously apply arguments from silence
to the possibility that the Euboians may have settled elsewhere in Corcyra.
Even if they had liked the area of Palaiopolis, their having settled half a

57. Strabo 6.270.
58. Cf. Morgan and Arafat 1995.
59. Personal communication by Tony Hackens.
60. Kallipolitis (1984: 74–75, figs. 8–9) tentatively identifies sherds from three Eretrian vessels in a deposit at Palaiopolis. Morgan 1995 claims that these are likely to belong to the early seventh century and may even be local.
61. See the annual reports in the *Archeologikon Deltion*. The sites of Figaretto and
Almyras Peritheias are equally helpful for the question I am raising.

kilometer away from the salvage excavations would explain the total lack of evidence. Finally, again, the settlement itself must have been too short-lived for its members to have left much behind.

The Euboian situation on Corcyra was perhaps analogous to what Thucydides describes as the Phoenician presence in sites around Sicily before the Greek colonization; no material evidence corroborates this presence, and one is left with assessment of probabilities, which, in turn, sometimes depend on the general attitude of scholarship at a given time. In the sixties the Phoenicians were out of fashion; now they are back in full force, and scholars will be more ready, I think, to acknowledge various forms of their presence. We also have no satisfactory material evidence for the first phases of Corinth's colonization on the island, which leaves the archaeological situation inconclusive. Blakeway claims that the cow suckling a calf on Corcyrean coins is a legacy of Euboian presence on Corcyra. There are also two onomastic indications: the peninsula of Palaiopolis (the site of the city of Corcyra) was called Makridies, a Euboian name,[62] and there was also a place called "Euboia" on the island.

The date of Corinth's colonization of Corcyra is our only point of reference for the previous Eretrian colony. There are, however, two contradictory dates for this Corinthian colony. Eusebius places it in 708; a fuller narrative version places it earlier, in 733. The difference is significant. We are told that two Corinthian aristocrats of Herakleid descent, Chersikrates and Archias, founded Corcyra and Syracuse in a single colonizing thrust. The synchronism seems suspicious a priori, but several considerations may support it. First, conquest and colonization involved the expulsion not only of the Eretrian colony; as we have seen, Liburnians, probably settled at different sites on the island, were also expelled. The Liburnians may have been expanding toward the south since the ninth century.[63] They were maritime peoples who, although the term "thalassocracy" used by some Albanian scholars may be an exaggeration, should be seen as a vehicle of interconnections between the shores of the Adriatic and Italy. Some would attribute to them the diffusion of Devollian pottery (named after the valley in Albania) to Messapia.[64] In short, it seems that Corcyra was being colonized by

62. Strabo 10.449; cf. Blakeway 1933: 205.

63. Hammond 1982b: 266; Hammond, however, sometimes confuses pottery movement with migration.

64. Mano 1983. Mano suggests that an Illyrian thalassocracy hindered Greek colonization, but relations with the Illyrians may sometimes have been very good. This seems to have been the case in the seventh century with the Corinthian colony to Epidamnos (App. *BCiv.* 2.39), which also had a special magistrate to deal with the native (a *poletes*: Plut. *Mor.* 297F); cf. Cabanes 1988: 52–55.

both Eretrians and Liburnians.[65] To succeed in this double enterprise of ex-pelling both Euboian Greeks and the Liburnians, the Corinthian contingent must have been considerable, and thus makes the story of a major Corinthian expedition that first took Corcyra and then proceeded to Syracuse seem more credible.

Second, the maritime route (here the term is quite justified) between Cor-cyra and Syracuse is a natural one: it was the route of the fifth-century Athe-nian navy that set out to blockade Syracuse, and today, too, boats ride be-fore the northeasterly winds from Corcyra to Sicily. With these winds one reaches the first natural landfall in Sicily—Naxos (the first Greek colony in Sicily), founded by the Chalkidians of Euboia in 734—and may then proceed to Syracuse. In fact, one may see in Corinth's colonization of both Corcyra and Syracuse a reaction to what it could have perceived as a new pattern of Euboian expansion. Instead of trading, now the Euboians actu-ally colonized both Corcyra and Naxos. The Euboian Corcyra-Naxos route between the two new Euboian colonies was replaced by the Corinthian Corcyra-Syracuse one just a year after Naxos's foundation. Whether or not one accepts this reconstruction, the foundation dates for Naxos (734) and Syracuse (733) are well established and archaeologically confirmed.[66] Cor-cyra is implied in all this, and since one has to choose between 733 and 708 the overall case seems in favor of the earlier date. The Eretrians, therefore, apparently settled on Corcyra before 733, around the mid-eighth century, and thus probably belonged to the same generation as the Euboian settlers in Pithekoussai.

There is another geographical dimension to this Euboian colonization. It may have been around this time that the Euboians settled Orikos (Pasha Liman), an island in the Bay of Valona. Orikos is just opposite Otranto, where there is a notable presence of Greek pottery beginning with Middle Geometric II.[67] It is mentioned by Hekataios as part of his description of

65. It is unnecessary to postulate a combined Eretrian-Liburnian settlement on Cor-cyra (Hammond 1982b: 269). The island is very large and could have contained two sep-arate populations; cf. Calligas 1982. There is no evidence from the mainland until colo-nial times. The date of the "prehistoric" handmade wares from the sanctuary at Aphionas may be open to revision and downdating. On the mainland, Albanian scholars have pre-ferred a Bronze Age date for similar wares from their own sites, but the duration of the ware remains an open question. A comparable date for the Aphionas pottery would, on the basis of its similarity with Albanian wares, make the island "Illyrian." Further study is clearly required.

66. Graham 1982: 103–13.

67. D'Andria 1990: 283 sees this is a confirmation of Beaumont's suggestion (1936: 164) that Orikos was founded at this time.

Epirus,[68] and the name seems to signify the whole gulf, indicating that the settlement was of some importance.[69] Hekataois mentions it together with Bylliake, probably the port of the Bylliones, who claimed descent from Neoptolemos, son of Achilles.[70] According to Pseudo-Scymnus's description of the coastal region from Corcyra to Apollonia, it was founded by the Euboians after the Trojan War; like Odysseus, they had been driven there by the winds.[71] A dedicatory inscription of Apollonia at Olympia, dating to the early fifth century, calls the area Abantis, a Euboian name. It is cited by Pausanias, who tells of the destruction of Thronios (also in the bay) by Apollonia (see chap. 4).[72] This also seems to be reflected by Lycophron, who claims in his *Alexandra* that Elpenor and the Abantes from Euboia[73] went to the island Othronos and were driven by swarms of snakes to the city Amantia (also in the Bay of Valona, in the modern district of Vosjë).[74] This island Othronos seem to be a confusion with the Thronios just mentioned. This is a variant *nostos,* since the Homeric Elpenor, leader of the Abantes, died at Troy.[75] Another Hellenistic author, Apollonius of Rhodes, says that the previous inhabitants of Corcyra were Colchians (see also chap. 8) who stayed there with the Phaiakians until the (Corinthian) Bakchiads came to settle it and then crossed over to the "opposite island" and from there to the Keraunian Mountains (= the peninsula of the Bay of Valona) of the Abantes to the Nestaei and to Orikos.[76]

Unlike the "Illyrian" Bylliake or the "Lokrian-Euboian" colony Thronios,[77] Orikos was an island, well suited to trade and self-defense. As Beaumont observes, it had easy access to the small harbor Panormus, across the peninsula through the Logará Pass, and therefore good communications with Corcyra and the Euboian position on the mainland opposite Corcyra.[78] Un-

68. *FGrH* 1 F 104 with Hammond 1982b: 268.
69. Beaumont 1936: 165.
70. Strabo considers them Illyrian. 7.316, 326.
71. Ps.-Scymn. 442–43.
72. Paus. 5.22.3–4; cf. Plin. *HN* 2.204.
73. Cf. *Il.* 2.540.
74. Lycoph. *Alex.* 1044–45 with *Il.* 2.536.
75. Tzetzes, in his commentary, says that Othronos was near Sicily.
76. Ap. Rhod. 4.1206–7 with Delage 1930: 247–53 (at 251 for the precise siting, in Apollonius's description, of the Colchians on Corcyra).
77. Paus. 5.22.2 speaks of a joint foundation by Lokrian and Euboian Nostoi.
78. I see no justification for Hammond's claim (1967: 416 n. 2), contra Beaumont 1936: 165, that what is meant by schol. Ap. Rhod. 4.1175 is the positions across from Palaiopolis on Corcyra itself. There would have been no point in making that remark. One wonders if Butrint (Buthrotum) is meant. See, on the archaeological indications of Corcyraean contacts, Morgan and Arafat 1995.

til its foundation of Epidamnos and Apollonia, Corinthian involvement with the inland areas north of Corcyra may have declined somewhat during the last third of the eighth century and the first two-thirds of the seventh,[79] and the Euboian colony at Orikos seems to have held on. Its being an island probably saved it from the fate of Thronios.

The sources we have for the foundation of Orikos are *nostoi*, and one can only infer its historical context. It is highly unlikely that it was founded later than the Corinthian thrust to Epidamnos and Apollonia (seventh and sixth centuries). As for Eretria and Chalkis, their role as international colonizing states seems to have ended at the close of the eighth century, and the Euboian presence must therefore be pushed back at least to that time. Since an Eretrian presence on Corcyra seems to be acceptable, Orikos was founded either by Euboians (probably Eretrians) in the mid-eighth century or by Eretrian refugees from Corcyra after the Corinthians had conquered it (although, as we have seen, Plutarch says that these tried to return to Eretria and later settled in Methone). It is possible but highly uncertain to read such an interpretation into the verses of the *Argonautica* mentioned above. It remains to conclude that Orikos was already in existence by 733.

The Euboians have been called the first western Greeks because of their colony on Pithekoussai in the Bay of Naples. They were literate and knew enough of Homer to make Homeric jokes in their symposia (chap. 5). The priority of Pithekoussai is now well established among historians of Greek colonization, especially since the significant archaeological discoveries on the island.[80] Nothing comparable archaeologically exists on Corcyra. What has not been sufficiently emphasized is that Euboian colonization of Corcyra is not far removed in time and may even be regarded as contemporary.

Pithekoussai's priority has also created the impression of a "great leap" in the history of Greek colonization, since it has made it appear that the earliest colony in the west was also the most distant. All colonies established up to ca. 600 were founded closer to "Greece." In contrast to Pithekoussai, Corcyra projects a more conventional and, in terms of distances, somewhat less adventurous story: it was just around the corner, so to speak, north of Ithaca, on a natural maritime route to the north (the Strait of Otranto) and to Sicily, and facing Epirus. Thus "the first western Greeks,"[81] the Euboians of Pithekoussai, should be considered "first" in a more nuanced picture. Euboians seem to have been "first" on both sides of Italy—in the Bay of Naples and in the Ionian Sea. The Mycenaeans notwithstanding (see below), what emerges from the archaeological evidence, especially in Albania, Messapia/

79. Morgan 1988: 338; however, there is no positive evidence for this.
80. Buchner and Ridgway 1993 and chap. 5.
81. See the title of Ridgway 1992.

Iapygia (the Salentine peninsula in Italy opposite Albania), and the Strait of Otranto, is that Greeks were frequenting and trading with these areas as early as the first half of the eighth century, thus being at least contemporary with the colonists of Pithekoussai. Moreover, at least some of these were the "same" Greeks: the Euboians. This should not make the contemporary Pithekoussai story less exciting; rather, it places the protocolonial contacts with Etruria and Campania, as well as the founding of Pithekoussai, in a wider Euboian context.

Who were the Euboians in this region? It appears that the Chalkidians were active more in western Italy and the Eretrians more in the Ionian and Adriatic Seas, but they seem to have cooperated on Pithekoussai. It is possible that the foundation of Eretrian Corcyra and Chalkidian Kyme (on the mainland across from Pithekoussai) sharpened the confrontation between the two Euboian cities. By the end of the century they were fighting the Lelantine War, which resulted in the decline of both. In the west, however, there was one marked difference in favor of the Chalkidian colonies: Corinth, intensively active since the third quarter of the eighth century, directed its attention to northwestern Greece and to Sicily. Eventually, its "empire" would embrace Ambrakia, Leukas, and Corcyra[82] and later, sometimes indirectly, extend into the Adriatic (Epidamnos, Apollonia). Corcyra, as we have seen, was colonized with a view to Syracuse, and the Eretrians disappeared in the face of the Corinthians. By contrast, the Chalkidian colonies in western Italy did not have to confront the Corinthians, and Syracuse was to become involved with Kyme only in the fifth century, when it came to its aid against the Etruscans. This relatively favorable subsequent history of the Chalkidian colonies seems to have pulled a veil over the early history of Eretria in the Ionian and Adriatic Seas and caused the first western Greeks to be regarded more in Chalkidian terms (Pithekoussai was founded, it seems, by both Eretrians and Chalkidians, but it had a relatively short life).

This reconstructed colonization history directly bears on Odysseus: he was known to the Euboians of Pithekoussai and therefore also to the Euboians who sailed the Epirote coast and then settled Corcyra and Orikos, making dedications in Ithaca en route to these places and to Otranto.

OTRANTO AND MESSAPIA

During part of the ninth and the first half of the eighth century the Strait of Otranto (see map 5) seems to have functioned not as a divider but as a region of trade and contact for both Greeks and non-Greeks.[83] The sea

---

82. Graham 1983: chap. 7 and appendix 1.   83. Cf. Greco 1992: 3–5, 123–24.

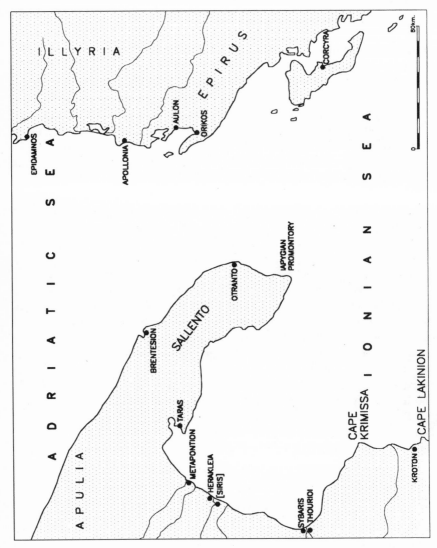

Map 5. The Strait of Otranto.

between Italy and Albania functioned in history as seas and rivers often do: either obstructing the passage between the shores or pulling them together as riverbanks.[84] Beyond Otranto, the Italian region concerned is the Salentine peninsula, variously named Messapia or Iapygia in antiquity.[85] Mycenaean contacts are already evident on both sides of the strait.[86] For example, the tumulus at Torre S. Sabina north of Brindisi, which seems of an Albanian type (i.e., from across the strait), contains Mycenaean material. Some hiatus between the Mycenaean material and Protogeometric pottery is apparent here as elsewhere (e.g., at Scoglio del Tonno near Taras).[87] If we are concerned with the resumption (rather than continuity) of contacts, the evidence for this applies at the moment to the end of the ninth century.

This century also seems to have witnessed trade and possibly migration of non-Greeks. Therefore, from a non-Greek point of view as well these areas provide an impression of contact of material culture and movement of populations on both sides of the strait. Greeks were probably entering existing networks[88] as well as shaping these networks. Non-Greek, "Illyrian" contacts between northern Epirus and southern Italy could also serve as a context for the transmission of folk motifs and Homeric stories. In some late sources the "Illyrian *koinē*" of the Strait of Otranto was articulated in terms of ancient "Arkadian" migrations to Epirus and Italy. Genealogically the Arkadian Lykaon could be considered the progenitor of Thesprotos and Ambrax (Epirus), Peuketios, Iapyx, and Daunos (southeastern Italy), and Oinotros (southwestern Italy). Supposedly, argues Paul Fabre, the "primitive conditions" of the Peloponnesian Arkadians (who were thought to have been there before the return of the Herakleidai) were found replicated in Epirus and Italy, where people were different from Greeks—but not entirely.[89]

Non-Greeks seem to have been using the shores of the Strait of Otranto as connecting banks. Iapygian (non-Greek) "Early Geometric" seems to have been imported from central Albania; Liburnians and other Illyrians, as well

84. Cf. Lamboley 1987. Specifically, Lamboley suggests the extension of the overland route to the east, connecting even Asia Minor with Italy through the Pindus Mountains and the Strait of Otranto.

85. The terms do not overlap precisely; see Nenci 1978.

86. In general, *Magna Grecia e il mondo miceneo* (1983). D'Andria 1983: 288; 1990: 282; Kilian 1990: 461; Bietti Sestieri 1992.

87. The extent of the hiatus and its significance are unclear. Much depends on appreciation of both the Late Helladic III C and the Protogeometric wares as "Greek" or "local." See also Korkuti 1984; Jones and Vagnetti 1988; 1992. Sueref 1987 tends to conflate pots and people, both Greeks and non-Greeks.

88. Morgan 1995.

89. Fabre 1981: 36–40; cf. Asheri 1995.

as Iapygian/Messapians, seem to have been moving and migrating between the banks.[90] Certain place-names, such as "Iapygia,"[91] were common to both the Albanian and the Italian shore. Place- and personal names in fact point to some Illyrian origins, but one must be careful not to apply toponomastic and onomastic methodology too rigidly.[92] Non-Greek pottery, matte-painted with hatched triangles, that was common to Makedonia and Illyria (especially Vitsa and Dodona) arrived in Salento in the first half of the eighth century. Some argue that the diffusion of this pottery was the result not so much of trade as of individual migration.[93] The general conclusion that Messapia was a crossroads of east-west routes from Italian Campania to Makedonia and north-south routes along the Adriatic coasts seem to derive also from the record of bronzes found in Messapia.[94]

It is unclear what Greeks thought about the ethnic identity of the Messapians in the eighth and seventh centuries. There was probably something that marked them as distinct, for their ethnography is neither Trojan, Pelasgian,[95] nor Arkadian. Herodotus, who seems to have had a somewhat broader, "Ionian" concept of Messapia,[96] considered them Cretan in origin (although in later sources the eponym Iapyx was a son of Daidalos).[97] Hellenistic writers, perhaps attempting a more scientific view, identified them with Illyrians, and they may have been right.[98] What matters is, first, the distinctness of the Messapians in Greek eyes and, second, their image as a people belonging to a maritime region that encompasses both Italy and Epirus. Greek popular etymology explained their name as "those who live between two seas." The etymology is worthless but the observation pertinent: the two sides of the sea constituted a "region."[99]

The end of the ninth and especially the first half of the eighth century become highly significant for Greek contacts. For the first half of the eighth

90. On the considerable intercourse between Illyrian communities on both sides of the Adriatic, see Hammond 1982b: 266; cf. Greco 1992: 123–24.

91. Hekataios *FGrH* 1 F 86 (Steph. Byz. s.v. Ἰαπυγία): "Two cities, one in Italy, the other in Illyria."

92. Cf. De Simone 1989: 107–110.

93. See Sueref 1991: 211–12 with D'Andria 1990: 284 n. 12; cf. Greco 1992: 123–24. Caution is due, however, since inferring migration may be the result, again, of conflating pots with people.

94. Rolley 1991.

95. On a Pelasgian element, see Pherecydes fr. 156 J; Dion. Hal. *Ant. Rom.* 1.11; Strabo 6.283.

96. Lepore 1979.

97. Hdt. 7.169–171. See Lombardo 1991: 35; cf. 1992; Nenci 1978: 50 ff.; 1990; Ampolo 1990.

98. See the discussion in Lombardo 1991: 59; cf. Nenci 1978: 51 with n. 25.

99. Nenci 1978: 47; De Juliis 1988: 31.

century these contacts are apparent at Otranto and throughout southern Salento and the Cape of Leuca. The intensity of circulation of Greek material in this area is "unparalleled elsewhere in Italy."[100] Recent work, especially by Francesco D'Andria, Mario Lombardo, and Jean-Luc Lamboley, has provided a new and important perspective on the history of Messapia.[101] Some Corinthian poetry of Middle Geometric I and II has been unearthed at Otranto,[102] Vaste (somewhat inland),[103] and Porto Cesareo (on the Ionian side of the peninsula).[104] Late Geometric material and vases of the protokotyle type marking the transition to Late Geometric I have been found at Otranto,[105] Vaste,[106] Cavallino,[107] and Porto Cesareo.[108] There is some Late Geometric Euboian pottery, mostly at Otranto.[109] A parallel development is noted with the non-Greek, Devollian-type pottery that is found both in Albania and on the Salentine peninsula, especially at Otranto.[110]

It is particularly noteworthy that both the Corinthian and the Euboian pottery is similar in range, shapes, and dates to that discovered at Ithaca.[111] This brings Ithaca yet again, either directly or as a point of passage, into the region of significant Greek contacts with Epirus and Italy.[112] Although in terms of chronology, vessel forms, apparent exchange structure, and so on, the inland Epirote contacts apparently differed from the seaborne ones, the island seems to have been tapping into both.

The most important implications of the Greco-Messapian discoveries have not yet come into sharp focus. The conclusions of D'Andria and Lombardo signify, in my view, nothing less than a revolutionary approach to the early history of Greek colonization in the west. It used to be thought that it was Taras, the Spartan colony founded in 706 B.C., that was responsible for the

100. D'Andria 1990: 283.

101. D'Andria 1979; 1983; 1988; 1989; 1990a; 1990b; 1991; Yntema 1982; 1991; De Juliis 1988; Moscati 1989; Whitehouse and Wilkins 1989; Lombardo 1991 and other articles in *I Messapi* 1991; Van Compernolle 1989; Lamboley 1987; 1996. For the sources see Lombardo 1992; cf. Susini 1962.

102. Melissano 1990: 36–38.

103. V. Melissano in D'Andria 1990b: 53–54.

104. D'Andria 1983: 288–89; Lo Porto 1973: 222–28.

105. Melissano 1990: 39–42.

106. P. Cagia in D'Andria 1990b: 54–55.

107. P. Cagia in D'Andria 1990b: 205–7.

108. F. G. Lo Porto in D'Andria 1990b: 229–230.

109. Melissano 1990: 42–43.

110. P. Cagia in D'Andria 1990b: 34–36.

111. Melissano 1990: 41–42; cf. Greco 1992: 123–24.

112. D'Andria 1983: 289–90.

Greek penetration (and, for some, the "Hellenization") of Messapia.[113] It now seems evident, however, that contacts with Greeks began about a century earlier and that Greek colonization should be seen as beginning with Pithekoussai.

The Greeks involved in these contacts were probably traders: Corinthians, Euboians, and perhaps northwestern Greeks, notably from Ithaca. It has been suggested that there were tiny enclaves of Greek traders and artisans (Corinthian?) settled in Messapia by the mid-eighth century.[114] It seems likely that, somewhat later, exiles from the colonies also settled there; there is, for example, the tradition about the exile of Phalanthos, the founder of Taras, in Brindisi, and the one about the Tarentine Gillos.[115] As we shall see in the case of Diomedes, the presence of individual Greeks—settlers, exiles, artisans, and so forth—could have been instrumental in spreading Greek *nostoi*. The relatively significant quantities of Corinthian material seems to point to active participation of Corinthians in addition to the presumed presence of Euboians. Once the network of contacts had been established, the active participants and the origins of the goods carried may have varied. There can be little doubt, however, about the intensity of the contacts with the Salentine peninsula and the implied Corinthian contacts there. During the period between the foundation of Syracuse (733) and Corcyra and the foundation of Epidamnos (627) and Leukas,[116] Corinth seems to have lost some of its interest both in inland Epirus and in Messapia, where Sparta founded Taras in 706.

This short summary and reconstruction of eighth-century Greek presence in the Ionian and Adriatic Seas indicates, even before we move on to the seventh century, that all the necessary conditions for familiarity and contacts with native populations already existed by the time the Nestor cup bearing an inscription alluding to Homer was placed in the Pithekoussai tomb. In both cases we are dealing with Euboian Greeks, and, more narrowly, Eretrians were present in both Pithekoussai and Corcyra. Homer was known to these Greeks, as the Nestor cup and some of the iconographic evidence will indicate (see chap. 5). There is no a priori reason, therefore, to assume that the localization of Odyssean itineraries must have begun later than the eighth century. In fact, as we shall observe, our earliest such localizations are found in Hesiod, ca. 700. His various references to the west— Odysseus as the progenitor of the Latins and Etruscans, the sites of the Sirens

113. Dunbabin 1948a: 149.

114. On nuclei of settlements, see D'Andria 1991: 433–36 and his discussion-comments in *I Messapi* 1991: 312–15.

115. Malkin 1994a: 133–39 (Phalanthos); Hdt. 3.134–38 (Gillos).

116. Founded probably by Gorgos, son of Kypselos (Strabo 10.452) or Periander. Graham 1983: 30.

and Circe—have all been doubted and their authenticity denied on a priori grounds. These doubts, with our new context, will appear irrelevant.

To sum up: a colonizing Euboian presence on both Corcyra and Orikos now seems acceptable at least for the mid-eighth century, replaced on Corcyra by Corinth probably ca. 733 (or possibly some twenty-five years later). The archaeological evidence from Otranto seems to suggest that this Greek presence was preceded by protocolonial traffic and was directed not only to the Epirote lands and the Ionian Sea but also across the Strait of Otranto to Italy and possibly also to the Adriatic. The evidence points to contacts as early as ca. 800 and the first half of the eighth century and may be thus termed protocolonial. When we observe the fascinating Adriatic identifications of Odysseus and other Nostoi, especially Diomedes, Philoktetes, and Epeios, along the shores of the Strait of Otranto, their context will begin to come into focus. Odysseus, for example, penetrated Campania, Latium, and Etruria via Pithekoussai; he probably entered southern Italy from the Ionian Sea.

THE OTRANTO CONTEXT AND THE NAME OF ODYSSEUS

A linguistic hypothesis traces the introduction of Odysseus's name into Italy via Messapia.[117] It has long been claimed that whereas the oldest form of the name "Odysseus" in Etruscan, Utuse, seems to derive from Ionian (Euboian) Greek, the Latin form Ulixes/Ulysses cannot have been borrowed directly from the same source. It has been suggested that Ulixes is a Messapian (Illyrian) form, reaching the Romans directly,[118] in a way similar to the borrowing of other Greek names, for example, via Oscan. The fullest study of Etruscan borrowings from Greek, by Carlo de Simone,[119] confirms that Etruscan variants of Odysseus's name markedly differing from Utuse/Odysseus (Uθste, Uθuste, Utzte) do not appear before the fourth century and should not enter the discussion. By contrast, the older forms (Utuse, Uθuze, Utuśe) clearly derive from the Ionian/Euboian.

It used to be thought that "Odysseus" was an earlier form of "Olysseus," but study of all the vase inscriptions bearing the (surprisingly great) variety of the names of the hero has left little doubt that this is not the case.[120] The Corinthian (and Boiotian) variants use the form Olytteus ('Ολυττεύς, 'Ολυσσεύς).[121] Given that the presence of Corinthians was not considered a relevant question for Messapia during the first half of the eighth century, no one was in a position to suggest that it was Greek contacts at that time

117. Phillips 1953: 65–66.
118. Altheim 1938: 128; Phillips 1953: 65–66.
119. De Simone 1968; 1970, esp. 126–28.
120. Brommer 1982–83; cf. Stanford 1992 (1963): 8.
121. De Simone 1970: 126; Brommer 1982–83; 89–90.

and in that region that introduced the story of Odysseus to Italy. Phillips's suggestion [122] that the Messapians were responsible for the transformation of the name of Odysseus into the Latin Ulysses is therefore correct but for the wrong reason and in a different manner from the one he envisages. One need not imagine, as does Phillips, that independent Illyrian or Messapian *Odyssey* epics account for this. Having observed the Greek context of contacts and possible individual migrations, it seem that it was a Greek rather than a Messapian Odysseus or an Illyrian *Odyssey* that were transferred by the Messapians to the Latins. He was not necessarily "Corinthian" (the "l" element in "Olytteus"); if Messapians heard both Euboian and Corinthian versions, it may simply be that one stuck and the other did not.

THE "CAPTAINS"

We have no idea who, individually, the Greeks were who sailed up to the Strait of Otranto in the ninth and the first half of the eighth century. It seems probable that prominent among the entrepreneurs were Euboian and Corinthian aristocrats or "princes." The term "aristocrats" may suit them, but it is too wide-ranging and is equally applicable to later periods and different historical contexts. The French term *prince* has been used, for example, to describe the prominent Euboians given "heroic" burials at the West Gate of Eretria. Considering views articulated mostly in anthropological terms of "big men" or "chiefs" [123] to describe the personal status of "aristocrats" in Dark Age society—before or during periods of state formation— "princes" may seem adequate. Admittedly impressionistic, it avoids the irrelevant associations of "big men" while retaining enough of a Viking flavor to account for the sailing context (trading, gift exchanging, raiding, etc.) in which we see the evidence for the activity of some of these "chiefs." "Princes" is, however, increasingly used in specific interpretive contexts of European archaeology. I opt, therefore, for the term *archos*, "captain," which I take from a particularly apt context in the *Odyssey*.

The powerful individuals operating along the coasts discussed in this book before the first half of the eighth century may have been "captains of sailor-traders," [124] leading expeditions with subordinate adventurers-traders who could expect a share in the profits. We are reminded of the Cretan Odysseus, in the story told to Eumaios, or Mentes, prince of the Taphians, who in the first book of the *Odyssey* stops over at Ithaca. From a narrative point of view he is Athena in disguise, but because he is meant to be plausible both to Telemachos and the suitors and to Homeric audiences this indicates that

122. Phillips 1953: 65–66.   124. *Od.* 8.162.
123. Cf. Donlan 1985; 1989.

such a stopover *at Ithaca* by a captain belonged to a familiar and acceptable frame of reference. Ever since Finley's *The World of Odysseus,* Mentes has been seen as the *Odyssey's* first example of a guest-friend,[125] but the way in which his identity is articulated, his habits, and his itinerary are of no less importance. Mentes is asked about his name, his place of origin, his city, and his parents; Telemachos also asks on what kind of ship he reached Ithaca and who brought him there, implying that he could have been a trader passenger rather than the owner of the vessel. Such a category is implied in the dialogue between Odysseus and the Phaiakian Euryalos. The latter asks Odysseus whether he is a "captain of sailors who are traders" (ἀρχὸς ναυτάων οἵ τε πρηκτῆρες ἔασιν).[126] It is also implied in the voyage of the Cretan Odysseus, who is persuaded by the Phoenician to go on the Phoenician's ship to Libya, where both may profit.[127] Finally, Mentes is asked whether he has been in Ithaca before and is a friend to Odysseus's house, "for many were the men who came to our house as strangers, since he, too, had gone to and fro among men." Ithaca, therefore, is perceived as a place frequented by traders, and in the case of Mentes a "regional" northwestern navigation is implied.

There is no "aristocratic shame" attached to his involvement in trade; Mentes's self-presentation and Telemachos's questions make it appear quite normal. Similarly, that Euryalos the Phaiakian taunts Odysseus for seeming not a man "skilled in contests" but a "captain of sailors who are traders" does not, as has been thought, indicate any general derogation of trade.[128] In one of the lying tales Odysseus makes a point of attributing to himself the reputation of being a superb profit maker.[129] It shows, rather, that the conflict of values between aristocrats who preferred the hunt and the hall, such as the brothers of the Cretan Odysseus, and entrepreneurs was much earlier than its echoes in Archaic poetry.[130] Odysseus, in his Cretan guise, is a bastard who becomes a successful pirate-trader-mercenary because he was shortchanged when his brothers divided their patrimony. It is to be expected that such men, perhaps scorned by contemporaries whom they considered their peers, were all the more eager to identify themselves with a Homeric hero such as Odysseus.

The first individuals whose names we know belong to the second half of the eighth century and seem to illustrate the overlap between prominent

125. Finley 1979: 65.
126. *Od.* 8.159–64 at 162.
127. *Od.* 14.295–96. Cf. Hesiod *Works and Days* 643 with other implications in the maritime passage for sharing cargoes.
128. Hainsworth in Heubeck, West, and Hainsworth 1988 on *Odyssey* 8.161–65.
129. *Od.* 19.285.
130. Donlan 1980: 35–75, 77–95.

individual status and the political context within which they were operating. Chersikrates and Archias, the founders of Corcyra and Syracuse, were certainly aristocrats in a social-genealogical sense: they belonged to the ruling clan of the Bakchiads and were regarded as Herakleidai, descendants of Herakles.[131] Their action (about 733 at the earliest) in founding colonies that seem to have been planned even vis-à-vis each other, linking Greece with Sicily via Corcyra, is already characterized by political organization and state interests.[132]

The foundation lore about Archias, including a late (probably Hellenistic) adaptation of the Aktaion myth that makes Archias responsible for tearing a small boy limb from limb, is beside the point here.[133] Here was certainly enough of an *autokrator* (the term is applied in the fifth century to the powers of a founder)[134] to make the decision to include displaced groups in his colonial enterprise.[135] However, some have preferred to see Archias less as a Corinthian than as an individual aristocrat who led a specific band of colonists from the village of Tenea to colonize overseas. In fact, Tenea has become an example in the history of colonization for regional hunger and overpopulation.[136] One wonders where this idea came from. The information about Tenea comes from a passage in Strabo[137] in which we are told that Archias departed for Syracuse *from the temple* of Apollo at Tenea: "It is said that most of the colonists who accompanied Archias, the leader of the colonists to Syracuse, set out from there (ἐντεῦθεν συνεπακολουθῆσαι)." One can either reject the information altogether or, since it is not of the same order as the late concoction about Archias as a murderer, retain its essentials: the name "Tenea" and that of its temple. The straightforward meaning of the text implies that the temple of Apollo was the point of departure for the colonists, who would be not "Teneans" but Corinthians. The reason for departing from Tenea was probably religious: Tenea was known as a place of good fortune (not of misery and hunger), and Apollo was also

131. Graham 1983: 220.
132. On the character of Corinthian colonization, see Graham 1983: chap. 7 and appendix 1.
133. Plut. *Mor.* 772d–773b with Diod. 8.10.1–3 and schol. Ap. Rhod. 4.1212 (where the entire Bakchiad clan is exiled); see Bérard 1957: 119. Will 1955: 180–87 claims that this is an adaptation of the Aktaion myth. Dougherty (1993: 31–44) considers this anecdote a paradigmatic Greek representation of founders (curiously missing both Diodorus and the scholiast and seemingly unaware of Will's interpretation or mine [1987a: 42]).
134. Graham 1983: chap. 3.
135. Strabo 6.270; Ps.-Scymn. 277–78.
136. Cawkwell 1992: 297. Dougherty 1993 misses this issue, as well as his joining the displaced group of failed colonists, entirely.
137. Strabo 6.380.

Apollo Archegetes, the god of colonization.[138] If Diodorus is correct in stating that the Bakchiad revolution took place around 747 B.C.,[139] this was also a further step in making overseas trade (and henceforward also settlement) "political." The date implies a change in the character of Corinth's overseas operations about the mid-eighth century.

By contrast, it stands to reason that the captains who traded rather than colonized during the first half of that century were somewhat less representative of their community (even if that community consisted mostly of other Bakchiads, rulers of others). Williams has suggested that what we call early Corinthian contacts with the west were conducted by independent aristocrats, perhaps acting in mixed groups.[140] Some of the modern discussions of early Corinth in fact envisions its society in the early eighth century in terms of strong families rather than a "city." Members of such families, it is argued, should be regarded as responsible for most (or some) of the Corinthian precolonial material found in Ithaca, Epirus, and Italy (and especially Otranto).[141]

The conclusions of a recent study of the Euboian aristocracy in the Dark Age seems to be compatible with this image of the captains.[142] During the tenth and ninth centuries the Euboian elite had privileged access to the import and exchange of foreign goods, especially from the east. Such fruitful long-distance connections were important for status enhancement. It is claimed that, for example, prestige goods found in Lefkandi had their individual biographies, which may have corresponded to individual histories, and that new regions of contacts may have provided fresh symbols of prestige. Thus, by the beginning of the eighth century it can be said that prestige had been accruing to objects in direct relation to the distance of their provenance and the effort involved in getting them. Special emphasis is thus placed more on the adventure-prestige activity than on profit or economic activity as such.[143] "Sailing and travelling in themselves probably became prestige-providing activities."[144]

138. Ibid.; see Malkin 1984–85; 1987a: chap. 1.
139. Diod. 7.9.
140. Williams 1982; n.d. Morgan (1995) now argues for three strands of Corinthian interest: (1) Late Protogeometric contacts through Medeon (north of the Corinthian Gulf) to land trade in the north, (2) contacts at Delphi and on the gulf up to Ithaca and in Epirus, and only then, rather tentatively, (3) links with the west along long-established routes.
141. The question of "state" versus individual-family trade was also debated at the 1994 Taranto conference. See Morgan 1994; 1995.
142. Crielaard 1996.
143. Cf. Van Wees 1992: 249–58.
144. Crielaard 1996 convincingly adduces anthropological evidence from Oceania suggesting that "adventure, curiosity, wandering, and exploring cannot be strictly sepa-

We cannot be certain about the identity of the agents who brought wealth to Euboia from the east. These could have been Euboians themselves, "Cypriotes," "Phoenicians," or all of the above. Skirting the issue, I feel safer in saying that with regard to the west, in contrast, we can be fairly certain that the wind that filled the sails of the ships came from Euboia. After the period of protocolonization, when new cities were founded in the west, founders such as Thoukles the Euboian or Archias the Corinthian would also come from the milieu of the captains. The "heroic burial" perhaps practiced in exceptional cases in Euboia as early as the tenth century would be converted into an annual cult of colonial founders, which, in itself, became an object of ambition for powerful persons.[145] Whereas the act of founding a new city was certainly communal (with respect to both the mother city and the community of settlers) the personal-aristocratic status of the founder was enhanced both in life and in the heroic cult accorded him after death. It is also possible that, already with the powerful protocolonists, the heroic terms in which some of these actions were cast converged with mythic associations of which the captains were aware.

In sum, whether initiatives of penetration into the Ionian Sea were individual or communal and whether they took place in the period of protocolonization or at the beginning of the colonization era, it was the individual captains who reached Polis Bay in Ithaca, disembarking in front of the cave of the tripods. They faced it as individuals, masters of their ships and probably of other traders, making personal dedications.

CONCLUSION

The basis for a new, protocolonial history of Greeks sailing up, down, and around the Ionian (and possibly the Adriatic) Sea now seems to be established for the ninth and eighth centuries. This conclusion may be evident to some archaeologists, but it appears that the implications of their work have yet to be integrated among historians. It seems clear, at any rate, that the basis of our understanding of Greek maritime activity must be substantially revised. Ithaca itself appears as a player, functioning, first, as "colonial"—an offshore island in relation to Epirus—and, second, as a stop on the maritime route to the north for those sailing both around the Peloponnese and (especially) through the Corinthian Gulf. That it did not remain a mere passive way station seems probable. In terms of material culture it

---

rated from trading ventures, assertion of traditional authority, or raiding." Moreover, "knowledge" gained in long-distance travels attaches awe and potency to its bearers, important traits in the implied rivalry among "chiefs."

145. See Malkin 1987a: 254–60 and pt. 2, passim.

certainly partook both of its regional, northwestern *koinē* and of some of the Epirote and Italian material. It was certainly important for the Euboians and Corinthians, some of whom probably dedicated tripods to Odysseus in the cave on Polis Bay, where they must have stopped en route north and on their return. By the mid-eighth century colonization enters the picture, especially with Corcyra. A reconstructed history of Eretrian colonization has been suggested, with a significant role for these Euboians also to the north, at Orikos in the Bay of Valona. These Eretrians were as much the first western Greeks as their compatriots (with the Chalkidians) at Pithekoussai in the Bay of Naples. The principle current in writing on Greek colonization that the farthest is the earliest may accordingly be in need of revision. Since the Euboians of Pithekoussai around the mid-eighth century were clearly aware of Homer, this presence up, down, and around is highly significant for the myths of the Nostoi: they would most certainly have been current in these parts.

Corinth, in particular, is evidenced at Otranto and in Messapia. It was not alone: these areas, encompassing both shores of the Ionian Sea, indicate the moving about (commerce, migration) of various Illyrians. Another *koinē*, therefore, seems evident and meshed with the Greek presence in these parts. That Illyrians too, just like the Greek Epirotes, with whom they had much in common (see chap. 4), may have been responsible for the dissemination of *nostoi* appears a viable proposition, against which should be assessed the penetration of the non-Euboian form of the name of Odysseus (e.g., the Corinthian Olytteus-Ulysses) into Italy.

THREE

Ithaca and the Cult of Odysseus

Perhaps the oldest heroic cult in Greece was discovered in Ithaca, Odysseus's homeland. Between the beginning or the middle of the ninth century and the end of the eighth, at least twelve or thirteen rich and ornate bronze tripods were placed in a seaside cave at the far end of the island's Polis Bay. From any perspective these dedications are highly exceptional. It is one thing to find costly tripod dedications at great pan-Hellenic centers such as Olympia and (later) Delphi or Delos or even in great city sanctuaries such as the temples of Hera at Samos and Argos. In Isthmia, for example, there are six tripods, all dated no earlier than the second half of the eighth century. It is something completely different—in fact, unique—for more than twice as many such dedications to be found in a cave shrine on a tiny island in northwestern Greece.[1] That expensive ninth- and eighth-century bronze tripods should have been placed in the Polis cave and dedicated to Odysseus may seem counterintuitive to a historian of Greek religion, and there is, in fact, room for reasonable doubt: we shall see that there is good evidence of a fourth-century reorganization of the cave (implying rearranging or, one might claim, importing the tripods), and the explicit epigraphical evidence for Odysseus is no earlier than the second century B.C. The case for a late, Hellenistic Odysseus cult needs to be seriously confronted in the light of some new considerations. The balance, I shall argue, should result in favor of Odysseus as the recipient of the tripods in the ninth and eighth

---

1. The Idaean cave in Crete was not a heroic shrine. See Sakellarakis 1988: 174–77 (for a discussion of a miniature gold tripod, a unique case); Burkert 1985: 48; cf. 280, 284. On other caves sacred to nymphs with no tripods, see Amandry 1984. On Isthmia, see Morgan 1996 with n. 3.

centuries. In the light of the previous chapter, in which a newly evaluated independent history of the island of Ithaca during the Geometric period has been suggested, Polis Bay and its sacred cave will now provide a fresh perspective for understanding the role of Odysseus and the range of evocations of the *Odyssey* in the western Mediterranean.

POLIS BAY AND THE MARITIME CONTEXT

One could argue, either today or—what may be more important for our purposes—in antiquity, that it was Odysseus himself who dedicated the tripods found at Polis. In the land of the Phaiakians King Alkinoös urged his fellow aristocrats, "Let us give Odysseus a great tripod and a cauldron, each man of us." There should have been, therefore, thirteen tripods—that of Alkinoös and one for each of the twelve Phaiakian elders (if they are what is meant by "each man of us")[2]—and it could be argued that, since this is also the number of tripods found in the Polis cave, therein lies the proof.[3] The Phaiakian ship brought Odysseus to the Bay of Phorkys, a place familiar to them from previous visits to Ithaca[4] where there was also a cave sacred to the nymphs (there are repeated references to this cave).[5] They placed Odysseus, asleep, on the ground and laid his treasure by an olive tree. When the hero woke up alone he suspiciously counted everything, including the "beautiful tripods."[6] We are not told their number. After Athena had revealed herself to him she pointed out the cave of the Naiad nymphs, familiar to Odysseus of old, and instructed him to hide the tripods "in the innermost recess of the cave."[7]

Homeric descriptions of Ithaca are notoriously at once imprecise and specific, bewildering modern scholars who attempt exact identifications.[8] Such attempts may be seen as justified, since unlike the fantastic places of the adventures told to Alkinoös Ithaca still belongs to the world of concrete topography. The cave of the nymphs, for example, is also pointed out today

2. *Od.* 13.217–18 with *Od.* 13.13.
3. See Heubeck and Hoekstra 1989 on *Od.* 13.217–18 with regard to this possibility: "a large part of the *Od.* would begin to look more like a historical novel than an epic poem."
4. *Od.* 13.113.
5. On the cave and its recalling of nymphs and caves in the *Odyssey*, see the sensitive discussion of Segal 1994: 51–53.
6. *Od.* 13.215–18.
7. *Od.* 13.363.
8. Stubbings in Wace and Stubbings 1962: 398–421; Luce 1975: 141–56; Symeonoglou 1984.

at a site much closer to Vathi, in southern Ithaca—an impressive stalagmite cave (Marmarospilia) with clear evidence of a cult to the nymphs.[9] But such cave cult was never exclusive,[10] even in Ithaca; there are dedicatory inscriptions to the nymphs in the cave on Polis Bay, and there is a sacred grove and altar to the nymphs near the sacred spring outside of the city of Ithaca.[11] Also, for what it is worth, Artemidoros of Ephesos and Porphyri identified the cave with that of Polis Bay;[12] the Bay of Phorkys, the Old Man of the Sea, has "at its mouth two projecting headlands sheer to seaward, but sloping down on the side toward the harbor. These keep back the great waves raised by heavy winds," and so on. Such a description of a safe haven fits Polis Bay marvelously. It is a surprisingly deep-water shelter, well protected by its headlands and by Kephallonia across the strait. However, it also fits numerous other bays in Ithaca or elsewhere in the Ionian islands.[13] Whatever the case, if someone, say, in the seventh century had wished to believe that it was Odysseus himself who had placed the tripods in the cave on Polis Bay, the topography of Ithaca would have lent itself to such an identification.

The obvious difficulty with this approach, however, is that Homer clearly says that Odysseus only hides the treasure (including but not exclusively consisting of tripods) in the cave, implying that he intends to come back for them. This difficulty is overlooked by the advocates of an approach that is the reverse of my line of argument. According to this view, Homer, an aitiologist, had either seen or heard enough about Ithaca and its topography to have included much convincing detail about the island in the poem he composed.[14] Knowing about the cave with the thirteen tripods, he concocted the details about Phaiakia, Alkinoös, and his twelve elders.[15] There are, however, serious objections to this view. First, as we have seen, a case is

9. Stubbings in Wace and Stubbings 1962: 416. However, the cave is not in the immediate neighborhood of Dexia Bay, which Stubbings identifies as the Bay of Phorkys, nor is it by the water as it should be following *Od.* 13.

10. Malkin 1996b: 1056.

11. *Od.* 17.204–11, 240–43.

12. Porphyri 58 (Lamberton 1983: 26) quotes Artemidoros as saying that the cave and the harbor of Phorkys were twelve stadia east of Kephallonia.

13. Hoekstra in Heubeck and Hoekstra 1989 on 13.96. Thus I am less confident about precise overlaps with what the *Odyssey* has to say about particular sites in Ithaca than with Symeonoglou (1984).

14. Heubeck and Hoekstra 1989: 177 on *Od.* 13.217–18; Waterhouse 1996: 310–15. The vague and "mistaken" details in Homer's description of Ithaca (Sieberber 1990) prove nothing either way. Even the best-intentioned travelers cannot re-create from memory precise features and contours of landscape. Homer, who was not writing a travelogue, was probably not interested.

15. Heubeck and Hoekstra 1989: 177 on lines 217–18: Alkinoös and his twelve kings (*Od.* 8.390) equal thirteen tripods.

often made for identifying the stalagmite cave of Marmarospilia, at the opposite end from Polis, with the cave of the nymphs of the *Odyssey*.[16] But no tripods were found in that cave, and if the details in the *Odyssey* were based on concrete information (related to the peculiar rock formation of the cave), then the tripods at Polis could not have been the basis for aitiology. If Marmarospilia lies at the heart of the Homeric description (as mentioned above, I have my doubts), then it both indicates the priority of this description to the placing of the tripods in the Polis Bay cave in the ninth century and illustrates that the tripods were placed there because of sailing practices. Second, Sylvia Benton, who excavated at Polis, says that Homeric descriptions of tripods fit not Mycenaean but Protogeometric ones, and therefore she too would see the *Odyssey*'s text as following the Ithaca tripods.[17] But this is a weak argument, since the Argive-style tripods of the Olympia type found on Ithaca at least from the beginning of the ninth century must have reflected the standard for luxury tripods.[18] Homer need not have seen actual tripods *at Ithaca* to envisage the tripods he describes. Claiming that Homer's text is an aition of the Ithaca tripods seems oversophisticated and hypercritical. Between the tenth and eighth centuries, references to tripods (as prizes, gifts, and cooking utensils) are not anachronistic.[19]

The aitiology thesis relies heavily on the number thirteen, but Homer does not speak of "the thirteen tripods"; the number is the result of calculations by modern commentators. Where Alkinoös and the twelve prominent Phaiakian elders are mentioned, each one is supposed to give a robe, a tunic, and a talent of gold, but there is no mention of tripods.[20] This becomes a fait accompli before the departure of Odysseus.[21] Later, just before Odysseus sets out, Alkinoös suggests that each man give him a great tripod and a cauldron and says that "we" will be compensated for this by a collection among the people.[22] No number either of tripods or of elders is specified. Also, when Poseidon complains to Zeus about the Phaiakians, he says that they have given Odysseus "gifts beyond telling," hoards of bronze, gold, and woven clothings. That they are not enumerated is what matters here.[23] Else-

16. See above with Gigante 1990: 138–41.
17. Benton 1934–35a: 53; 101 ff. Cf. Stubbings in Wace and Stubbings 1962: 419; Coldstream 1977: 347.
18. On the value of metal dedications, see Morgan 1990: 194–203.
19. Raubitschek 1992: 102.
20. *Od.* 8.388–93.
21. Odysseus receives a chest with the clothing and the gold "that the Phaiakians had given": *Od.* 8.440; 13.10–12.
22. *Od.* 13.13–15. On ἀνδρακάς see Hoekstra in Heubeck and Hoekstra 1989 on 13.12–14. Hoekstra rightly places a question mark by the "Twelve."
23. *Od.* 13.135 (ἀγλαὰ in some manuscripts).

where, both in the *Iliad* and in the *Odyssey*, when tripods are mentioned in a list of gifts they are counted.[24] Had the poet deduced the story from that figure we might expect the number thirteen to be more prominent. Odysseus, after all, "counted the tripods." Apparently the poet paid little attention to this. Even when, in the first person, Odysseus repeats the story and tells of the gifts of the Phaiakians, he neglects to specify a number or to privilege the tripods.[25] From the archaeological point of view we cannot even be certain that the tripods in the cave numbered thirteen, in spite of what is often said;[26] there may have been more.[27] We should also remember that they were dedicated not all at once but over a period of almost two centuries. In sum, what Odysseus received at Phaiakia was not a "treasure of thirteen tripods" but a treasure that included, among other things, an unspecified number of tripods, and we cannot be certain that only thirteen tripods actually existed. The number thirteen is a red herring washed into the seaside cave by a wave of modern scholarship.

The correct approach to the problem, in my view, is neither to look for the real Odysseus nor to reduce the *Odyssey* to an *aition* but rather to see it in terms of life being articulated through art, of ritual following myth—all this in the historical context in which the evocation of Odysseus at this particular seaside shrine would have been most meaningful to the widest circles of those who frequented it: the Ithacans, the Euboians, and the Corinthians of the ninth and eighth centuries and perhaps also the Achaians of the eighth. What is of importance is whether it could have been believed, sometime in the ninth century, that this was where the Phaiakians landed Odysseus and that it was in this cave, sacred to the nymphs, that he (but only temporarily, to conceal them) placed his tripods. Dedicating tripods at that cave constituted—in addition to an offering—a ritual imitating what Odysseus had done.

I shall suggest that the similarity of the finds to the text of the *Odyssey*—costly tripods placed in a cave—is too close to deny any Odyssean connection. Everything points to a deeply significant identification involving exceptional dedications. The Greeks who dedicated tripods to the One-Who-Once-Placed-Tripods-in-the-Cave were effectively repeating the first act of Odysseus himself when he was landed at Ithaca by the Phaiakian sailors.

---

24. For such lists compare *Il.* 9.122–28 (seven tripods); 24.229–34 (two tripods); *Od.* 4.128 (two tripods); see also (with no tripods) 4.590–615; 24.274–77.

25. *Od.* 16.229–31; 23.341.

26. Repeated even by Raubitschek (1992: 101), who writes against the aitiologists.

27. Claude Rolley thinks, for example, that the tripods may have been dedicated in pairs (Magou, Philippakis, and Rolley 1986: 127).

THE CULT AND THE TRIPODS

The most outstanding aspect of the cult in the Polis cave is the tripods. When Schliemann visited Ithaca, in 1868 and 1878, searching for confirmation of the Homeric epics, he noticed that a private excavation was taking place in the cave. However, the site, as different from a grand Mycenaean palace as one could be disappointed to find, did not attract much of his attention.[28] Mr. Louisos, the proprietor, had discovered the cave while digging a pit for a limekiln. In the early 1930s, when Sylvia Benton of the British School at Athens conducted her important excavation at Polis, she interviewed one of Louisos's workmen and learned that a complete bronze tripod has been unearthed at the cave but had been melted down to avoid detection. The story seems to be confirmed by the son of Schliemann's host at Ithaca, who also saw a tripod (probably the same one).[29] It should be noted that Vollgraff too dug in the cave in 1904 without discovering any tripods and that by the time of the British expedition much of the delicate stratigraphy had been disturbed.[30] Schliemann chose to concentrate on the site of Aetos, where he claimed to have identified the Mycenaean remains of the palace of Odysseus.[31] Schliemann-bashing has become a favorite pastime for some scholars,[32] but whereas some of the charges leveled against him may be valid, the fact remains that he did make important discoveries. Perhaps some of the forces that moved him would not have been too alien to Greeks in the Archaic period, who also searched for topographical identifications of their—in fact the same—heroes. It is their perspective more than the realities of the Mycenaean period that concerns us here.

Greeks at the close of the ninth century and during the eighth may have imbued Ithaca and its cave with Odyssean evocations. Excavations inside the cave have demonstrated its continuous use from the Mycenaean to the Roman periods, although it can be clearly identified as a place of cult since the ninth century. In the fourth century the cave was rearranged internally (a step and a retaining wall were built). The site seems to have been sacred primarily to the nymphs, as such caves often are. An inscription mentions together Athena Polias and Hera Teleia;[33] there are also representations on masks showing Artemis with bow and quiver.[34] Votives, especially of female

28. Benton 1934–35a: 46; cf. Schliemann 1963 (1869): 44–47.
29. Benton 1934–35a: 46–47.
30. Vollgraff 1905 with Antonaccio 1995: 152.
31. Schliemann 1963 (1869), basically followed Gell's identification (1807). For a good review of the attempts to locate Mycenaean Ithaca, see Symeonoglou 1984.
32. Calder and Traill 1986; cf. Calder and Cobet 1990; Traill 1993; Masson 1995.
33. Boustrophedon inscription (550–525?): Jeffrey 1990: 231.
34. Benton 1938–39: 43, nos. 62–64; 56.

figurines, are plentiful. From the Hellenistic period there are nymph-reliefs and three inscribed dedications to the nymphs. The explicit references to Odysseus are few and late (which is not exceptional: inscribed names are scarce even in well-attested cult places).[35] An inscription from Magnesia records the Ithacans' response to an invitation to participate in the games of Artemis Leukophryne at Magnesia, instituted in 206 B.C.[36] The Ithacans, in return, invite the Magnesians to the "Odysseia" and order the inscription to be set up in the Odysseion, which Benton regards as a hero shrine (*heroön* building) separate from the cave.[37] A series of masks dating to about the second century was dedicated in the cave. One of them, mentioned above, reads εὐχὴν 'Οδυσσεῖ (a "prayer" or "votive offerings" to Odysseus) and in another direction [ὁ δεῖνα ἀνέθ]η[κε]ν (so and so dedicated it).

Benton interprets the "Odysseia" as ancient games and the tripods as victory prizes. This is certainly possible, although the proximity in the inscription to a Magnesian cult instituted in 206 B.C. renders it suspicious. No games or competitions are mentioned, although these are explicit in the answer of Ithacans' neighbors, the Kephallonians, to the same invitation. However, the Kephallonians reciprocate by inviting the Magnesians for the sacrifices and games of their eponym, Kephalos.[38] The difference between the Kephallonian and the Ithacan answer may mean either that even in the Hellenistic era there were no games for Odysseus or that these were simply self-evident and implied in the term "Odysseia." In any case, one does not need the unlikely extension of Hellenistic Odysseia (= games) to the ninth and eighth centuries, since the tripods may be interpreted simply as dedications.

The evidence just mentioned plays a major role in the argument, most recently advanced by Carla Antonaccio, that the attachment of Odysseus to the cave at Polis was a Hellenistic phenomenon.[39] The case rests on the following points: (1) The earliest explicit attestations are the inscription of the Hellenistic terra-cotta mask and the Magnesia inscription from 206. (2) The fourth-century rearrangement of the cave may indicate that Odysseus was only then identified with the cave. (3) Other deities, notably Hera and Athena, are mentioned much earlier. (4) Tripods are not reserved for male deities or heroes and are better seen as prestigious dedications. Her conclusion: "In the absence of clear evidence to the contrary, Odysseus is best regarded as a relative late comer to the cave. The earliest deities that

35. Antonaccio 1995: 108 (although this lack is used here mainly to argue against the identification of a hero cult).
36. Kern 1900: no. 36, esp. lines 15–16, 28–29.
37. Benton 1934–35a: 55.
38. Kern 1900: no. 35 lines 34 ff.; Antonaccio 1995: 154 n. 32.
39. Antonaccio 1995: 152–55.

can be certainly associated with it are Hera and Athena; next are the Nymphs, and Odysseus last."

There are, however, several considerations that have not been sufficiently discussed. First, on general grounds, continuity of a cult at a sanctuary during the Archaic and Classical periods often implies continuity in the identity of the cult recipient.[40] Greek sanctuaries, at least since the Archaic period, seem for the most part to demonstrate such continuity. The old distinction implying that "chthonic" powers (heroes, nymphs) precede "Olympian" ones at chthonic sites such as caves and springs may still be useful for certain categories in Greek religion. Thus, it is legitimate to regard the deities associated sporadically with the cave—Athena, Hera, Artemis—as additions to a place previously sacred to the nymphs and to the hero. In short, arguing for continuity of cult backward from the third-century identification is an acceptable methodology. However, in itself it is an insufficient general argument, admitting of exceptions.

Second, it is misleading to view the Hellenistic inscription mentioning Odysseus in isolation from other Ithacan evidence. It is not true that the earliest attestation of Ithacan identification with Odysseus is Hellenistic, based only on the mask.[41] Ithaca apparently never contained more than a single political community. In Homer too the name of the city and that of the island are the same.[42] Ithaca began minting its coins in the early fourth century, and Odysseus, sometimes with Athena on the obverse, was clearly Ithaca's national symbol, the emblem of its collective representation, right from the first.[43] There is no reason to assume that this was a novelty of the Classical period.

Third, again considering Ithaca as a community, Aristotle (in his *Constitution of the Ithakesians*) implies a ritual of annual gifts from the people of Ithaca to Odysseus. Neoptolemos, he says (see chap. 4), came to Ithaca to arbitrate between the suitors' relatives and Odysseus; the hero was made to go into exile, but the relatives had to pay him compensation. This was transferred to Telemachos, obviously as a kind of caretaker for his father.[44] The

40. This is a familiar point. See, e.g., Coldstream 1985: 67–69; cf. Roux 1984: 153–71; Burkert 1988: 27–48.

41. Antonaccio 1993; 1995: 152–55.

42. *Od.* 3.79–81; 21.251–52.

43. Head 1911: 428. Dion 1977: 79 is mistaken in stating that only Mantineia had coins showing Odysseus.

44. Such offerings could go on for centuries, as Plutarch illustrates with regard to a fellow student at the School of Ammonios at Athens, who was a descendant of Themistocles and was receiving tangible honors from the Magnesians centuries after the latter's death. Plut. *Them.* 32.5.

ritual aspect of the gifts is clear: they were an annual affair that continued to Aristotle's day. The gifts consisted of barley meal, wine, honey in the comb, olive oil, and sacrificial animals. He does not specify where these were given, but it is reasonable to expect such offerings to have been placed in the cave at Polis (where they would have perished and became invisible to archaeologists except, perhaps, for the ash layer).[45] Aristotle himself seems to have been well acquainted with particular aspects of the Odysseus lore of the region of Ithaca.[46] We do not know when, before the fourth century, the custom of giving annual gifts and sacrifices to Odysseus originated. The early fourth-century coinage just mentioned implies an earlier prominent place for Odysseus. It is reasonable to assume that Aristotle is referring to a cult predating at least the fifth century, since at that time Corcyra had a well-established cult in a sacred grove (*alsos*) to Alkinoös.[47] Also, at some uncertain time one of Corcyra's ports was named "the port of Alkinoös."[48] Alkinoös, of course, is a figure totally dependent in myth on Odysseus; therefore, one may infer a fortiori that a cult to Odysseus also existed on Ithaca, the island en route to Corcyra, when Alkinoös had his cult there.

Fourth, the magnificent tripod dedications discovered in the cave would not have been placed there merely for nymphs; their kind of cult did not involve that kind of dedication.[49] Nymphs are often associated with caves, and the Polis Bay cave contains inscriptions to them and nymph reliefs. The predominant feminine-type dedications in the cave at Polis (figurines, masks) are easily explained in terms of nymphs. At the Corycian cave near Delphi, sacred to the nymphs and Pan, some eighty to ninety percent of the figurines discovered (some fifty thousand fragments altogether) were feminine in type.[50] In spite of the warning not to assume too close a relationship between the nature of the object dedicated and the deity-hero-nymph receiving the dedication, reemphasized by contributors to an exemplary study

45. Fr. 507 Rose = Plut. *Quaest. Graec.* 14 with Halliday 1975 (1928): 81. Literally, it seems that Odysseus "dedicates" the gifts to Telemachos, possibly hinting at a family of priests that traced its descent to him. Cf. Antonaccio 1995: 153.

46. *Poet.* 25.16.1461b.

47. This is implied by Thuc. 3.70.4, referring to it as a matter of fact rather than as something new; cf. Ps.-Scylax 22.

48. Eust. ad Dionys. Per. *GGM* 2.310.

49. A possible exception: at Oropus, at a shrine of the nymph Halia, victorious Choregoi dedicated tripods between the fourth and the second century (inscriptions on tripod bases). There is obviously a very significant difference in time between the Ithaca tripods (ninth and eighth centuries) and these. Also, some have suspected that the nearness of the shrines of Amphiaraos and Halia enhanced the latter's status; see Schachter 1986: 184. I thank Emily Kearns for drawing my attention to this. Cf. Malkin 1996b.

50. Amandry 1984: 402.

of this cave,[51] the difference between tripod recipients (gods, almost exclusively) and nymphs is still sufficiently significant to imply at least two distinct categories of dedication recipients. Amandry compares thirteen other caves associated with nymphs throughout the Greek world.[52] As at Ithaca, they are not exclusive to the nymphs but often associated also with other deities and heroes. At Pharsalos, for example, a cave was sacred to the nymphs, Pan, Hermes, Apollo, and Herakles.[53] None of these caves contains a tripod.

One could object that hero shrines also rarely have tripods dedicated in them, but here the case is more nuanced, especially since the category of heroes is much wider than that of nymphs. Already in the "heroic burial" at Lefkandi (tenth-century) one finds traces of a tripod; roadside cuttings suggest that a monumental tripod cauldron was placed there, and cauldrons seem to mark the eighth-century "princely tombs" at Salamis in Cyprus, Kyme in Italy, and Eretria in Euboia.[54] These examples are not from hero shrines but from heroic-style burials possibly emulating heroic ("epic"?) notions.[55] However, they do illustrate an association that nymph cults seem not to have between tripods and elites and notions of the heroic. Even acknowledging the lack of evidence for tripod dedications for both nymphs and heroes, the major point is that ninth- and eighth-century tripods do occur in the Polis cave and thus seem to call for an explanation specific to that place.

Ithaca with its numerous and early tripods seems exceptional in the Greek world as the only cave sacred to nymphs that contains any tripods. The two classes of dedications—feminine figurines and masks and tripods—appear therefore to indicate multilayered cult activity. Antonaccio claims, as we have seen, that first deities were worshipped at the cave, next the nymphs, and fi-

51. Amandry 1984: 401 ff. with the pertinent remarks in the same volume by Anne Jacquemin (p. 166) and Claude Rolley (p. 261).

52. Amandry 1984: 404–8: In Attica, Vari, Marathon, Pentelica, Parnes, Daphni, Athens, sanctuary of the Nymphs; elsewhere, Pitsa, Lera (Crete), Pharsalos (nymphs, Pan, Hermes, Apollo, Herakles), near Aphytis (Chalkidike), Nea Herakleitsa (eastern Makedonia), Aliki (Thasos), Lokroi (Italy). Cf. Sourvinou-Inwood 1993: 5.

53. Cf. Borgeaud 1979: 75–81; Malcolm 1985: 19–27.

54. Popham, Themelis, and Sackett 1980: 214. The tenth-century Lefkandi tomb, tentatively called a *heroön* by the excavators, does not seem to indicate continuous use and may be regarded, at best, as a "heroic burial." Popham, Touloupa, and Sackett 1982 with Calligas 1988: 232; cf. Blome 1984. See also Popham, Themelis, and Sackett 1980; Catling and Lemos 1990; Popham, Calligas, and Sackett 1993; Antonaccio 1995: 236– 40 (against a *heroön*). See now also Coulton 1993: 49; Popham now phrases it (in Popham, Calligas, and Sackett 1993: 99) "*Heroön* at least in the sense that it was built to honour a warrior who was given a funeral closely corresponding to those given to a hero in the Homeric epic."

55. De Polignac 1995: 128–38.

nally Odysseus,[56] implying a wide-ranging chronological order of cult accretions. However, in the nymph cave shrines I know of (including those listed by Amandry) the cult of the nymphs is usually the primary cult, with other deities having been attached later.[57] I will claim that the dedications of tripods to Odysseus began at the cave because it was sacred to the nymphs, since in the landing scene of Odysseus's return (which we know as *Odyssey* 13) he prays to them, mentions gifts he used to give them,[58] promises some more, and hides the gifts of the Phaiakians in the cave of the nymphs on Ithaca.

What seems to be of crucial importance but has been overlooked[59] is the ritual that Odysseus performs on first leaving Ithaca after the slaughter of the suitors: "Odysseus, after sacrificing to the nymphs, sails away to Elis."[60] This detail belongs to the first book of the *Telegony*, a sequel to the *Odyssey* written during the first half of the sixth century, the first book of which was based on a seventh-century poem, the *Thesprotis*. Why would Odysseus's initial departure from Ithaca have involved the nymphs? It could have been the fulfillment of a promise he had made to the Naiads in the thirteenth book of the *Odyssey* (358–60): "but I will also give you gifts, as I used to before, if Athena . . . freely grants me to go on living here myself, and sustains my dear son." However, such gifts appear as rewarding his remaining at rather than leaving Ithaca. The *Telegony* mentions sacrifice (not "gift"), which seems to indicate rather a departure sacrifice precisely at the point where Odysseus has landed. Nymphs are not the obvious choice for embarkation and sailing rites. Apollo Embasios, for example, or some other deity of the sea would have been the more appropriate choice.[61] But Eugammon seems to be drawing on an early tradition closely linked to Ithaca and its cave of the nymphs at Polis Bay. Since the sacrifice to the nymphs is probably taken from the seventh-century *Thesprotis,* it implies that the cave of the nymphs was already regarded not only as the point of the return of Odysseus but also as the site of his second departure from Ithaca. As a point of arrival and departure, the cave could become the proper site for dedications—expensive dedications—to "Odysseus *and* the nymphs," by those sailing to and from

56. Antonaccio 1995: 154.

57. Cf. Rouse 1902: 44–48; Borgeaud 1979: 75–81 (for the examples of Apollo Nomios and Hermes).

58. Cf. *Od.* 17.240 ff. with Segal 1994: 53; Gigante 1990: 134–37 and Papadopoulou-Belmehdi 1994: 96–102 on nymphs and caves in the *Odyssey*.

59. Here I differ from Segal 1994: 59; whereas I agree that the gifts in the cave are another stage of the "transition," the disregard of them later in the *Odyssey* calls for another explanation in my view.

60. *Telegony*, Bernabé 1987: argumentum 1.

61. Malkin 1986.

Ithaca and anchoring in the bay. It is not impossible that the gift of tripods (aside from the more modest gifts of the people of Ithaca) was regarded as a fulfillment of the promise of gifts made by Odysseus but never fulfilled in the *Odyssey*. It is as if his action (placing tripods) and his promise of gifts initiated a ritual to be practiced thenceforward.

Fifth, it is implausible that the tripod dedications were offered to Olympian deities, for these are not usually worshipped in caves.[62] The Idaean and Dictaean caves in Crete and the cave of Eilytheia at Cretan Amnisos are notable exceptions, as are the Arkadian cults (sometimes associated with myths of divine births) of Rhea, Demeter, Hermes, and Selene.[63] Elsewhere when caves are associated with Olympian deities it is not as the major sanctuary sites (the tripods at Ithaca imply a major cult).[64] We should also remember that Ithaca's major cult complex in this period (from at least the eighth century on) was Aetos, not Polis, and that major dedications to Olympians could be expected to be found there. Again, Polis appears in need of an explanation specific to that cave. The deities' names on the sixth-century inscription (whose context is uncertain) are made jointly to goddesses whose cults are not usually linked; it seems that the cult titles had something to do with the magistrates making the dedications but not as part of priestly ritual.[65] The representations of Artemis are too late to be brought into consideration here, and, again, tripods (rarely dedicated to that goddess) were placed in more important sanctuaries.[66]

62. Thus the issue of having tripods dedicated to female deities in major sanctuaries (not caves) is not quite applicable here as Antonaccio thinks (1995: 154), relying on Maass (1978: 4 n. 24) who lists such dedications, for example, to Athena Lindia in Rhodes, Athena Polias in Athens, Hera at the Samian Heraion, and so on. See also the survey by Hiller 1991: 75–77.

63. Borgeaud 1979: 80 n. 52; the most famous cave cult in Arkadia was that of Demeter Melaina (Paus. 8.42.4–5).

64. Cf. Poseidon at Tainaron (Pompon. Mela 2.51; Strabo 8.363), Aphrodite's grotto at Naupaktos (Paus. 10.28.3); the Thaumasion of Rhea in Methydrion (Paus. 8.36.3), the cave of Demeter at Phigaleia, with an altar outside it (Paus. 8.42.11), and the grotto of Hades at Eleusis. The possible cave (cleft in the rock) at Brauron was distinguished from the main temple; similarly distinguished were Apollo's cave within the sanctuary at Klaros, the cave at Ptoion (Martin and Metzger 1976: 34–45), and the cave in the northeast corner of the *temenos* (precinct) of Aphaia at Aegina (considered by Thiersch 1928: 140–150 to have been the shrine of Aiakos). Apollo had several sacred caves, especially in Asia Minor (Nilsson 1976: 74), but his major sanctuaries were not cave sanctuaries.

65. This is a tentative conclusion. Jeffrey (1990: 101) mentions an inscription to Hera and Athena at Phokis (where the goddesses were apparently given iron spits) but with no cult titles as at Ithaca.

66. Such are the tripods at the sanctuary of Ortheia (Artemis at some point?). Maass 1978: 4. At Kalapodi one is uncertain whether the tripod discovered there was for

What is the significance of the apparently exceptional number of tripods found in the Polis cave? Comparing quantities of archaeological finds, of course, is a relative matter. Much depends on the conditions of preservation, which may vary from site to site; there was also a practice (although less common for tripods) of melting down discarded metal objects,[67] and looting often took place. With all this in mind, Polis remains exceptional, especially considering that the tripods were found not in Ithaca's central sanctuary of Aetos but in a peripheral seaside cave shrine. One could claim that in the course of more than a century and a half the dedication of thirteen tripods does not seem extravagant. In the Hall of Hephaistos Homer imagines the fantastic number of twenty tripods, which puts things in some perspective.[68] One suspects that at Polis too there were more tripods than twelve or thirteen and that during the fourth-century rearrangement only what seemed like the best of them were relocated in prominent positions inside the cave. The fact remains that even when we compare only the six or nine tripods that precede the 750s with other tripods found in Greek sanctuaries (at Olympia, Aegira, and Kalapodi),[69] their number is still strikingly exceptional, especially in terms of the nature of the site in which they were found.

Finally, the exceptional number of the tripods, their varied types, and the chronological differences among them also seem to disprove another suggestion: that someone in the fourth century (when a new retaining wall was built in the cave) had placed the tripods there in order to imitate the Homeric text. Such a person would have to have gone to a great deal of trouble to find precisely this series of Middle Geometric and Late Geometric tripods, among the earliest ever discovered.[70] The fourth-century rearrangement of the cave probably did involve a reordering of the tripods, but it seems very unlikely that they were brought there from another sanctuary. Such ancient tripods must have been well known for centuries as prominent dedications, and normally one did not remove dedications from a shrine.

As an interim conclusion, explicit evidence (coinage, the Ithacan ritual), exclusionary considerations (tripods not for nymphs, dedications to gods not in caves), and arguments from the specific religious practices at Ithaca as well as in Greek religion in general point to Odysseus as the most likely

---

Artemis or Apollo. Felsch and Kienast 1975: 19, figs. 18 and 19. I am grateful to Christianne Sourvinou-Inwood for advice here. Cf. Ellinger 1993: 28.

67. Cf. Linders 1989–90.

68. *Il.* 18.373–77.

69. On Olympia, Morgan 1990: 43–47; on Aegira, Morgan 1990: 65; Morgan and Hall n.d.: 172–73; Alzinger 1981–82: 12, fig. 4; Alzinger 1985; cf. Amandry et al. 1987; Ellinger 1993: 27–28.

70. De Polignac 1996.

recipient of the tripod dedications in the cave on Polis Bay during the ninth and eighth centuries.

THE NATURE OF THE CULT

The tripod dedications to Odysseus at Polis imply a ritual action that we may tentatively call a "heroic cult" rather than a hero cult *tout court.* The Hellenistic "Odysseia" and Odysseion imply games for the hero and an official *heroön;* hence Benton infers that the tripods were prizes. However, this stretches the games to the ninth century, which is not impossible but may be going too far. The gifts and sacrifices to Odysseus, as I understand Aristotle, would certainly make this a full-fledged hero cult. Following the implications of the Ithacan coinage and the cult to Alkinoös at Corcyra, a full hero cult to Odysseus at Ithaca may therefore be dated at least to the fifth century. But how much earlier? I would like to be very careful in applying categories here, since we do not have sufficient parallel evidence for hero cults as early as the ninth century. Cults to heroes in Greek religion present a bewildering variety of types, both in terms of cult sites and in terms of recipients, from the anonymous through local figures who "hold the land" to epic and pan-Hellenic ones. It may be dangerous to argue backward from later practices in order to lump Odysseus with "hero cults in Homer."[71] With just the evidence of the tripods and the echoing of the landing scene of the *Odyssey,* one should opt for a minimalist approach.

What we know of the cave does not fit the political and social categories around which recent discussions of eighth-century hero cults revolve. The heroic cult to Odysseus seems neither to have implied any idea of a hero's tomb nor constituted a "node of power"[72] or a territory-delimiting cult[73] or an ancestor cult, nor, as far as we know, did it legitimate the status of any particular clan or class within the community of Ithaca itself. Yet it did belong to the historical community of Ithaca, as well as to other Greeks, contextualizing hopes, actions, or rewards and juxtaposing these with a heroic past. I claim that both Ithacans and Greek visitors, through dedications to Odysseus, evoked a range of associations centered around that hero.

Odysseus belongs to the class of Homeric heroes, including Menelaos, whose cults were not linked to a tomb or a cenotaph.[74] Not all hero cults need graves, especially cults to epic heroes.[75] In fact, no tradition identifies

71. Such as the tomb of Ilos at Troy: *Il.* 10.414 with 11.166, 371; 24.350. Cf. the tomb of Aisyetes 2.786–87 with Hadzisteliou-Price 1973: 129–30.

72. Morris 1988: 750.

73. De Polignac 1995, esp. chap. 4.

74. Malkin 1994a: 6, 47; Antonaccio 1995: 157–66; cf. Morris 1988.

75. Nagy 1979: 115–16, 159–61; Snodgrass 1987: 159, 164; 1988; Kearns 1989: 1–9; cf. 1992. There were exceptions, too, such as the cult accorded the Argonaut Idmon in

any tomb of Odysseus in Ithaca. The only comparable situation—but more in terms of the type of location than of its content—is a cave at Koukounaries in Paros, where there is evidence for cult activity and dedications in the mid-ninth century. The cave was used for burials in the Bronze Age, but it is uncertain whether people then were commemorating an ancient hero. Too little is known about this cave, although the possibility that some sort of heroic cult was practiced there about the same time as in Ithaca is intriguing.[76]

There have been some rewarding discussions of the issue of heroic cults following Farnell's suggestion that cults to epic heroes were instituted because of the dissemination of the *Iliad* and the *Odyssey*. Nicholas Coldstream, in a seminal article evaluating offerings placed in Mycenaean tombs, has revived the thesis. In contrast, Anthony Snodgrass has argued that such offerings should instead be viewed in terms of staking claims to lands and territories.[77] James Whitley places more emphasis on the regional division and the political implications of such cults.[78] Ian Morris, also arguing against the Coldstream thesis, elucidates the ambiguity implied in tomb cults with regard to who Greeks thought might have been buried in the tombs,[79] whereas Carla Antonaccio has refined our distinctions, differentiating the tomb cult (either single offerings with no evidence of continued cult or repeated offerings linked with ancestors) and the (named) hero cult.[80] I have added to the discussion on the cult accorded to founders of colonies[81] and in denying that such cults professed landownership.[82] One should retain a broad perspective, emphasizing (as does Emily Kearns) the variability of hero cults.[83]

The cult at Polis, which has nothing to do with a tomb, is partially comparable with the Dorian cults instituted for Menelaos (and possibly Agamemnon) over a century later, at the end of the eighth century. The Menelaion implies a similar purpose: identification with a Homeric past recognized by

---

the context of the colonization of Herakleia Pontike; his tomb was in the agora. Ap. Rhod. 2.846–50; cf. Malkin 1987a: 73–77.

76. Schilardi 1975: 92; 1976: 289.

77. Farnell 1921; Coldstream 1976; Snodgrass 1982; 1986; 1988; 1991.

78. Whitley 1988.

79. Morris 1988.

80. Antonaccio 1993; 1995.

81. Malkin 1987a: pt. 2.

82. Malkin 1993; cf. de Polignac 1995: 140.

83. Kearns 1989; 1992.

84. Malkin 1994a: chap. 2. It is noteworthy that Antonaccio (1995: 155–66), in spite of her general skepticism, acknowledges the Spartan Menelaion as genuine. She makes a good case for doubts concerning the Agamemnoneion (1995: 147–51).

other Greeks and linked especially with the locality.[84] It therefore provides a strong parallel for cultic activity, probably with communal implications, centered around a pan-Hellenic figure of an epic hero. However, in comparison with that of Odysseus, the strong local significance of Menelaos (king of Sparta) was more problematic: it belonged, after all, to a time before the return of the Herakleidai and the coming of the Dorians, thus serving a (Dorian) Spartan "overreaching" to a pan-Hellenic local hero that predated Dorian Sparta and lacked any direct genealogical continuity (Menelaos was no Herakleid). At the same time, Menelaos was not only a king of Sparta and husband of Helen but the most famous Nostos after Odysseus, one whose story is told in the *Odyssey* and whose presence in North Africa and in the western Mediterranean played a role in Spartan colonial articulations of attitudes to territory and native populations.[85]

Well aware that the tripods in the Polis cave can be compared in terms of their early dates to those of Olympia, François de Polignac suggests that the latter were dedicated to Pelops, the eponymous Peloponnesian hero and founder of the chariot races, with whom the princes identified.[86] Pelops and Odysseus, he thinks, served similar purposes: the one a focus for the Peloponnesian aristocracy, the other for the Greeks sailing to the northwest. This fits de Polignac's model of the Greek sanctuary as a point of social convergence and mediation. He also emphasizes the prestige attached to the objects as increasing in direct proportion to their distance from the home of the dedicator; Ithaca was remote, yet frequented, and it was precisely its remoteness that encouraged expensive dedications.[87]

Olympia was a Peloponnesian center with "convergence" literally signifying turning toward some focal point from the "outlying" cities. By contrast, Ithaca, perhaps like Samos in the east, was a different sort of "center": a maritime, diffusive convergence, not a center for common rites and games. I am therefore less convinced that Odysseus's function can be compared to that of Pelops, especially in de Polignac's sense of (Peloponnesian) *souveraineté efficace*, except for the general association with a mythic hero whose *story* is directly connected with how those making the dedications may have perceived their presence at the site of the dedication. Odysseus's function was perhaps comparable rather to Menelaos's in terms of what he may have

85. Malkin 1994a: chap. 2.

86. De Polignac 1996. Following Morgan (1990: chap. 3), Antonaccio (1995: 170–76) claims that the cult was late, not before the Archaic period. See Herrmann 1979: 49–59; 1980; Mallwitz 1972: 133–37; and especially Kyrieleis 1990; 1992. Kearns (1992: 67) emphasizes that Pelops's bones were not in his *heroön* at Olympia but in a chest in a small building beside the sanctuary of Artemis Kordax at Pisa (Paus. 6.22.1 with schol. ad Pind. *Ol.* 1.149.).

87. Morgan 1990: 45 makes a similar point regarding Olympia.

meant for the community of Ithaca. But he was also a hero of convergence for other Greeks. What converged for them was mythic associations, Odysseus's heroic precedent (both that of his Ithacan identity and his specific action of placing tripods in a cave). What also converged was the visiting aristocrats themselves and what they were doing: showing off to each other, sailing to the beyond and back, crossing and recrossing, at Ithaca, the frontiers articulated through Homeric geography.

Keeping in mind that actual tripods were placed in the cave during the ninth and eighth centuries and that Odysseus's myth, implying an association with Ithaca and with the cave of the nymphs, was probably also known in that period (although perhaps the text of the *Odyssey* as we have it was not), we may formulate another interim, minimalist statement. Tripods were dedicated in a cave on a bay at Ithaca to the Ithacan hero who himself had placed tripods in a cave on a bay at Ithaca. Greeks, both local Ithacans and visitors, invoked Odysseus, and, especially, the landing scene at Ithaca at the point of disembarkation where Odysseus was placed by the Phaiakians on the shore, signifying the end of his *nostos*.

TRIPODS AS DEDICATIONS

The tripods probably served the usual purpose of dedications: self-advertising (impressing others), a personal "letting go" (*aphienai*) of wealth in order to eternalize it in a place that many others would frequent but far from home, and a deep, personal significance that usually eludes the modern scholar. Insofar as dedications were made by visitors, probably adventurers and traders, the dedications to Odysseus must have expressed something personal.

It is a pity that there are no inscriptions on the excavated tripods. We could have learned much more had they been like the tripods Herodotus saw at the temple of Apollo Ismenios at Thebes, which were inscribed in archaic script, in "Kadmeian, Ionian-like letters." One of them pretended to be dedicated by a mythological hero—"Amphytrion dedicated me," clearly a case of ritual dedication imitating myth. The other two inscriptions advertised the donors: Skaios the boxer and Laodamas the monarch.[88] It is just possible that some of the various donors of tripods in the cave on Polis Bay also declared them to have been gifts of Odysseus to the nymphs.

An analogy regarding a mid-seventh-century historical figure may provide another perspective. Kolaios the Samian, while on his way to Egypt, was carried by easterly winds all the way to Spain, beyond the pillars of Herakles (Gibraltar). Having made enormous profits on the wares originally in-

---

88. Hdt. 5.60–61 with Raubitschek 1992: 102.

tended for Egypt, the Samians invested the magnificent sum of six talents in an elaborate bronze cauldron that they dedicated at their Heraion. In telling the story Herodotus[89] shifts freely from the individual Kolaios to the Samians, whose dedication consisted of one-tenth of their newly acquired wealth. The glory and the adventure story were individual; the dedication was a state affair. This overlapping between trader-adventurer and polis may have been less clear in the earlier centuries, but the pattern is similar. Captains of sailor-traders sailed to the lands of the beyond in the eighth century and probably also in the ninth. Some became wealthy; some dedicated tripods.

Investment in the divine, combined with self-advertising, can be expressed in the form of thanks, with the expectation of further rewards. In addition to the "state" dimension (the story of the Siphnians and their treasury at Delphi comes to mind),[90] there was also a whole range of personal thanks dedications that may afford a glimpse of the range of expectations of these captains. A little bronze hoplite of the early seventh century found at Thebes, for instance, declares: "Mantiklos dedicates me to the Far-shooting Silver-bowed one as his tithe. Phoibos, make him [Mantiklos] a pleasing return-gift for it";[91] on a marble column from the Athenian acropolis of the early fifth century that once supported a statue we read (in verse, as is Mantiklos's dedication) "Maiden, Telesinos son of Ketis dedicated this image to you on the acropolis: may you take pleasure in it, and allow him to dedicate another."[92] These personal dedications illustrate the quid pro quo aspect of dedications in general and what may have been important to traders in particular.

Another perspective on the Ithaca dedications has to do with Corcyra. It is impossible to know how the island was perceived by the early Greek traders, but once we begin to have some sources it was unanimously identified with Scheria, Homer's land of the Phaiakians.[93] Homer's most explicit description of the foundation of a city[94] refers to Scheria: because their neighbors, the Cyclopes, used to plunder them, "Nausithoös . . . had removed them and led and settled them in Scheria. . . . about the city he had drawn a wall, he had built houses and made temples to the gods, and divided the plough-land." However, in spite of this prosaic colonization story, Homeric Scheria

89. Hdt. 4.152.
90. Hdt. 3.57.
91. Powell 1991: 168–69; Robb 1994: 57–59.
92. Hansen 1983: nos. 326, 227.
93. See Hornblower 1991 on Thuc. 1.25.4; 3.70.4. Hellanikos *FGrH* 4 F 77.
94. Malkin 1987a: 98 on *Od.* 6.7–10.
95. I am fully convinced by Segal 1994: 12–64 on the role of Phaiakia in the *Odyssey*. One may add that their colonization from the Land of the Beyond (Hypereia) to Scheria is also a transition toward the "real" world (contra Hainsworth in Heubeck, West, and

does not belong to concrete topography.[95] In the *Odyssey* Poseidon punishes the Phaiakians for having done Odysseus a favor and seals them off from the rest of the human world. By contrast, the real Corcyra was colonized first by Euboians and then by Corinthians. In apparent contradiction with Poseidon's punishment, an accessible Corcyra was identified with "Phaiakia" and Alkinoös, as we have seen, received cult there.

The symmetry is remarkable: Scheria, the last point of otherworldliness in Homer on the way down to Greece, was also one of the first sites in the west to be settled beyond the pale of Homeric Greece on the way up. For Greek traders or aristocrats of the eighth century such as Chersikrates the Herakleid, the founder of Corinthian Corcyra, both Ithaca and Corcyra were Homerically connected. In their experience Corcyra-Scheria was also the source of Odysseus's tripods. All this seems connected in terms of both ritual imitation and symbolic content: a tribute was paid to Odysseus in Ithaca, at the point of his return and their exit to the new world of commerce and colonization.

THE DEDICATIONS: ORIGINS IN ITHACA?

One's first impression[96] might be that the people of Ithaca had very little to do with the actual tripod dedication and that the varied origins of the tripods themselves point to the external origins of the dedicants. This may be true especially after ca. 760 with regard to the Delphic-Ithacan type of tripod, since there can be little doubt that at Delphi the tripods were not dedicated by the Delphians themselves. But Ithaca was not Delphi, and there may be reason to consider the role of its own people. One possibility is to regard the dedications in the Polis cave as an element of Ithacan interconnections with Aetos—a peripheral shrine in relation to the central settlement and sanctuary.[97] Some Ithacans may have dedicated tripods that they had received, for example, from visiting Corinthians as gifts of guest-friendship, although it is hard to conceive of the entire series of tripods in the Polis cave as having originated in this manner. Moreover, Aetos, not Polis, would seem to have been the more appropriate place for *xenia* dedications, a point supported by the lucky find of the *xenia* inscription from Aetos on a wine jug from the close of the eighth century: "guest-friend dear and trusted comrade" (chap. 2).[98] Kevin Robb goes so far as to say that the

---

Hainsworth 1987 on *Od.* 6.4–10); otherwise the point of the name "Hypereia" is lost. For other ideas regarding the name, see Germain 1954: 290–94.

96. Except Morgan 1988.

97. Cf. Morgan 1988: 315; Waterhouse 1996: 309.

98. Robertson 1948: 82; Robb 1994: 49–52.

inscription provides "compelling evidence . . . on the island, in the closing years of the eighth century, [that] Greeks regularly received other Greeks from afar . . . according to the properties and in the specialized language of 'Homer.' Only contemporary oral singers could have taught them to behave in this way."

Some individual Ithacans may have been prosperous in their own right, and it is even conceivable that at some point dedications were made on the communal level. The existence of the Aetos sanctuary with its varied dedications as well as the shrine at Polis (containing expensive dedications), on the one hand, and the small size of the island, on the other, seem to imply some kind of single communal sacred management rather than several communities. Pending further archaeological reassessment of the role of Ithaca in the ninth and eighth centuries, I am inclined to see the tripod dedications in terms of a mixture of dedications by protocolonial and colonial traveling entrepreneurs (the Ithacans could be counted among them) and the local communities of Ithaca itself and possibly the surrounding islands.

The cave was apparently a focus of Ithacan pride, and we know that it had been an active cult place down to the Roman period. By the Classical period, as we have seen, Ithacans were annually commemorating Odysseus with gifts and sacrifices, although we cannot tell when this began. Ithacans probably had a role in managing the sacred cave at least from the ninth century on. Its valuable contents imply some form of political control and management; the shrine on Polis Bay simply contained too costly a treasure to be left unguarded. At this point one cannot advance beyond such a general inference, since the subject of temple guards (*nauophylakes*) seems under-investigated. Dedications, and tripods in particular, were not to be removed from a sanctuary.[99] Some inscriptions from temples do contain a provision to the effect of "Do not steal the votives," which may imply that one could if one had a mind to. One cannot really doubt, however, that sanctuaries that attracted real wealth locked it up, as, for example, the "key," that standard badge of priestly office, seems to imply.[100]

As I have pointed out, Ithaca was prosperous and enjoyed its position on the maritime routes as well as its own role in the northwest context. Its local, regional, and interregional status should therefore be taken into account. In the Ionian Sea Ithaca provides the clearest evidence for continuity of settlement from Mycenaean times.[101] If the neighboring islands were undergoing processes of repopulation and strengthening of communities

99. Cf. Hdt. 144.
100. Note also the "sealed rooms" of *IG* I^3.4; cf. Jordan 1979: 23–28 with Arist. *Pol.* 1322b (*nauophylakes*).
101. Desborough 1972: 88–89; 245–47 and see chap. 1.

during the Dark Age, the figure of Odysseus could have served as the focus for the communal identity of Ithaca's surrounding islands as well. These were said by Homer to have been included in his domain. This may be especially true of Kephallonia,[102] whose name is used in the *Iliad* and *Odyssey* as the ethnic appellation for all of Odysseus's men. Later traditions, mentioned in Aristotle's *Poetics*,[103] claim that Penelope's father (Ikadios rather than Ikarios) was Kephallonian. Some of the early tripods, therefore, may have been commissioned for Odysseus as a hero of the Ionian Sea, with his regional reputation extending also to Messenia, Elis, and Achaia—areas that may have shared some of their material culture with Ithaca. Thesprotia (see chap. 4) may also be included in this circle.

In sum, the role of foreign traders must not be allowed to overshadow that of Ithaca itself. It seems likely that the material found in the cave dating to Mycenaean and early Protogeometric times is local, although we do not know whether it was votive in nature. From the seventh century on, with the decline in the importance of Polis, the material in the cave again seems to be local, but the ninth and eighth centuries had been unquestionably exceptional. I am therefore inclined to see Polis as a local Ithacan shrine that acquired an "international" dimension during those two centuries. It is possible, too, that the earliest tripods were actually the result of local prosperity and only the later ones (from ca. 800) were dedicated by foreigners. This would fit the pattern at Otranto (chap. 2), where so far the protocolonial activity is evidenced from around 800, whereas the tripods at Ithaca begin earlier. However, we may yet find earlier Greek material at Otranto.

TRIPODS, EUBOIANS, AND CORINTHIANS

The tripods themselves may one day furnish some clue once a complete metallurgical trace analysis is conducted. What has so far been achieved is a general confirmation of Benton's identification of various tripod pieces (with some exceptions).[104] Some doubt has been expressed that the series begins as early as Benton thought, since judgment is ultimately based on stylistic analysis.[105] Claude Rolley claims that the percentage of tin may be a vital point: whereas the use of tin in the making of bronze (a variable composition of copper, tin, arsenic, lead, and iron) was known to the Mycenaeans

102. Cf. Snodgrass 1971: 170.

103. *Poet.* 1461b 5–9.

104. See Rolley 1977: 16–20, 94–95; Magou, Philippakis, and Rolley 1986; Rolley 1992. Snodgrass's general objections (1971: 281–86) to stylistic dating should be taken into consideration, although the Lefkandi tripod molds (ca. 900; see below) and the Olympia tripods attest to the tenth-century tradition.

105. Cf. Snodgrass 1971: 281; Morgan 1990: 30–31, 198.

THE CULT OF ODYSSEUS

in the second millennium, its use in Greece seems to have disappeared and been recovered from the Near East only in the eighth century. Argive bronzes of the ninth century, for example, which constitute some of the tripod dedications at Olympia, lack tin. Argos adopted the technique very gradually, adding increasing percentages of tin during the eighth century. By contrast, Corinthians began using tin about the second quarter of the eighth century, but their use of it was somewhat irregular and inconsistent in terms of percentages. Thus it should be possible to distinguish Corinthian bronzes in Ithaca from Argive or Euboian ones. Others may disagree, saying that tin content was a matter of manipulation for achieving visual effect; Richard Jones's analysis of the tin content in the Lefkandi bronzes is a case in point.[106]

The earlier tripods (Benton nos. 1–5) are closer to the Argive "massive type" dedicated at Olympia (which does not mean that they came from Argos). Could they have been Achaian or Euboian? In his discussion of the tripod molds found in Lefkandi, Catling claims that Late Geometric tripods, usually thought to have been a revival due to influences from the east, may have been derived from a continuous tradition represented as early as tenth-century Lefkandi. There "parallel relief ridges and running spirals appear in almost the same kind of juxtaposition as the ornament of some of the tripod cauldron legs from Olympia"; they are also very close to one of the legs of the Ithaca tripods.[107] The Euboians will prove significant in connecting the tripods of Odysseus with our earliest explicit and external evidence for Greek knowledge of the content of the Homeric epics, the Nestor cup from Euboian Pithekoussai (chap. 5). We have already discussed the trading and colonial activity of Euboia itself in Corcyra and Orikos. Thus it seems that in Euboian terms the site of Odysseus's cult was particularly significant: it was on the way to Corcyra, the key to the Strait of Otranto and the crossover (with the northeast winds) to Sicily.

Determining provenance is not the same as determining who made the dedications. Tripods could have been ordered and imported. Moreover, artisans could have been brought in to produce the tripods on the spot. Even if it could be determined whether the tripods were made in Ithaca or imported, one would still need to ask for whom they were made. Analysis of the tripods and in particular the horse attachments indicates that from ca. 760 they may be classified as Delphic-Ithacan (certainly Benton nos. 6, 7, and 9), since similar Corinthian tripods were found at Delphi and one at Corinth itself and a terra-cotta copy was dedicated at Perachora (Benton

106. Jones 1980 with fig. 1.
107. W. Catling in Popham, Thelemis, and Sackett 1980: 97. Rolley objects, claiming that, as strange as it may seem, Euboia's ninth-century contacts were mainly with Crete (personal communication).

nos. 10 and 11 are purely Corinthian). It may be argued, therefore, that Corinthian dedications at both Delphi and Ithaca belong to a context of the extension of Corinth's inland and maritime routes. One may tentatively draw the conclusion, therefore, that the later tripods were made by or for Corinthians.[108]

THE DECLINE OF POLIS

It is clear that, unlike Aetos, the Polis cave was never a major sanctuary. In the seventh century it saw no more expensive tripod dedications. It may well have lost its special allure when maritime contacts became more frequent, organized, and oriented toward colonization. Corinthian colonization first in Corcyra (and Syracuse) and then in Leukas and Akarnania, Epidamnos and Apollonia, illustrates how commercial routes became colonization routes without the special appeal of the setting out and returning characteristic of Odysseus. Also, by the seventh century Corinth had sufficient political control over Leukas to make navigation through its channel safer (in fact, the Leukas channel was probably dug only then), and thus the Ithaca-Kephallonia channel (where one would stop at Polis) must have been much less frequented. Ithaca's local claim to Odysseus, particularly impressive with regard to other Greeks, must also have lost some of its internal Ithacan appeal once fewer Greeks from abroad regarded the island as the threshold to the Odyssean Beyond. The historical followers of Odysseus in western waters had become more numerous, politically controlled, and no longer new. During the period 700–550 B.C. only a thin stream of rather insignificant dedications persists. The cult had obviously become local and as a sacred spot (not a *temenos*) attracted various ritual actions, which explains why although sacred to Odysseus and the nymphs it also saw names of other deities.

The novelty of Greek penetration northward and the crossing and recrossing of the mythical boundary drawn by Homer between the real world and that of the Phaiakians had eventually worn off. The shrine, always a nymph place, continued as a local/sailors affair but no longer something for captain-princes. The princes themselves seem to have been replaced by

---

108. The nature of the early Corinthian trade and the degree of individuality of Corinthian traders is still unclear. Aside from adventurers' trade, the presence of olive-oil amphorae in Messapia during the first half of the eighth century may indicate some kind of organized trade, perhaps implying stronger community organization at Corinth than has so far been supposed. The issue was debated at the 1994 Taranto conference. It needs to be discussed, naturally, along with other Corinthian questions such as the Late Geometric II burials and the evidence from the extensive defensive wall (no later than the second half of the seventh century). See Williams 1982. I am grateful to Claude Rolley for information about this and other matters regarding the tripods.

more organized political activities of trade and colonization. More specifically, Euboians such as the "hero of Lefkandi" or Amphidamas of Chalkis,
during whose funeral Hesiod had won the bronze tripod as first prize, or
those buried in the princely tombs at Eretria's West Gate or at Kyme in Italy
were gone.[109] Both Chalkis and Eretria declined, at least in terms of overseas colonization and lavish metal wealth at home, after 700 B.C. The class
of individuals who, in the later eighth century, buried their dead heroically
with bronze cauldrons in their tombs disappeared or changed its habits.
The disappearance of the tripod dedications at Ithaca is therefore contemporary with that of princely burials. It was apparently such captain-princes
and those for whom they had set the tone who dedicated the tripods at Ithaca.

CONCLUSION

The historical Greeks were sailing north of Ithaca during the ninth and
eighth centuries hoping to return home, like Odysseus, with treasure. Ithaca
was precisely at the geographical point where departing from it or returning there could have been perceived as sailing in the wake of Odysseus, and
this perception was linked with the cult at Polis. The dedications in the cave
there seem to imply not just a local Ithaca cult but also what we may call a
proto-pan-Hellenic one, since the hero was shared by other Greeks. The tripod dedications of Ithacans and Greek visitors corresponded to a custom of
prestige dedication at sanctuaries and apparently also reflected an allusion
to particular tripods and to a specific placement of tripods in a cave of which
the *Odyssey* tells us.

I do not claim that those dedicating the tripods had a Homeric text in
hand or even that the verses of a bard were fresh in their minds. People dedicate, bury, and perform a multitude of ritual actions according to perceptions and concepts—or according to stipulations in ritual texts. The latter
hardly exists as a general phenomenon in Greek religion. By contrast, in
saying that there had been an epic influence on the perception of the
heroic one does not need a textual Homer. Thus, for example, saying that
the princely burials in Cyprus cannot be influenced by Homer because they
are too early (ca. 800)[110] is an oversimplification. What matters is both the
general notion of the heroic and the likelihood that the specific myth (not
necessarily its final textual rendition) had had sufficient impact to create
the wish to emulate not merely a general heroic concept but also quintessential episodes in the lives of the heroes emulated. Touching land after
twenty years of *nostos* must have been such an episode.

With Odysseus the issue is not the archaeology of death in the later

109. Bérard 1970; 1978; cf. Malkin 1987a: 264; de Polignac 1995: 128–43.
110. Antonaccio 1995: 228.

eighth century and its social implications around which so much discussion (justifiably) revolves. Rather, the choice of a specific hero, such as Menelaos or Odysseus, depended on the salient story of such a hero that tied him to a specific place,[111] but it also had meaning beyond it. Menelaos was a pan-Hellenic Homeric king of Sparta, not just someone in the Spartan king list. However, one doubts that the Menelaion was frequented by Greeks from outside Sparta. By contrast, Odysseus's heroic cult touched both Ithaca and its (mainly Euboian and Corinthian) visitors, and in this sense he was a proto-pan-Hellenic hero.

In summary, I have argued for the identification of Odysseus as the cult recipient at the cave, using positivistic, exclusionary, and context-oriented evidence. The cult at Polis seems to have emerged as a local affair, attracting expensive dedications when Ithaca itself became prosperous and when traders/adventurers/explorers would stop there en route to the coasts of Epirus, Corcyra, and Italy and back. Before the mid-seventh century, when control of Leukas (and probably the cutting of the Leukas channel) had been achieved, maritime conditions would have encouraged Greeks to sail via the Ithaca-Kephallonia channel, where the only anchorage place is Polis Bay. This facilitated the identification of that bay as the site of Odysseus's landing scene, the end of the hero's *nostos*. Both the framework of the story of Odysseus's return and the specific details of a particular scene in the *Odyssey* (the promise of gifts, the placing of treasure in the cave) are implied in the emulative aspect of the dedications.

We do not have the means to understand the personal experience of the dedicators, whether Ithacans or captains of sailors-traders, but arguing from the role of dedication in general we may glimpse aspects of personal thanks offerings (either following success or hoping for it), ritual investment and personal enhancement, and the overlap (as in the analogy of Kolaios) of individual success and the community's reward and sharing. Ithacans were probably among those making dedications. They managed the shrine (probably also guarding its treasure) and, at least in the Classical and Hellenistic periods, worshipped Odysseus in a full hero cult, including annual gifts and sacrifices (and possibly games). It seems that the salient feature of the Odysseus cult, as its seaside location also suggests, was directed not primarily to the territorial and social cohesion of the political community of the Ithacans (Aetos did that) but to that of the community in its pan-Hellenic maritime context. The importance of Polis probably depended on the recognition by other Greeks, which partly explains the decline of the shrine following the seventh century, when conditions had changed.

In the context of renewal of maritime contacts by mainland Greeks to-

111. On the range of significations of "place" in religious experience, see Smith 1987.

ward Corcyra, Illyria, and Italy, the identification of Corcyra with Phaiakia reinforces the impression that Greeks were aware of the reversal of the return of Odysseus implied in their own sailing north of Ithaca. They would not have wished to find Sirens and Cyclopes, but they might have hoped to replicate other itineraries such as his journey to Thesprotia to make profits and return home. The reversal of Odysseus's return encapsulates a condensed, poetical opposition that we do not find in later colonial uses of myths. In North Africa colonists landed in what they identified as "the port of Menelaos," where the famous Nostos had set the precedent of a landing. In Herakleia Pontike the city was founded around the tomb of the Argonaut Idmon. These identifications constituted a bringing down to earth of what were essentially atemporal and atopographical myths of travel in order to articulate a political geography of settlement. By contrast, the dedications to Odysseus at Polis begin in a protocolonial period in which what was essential for the traders-adventurers was the travel itself—travel along real coasts and maritime routes but also along the paths of the imagination, where the imagery of traverse could be at once fantastic and concrete and where the climactic feature of Odysseus's *nostos,* touching the shore of his homeland, would be most meaningful.

Once Euboians and then Corinthians had settled in Corcyra and farther north, the tripod dedications became meaningful also in colonial terms. With the Euboians we can be fairly certain of their awareness of the Homeric epics by the last third of the eighth century. The colonial Euboian context of both Corcyra and Pithekoussai may serve as a *terminus* for assessing the protocolonial significance of the tripod dedications for which I have been arguing. These dedications therefore indicate both a local, Ithacan, significance and a universal one, each informed by the other. Odysseus was a model for those living the reality of early Archaic Greece. "As distinct from the Iliadic hero, who sets an example of how one ought to die, all Odysseus's life-experience demonstrates how one ought to live."[112] For Greek protocolonists, leaving behind them the conceptual borders of the concrete geography of the epos and actually (not only mentally) entering an alien world, Odysseus came to express the point of contact between the two worlds.

112. Finkelberg 1995: 10.

FOUR

The *Odyssey*'s Alternatives:
Ethnicity and Colonization in Epirus

The geography of Odysseus's travels in the *Odyssey* is heroic, mythological, and exceptional among *nostoi*. Almost all other Nostoi in the non-Homeric sources and even those in the *Odyssey* itself (such as Nestor and Menelaos) move about in recognizable geography. But Odysseus reaches terrible and nonhuman places, such as the lands of the Laistrygonians or the Cyclopes.[1] For a sailor in the historical periods such lands were nightmares, not travel goals. In contrast to the *Odyssey*, however, there was an altogether different kind of Odysseus *nostos* that was compatible with most other, human and topographical *nostoi*. Whereas the *Odyssey*'s *nostos*, especially its final leg, relates to a maritime route along the coasts, the non-*Odyssey* alternatives and sequels that relate a human and topographical Odysseus *nostos* emphasize routes radiating from Ithaca to the lands opposite it. These lands included that which came to bear the name of "the mainland," "Epirus," as well as Aitolia, Elis, and Arkadia.

Unlike the stories told to Alkinoös, Odysseus's adventures in Epirus after his second departure from Ithaca have nothing fantastic about them. The Epirote exploits belong to the more common type of *nostos*, recounting precise wanderings and encounters with human beings (not monsters), and in them Odysseus sometimes becomes a progenitor of royal houses or entire nations. Strictly speaking, it could be argued that we are no longer concerned with a *nostos*, because the return of Odysseus had been accomplished once he came to Ithaca, slaughtered the suitors, and rejoined Penelope. However, anything that happened in a life of a hero who participated in the Trojan War belongs to the category of *nostoi*. Homer too is explicit on this: the

1. Cf. Dion 1969.

120

"full" return of Odysseus could not be accomplished until the prophecy of Tiresias had been fulfilled. That prophecy, in the eleventh book of the *Odyssey*, speaks explicitly of a sequel: it specifies that Odysseus will have to depart from Ithaca once more. In the passage in the eleventh book in which Odysseus consults with the dead, the prophet Tiresias tells him:

> But after you have killed those suitors in your own palace,
> either by treachery, or openly with the sharp bronze,
> then you must take up your well-shaped oar and go on a journey
> until you come where there are men living who know nothing
> of the sea, and who eat food that is not mixed with salt, who never
> have known ships whose cheeks are painted purple, who never
> have known well-shaped oars, which act for ships as wings do.
> And I will tell you a very clear proof, and you cannot miss it.
> When, as you walk, some other wayfarer happens to meet you,
> and say you carry a winnow-fan on your bright shoulder,
> then you must plant your well-shaped oar in the ground, and render
> ceremonious sacrifice to the lord Poseidon,
> one ram and one bull, and a mounter of sows, a boar pig,
> and make your way home again and render holy hecatombs
> to the immortal gods who hold the wide heaven, all
> of them in order. Death will come to you from the sea [or "far from the sea"],[2] in
> some altogether unwarlike way, and it will end you
> in the ebbing time of a sleek old age. Your people
> about you will be prosperous. All this is true that I tell you.

The prophecy is seemingly out of tune with the *Odyssey*'s ending as we have it, where peace and happiness reign over Ithaca. However, it is no news that Tiresias's prophecy and the last book and a half of the *Odyssey* thoroughly contradict each other, and editors since antiquity, following a nonoral, textual-criticism approach, have been claiming that the ending of the *Odyssey* is a later continuation.[3] Accordingly, Tiresias's prophecy, which shows awareness of a post-*Odyssey* story, has also been suspected as an interpolation.[4] But suspecting interpolations is easy and almost impossible to prove, and the suspicion is more often based on a misguided notion of order and consistency than on an acknowledgment of the oral complexity of the Homeric poems. The point to remember is that the *Odyssey* presupposes not only the genre of *nostoi* but also the specific alternatives and sequels of the *Odyssey* itself (chap. 1).

2. For parallel passages in Homer see Ballabriga 1989: 294.
3. See Russo, Fernandez-Galiano, and Heubeck 1992 on 23.296; cf. on 24.413.
4. Merkelbach 1969: 151–52, 144 n. 2, 228 n. 1.

Stanford has shown how the prophecy of Tiresias permitted a host of poets, from Eugammon of Cyrene in the sixth century B.C. to Nikos Kazantzakis in the twentieth century A.D. to write sequels to the *Odyssey*.[5] But perhaps we should not be too quick to judge the raison d'être of the ancient sequels in light of the later ones. The assumption that a sequel was composed after the work whose narrative content it follows or that the authority of the Homeric texts preceded that of the sequels so that Tiresias's prophecy could "permit" them to be born rests on the narrative fallacy that what happened later was also composed later. It seems rather that the prophecy assumes that such a sequel already exists, just as the *Odyssey* assumes the existence of an *Argonautica* or an *Iliad*. As I have argued, since the *Odyssey* is consistent in its references to epic poets and poetry, to specific scenes in the *Iliad*, and to what "preceded" its own narrative, there seems no good reason not to assume that it also implies awareness of at least some of its narrative sequels. Just as the *Iliad* presupposes the judgment of Paris (a pre-*Iliad* element) and the destruction of Troy (post-*Iliad*), although neither of the scenes is detailed there, the post-*Odyssey* scenes should be assessed along the same lines. To reiterate an example: some version about a sequel concerning Odysseus's death must have been known at the time the *Odyssey* was sung.

That Tiresias's prophecy implies awareness of post-Ithaca stories has already been successfully argued.[6] Conversely, a useful yardstick for early elements in stories about the non-*Odyssey* Odysseus would be their adherence to the main elements of the prophecy of Tiresias. A sequel that removes Odysseus permanently from Ithaca, for example, is suspect as a later creation because Odysseus, after the sacrifice to Poseidon in a hinterland oblivious of the sea, should then return to Ithaca and sacrifice there to all the Olympians in turn. Death, therefore, ought to find him at Ithaca with those around him prospering. Let us first observe the *Odyssey* itself.

Tiresias's prophecy is repeated almost verbatim by Odysseus,[7] prefaced by his telling Penelope, "Lady, we have not yet come to the end of all our trials, but still hereafter there is to be measureless toil, long and hard, which I must fulfill to the end; for . . . the prophet told me to go among mortals, city by city (ἐπὶ ἄστε')."[8] Penelope answers that if the gods are to give him old age, they can both hope for the day when they will be free of their troubles.[9] Dying at an old age in Ithaca is compatible with the *Odyssey* and some of the Trojan Cycle poems. However, "city by city of mortal men" is

---

5. Stanford 1992 (1963): 87–88 and passim.
6. See Ballabriga 1989 with previous discussions.
7. *Od.* 23.269–84, that is, before the so-called continuation.
8. *Od.* 23.248–50, 267–68.
9. *Od.* 23.286–87; cf. 212.

rather curious in terms of the *Odyssey* itself. In the *Telegony* Odysseus goes off to Elis to check on his cattle, returns home to perform the sacrifices ordained by Tiresias, and then goes off for further adventures in Epirus before finally returning to Ithaca, where he dies an old man. It is as if Tiresias's prophecy had been split in two, with the sacrifices to all the Olympian gods taking place after the return from Elis (implying that the condition of the oar had already been fulfilled) and all other adventures, city by city, taking place later. The words "city by city" exist in Odysseus's paraphrase but not in the prophecy (which stipulates only going as far inland as possible) and therefore seem to refer to other episodes. The words are compatible with the curious statement about the "many cities he saw" in the introduction to the *Odyssey* and in the various stories that the lying Odysseus tells. To Eumaios, for example, he says, "wandering through the many cities of men I come here" (αὐτὰρ ἐγώ γε πολλὰ βροτῶν ἐπὶ ἄστε ἀλώμενος ἐνθάδ᾽ ἱκάνων).[10] Moreover, Odysseus (the "real" Odysseus) is expected to have visited many cities: that is what Alkinoös expects to hear from the hero instead of a story of fantastic wanderings.[11] Except for Ismaros, which Odysseus promptly sacked once he left Troy, the "real" Odysseus saw mostly a world whose salient feature was lack of cities of mortal men.[12] Thus, even for those who see the *Odyssey* as necessarily primordial in respect to any "sequel" that verse too should be interpreted as providing an "opening" (in my view an allusion) to the sequels of the *Odyssey*.

"City by city" also seems to refer to the image of an immense Epirus that we find in the Hesiodic description of the "innumerable inhabitants" of the land of Dodona[13] or in Pindar's description of Neoptolemos's kingdom,[14] extending from Dodona to the Ionian Sea, as Ἀπείρῳ διαπρυσίᾳ, "vast, far-stretching Epirus." "Immense, unlimited Epirus" can be a play on words in Greek, and it recurs in an isolated verse of Euripides, Ἤπειρον εἰς ἄπειρον.[15] This image will prove important when we come to discuss the dimension of ethnic self-definition.

The exile of Odysseus, whether voluntary or compulsory, is common to most post-Ithaca stories, but the issue is also raised a few times in the *Odyssey* itself. Whereas in the "continuation" (24.482–86) Zeus tells Athena that

10. *Od.* 15.491–92; cf. 16.63–64; 19.170: πολλὰ βροτῶν ἐπὶ ἄστε᾽ ἀλώμενος, ἄλγεα πάσχων, which is even closer to the introduction (1.3–4) πολλῶν δ᾽ ἀνθρώπων ... ἄστεα and πάθεν ἄλγεα.
11. *Od.* 8.572–76.
12. The qualifying "mortal men" excludes such places as the "community" of the Cyclopes or the city (?) of the Laistrygonians.
13. Merkelbach and West 1967: fr. 240.
14. Pind. *Nem.* 4.51–53; cf. 7.35, 103; *Paean* 6.102.
15. TGF fr. 1010; cf. Dionys. Per. 5.430; following Ballabriga 1989: 298.

erasing the memory of the slaughtered will resolve the civil strife and ensure the reign of Odysseus forever (thus foreshadowing Renan's famous dictum about common forgetfulness being the condition for national unity),[16] this is not the impression one gets from earlier assessments of the realistic option of exile. In a sense, Odysseus's slaughter has a basic tragic aspect somewhat similar to that of Orestes in fifth-century tragedy: to regain his position and avenge the dishonor to his household he must kill, yet he must also pay for this action. "For when one has killed only one man in a community," says Odysseus to his son after the massacre, "and then [or "even when"] there are not many avengers to follow, even so, he flees into exile, leaving kinsmen and country. But we have killed what held the city together, the finest young men in Ithaca." This is told to a Telemachos just returning from his voyage to the Peloponnese with a fugitive, "exiled" murderer (Theoklymenos) on board.[17] This sober assessment of Odysseus's is closely related to what Odysseus in disguise, the Cretan Odysseus, tells Athena: "I have fled, an exile, because I killed the son of Idomeneos." He also provides reasons: "He tried to deprive me of all my share of the plunder from Troy, and for the sake of it my heart suffered many pains: the wars of men; hard crossing of the big waters; for I would not do his father favor, and serve as his henchman in the land of Troy, but I led others, of my own following."[18] The Cretan Odysseus then departs, of his own accord, before the arrival of the avengers. Exile, therefore, may be tantamount to escape. Basic heroic conflicts are apparent in this story: Idomeneos and his sons seem to expect the Cretan Odysseus to serve them, but he refuses; depriving him of his booty,[19] as the *Iliad* illustrates, is a justified grievance; finally, the "heart" (*thymos*) of the hero, very much like that of the real Odysseus, suffers generally from war and sea voyages, but it is also what may move him—without apparent cause—to further wanderings. The Cretan Odysseus whose story is told to Eumaios returns home to his wife and children after many wanderings only to be awakened again by his *thymos* to go off again, to Egypt.[20] The *Odyssey*'s "Cretan Odys-

16. Renan 1882: 11: "The essence of a nation is that all individuals have many things in common, and also they have forgotten many things. No French citizen knows whether he is a Burgundian, an Alan, a Taifale, or a Visigoth, yet every French citizen has to have forgotten the Massacre of Saint Bartholomew."

17. *Od.* 23.118–22; 15.272–78. The latter passage is often regarded as an interpolation, mainly because it serves no apparent purpose (for references and summary see Hoekstra in Heubeck and Hoekstra 1989 on 15.223–81). But it does: the theme of murder and consequent exile, the counteroption to the end of the *Odyssey*, seems to be mounting gradually from Odysseus's own lying tales (like Theoklymenos, he gets a ride on a ship) through the Aitolian murderer (*Od.* 14.379) to Theoklymenos.

18. *Od.* 13.259–65.

19. Cf. Van Wees 1992: chap. 7.

20. *Od.* 14.244–46.

seuses," as Merkelbach observes,[21] may "argue against" other versions of the *Odyssey* or simply reflect them as (ironic and intertextual?) alternatives.

In some non-*Odyssey* sequels we observe endings that are different from the prophecy of Tiresias. According to one version, Odysseus goes to Kalydon in Aitolia, marries the daughter of Thoas, and dies happily next to the son born of that union, Leontophonos.[22] A fragment of Aristotle's *Constitution of the Ithakesians* mentions an oracle (*manteion*) of Odysseus among the Aitolian Eurytanes.[23] Another fragment[24] has been emended accordingly: instead of migrating to Italy, as the text says, Odysseus is supposed to go to Aitolia. However, for "Aitolia" to belong to the *Constitution of the Ithakesians* makes little sense, and the presence of Odysseus in Italy is richly attested as early as in Hesiod (chap. 6). Not everything has to be consistent; it would appear that the *Constitution of the Ithakesians* was a compendium of conflicting traditions, since Aristotle also has Telemachos marrying Nausikaa.[25] The Aitolian story ends with Odysseus dying away from Ithaca, which is obviously not what the Ithacans who minted Odysseus coinage and were contemporaries of Aristotle had in mind. The story thus seems to be an Aitolian appropriation of the hero, perhaps ennobling some princely family or reflecting some attempt at Aitolian colonization in the Adriatic (see chap. 8).

The Arkadian connection of Odysseus[26] seems surprisingly rich—in fact, too rich—and points to an independent, perhaps not even epic route with more emphasis on Penelope than elsewhere. Her tomb was shown there,[27] and according to a tradition known to Herodotus she and Hermes were the parents of Pan, a characteristically Arkadian god.[28] A more direct link to Tiresias's prophecy is indicated by coins from Mantineia (after 370) showing Odysseus planting his oar, with the altar of Poseidon on the reverse.[29] We have no idea whether these Arkadian episodes and the establishment of a cult to Penelope evolved before the Classical period. They probably did not. George Huxley[30] suggests that since the arbiter sent to Cyrene in the sixth century was Demonax of Arkadian Mantineia, the unknown part of the sequel to the *Odyssey* by the Cyrenaean poet Eugammon brought Odys-

---

21. Merkelbach 1969: 224 ff.

22. Apollod. *Epit.* 7.40; Eust. p. 1796 51.

23. Fr. 508 Rose = Tzetz. *ad* Lycoph. *Alex.* 799.

24. Fr. 507 Rose = with Halliday 1975 (1929) on Plut. *Quaest. Graec.* 14.

25. Aristotle fr. 506 Rose with Hellanikos *FGrH* 4 F 156.

26. There is no reason to regard Epirus and Arkadia as equivalent. Cf. Hansen 1977: 33.

27. Paus. 8.12.5–6.

28. Hdt. 2.145 4; cf. Borgeaud 1979: 85 n. 75 with Jost 1985: 287 n. 4, 463; Ballabriga 1989: 289 n. 13.

29. Head 1911: 449–50; cf. Paus. 8.9.2.

30. Huxley 1959; 1969: 170–71.

seus to Arkadia, where—away from the sea—he performed the sacrifices ordered by Tiresias. This, however, seems to disregard the fact that the Arkadian versions concerning Penelope totally contradict what we know of Eugammon's sequel regarding Penelope. Moreover, Huxley apparently overlooks the independent routes taken by some of the *Odyssey* sequels, such as the Aitolian one. Finally, an echo of a Thesprotian fulfillment of Tiresias's prophecy is found in the tradition that Odysseus founded an oracle at Trampya near the Pindus Range, far from Arkadia.[31]

In sum, most of these versions, notably the Aitolian and the Arkadian ones, seem to have been later and independent developments from the post-Ithaca story implied by the prophecy of Tiresias. By contrast, Thesprotia in Epirus appears much closer to the *Odyssey*'s implied sequel.

THESPROTIA

The existence of a poem called *Thesprotis* is attested in a reference by Pausanias,[32] and Clement of Alexandria accused the author of the *Telegony*, Eugammon of Cyrene (fl. 566–63 B.C.), of having stolen an entire book from the *Thesprotis* written by Mousaios, a poet probably active in the seventh century.[33] It seems clear, therefore, that the subject matter of the *Thesprotis* was Odysseus, that the episodes had to do with Thesprotia, and that these were the subject of poetry sung earlier than Eugammon in the seventh century. For the *Telegony*, the sequel composed by Eugammon of Cyrene, we have only a plot summary by Proclus. Some are appalled by the *Telegony*'s melodramatic ending with the return of Odysseus to Ithaca and his death at the hands of his own son by Circe, Telegonos ("born far away"; cf. Telemachos, "he who fights from afar"). Telegonos, in search of his father, comes to Ithaca but apparently does not recognize the place and plunders it; Odysseus dies defending the land. Sad recognition follows, and the final scene is the marriage of Telegonos to Penelope and of Telemachos to Circe. However, plot summaries can be unfair; one wonders what our impression, say, of Euripides would be if such a summary were all we had of *Medea*. In fact, Sophocles, whose plot summary of *Oedipus* could be represented as equally embarrassing, apparently wrote a tragedy about the death of Odysseus, probably along similar lines.[34]

---

31. Schol. Lycoph. 800; schol. *Od.* 11.121; Steph. Byz. s.v. Βούνειμα.

32. See Paus. (8.12.5–6), who mentions another son (Poliporthes) of Odysseus and Penelope.

33. Clem. Al. *Strom.* 6.2.25.1; cf. Severyns 1928: 409–16.

34. *TGF* p. 141, 194. For the argument only, no fragment, see Parth. II *Erot. Path.* 3. Another version (Eust. *ad Od.* 16.118) has Telemachos kill him.

But Telegonos and the end of the *Telegony* are of lesser importance here. It is the first part of the *Telegony* that should concern us, especially since there is a good chance that it is derived from a seventh-century poem. Proclus says that the *Telegony* consisted of two books, and since the first apparently dealt with Epirus its link with the *Thesprotis* seems secure. The *Telegony* starts with the burial of the suitors, thus overlapping with the end of the *Odyssey* but perhaps only up to verse 413 of book 24, before the pacification of Ithaca.[35] Unlike other sequels, in this first book of the *Telegony* there seems to be nothing that forces Odysseus out of Ithaca: neither is Penelope unfaithful nor is there a *stasis* resolved by Odysseus's exile. None of the "elaborations"[36] that distinguish some of the *nostoi* from Homer is apparent here. In contrast, the second book of the *Telegony* should be counted among these elaborations: a Cyrenaean touch is added, with the name of Arkesilas as another son born to Odysseus, and there is a crescendo of marriages at the end.

A remarkable example of elaboration (again, incompatible with the Tiresias prophecy) is the motif of Penelope's unfaithfulness, in yet other versions a prime cause for Odysseus's disgusted departures.[37] The most disparaging, the one by Duris of Samos,[38] claims Penelope slept with 129 suitors and accordingly named the son born to her Pan ("all"). In a less contemptuous version, found in Herodotus, Pan (the god) is her son by Hermes. Herodotus also has Penelope return to her father, Ikarios.[39] It seems that this is a literary development, perhaps adjusting Penelope's role to that of Clytemnestra. Closer to Phaedra is her role as the one responsible for making Odysseus kill his own son, Euryalos. Here Odysseus leaves Ithaca and finds refuge with the Epirote king Tyrimnas. Odysseus has several sons by the king's daughter Euippe: Doryklos, Leontophonos,[40] and Euryalos. Odysseus returns to Ithaca; Euippe sends him the adolescent Euryalos; Penelope arranges for Odysseus unknowingly to kill him. This was apparently the plot of Sophocles's *Euryalos*.

Odysseus's departure from Ithaca is not a straightforward one in the *stasis* version from the *Greek Questions* of Plutarch, who relies, at least for one detail, on Aristotle's *Constitution of the Ithakesians*.[41] Here Neoptolemos, the son of Achilles (who in the poem called *Nostoi* meets with Odysseus in Thra-

---

35. Huxley (1969: 171) speaks of 14.417. See Russo, Fernandez-Galiano, and Heubeck 1992: 405–6.
36. Griffin 1977.
37. On this motif, see chap. 8 on Diomedes.
38. Tzetz. ad Lycoph *Alex.* 772; Lycoph. *Alex.* 771–73 and scholia.
39. Hdt. 2.145; cf. Apollod. *Epit.* 7.38; schol. ad Theocr. 1.3 and 123.
40. Lysimmachus ap. Eudocie *Viol.* 191 and Eust. ad *Od.* 16.118.
41. Fr. 507 (Rose).

cian Maroneia and settles among the Molossians),[42] arbitrates between the relatives of the slaughtered suitors and Odysseus. Odysseus was to be exiled from Kephallonia, Zakynthos, and Ithaca. For their part, the relatives and friends of the suitors were to make an annual payment for the wrongs they had done Odysseus (chap. 3) consisting of barley meal, wine, honey in the comb, olive oil, and sacrificial animals. The hero then migrated to Italy and transferred the payments to his son.

As we have seen above, the motif of exile seems to be foreshadowed in the *Odyssey* itself, which may therefore allude to this version as well. Since the story lays the emphasis not on the destination but particularly on the reason for departure, contradicting both the end of the *Odyssey* as we have it and Eugammon's *Telegony*, it seems likely that the arbitration of Neoptolemos reflects an Ithacan version. It is the only one that lists (some of) the other Ithacan islands and provides a "local," evenhanded resolution of the conflict, different from Athena's divine intervention in the "continuation" of the *Odyssey*. Aristotle himself seems to have been well acquainted with particular aspects of the Odysseus lore in the region of Ithaca. In the *Poetics*[43] he wonders why Telemachos did not visit his father-in-law when he went to see Menelaos in Lakedaimon. Perhaps, he says, the Kephallonian version about Penelope's father should be believed, since Ikadios (his spelling) was a Kephallonian and therefore so was Penelope.[44] Kephallonia is also mentioned in Neoptolemos's arbitration. The particular detail, therefore, may have been a Kephallonian attempt to usurp the preeminence of its neighbor Ithaca, perhaps also relying on the Homeric appellation "Kephallonians" for all of Odysseus's men.

Athena says[45] that Odysseus was in (Thesprotian) Ephyra, where he stayed with Ilos, son of Mermeros.[46] Mermeros's home was probably in the northwest: Pausanias places him in Corcyra and the mainland opposite, and Ephyra could be easily reached from Ithaca.[47] In another poem that takes up themes from the *Argonautica*, the *Naupaktia*, it is said that after the death of Pelias Jason settled in Corcyra,[48] and his son Mermeros was killed by a lioness while he was hunting on the (Epirote Thesprotian) mainland opposite. In later versions this Mermeros is supposed to have been killed by his

42. Bernabé 1987: 94 (argumentum).
43. Arist. *Poet.* 1461b 5–9.
44. Cf. schol. *Od.* 15.16.
45. *Od.* 1.259.
46. *Od.* 1.259.
47. Paus. 2.3.9; *Od.* 1.257 ff.; 2.326–28. On Thesprotian Ephyra, see *Il.* 15.529–31: a (bronze?) breastplate was brought from Ephyra by Phyleus, father of Meges (on his kingdom, see *Il.* 2.625–30).
48. Paus. 2.3.9

mother Medea in Corinth.[49] The Corcyrean localization has obviously been created after the Greeks settled there (ca. mid-eighth century), but Ephyra, the land of the oracle of the dead, explicitly mentioned in the *Odyssey*, clearly points to a version at least contemporary with the *Odyssey* itself. In sum: since Mermeros's home in Ephyra appears to have been common to the *Odyssey* and the early *Argonautica* and since both refer to Epirus, it would appear that the case for the *Odyssey*'s allusions to Epirote traditions is now more secure.

In the fourteenth book of the *Odyssey* Odysseus appears before Eumaios as a Cretan who recounts his life as a bastard son and adventurer up to the point where, shipwrecked from a Phoenician ship bound for Libya, he reached Thesprotia. The Thesprotian king, Pheidon, showed him the enormous treasure that Odysseus had left in his keeping before going to Dodona to ask the oracle whether he should return home openly or in secret. Since there happened to be a Thesprotian ship setting out for Doulchion (part of Odysseus's kingdom), the "Cretan" joined it, sent by the Thesprotian Pheidon to King Akastos. The sailors, however, planned to sell the Cretan into slavery; when they landed in Ithaca for their supper, he managed to slip away and thus appeared, looking wretched, before Eumaios.[50]

The story, told to a man living in Ithaca (Eumaios) and retold later along similar lines to Penelope,[51] presumes that Odysseus and the Thesprotian king had trustful, probably close relations (a point made explicit by Penelope). Thesprotia would have been the last place on Odysseus's return before going to Ithaca except for Dodona. If Dodona's answer had been "Return in secret," according to this hypothetical and unrealized *nostos,* Odysseus's treasure would presumably have been kept in Thesprotia a while longer. Thus Thesprotia, the region of Epirus across from Corcyra, fulfills the function of the cave of the nymphs in the "real" story. It signifies an assumed Ithaca-Thesprotia-Dodona relationship that Eumaios, Penelope, and the *Odyssey*'s audience would find convincing and realistic (the Thesprotians seem to have been the influential force in Dodona before the Molossian hegemony in the fifth century).[52] Moreover, in what happened to the Cretan Odysseus we learn that a Thesprotian boat "happened to be setting out for Doulchion" and when it did it stopped at Ithaca for refreshments. The story, then, is now dealing not with possibilities but with acceptable reality. The villainy of the sailors and the presence of a foreigner were the exception; the trip itself was routine. In general, the *Odyssey* gives the im-

49. Apollod. *Lib.* 1.9.28.
50. *Od.* 19.285–359.
51. *Od.* 19.270 ff.
52. Strabo 7.7.11. 328; cf. Theopompus *FGrH* 115 F 382 and F 319. See Lepore 1962: 63–64.

pression of many comings and goings between Ithaca and the coasts of north-western Greece and especially Thesprotia. When Penelope reproaches Antinoös for plotting against her son,[53] she reminds him of past favors. Once Antinoös's father sought refuge with Odysseus because (together with Taphians) he had raided the Thesprotians, who were allies of the men of Ithaca, and the angry Ithacans wanted his blood. Against this background we may understand the normality of Thesprotian ships' happening to be sailing to Ithaca.

There are other interesting indications. Eumaios, lamenting the wastefulness of the suitors, tells the Cretan Odysseus how much property his master used to have. No one could compare, he says, either in Ithaca itself or on "the dark mainland" (Epeiros),[54] where Odysseus kept herds of cattle, sheep, goats, and swine and *xenoi* and his own men attended them. This is a slice of reality, a symbiosis between islanders and mainlanders, Ithacan herdsmen residing (seasonally?) on the mainland and herding together with non-Odysseus men (*xenoi* does not mean barbarians here). Today too one can often see goats being moved about on small vessels between islands and mainland. The *Odyssey* is explicit: a barren cow and fat goats are brought to the suitors' banquet by ferrymen from across the waters.[55] The symbiosis may not have always been easy or normal; Laertes laments his youth, when he was strong and conquered Nerikos, "the strong-founded citadel on the mainland cape" (ἀκτὴν ἠπείροιο).[56] The mainland is usually taken to be Akarnania and perhaps Aitolia.[57] This may be the case, although the straightforward mention of Elis in the *Telegony* may indicate that aside from areas of direct control or immediate access "mainland" could indicate more distant regions. Elis is also mentioned as a matter of course in the speech of Telemachos comparing his authority with that of those in Ithaca or in the "islands off horse-pasturing Elis," and the relatives of the dead suitors stress the need for haste lest Odysseus go to Pylos or Elis.[58]

In the first book of the *Telegony* Odysseus simply goes to Elis "to inspect the herds of cattle," probably his own.[59] Ithaca, as Telemachos replies to Menelaos when offered some horses, has no plains and little grazing,[60] and the story is compatible with the need, articulated by Eumaios, to have herds on the mainland. If the kingdom of Odysseus included one of the Echi-

53. *Od.* 16.424–27.
54. *Od.* 14.97–100.
55. *Od.* 20.187–88.
56. *Od.* 24.377.
57. Oberhummer 1887: 47, 49, 239; cf. Lepore 1962: 8 n.2.
58. *Od.* 21.347, 24.430.
59. Probably not the herds Odysseus plans to raid in *Odyssey* 23.356–58.
60. *Od.* 4.600–608.

nades, facing Elis,[61] this would explain the straightforward manner in which a trip to Elis was perceived in terms of the *Odyssey*. After Elis the Odysseus of the *Telegony* returns to Ithaca "to perform the sacrifices ordained by Tiresias." Apparently the condition laid down by the prophet in the eleventh book of the *Odyssey* has now been fulfilled, although Proclus says nothing about this. Elis plays a part also in the thirteenth book of the *Odyssey*, where the Cretan Odysseus seeks refuge there. Such a story underlines the accessibility and proximity of Elis and would have appeared natural for someone from Ithaca.

In short, Thesprotia in the *Odyssey* and Elis in both the *Telegony* and the *Odyssey* seem to indicate both an allusion of the *Odyssey* to its sequels and alternatives[62] and a reflection of Ithaca's multiple real-world connections with its various mainlands (Epirus and the Peloponnese). We are now in a better position to observe more closely the poetic role of Thesprotia.

Eugammon is consistent with the remarkable passage in the *Odyssey* in which Odysseus encounters Penelope as a Cretan and tells her what happened to Odysseus, lying yet including "real" details.[63] In the land of the Thesprotians, he says, he heard that Odysseus had reached the land of the Phaiakians. Here the story deviates, drastically changing the character of the *Odyssey*'s geography. The Phaiakians, he says,[64]

> gave him much, and they themselves were willing to carry him
> home without harm. So Odysseus would have been home a long
>   time
> before this, but in his mind he thought it more profitable
> to go about and visit much country, collecting possessions.
> For Odysseus knew profitable ways beyond all other
> men who are mortal, no other man could rival him at it.
> So Pheidon, king of the Thesprotians, told me the story.

Homer shows here that he is aware of an alternative to the looking-glass geography of the *Odyssey*. Phaiakia is no longer the utopia through whose mist Odysseus returns to the real world. Obviously, Odysseus has rejected the Phaiakians' offer and chosen to go to Thesprotia instead, and their role is played, rather mundanely, by the king of the Thesprotians. Once Odysseus returns from Dodona the king, guarding his treasure for him,[65] will send him to Ithaca on a Thesprotian ship. The story seems to be implied in the scene when the bewildered Odysseus wakes up in Ithaca after the Phaiakians have

61. Strabo 100.452–53, doubted by Hope Simpson and Lazenby 1970: 104.
62. Ballabriga 1989: 297.
63. *Od.* 19.270 ff.
64. *Od.* 19.281.
65. Similarly, the gifts that Telemachos received in the Peloponnese are guarded for him in a friend's house. *Od.* 16.327.

left him asleep on the shore. He cries out, "I wish I had stayed among the Phaiakians, just where I was, and I would have visited some other powerful king, who then would have been my friend and seen to my journey."[66] The poet of the *Odyssey*, yet again, is playing with options and alternatives.

All this is so compatible with the Thesprotian non-*Odyssey* stories that it is easy to see how such passages were considered suspect as interpolations, especially since Corcyra, which faces Thesprotia, was identified as Scheria, the land of the Phaiakians. In fact, the passage in the *Odyssey* seems to imply that identification. Was this identification created because Greeks settled in Corcyra? It is curious how the argument "This or that could have not been so and so until Greeks had actually settled Corcyra" is sometimes employed by literary critics. Such a priori historical argumentation disregards the historical role of *proto*colonization. Odysseus, who "knew profitable ways beyond all other men who are mortal," was the epitome of such a protocolonist, a "captain", an explorer, raider, and gift receiver.[67] Here, in the Cretan-Odysseus version we see the poet introducing a character more typical of the poetry of Hesiod or Solon. Poetically, this is ingenious, since it is precisely the difference between what really happened to Odysseus (namely, the fantastic) and the lies of the Cretan Odysseus (namely, the reality) that creates the multiplicity of options in the *Odyssey*.

The first actions of Odysseus in the *Telegony* tie in with the end of the *Odyssey:* he buries the suitors and sacrifices to the nymphs, perhaps fulfilling the promise he had made them. The departure and the rite have a particular northwestern, Epirote aspect: Odysseus departs for the mainland. The significance of this ritual act has been discussed above in the context of the cult to Odysseus at the cave of the nymphs on Ithaca, attested from the ninth century. If this connection is accepted, and keeping in mind that the cave no longer saw significant tripod dedications after ca. 700, the mention of the act in the *Telegony* strengthens the claim that it reflects pre-seventh-century traditions.

From here on the *Thesprotis/Telegony* becomes localized. Among the Thesprotians Odysseus marries their queen, Kallidike, and has a son with her, Polypoites. A war breaks out with the Brygi, who are supported by Ares; Athena helps Odysseus, and the conflict is resolved through Apollo's arbitration. After the death of his Thesprotian wife, Odysseus leaves the throne to his son and returns to Ithaca.[68] The Brygi are intriguing, since they point to a use of the Odysseus myth as legitimation of conflicts with peoples that seem to be non-Greeks. They are probably the same as the Briges, previous

---

66. *Od.* 13.204–6.
67. Cf. Van Wees 1992: chap. 4 and Crielaard 1996.
68. The story also appears in the *nostoi*. Bernabé 1987: 94–95.

settlers of Epidamnos and the reputed ancestors of the Phrygians.[69] In Thesprotia, therefore, Odysseus seems to have played a role comparable with that of Herakles both for Greeks and for non-Greeks as the progenitor of the Thesprotian royal house and the defender of the realm. Whereas the Greekness of the Thesprotians may have been a matter for debate, the ethnicity of the Brygi is clear: they were barbarians. Odysseus fought and repelled them with the help of the Greek goddess of (hoplite) war, who is juxtaposed with the most "barbarian" of the Olympians, Ares.

Why were the Thesprotians drawn to Odysseus? Their interest seems to have extended to attributing to Odysseus the foundation of a city at the foot of the Pindus Range (Bouneima) and an oracle at Trampya in accordance with Tiresias's prophecy.[70] We can only speculate about the factors involved. At some point they had become exposed to Greek values attaching ennobling importance to genealogical links with the Nostoi. An Odysseus connection would have worked well for the merchants of Ithaca operating in the region, and the Ithacans for their part may have regarded this as a form of flattery of the Thesprotians, oiling their connections. In relation to other peoples of Epirus (except, perhaps, the Molossians and the Chaones), descent from Odysseus allowed the Thesprotians greater antiquity, and in fact they claimed it.[71] The Molossians and Chaones, however, seem to have repaid them in the same coin: they, too, were descendants of Nostoi. It is remarkable how Greek categories of group definition following the genealogy of a Greek hero could take over and contribute to some notion of common heroic origins, later (but only later) to be articulated in terms of common Hellenism.

Appropriations of Odysseus were not unique to Epirotes. It seems that whereas no one could bring Odysseus himself to Euboia or Corinth, one could play with his own genealogy and make him a Euboian or a Corinthian. The details are somewhat free-floating in time, since they come down to us from late sources. The conventional genealogy of Odysseus makes him descend (on his father's side) from Laertes, Akrisios, Kephallos, Deion, and Aiolos.[72] Others make Kephallos, a grandson of Kekrops, his grandfather.[73] Odysseus is also said to be the son of King Pandion.[74] Thus the hero is linked either with the Athenians or with the Abantes (Euboians). But Odysseus

---

69. App. *BCiv.* 2.39; Strabo 14.680–81. Appian describes the foundation of Epidamnos as a joint effort of Corcyra and a non-Greek people against the Liburnians.

70. Schol. Lycoph. *Alex.* 800; schol. *Od.* 11.121; Steph. Byz. s.v. Βούνειμα.

71. Strabo 7.328.

72. Cf. *Od.* 16.118; 24.270, 517; Apollod. *Bibl.* 1.112. For variants see schol. *Il.* 2.173; Eust. 1796, 34 ad *Od.* 19.118 and schol. ad loc.

73. Apollod. *Bibl.* 3.14.3.

74. Apollod. *Bibl.* 3.14.7.

may also be a Corinthian as the son of Sisyphos.[75] In spite of its prominence and maritime activity, Corinth was not "interpolated." In the *Catalogue of Women* "wealthy" (ἀφνειός) Corinth forms part of Agamemnon's kingdom. There was one Corinthian who was killed by Paris.[76] With such little representation Corinthians may have wanted to compensate, and Eumelos may have reworked the *Argonautica* and brought Medea to Corinth accordingly. It is also possible, as Dunbabin (followed by Huxley) claims,[77] that Eumelos appropriated Epirote Ephyra with its Corinthian namesake.[78]

ODYSSEUS AND EPIROTE ETHNICITY

Sailing to and beyond Ithaca and Corcyra, *nostoi* would often articulate the identities of royal houses or of entire populations. Whether in Epirus or in western Italy, the *Odyssey*, its alternatives, and other *nostoi* functioned as an organizing, explanatory model for encounters with various populations and relationships with their rulers. A significant pattern emerges, for example, when we observe that the most common device for articulating identity is the heroic genealogy. The Greek hero ubiquitously associated with heroic progeny is Herakles, but with regard to non-Greeks he is interestingly almost absent from Epirus, the Adriatic, and Campania and Etruria. We do not find Herakles siring royal genealogies as he did, for example, in Epirus's neighbor Makedonia and throughout the world. Rather, the significant progenitors, especially in the regions facing Corcyra (Epirus) and Pithekoussai (Campania), were the Nostoi and especially Odysseus. This pattern indicates, I think, that the distribution of *nostoi* that were used as articulations of genealogies and ethnicities is directly linked with the historical context of Greek sailing and colonization in the Geometric and Archaic periods. The Nostos articulations thus appear to be the result not of late erudite guesses but of historical encounters.

One finds two commonly used mythic devices for explaining ethnicity in the Greek Mediterranean world (chap. 1): heroic genealogy and quasi-historical heroic myths of migrations. As an example of the latter we may note the story about the Cretan king Minos, who pursued Daidalos to Kamikos in Sicily and was murdered there by Kokalos. His now leaderless

---

75. Schol. Lycoph. *Alex.* 344; Hyg. Fab. 201; schol. *Il.* 10.266 and also Soph. *Aj.* 190; schol. Sophocles *Philoct.* 417, 1311, fr. 142; schol. Eur. *Cyc.* 104; *Iph. A.* 524–1362; Ov. *Ars Am.* 3.313; *Met.* 13.31; Serv. ad Verg. *Aen.* 6.529. Why the Corinthians should have been interested in such appropriation of the hero should by now be readily understood. It may be added that Corinth is not mentioned at all in the *Odyssey*.

76. *Il.* 13.660–72.

77. Dunbabin 1948c: 60; Will 1995: 118–29; Huxley 1969: 19.

78. On Ephyra, see n. 47 with Ballabriga 1986: 37; cf. Dion 1977: 76–78.

Cretans escaped from Sicily and ended up as settlers in Iapygia, in southern Italy, ánd it was their descendants whom the Greek colonists of the eighth and seventh centuries met upon their arrival. Aside from the Cretans, Greek myth ethnography could use models of migrations of Arkadians, Pelasgians, and so on.[79] However, *nostoi* were individual myths, and for the most part we observe only the genealogical model of articulation. The main issue will therefore be whether Greeks created *nostos*-"ethnicities" for others, and, if so, why they did so and to what extent these ethnicities were adopted and internalized by non-Greeks. In order to approach the subject we shall need to say a few words about specific, Epirote categories of ethnicity, since the subject is far from self-evident. It involves ancient perceptions of Greek ethnicity: how Greeks perceived ethnicity—their own and that of others—and whether that question is at all legitimate for the Archaic period. It also involves our own categories of thinking about ethnicity and ethnogenesis in general (chap. 1). These categories are often conditioned either by analogies with encounters with "absolute others" in the vein of Columbus or Captain Cook or by the role of ethnicity in modern nationalism. Briefly considering some of these categories may both help us to avoid anachronistic pitfalls and sharpen the contours of what it is we are looking for.

Were the Epirotes Greeks? Or, rather, did the question matter to them or to other Greeks, and, if so, when and to whom among them, precisely? It is clear that most of the Epirote "tribes" (Theopompus counted fourteen) [80] were not regarded as Greek by the few Greek writers who cared to address the question. The name of the land, Epeiros (Epirus), which first appears in Hekataios,[81] is not an ethnic appellation but one of the few names in Greek coined from a maritime-geographical perspective: "the mainland." Regional names, not implying an indefinite view of the land ("mainland" is indefinite), appear much earlier, as we have seen with Homeric Thesprotia.

From the indigenous points of view (and these were varied and numerous) a general distinction may be drawn between Epirote cities, usually coastal ones, that attributed their foundation to a Greek hero (e.g., Byllis, a foundation of Neoptolemos) and particular royal houses that did the same. Such cities, it seems, were following the pattern of self-definition of Greek city-states, which were more concerned with foundations than with the genealogies of royalty. For the royal houses in question, in contrast, the point was not to Hellenize the ethnic origins of their peoples but to heroize their own. This was apparently sufficient and not extraordinary in Archaic Greek terms. The Herakleidai at Sparta or Corinth, for example, defined them-

79. Fabre 1981; Briquel 1984; 1990; 1993.
80. Strabo 7.323–24.
81. *FGrH* 1 F 26, 119.

selves (and were universally regarded) not as Dorians but as direct descendants of Herakles.[82] It is noteworthy that a Bakchiad, Arrabaios, a little over two centuries after the demise of the Bakchiad regime in Corinth surfaces as a king of the Epirote Lynkestai.[83] (His origins may be sought in one of the Corinthian colonies.)

Strictly speaking, therefore, the proper term for the use of Greek heroes as progenitors of royal houses is not "Hellenization" but "heroization" (in Greek terms). Greeks applied similar heroic genealogies to various barbarian peoples, such as Perseus and the Persians.[84] It is unlikely, however, that the Persians took much notice of such attributions. The point becomes relevant for Hellenization when a non-Greek people or royal family acknowledged and took pride in its Greek origins. Whereas this did not happen with the Persians or the Egyptians, it did with the Molossians (who were probably ethnically/linguistically Greek—see below). In other words, what may have begun as poetic or erudite inventions caught on. For the Molossians, for example, Greek heroic origins ceased to be merely a matter for Greek-centered erudite "ethnography of the Other" but were incorporated and adopted by that Other.

The ancestor of the Molossian kings, farther inland, was another Nostos, Neoptolemos/Pyrrhos, son of Achilles. According to one version he was joined by the widow of Hektor, the Trojan Andromache.[85] This too contradicts the *Odyssey*, in which Neoptolemos ends up living in his father's domain in Phthia.[86] Hagias of Troizen in his *Nostoi* (seventh-century?) brings Neoptolemos to the Molossians before continuing to Phthia.[87] Pindar sings of Neoptolemos who rules Epirus from Dodona to the Ionian Sea.[88] In the sixth *Paian*[89] Pindar seems to adhere to an older tradition in which Neoptolemos crossed over by land to avoid the kind of maritime disaster other Nostoi were experiencing and came to Molossis near Mt. Tomaros. Later, Pindar finds another explanation and a compromise: Neoptolemos is buried in Phthia (as in Homer), but during his *nostos* his ship was driven by a storm to Ephyra, where he ruled the Molossians for a short time "and in his honor

82. Malkin 1994a: chap. 1.

83. Hammond 1967: 439.

84. Wilkes 1994: 58–66.

85. Paus. 1.11.1.

86. *Od.* 3.188; 4.5 ff.

87. Proclus in Bernabé 1987: 95; cf. Apollod. *Epit.* 6.12; Eratosthenes ap. schol. *Od.* 3.188.

88. *Nem.* 4.51–53.

89. Pind. *Paean* 6.110 with Radt 1958: 158–60.

his dignity was borne by his race forever."[90] In the *Paian* Pindar apparently offended both the Aiginetans and the Molossians, since he said that Neoptolemos (ultimately of the Aiakidai) was killed by Apollo at Delphi. The double insult illustrates the irrelevancy of categories of Greekness; no one doubted the Greekness of Aigina, whereas some, such as Thucydides, regarded the Molossians as barbarians. In the seventh *Nemean Ode* Pindar apologizes to both and says especially, "If any Achaian is near who lives above the Ionian Sea, he will not blame me, for I rely on my being their *proxenos* [public guest-friend]." The "Achaians" here were probably the members of the Molossian royal household, "Achaians" in the same sense as the Herakleidai.[91]

It is difficult to determine when the Neoptolemos origins of the Molossians were first articulated. Unlike the travels of Odysseus among the Thesprotians, which are opened by the two discussions of Tiresias's prophecy in the *Odyssey*, the poet seems to block the possibility of Neoptolemos's stay among the Molossians.[92] Before Pindar, the epics of the Trojan Cycle provide, as we have seen, different versions of Neoptolemos's return, with varying lengths of his sojourn among the Molossians. Lepore and others argue that the motive for Molossian interest was their conflicts with the Thessalians (themselves from the land of Achilles),[93] and this makes perfect sense. However, one should not regard these conflicts as the exclusive motivation. The Molossians also took control of Dodona and probably came into conflict with the Thesprotians as well. The early fifth century seems too late for the genealogical claim of the Molossian royal house, as Lepore would have it. He seems correct, however, in assuming that it was a post-*Odyssey* development.[94] My conclusion differs from his as follows: Earlier than the fifth century, probably as a reaction to Thesprotian claims on Odysseus (later enhanced by rivalry with Thessalians), the Molossians of about the middle of the seventh century discovered that they too were of Nostos descent. That is how Hagias's *Nostoi* could mention it. The chronology, however, is tentative, since the ethnic developments and movements that eventually resulted in Molossian expansion are unknown to us, as are the precise dates of the *nostos* compositions.[95] What seems significant is the priority of the Thesprotians in terms of both their presence in Dodona and their articulation of the Odysseus *nostos*. Unlike the Molossians, the coastal Thesprotians were much

90. Pind. *Nem.* 7.53–65; 34–40.
91. Hammond 1967: 384; Malkin 1994a: 42. On Delphi see Suárez de la Torre 1997.
92. *Od.* 3.188–89; 4.3–9.
93. Lepore 1962: 47–49, 54, with n. 83.
94. Lepore 1962: 44–55.
95. In fifth-century historiography (Hdt. 1.146.1) the Molossians are mentioned as one of the peoples composing the Ionians of Asia Minor.

more open to influences from Ithacan, Corinthian, and Euboian traders and colonists penetrating their hinterlands during the ninth and eighth centuries.

The Chaones, the third major Epirote group, pose a more complex problem, since they seem to have insisted on Trojan origins from Helenos, the captive Trojan seer, who accompanied Neoptolemos.[96] He was also regarded as the founder of Buthrotum.[97] The story seems to be attested first in Euripides and Theopompus.[98] It may have been a response to both Thesprotian and Molossian self-definitions, since in the fifth century traditions about Trojans, notably Aeneas, were already current with regard to Epirus.[99] The Trojan ethnic self-definition as an *opposite* model to that of the Greek lies somewhat outside the scope of our discussion, but certain elements of it may need mentioning. Indeed, Epirus may prove to be of the utmost importance to the whole issue, made famous by the Romans' insistence that they were not of common Greek-Trojan descent (Odysseus and Aeneas as cofounders of Rome) but only of Trojan origins (see chap. 6). The earliest testimony for the opposite model comes from an ancient Epirote monument, no longer extant.

In the early fifth century the Greeks of Apollonia set up a monument at Olympia commemorating their conquest of the land of Abantis and the city of Thronios. Pairs of heroes—a Greek confronting a barbarian (Trojan)— are portrayed, among whom are Odysseus and Helenos. This monument is remarkable in its articulation of victory in terms of Greek versus Trojan and in juxtaposing, among others, Odysseus and Helenos. A chronological distinction between Archaic and Classical attitudes seems to surface here. First, we have observed the Epirote pattern of Greeks and Trojans *together* (Neoptolemos and Andromache, Neoptolemos and Helenos), and this is compatible with the pattern of pairing a Greek and a Trojan in a *nostos* (Menelaos and Antenor, Philoktetes and Aigesthes, Odysseus and Aeneas). A later development, probably of the early fifth century, was the *opposition* between Greek and a Trojan as an articulation of the Greek-barbarian distinction and enmity expressed in the Apollonia dedication. In other words, the opposition, with all its complexity and conflicting myths, later to be made famous by Rome, seems to have preceded the emergence of this opposition in Italy (see chap. 6).

96. Apollod. *Epit.* 6; cf. Hammond 1967: 413.
97. Teucer of Kyzikos *FGrH* 274 F 1.
98. Eur. *Andr.* 1243–51; Theopompus *FGrH* 115 F 355; cf. Hellanikos *FGrH* 4 F 84.
99. Cf. Lepore 1962: 55–56.

At the same time, in the context of the great houses, less mindful of "national" origins, the old heroic language combining Greek and Trojans was sustained. A late claim (fourth-century) such as that of Olympias, Alexander's mother, seems indicative of the consistent trend current in Epirus since the first application of the *nostos* of Odysseus to that land. This daughter of the Molossian king was descended, she claimed, from both Achilles (through his son Neoptolemos/Pyrrhos) and the Trojan Helenos.[100] According to another tradition Molossos, the eponym of the Molossians, was born to the Greek Neoptolemos and the Trojan Andromache.

Evidently the Greek Apollonians, relative newcomers to these parts, did not appreciate such amalgamations of Greek and Trojan descent. Ironically, the Apollonians pitted Greek heroes against Trojans perhaps because they found such claims threatening: the city they attacked, Thronios, was reputed to have been settled by Lokrians and Euboian Nostoi. The *new* Greeks on the land, the colonists of Apollonia (founded ca. 600),[101] could thus claim superiority. In the world of the early fifth century, when the general opposition between Greek and barbarian had increased significantly, this juxtaposition had become part of the general Greek frame of reference.

It seems that the foundation of the Corcyrean and Corinthian colonies, first Epidamnos and then Apollonia, changed the nature of *nostos* articulations. Instead of tracing the origins of kings they became ethnic appellations, and the contrast Greek-barbarian/Trojan was born. Queen Olympias, a descendant of both (Greek) Neoptolemos and (Trojan) Helenos, may have cared little about all this. Others, such as the Chaones, perhaps insisting on some "difference" from the Thesprotians, who since the seventh century, at the latest, had been identified with Odysseus, also played the Trojan role. Therefore, it seems that the pattern of genealogical and ethnic identifications via *nostoi* had been in existence in the northwest by the seventh century, if not earlier. Eventually, the entire pattern, begun in Asia Minor and developed along different lines in Epirus, would be grafted upon the new colonial lands in the west.

Perhaps an analogy is in order. In fractal physics, the small basically resembles the large. Magnifying the forking pattern of the veins of a single leaf, for example, provides an overlap of the forking pattern of the branches of the whole tree; enlarging a section of a rugged coastline may provide a pattern for the entire coast, and so on. This seemingly chaotic forking pattern also provides a basis for prognosis, for example, corresponding to the way oil shale forces its way underground. Ithaca and Epirus may be said to be "fractals" of Greek colonization. Ithaca's position, as we have seen, is that

---

100. Theopompus *FGrH* 115 F 355.   101. Graham 1983: 130.

of a "colonial" offshore island in relation to the mainland; maritime trade and settlement routes passed through it to the north and back; the various peoples in Epirus were themselves Greeks or exposed to contacts with Greeks early on and especially to Greek genealogical and ethnic identifications in terms of heroic progenitors. But Epirus was also specifically connected with Nostos progenitors. Whereas elsewhere any hero would do, in Epirus and the Adriatic it was predominantly the heroes of the *Odyssey* and its related *nostoi*. As I have argued, the *colonial* juxtaposition of Greek and Trojan started there, where the need for self- and ethnic definition stemmed from ethnic ambiguities. In Epirus the juxtaposition does not seem to have been originally conflictual, as it became in later periods in the west and especially in Rome. It is not impossible that already during the period of protocolonization, especially in the first half of the eighth century, when Greeks must have wondered about the identity of the non-Greek peoples they met, existing patterns of genealogical and ethnic identification through Greek and Trojan Nostoi were grafted upon the new lands.

From at least the eighth century on, Epirus was a region of uncertain ethnic definition and various movements of populations. One hesitates to speak of the peoples concerned in terms of Greek versus non-Greek, even though one can be relatively certain that the Molossians, for example, spoke Greek. Greek ethnicity was not always defined in terms of language. This may sound a little harsh, especially for Athenocentric scholars familiar with the often-quoted phrase of Herodotus (actually a rhetorical declaration that he places in the mouths of the Athenians) that Greeks are those who share gods (sanctuaries and sacrifices), language, blood, and a way of life.[102] By contrast, for historians accustomed to discussing, for example, Epirotes and Aitolians, the ethnic criterion of language is not the answer but the question.

What complicates matters is the existence of two sets of groups constructing their identity (or ethnicity) differently. Local Makedonian groups, for example, tended mostly to be inward-looking and isolated. We have no way of knowing to what extent there was any notion of a Makedonian group identity. Thus the group-ethnos criterion often mentioned in modern treatments of ethnicity and ethnic change may itself be lacking. Epirote and Makedonian royal houses did, however, emphasize blood and kinship in order to construct for themselves a heroic genealogy that sometimes functioned also as a Hellenic genealogy. It was only when the oppositional model of the pan-Hellenic criterion was fully articulated in the fifth century that the genealogical-royal criterion could come into conflict with the general

102. Hdt. 8.144.

view of Greek ethnicity. For example, when Alexander of Macedon sought to participate in the pan-Hellenic Olympic games it was argued that he was not Greek; however, the Hellenodikai (the board of judges from Elis that supervised the games) acknowledged his claim that he was "Argive."[103] Like the Spartan kings, he could claim descent from Herakles.[104]

With this fifth-century oppositional model, aristocratic claims to pan-Hellenic identity could be compared to Gellner's model of prenationalist Europe, where members of the elite saw themselves as belonging to a broad international ruling-class culture distinct from the fragmented, localized peasant societies. That model too has its weaknesses, since the extent to which group identity is implied in the ruler identity has varied since as early as the Middle Ages. The Sallic Law in France, for example, helped articulate both the genealogy of the French royal succession and the nonelite identity of "Frenchmen," a viable collective term long before the modern era.[105] Tyrtaios in the seventh century B.C. is already playing with both the ruler genealogy and the identity of the entire Spartan people; in one place he stresses the distinction between the Herakleidai who led "us" from windy Erineios, and elsewhere he calls all of the Spartans "Herakleidai."[106]

Ascribing Nostos descent (whether Greek, Trojan, or both) to Epirote princes, which may have begun on an individual basis, would place the persons concerned in the pan-Hellenic myths of origins. These myths apparently also played a part in inter-Epirote relations. Thesprotians, Molossians, Chaones, Akarnanians, and others were all pressed against each other, and all seem to have resorted to some Greek definition of their ethnicities or, at least, of their royal houses. The Nostos identities seem to have served as whetstones for self-definition and, possibly, as a way of casting aspersions on others.

The communal-group aspect of Nostos descent must have been familiar to Greeks from the early Archaic period but not in relation to Epirus. *Nostoi* have been used to articulate the origins of entire Greek communities in Asia Minor, perhaps as early as the tenth and ninth centuries.[107] The pattern here was more complex: sometimes we find individual Nostoi, similar to the situation in Epirus (and Italy, as we shall see). Sometimes entire groups are supposed to have migrated directly; sometimes the return to Greece caused such havoc as to create the need to emigrate, as with some of the versions about the Ionian migration. The communal aspect came into a sharper focus for another reason: the contrast in Asia Minor between Greeks and

103. Hdt. 5.22; cf. Dascalakis 1965: 105–10; Hammond 1989: 19–21.
104. Cf. Hes. fr. 7 M-L; Hellanikos *FGrH* 4 F 74 on the genealogy of Hellen.
105. Guenée 1978; Barnavi 1983.
106. Fr. 8 Prato. For the precise meaning see Malkin 1994a: 39.
107. Vanschoowinkel 1991: chap. 9.

non-Greeks, between coastal (Greek) communities and a non-Greek hinterland, was probably sharply felt. The situation was inherently colonial, although the term "colonization" is usually reserved for the foundation of cities in the eighth century.

This was not the situation in Epirus, at least not before the eighth and seventh centuries, and even then colonies were few and sparse. In Epirus the peoples involved seem to have been Greek-speakers not universally regarded as "Greek" by other Greeks. By the fifth century some Greeks who happen to be more familiar to us even labeled them "barbarians." It seems that Epirotes, first the Thesprotians and then others, primarily turned to Nostos origins to enhance their royal genealogies. Thus an Alkon, for example, could move in the world of Greek aristocrats on a par with the rest of Agariste's suitors as late as the sixth century. Whether such origins were extended to the entire "people" may have been of little consequence, just as in Sparta the distinction between Herakleidai and Dorians was never abandoned. When group or ethnic "entities" began to matter, Nostos origins would play a role in the question of whether Epirotes were also Greeks.

"OBJECTIVE" EPIROTE ETHNICITY

Pindar, we may assume, sang to the Molossians in Greek. But, one could argue, the fact that French was spoken among Russian aristocrats of the nineteenth century does not make them French, and so the Molossians may have had Greek as a cultural language without being Greek. When Kleisthenes, the tyrant of Sikyon, wished to find a husband for his daughter (he made the proclamation at Olympia, where presumably only Greeks were present), one of the suitors was the Molossian Alkon, who is mentioned without a patronymic; perhaps he was of the royal house, perhaps not,[108] something that widens the circle of "Greek" Molossians. The episode is attributed to the beginning of the sixth century. By the fifth century we find Themistokles seeking refuge at the court of a Molossian king, Adenotos, whose son Tharyps (or Tharypas, Arrhybas) had been educated in Athens and taught Hellenic (Athenian?) customs to his people.[109] Crucial are the Molossian inscriptions regarding the organization of the entire Molossian ethnos-state, which were deposited at Dodona (under Molossian control since the early fifth century);[110] they are Greek inscriptions written not in a learned artificial language but in a northern Greek dialect. Finally, it is as-

108. Hdt. 6.127; cf. Cabanes 1988: 23–24.
109. The sources are late: Paus. 1.11.1; Just. 17.3; Plut. *Pyrrh.* 1 with Hammond 1967: 507.
110. See Hammond 1967: 368.

sumed that Greek was spoken at Dodona by—and to—the inquirers, and when Periander sent to consult the Nekromanteion in Thesprotian Ephyra it appears that he was consulting a Greek oracle.[111]

The question of "objective" Greekness applies not only to the Molossians but especially to the Thesprotians and the Chaones and is relevant to the problem of articulating ethnicity via Nostos ancestry. From the point of view of some modern scholars, some of the Epirote tribes that did not speak dialects of Illyrian should be regarded as Greek, especially if they spoke a dialect of the language.[112] But the difference between a dialect and a language may be in the eye of the beholder, as Ernest Gellner has demonstrated in his book on nationalism.[113] With unity comes "dialect," with separation "language," as, for example, the shifting definitions of Ukrainian and Russian in the twentieth century illustrate. Similarly, in the fifth century B.C. a language criterion for Greekness seems to have crystallized, although it is unclear whether a modern linguist might agree, say, with Thucydides that what was incomprehensible to Athenian ears was un-Greek. What should be relevant for the Archaic period is rather the face that some of the peoples under discussion presented to themselves and others and whether they were accepted by "proper" Greeks. Much has been written of the self-definition of Greeks, especially in relation to the "Other."[114] The Epirotes were not structural opposites as were the distant Scythians. According to one of our earliest (albeit late) sources, Hekataios,[115] they were—if a general term had to be found—"Molossian tribes," which seems as helpful as "Aitolian" and not much more.

At the same time, Epirotes, as well as Akarnanians and even Aitolians (and possibly also Ozolian Lokrians) could seem "other" and "opposite" to Thucydides and others. Pierre Cabanes has shown that, linguistically, Greek was spoken in southern Epirus and Illyrian in the north[116] and that there must also have been an area of bilingualism. What is more important, however, is that Illyrian-speakers and Greek-speakers in the regions of modern Epirus and Albania were more similar to each other in their modes of life (and in their habitats—mountains and rain) than to Greeks dwelling in poleis such as Athens or Corinth. Thus a mode of life that for Herodotus was one of the criteria for Greek ethnicity[117] actually serves as a line of de-

111. Hdt. 5.92.7.

112. Some Albanian definers, however, argue against distinguishing Epirus and Illyria, thus extending Epirus northward. Cabanes 1988: 20; cf. 33–46.

113. Gellner 1983: 44 ff.

114. See, e.g., Hartog 1988; Hall 1989; Cartledge 1993.

115. See discussion and references in Hammond 1967: 465.

116. Cabanes 1979: at 292–94; 196 for the evidence; see also Funke 1991b.

117. Hdt. 8.144.

marcation *among* Greeks. In her influential study *Inventing the Barbarians,* Edith Hall stresses mode of life as a contrast but misleadingly suggests that it distinguishes Greek and Chinese perceptions of ethnicity. For the Chinese, she says, the criterion for barbarism was a mode of life, such as nomadism; for the Greeks, it was language. In this she follows an established tradition in modern scholarship that, as we have noted, has been persuasively criticized by Jonathan Hall. Aitolians and Epirotes might in fact be called barbarians not because they spoke a language that was not Greek but because they were different in many ways—in their political organization, their pastoral economy, and the physical character of the land they inhabited.

The Greekness of the northwestern peoples was apparently a matter for debate, as the polemical tone of Thucydides indicates.[118] Aside from what he may have observed "objectively," Thucydides needed a barbaric mode of life for his anthropological argument that what he could observe in western Greece was the condition of the Greeks as it had once been in antiquity.[119] An excellent example, pertinent also to *nostoi,* is his digression on Argos Amphilochikon:[120] upon his return from the Trojan War (the Nostos) Amphilochos, dissatisfied with the situation in Argos, left his home city and founded Argos Amphilochikon on the Ambrakian Gulf. In a later period its inhabitants invited Ambrakiots to strengthen the colony and, adopting their language/dialect, thus became Hellenes (ἠλληνίσθησαν τὴν νῦν γλῶσσαν πρῶτον ἀπὸ τῶν Ἀμπρακιωτῶν ξυνοικησάντων). According to Thucydides, the rest of the Amphilochians were barbarians.[121] The passage is remarkable: for Thucydides the Amphilochians were, like the Chaones or the Molossians, of heroic Greek ancestry; their becoming "Hellenized" clearly signified a change not of blood but of language. It seems clear that although Thucydides thought that the name (and language?) of the Hellenes had spread only after the Trojan War, he considered the heroes of that war, Amphilochos of Argos included, "ethnically" Greek. Yet somehow the colonists were "barbarians" until some of them assimilated to the Ambrakiots and their (Doric) language. Being a "Hellene," as Thucydides makes clear in his introduction, meant the extension of the appellation from the original Hellenes of Thessaly. It also meant mutual recognition and understanding, possibly learning each other's language.[122] However, since all this took place

---

118. See Thuc. 1.5; 2.68.5; 2.80; 3.94.4–5.

119. Thuc. 1.6.1–2.

120. Thuc. 2.68; cf. Strabo 7.326; Apollod. *Bibl.* 3.7.

121. Thus. 2.83.5. Hammond, who discusses this passage (1967: 419), translates: "They were made Hellenes in the matter of their present speech then for the first time as a result of the Ambrakiots' living with them."

122. Hammond 1967: 420 against Gomme 1945 on Thuc. 1.3.4 ὅσοι ἀλλήλων ξυνίεσαν, "came to understand each other."

after the Trojan War, there is an inherent contradiction concerning the "Hellenism" of a Nostos such as Amphilochos.

The ambiguity regarding the Hellenic status of the "Greek" heroes of the Trojan War is a familiar point. If we wish to understand Archaic Greek thought about the ethnic and genealogical role of the Nostoi and other heroes, perhaps we should exclude the term "Greek" from the discussion altogether. Homer, except for calling one side Danaoi, Argeioi, and Achaioi and the other Trojan, disregards most distinguishing "ethnic" features between them, especially that of language (everyone speaks Greek) and religion.[123] The ancient historians, primarily Herodotus and Thucydides, insisted on the distinction between being Greek (an earlier state, without a general appellation) and being *called*, comprehensively, "Greeks" (Hellenes), a result of migration, diffusion, and acculturation. What is important is to realize that the ambiguity between the heroic and the ethnic was authentic not only in Homeric terms but also as a fundamental perspective of the Archaic period. Most significant, it provides a clue to the relative ease with which Greeks could perceive "their" heroes as "ethnically" populating the world with both Greek and non-Greek peoples.

When the Amphilochians came under Thucydides's scrutiny, their status appeared ambiguous, and he created a definition for them. It is clear from other references in his work that he could distinguish very well between various groups of Greeks, semi-Greeks, bilinguals, and non-Greeks;[124] perhaps the Amphilochians spoke "uncouth" Greek. But the point that emerges is precisely the ambiguity of the situation, which by his day had become rather fluid, with Greek colonization and Hellenization, various movements of populations within Epirus, and attempts at self-definition on the part of the three major Epirote groups: the Chaones, the Molossians, and the Thesprotians. Thucydides explicitly regards these groups as barbarians; Knemos the Lakedaimonian, he says, had with him Greeks from Ambrakia, Anaktorion, and Leukas as well as barbarian Chaones, Thesprotians, and Molossians.[125] His attitude to the Aitolians is more ambivalent. On the one hand, he treats the Ozolian Lokrians, Aitolians, Akarnanians, and continentals (Epirotes) as if they belonged to Hellas.[126] On the other hand, he reports that the Aitolians displayed traits of barbarism in their way of life (unfortified villages), their food (uncooked), their dress, their open carrying of weapons, and their incomprehensible language (*agnostotatoi*).[127] Thucydides on the whole does not seem to reflect any consensus on these issues.

123. Wathelet 1988.
124. Gomme 1945 on Thuc. 1.3; Hammond 1967: 419–22.
125. Thuc. 2.80.5.
126. Thuc. 1.5 with Antonetti 1990a: 71–76.
127. Thuc. 3.94.4–5.

That Epirus, regarded by some as a "barbarian" land, is also construed as the "original" home of the Hellenes is a remarkable paradox. Whereas the Hellenes of Achilles are supposed to be located in southern Thessaly (the northeast), the localization of the kingdom of his son, Neoptolemos, in Molossia (the northwest) may be due to the vagueness of the ethnography of the Hellenes in northern Greece. It may be misleading to pinpoint "Hellas" too precisely; the term itself may provide some clue. In the *Odyssey* we are told that Odysseus's name was famous "throughout Hellas and middle Argos."[128] Obviously, what is meant is not a small Hellas in Thessaly but something more comprehensive. Does Hellas signify here all of northern Greece, complementary to an "Argos" standing for the Peloponnese? Or does it mean only northwestern Greece?[129] Since "Argos" is mentioned,[130] "Hellas" certainly does not function as it does in Hesiod, where it seems to signify all of Greece.[131] (Hesiod, incidentally, uses the term in a Homeric context, as the land whence the "Achaians" [not "Hellenes"] set out for Troy.) Later writers, such as Dikaiarchos and Skylax, regarded "continuous Greece" (ἡ Ἑλλὰς συνεχής) as extending more or less south of the Ambrakian Gulf and the mouth of the Peneios and north along the Pindus and to the east of the Pindus Range but excluding Epirus.[132] Herodotus, however, included Thesprotia in "Hellas,"[133] and in cataloguing the Greeks he says that "all of the above came from countries closer than Thesprotia and the river Acheron. For the Thesprotians are neighbors of [or "march with"? ὁμουρέοντες] the Ambrakiots and the Leukadians who came from the most distant lands."[134] Finally, as we have seen, the Molossians appear to have been Greek-speakers.

The concepts of "Hellenes," "Hellas," and "barbarians" seem to mingle in the northwest. The trouble, of course, is the general ambiguity that exists in all historical periods between ethnic and territorial appellations, where the overlap is rarely—if ever—apparent. This is especially true for the modern regions of northern Greece and Albania, where, as Strabo observed, "the boundaries and the political organizations of tribes and places are always undergoing changes."[135] Already in the *Iliad*[136] we are told that Peleus gave

128. *Od.* 1.344; cf. 4.726, 816; 15.80.
129. Hall 1989: 8.
130. Cf. "Achaian Argos," *Od.* 3.251; *Od.* 4.174 (Menelaos would have given Odysseus cities in Argos).
131. Hes. *Op.* 653.
132. Ps.-Scyl. 26.
133. Hdt. 2.56.
134. Hdt. 8.47.1.
135. Strabo 7.433 (5.8).
136. *Il.* 9.483.

Phoinix the Dolopians who were on the edges of Phthia, indicating the changing status of populations. Perhaps the most relevant example is the Perrhaibians, who, according to Homer, "placed their homes around hard-wintered Dodona" (in Epirus). Later we find them in the northeast, near Olympus, north of Peneios and far from Epirus.[137] They may have been originally transhumants who came to settle down at one of their stops. An "ethnic" name may move with the people associated with it, as if brushing the land with recognizable paint. Thus the Perrhaibians provide a concrete example of how the "Hellas" of Thessaly and that of Epirus could have been confounded. Similarly, the *nostos* of Neoptolemos, whose father's kingdom was in the northeast, takes him to western Epirus, to the Molossians, who later came to rule "Achilles's oracle,"[138] Dodona. This is not a *nostos* that takes its hero to distant lands, such as Libya or Italy, where we would not expect the term "Hellas" to spread.[139] Rather, the very close proximity of Epirus renders the *nostos* plausible in a "Hellas" context in terms of fluctuating local and regional identities.

Unless we take the lines "throughout Hellas and middle Argos" as sufficient evidence, there is no general geographical concept of Greece (Hellas) in Homer, just as there is no concept of Greeks. The qualifying "middle Argos" adds to the impression that the poet of the *Odyssey* here has a more regional perception of what he is talking about, just as does the poet of the *Iliad* when Achilles says[140] that there are many Achaian girls to choose from "throughout Hellas and Phthia." "Middle Argos" seems to signify not a "plain"[141] but a region with political significance, probably that of "kingdom." As for "Hellas," as noted, it is inconceivable that Penelope is referring here to (one of) Achilles's regions. "Hellas," perhaps surprisingly, may have an even more specific northwestern localization.

Aristotle says that ancient Hellas (ἡ Ἑλλάς ἡ ἀρχαία) was around Dodona and the Acheloös, not in Thessaly; "it was there that the Selloi [Zeus's priests at Dodona] and those who were then called 'Graikoi' and now 'Hellenes' used to live."[142] The "Graikoi"—their name the source of the Latin "Graeci" and our "Greeks"—pose a fascinating problem. It used to be thought that "Graikoi" was the name of a Boiotian people, across from Euboia, that came to be known to the Romans in the west and hence the general appellation of "Greeks" was later attached to all other Greeks. It was assumed that these Boiotian Graikoi (inferred from either Graia in Euboia or

137. Aesch. *Supp.* 245–46; cf. Lepore 1962: 3–4; Parke 1967: 5; Hammond 1967: 371.
138. *Il.* 16.220 ff.
139. See Maddoli 1982.
140. *Il.* 9.395.
141. Hoekstra in Heubeck and Hoekstra 1989 on *Od.* 15.80.
142. Arist. *Mete.* 352a 33–34.

near Tanagra in Boiotia[143] but unattested) joined the Euboian colonization of Kyme.[144] The suggestion was never proven and seems rather dubious at first glance. Since the "first western Greeks," the Euboians, were responsible for the dissemination of the Greek alphabet and culture in Campania and Etruria at least from the mid-eighth century on, why would a freak accident such as the presence of a negligible Boiotian group of hangers-on be the source for the collective appellation of all Greeks? Why, if Euboian colonization in western Italy was the responsible factor, were Greeks not called "Euboians" or "Chalkidians," as was the case with the Eastern Ionians, whose name became equivalent with "Greeks" in Near Eastern languages? It is no news that "Yawan," "Yaman," etc., a comprehensive Near Eastern appellation found in a variety of sources and languages, derives from the Ionians of Asia Minor. For example, a raid by the Ionians (ia-u-na-a-a) on the Phoenician coast is reported to Tiglath Pileser III in a letter of the 730s found at Nimrud.[145] Such is the nature of external ethnic appellations: the Ionians were the first "Greeks" known in the Near East and thus their name was applied to all other Greeks.

For "Graikoi" there is to my mind an alternative explanation that is not new but has somehow been overlooked. Two of the three comprehensive names for "Greeks" that are still relevant today—Graikoi, Hellenes, and Ionians—were associated with Dodona and Epirus, a fact that encourages Hammond to contend that the origins of the Greeks (the "real" origins) were Epirote.[146] The Graikoi, a northwestern people who resided in the region of the oracle—which seems to have been a center whose influence and reputation extended far beyond its locality during the Dark Age—probably came to be known also across the Ionian and Adriatic Seas. It was by that name that they were known to Illyrians and Messapians, and it was via the latter that the name reached Latium (as has also been suggested for the route of the Latin form of the name of Odysseus, "Ulysses"). It is no accident, perhaps, that Hellanikos describes Aeneas's itinerary as "from the Molossians to Italy."[147]

Unlike the foreign name "Ionians," denoting all Greeks, "Graikoi" and "Hellenes" both seem to point also to a *self*-appellation of a comprehensive nature. Although "Hellenes" was clearly the name used by most Greeks, Aristotle's statement is in need of clarification, especially since the "Hellenes"

143. *Il.* 2.498.

144. See the discussion in *PW* 7.2 1693–95 (Miller). Bérard (1952) reviews the evidence but argues that since "Graikoi" was the earliest name of the Hellenes (Aristotle), its existence in Italy indicates that it had already reached that country by the Bronze Age.

145. Saggs 1963: 76–78; Braun 1982: 14–15; cf. Brinkman 1989.

146. 1967: 370 and passim.

147. Hellanikos *FGrH* 4 F 84; see chap. 6.

too seem to be particularly attached to Dodona. The Selloi, Zeus's priests, are alternatively called Helloi,[148] and Hesiod called the country of Dodona Hellopia.[149] Both Hammond and Parke,[150] among others, connect the Helloi etymologically with "Hellenes," and both demonstrate (Hammond the more systematically) that ethnic names that end in -*enes* are typical of northwestern Greece. With all the comings and goings of Epirote peoples, the shifting identifications between Hellenes of Thessaly and those of Epirus now become more than understandable. This is also why the name of Odysseus, already in the *Odyssey,* could be famous in a northwestern Hellas.

The idea of a comprehensive ethnic appellation for all Greeks took shape *among Greeks,* probably in the context of an interplay, on the one hand, of the type that Thucydides envisaged (mutual awareness and recognition) and, on the other, of significant contemporary encounters with non-Greek civilizations. Somehow—and we shall never know how—the terms "Hellenes" and "Hellas" caught on. The comprehensive term "Ionians" was too obviously a foreign appellation and in a Greek framework too specific (applying only to Ionian Greeks). "Graikoi" too seems to have been a term used by the neighboring Illyrians and Messapians. However, since Graikoi and Hellenes overlapped geographically and religiously, later Greeks thought it necessary to account for the mutually exclusive ethnic names. In some versions Graikos was made a son of Thessalos, "the woodcutter to whom they say the first dove showed the oracle [Dodona]," thus explaining both the Thessalian and the Epirote Hellenes.[151] In others, such as the version behind Aristotle's source, the more "scientific" explanation was put forth that "Graikoi" was simply the earlier name and the influence of Dodona seems to account for its special prominence among neighboring civilizations. Since the Hellenes were similarly connected with Dodona, either as occasional residents or through its priesthood (the Helloi), external (Graikoi) and self (Hellenes) appellations of the "Hellenic people" could, exceptionally, overlap.

Dodona connects the world of Odysseus with that of Achilles. The latter is the only hero in Homer to pray, in a rather peculiar, archaic formula, to Zeus of Dodona.[152] His son, Neoptolemos, moves variably between Phthia (and Hellas) and Dodona. His *nostos,* as noted, is connected with that of Odysseus, who is said to have met Neoptolemos at Maroneia in Thrace before

148. Parke 1967: 7 = Pindar (fr. 259 Bowra = Strabo 7.7.10.; Hesychius s.v. Ἑλλοί. Apollodorus supported "Selloi," citing *Il.* 2.659, 15.521: "he had brought her out of Ephyra from the River Selloeis."

149. Strabo 7.328 (*Ehoiai* fr. 134 1).

150. Hammond 1967: 372; Parke 1967: 8.

151. Steph. Byz. s.v. Γραικός.

152. *Il.* 16.220 ff.

he came to Epirus. We have seen how Odysseus, in the guise of a Cretan, tells Eumaios that he has been to Thesprotia, where he was told by the king that "Odysseus was going to Dodona, so that from the god's high-foliaged oak tree he might hear the will of Zeus . . . whether to return openly or secretly."[153] The suitor Amphinomos, discussing the plot to kill Telemachos, says that they should first ask the will of the gods to see "if the ordinances of great Zeus approve of it." Apparently Dodona is meant here.[154] Dodona therefore seems to belong to the world of both Thesprotia and Ithaca.

There are a few preliminary conclusions to be drawn from this: the ethnic self-appellation of "Hellas" and "Hellenes," which seems to be attested as early as Hesiod, does not appear as such in the *Iliad* or the *Odyssey*. However, its origins, whether or not these should be explained in terms of an "original home" of Greek peoples such as the Dorians (Hammond), seem to combine Thessaly and Epirus with some driving force that may be located in the god of the Greeks, Zeus of Dodona.[155] The oracle, sacred to "Zeus the Pelasgian" and to the Helloi, seems to exemplify the ambiguity of Epirus, with its non-Greek (or non-Greek-speaking) populations and royal houses. In modern ethnographic and national terms it may seem strange for the Hellenes to have originated around the oracle of a Pelasgian Zeus; in Aeschylus's *Supplices* the contours of Hellenic geography are also spoken of in terms of "Pelasgians," a term that seems to have functioned not necessarily as non-Greek but as pre-Greek.[156] It was around such a center, obviously sacred not to Greeks alone, that some dividing lines and definitions of who was and who was not Greek evolved. For the non-Greek west the name "Graikoi," stemming from the heart of the ambiguous area, prevailed. For the Greeks the name was "Hellenes," from the same area.

CONCLUSION

Metaphors and images, some might argue, may not constitute the conclusion to a historical argument, but perhaps they may be allowed to introduce one. Epirus, the land where Zeus the Cloud-Gatherer had his major oracle, evokes an image: just as a heavy rain cloud glides onto a mountainside and suffuses it with moisture until streams of water flow and seep into the earth, so the various *Odyssey* clouds float in their timeless, mythical ether until they touch some land, seep in, and transform its image. Epirus, in this chapter, is such a land, and it emerges from the discussion linking the poetical with

153. *Od.* 14.327, repeated in 19.296 ff.
154. *Od.* 16.402 ff.
155. On Dodona and its relations with Thessaly, see Lepore 1962: 58–66.
156. Cf. Aesch. *Supp.* 245 ff.

the concrete dimensions of myth. We have noted a quality that distinguishes the *Odyssey* from most *nostoi:* its geographical dimension is monstrous and mythological, whereas the variant Odysseus returns and the *nostoi* of other heroes (see chaps. 7 and 8) are human and topographical. It is the second that implies the familiarity of direct contact and absorption by native leaders or populations; the first belong to some protocolonization phase.

But it is not as if once trade and colonization began, myths suddenly altered. The active historical role of myths as mediators and definers of genealogies and ethnicities and the change of perspective for the Greeks who were sailing and settling was a gradual and particular process. We have seen, for example, how in the course of at least two centuries certain myths, such as that of Neoptolemos, a Greek Nostos, and Helenos, a Trojan one, could change their "use" from a mediating role to an articulation of oppositional hostility (Apollonia and the Greek-barbarian contrast). The *Odyssey* did not, for the most part, serve in Epirus as a territorial charter myth, nor did it offer a priori "irredentist" justifications. *Odyssey*-related myths could, however, sometimes provide genealogical charters for princely families, especially those of the Thesprotians, Molossians, and Chaones. It has been argued that some confusion between opening and civilizing myths applied to new lands (such as that of Herakles and Antaios), on the one hand, and political-communal myths (such as foundation stories), on the other, may have given birth to some blanket declarations about the "uses" of the *Odyssey* and *nostoi* as justification.

The *Odyssey*'s Odysseus does not found any city; the Odysseus of other *nostoi* sires royal families and founds some (Bouneima). The *Odyssey*'s Odysseus is supposed to travel, not settle, among cities of men. In fact he hardly does even that, but traveling "city by city" is foreshadowed in verse three of the first book and in Odysseus's own prognosis of what will happen to him when he departs from Ithaca yet again. Thus the *Odyssey* implies its own sequels, just as it alludes to its antecedents. What is meant by "sequel" is not a possible alternative to the narrative framework of the *Odyssey* itself, such as the postulated "realistic" version that may have taken Odysseus to Ithaca via Egypt, Crete, and Thesprotia. The implicit awareness of the non-*Odyssey* sequel stories emerges also with regard to the realistic option of exile from Ithaca (exile, in itself, is a recurrent motif). This awareness becomes explicit in the eleventh book, in Tiresias's prophecy. The prophet's words have been applied as a yardstick to assess other versions concerning the life of Odysseus after the return to Ithaca. The analysis of the sources has yielded the conclusion that both the Aitolian and the Arkadian version are late in comparison with the Thesprotian Epirote stories, which belong, at the latest, to the seventh century. An independent Ithacan version has also been identified, placing its emphasis on Ithaca's internal *stasis* and reconciliation.

Other elaborations, placing their emphasis less on locations (Aitolia, Thesprotia, Arkadia, Italy, Ithaca) than on personalities and characters (Penelope's unfaithfulness, Telegonos, Euryalos), should be kept distinct and assessed according to different criteria.

The *Odyssey* artfully proposes an alternative *nostos* itinerary crucial to the role of Epirus: instead of accepting the offer of the superb Phaiakian seamen to transport him back to Ithaca, Odysseus chooses to go by himself from Phaiakia to Thesprotia to gain profits and proceed to Dodona to consult the oracle. Phaiakia becomes mundane, no longer the looking glass through which the world of concrete topography is reentered. It seems identical with Corcyra, opposite Thesprotia and identified as Phaiakia by later Greeks. This is compatible with the general familiarity of Thesprotia in the *Odyssey:* the Thesprotians were allies of the Ithacans, as Penelope reminds Antinoös. Inquiries at Dodona seem acceptable along with regular maritime contacts. The Thesprotian king Pheidon is a civilized king, not the frightening Echetos of the "mainland," who mutilates his victims (as the suitors threaten both the beggar Odysseus and Iros). The seventh-century *Thesprotis,* recounting a second *nostos* of Odysseus in Thesprotia and closely associated with Tiresias's prophecy about the compulsion to go inland, is therefore beautifully contextualized through the *Odyssey* itself. The two texts (one lost, except in summary) "read" each other.

A pattern that will surface in my discussion of Italy may already be discerned here: it is not the areas of immediate contact but the peripheral ones that receive the mythological grafting. The frightening Echetos and Cape Nerikos, conquered by Laertes, seem to belong to a partly hostile "dark mainland" directly opposite Ithaca. Neighbors can be the worst enemies, and not because of any qualitative difference. The bodily mutilation that Echetos inflicts on his victims, cutting off their noses and ears, does not differentiate him as "barbaric" from the men of Ithaca; the suitors, after all, do not make good their threat, whereas the Ithacan Telemachos and the two herdsmen inflict precisely this punishment on Melanthios.[157] In short, he is simply an enemy. By contrast, the alliance with the more distant Thesprotians makes excellent political sense. This point seems to have confused most commentators. On the one hand, Thesprotia is localized opposite Corcyra, as all the ancient sources agree;[158] on the other, commentators seem to think it must include Ambrakia, opposite Ithaca (although it is kept distinct from Thesprotia by ancient sources) because Thesprotia in the *Odyssey*

---

157. *Od.* 18.79–81, 116; cf. 21.308 (cutting off the nose and ears of a centaur); on Melanthios, see 22.473–76.

158. Thuc. 1.46.4, 50.3, with Meyer in *Der kleine Pauli* s.v. "Thesprotia" p. 756.

is "near" Ithaca.[159] But Dodona, obviously reachable from Thesprotia in the
Odyssey but clearly distant from Ithaca, throws off the discussion yet again.
The solution is simple: there is no need to create difficulties because the
point about Thesprotia in the *Odyssey* is its distance from, not its nearness
to, Ithaca. Because it was distant it could be portrayed as friend and ally.

The offshore position of Ithaca was, as we have seen, naturally "colonial"
in relation to the mainland. Ithaca's relation with the mainland is also comparable to that of a colony stretching to a mainland *peiraia:* Ithaca is represented as attempting mainland conquests, with the site chosen (Cape Nerikos) reflecting maritime considerations. A symbiosis of a more mundane
kind surfaces in the *Odyssey* in illustrative detail. Herds are kept on the mainland and other islands and transported in boats, as in the case of the goats
brought over by ferrymen for the suitors' feast. Odysseus himself, says Eumaios, used to have his herds kept on the mainland. A constant coming
and going between Ithaca and various mainland shores is envisaged in the
Odyssey and ties in seamlessly with some of the sequels, where Odysseus, for
example, leaves Ithaca to inspect mainland herds as far as Elis. In short,
Thesprotia in the *Odyssey* seems to indicate both an awareness of the sequels
and alternatives and a reflection of the Ithacan reality of varied links with
its mainland. Possibly the friendlier contacts with the more peripheral
Thesprotia facilitated the adoption of Odysseus myths by the historical
Thesprotians.

In his Thesprotian, non-*Odyssey* story, Odysseus founds a city (Bouneima)
and establishes an oracle (Trampya), fights wars with the barbarian Brygi,
helps the local king, and sires a royal genealogy. Independent, Epirote traditions are apparent here, following the contact with Odysseus myths. Just
as archaeologists discussing the material artifacts of a certain provenance
ask who the carriers were, in discovering uses of myth one may ask about the
agents of contact. The distribution map of Odysseus identifications may
be revealing. The conspicuous absence of Herakles as a royal progenitor
(ubiquitous and as close as Makedonia) signifies that a special explanation
with Odysseus and his Ithacan home at its center is needed. Corinthians
may have been indirectly responsible, but they themselves seem to have appropriated Odysseus (as a son of Sisyphos). By contrast, Ithaca, properly belonging to the region, seems to have been responsible either directly or by
means of the other Greeks passing through it. The Epirotes were drawn to
Odysseus because of his Homeric status, associated with a nearby island (but
not a too-familiar, close neighbor), and translated his stories not in the vein

159. Hoekstra in Heubeck and Hoekstra 1989 on 14.315. All his other *Odyssey* references (14.335; 19.292; 16.427) are easily explained in terms of sailing not from a mainland opposite.

of Homer but in human, genealogical, and political terms. Ithacans and other Greeks may have regarded the grafting of Odysseus onto Epirote lands as a form of flattery, easing their contacts. But internal Epirote rivalries may also explain something: Thesprotians, Molossians, and Chaones all turned to Nostos ancestors, thus competing with each other for greater antiquity and heroic status. The purpose of Epirote royal houses was probably not to Hellenize the ethnic origins of their peoples but to heroize those of their dynasties. It is remarkable how Greek categories of group definition, sometimes beginning with poets or erudites and relying on a genealogy of a Greek hero, could take over and contribute to some notion of common heroic origins, later (but only later) to be articulated (or debated) in terms of common Hellenism.

The genealogical, heroic identities of Epirus have here been examined against the background of "objective" Epirote ethnicity, with the varying applications of the criteria of language and way of life. In terms of the language criterion Epirotes were Greeks, Illyrians, or both. In terms of way of life (and even natural environment), many appeared at once more alike than and very different from the Greeks of the city-state culture. The *nostos* and foundation of Argos Amphilochikon exemplifies the ambiguity in the (anachronistic) attitude of fifth-century Greeks such as Thucydides. Amphilochos its founder, a Greek hero of the Trojan War, somehow founded with his followers a city that became "Greek," in Thucydides's view, only centuries later. Thucydides insists on the distinction between being Greek and being called Greeks. He does, however, regard many Epirotes as barbarians. Similar to the case of Amphilochos is Neoptolemos, the common ancestor of Molossians ("barbarians") and Aiginetans ("Greeks"), as Pindar's poetry (which managed to offend both) illustrates. In fact, the ambiguity stems not from any objective, primordial reality of ethnicity but from the changing historical realities of group definitions—the change from the royal/heroic to the comprehensive political-group criterion.

Nostoi function as *archēgetai* (founders) and progenitors in the eastern Mediterranean, in Greece, and in the west. They can be identified as leaders of entire migrations or even as the primary cause for such migrations. In (proto?)historical thought they were the agents of Greece's major historical *kinesis*. Consequently, in the east they were also associated with the founding of cities, as in Cyprus. By contrast, in the northwest they were mainly progenitors (sometimes founders too) of what mattered, politically, in these areas. The superimposition of the two criteria, the heroic and the ethnic, is exemplified in the argument of Alexander I at Olympia: he was finally admitted to the games as a "Greek" because he was a Herakleid. A few generations earlier the distinction might have seemed irrelevant. Rising above the conflation of criteria, a more general understanding that emerges is that

Greeks could, with relative ease, perceive "their" heroes as "ethnically" populating the world with both Greek and non-Greek peoples.

Even when regarded as "barbarians," Epirotes did not function as a reverse image of Greekness and civilization as François Hartog has argued for
the Scythians in Herodotus. A conflictual situation, translating the various
nostoi into a dichotomy of Greeks versus barbarians and hence transforming (some) Epirotes into barbarians has been pointed out relatively late, in
the context of the more recent Corinthian colonization of Apollonia. Is
there a formula here—the more recent and less secure, the more explicit
the uses of myth for political purposes? In another book I have argued for
a direct proportion between the explicitness of *territorial* charter myths and
the degree of threat to their realization. Here we are concerned with the
emergence of an "ethnic charter myth" articulating the Other (= enemy)
as barbarian. But even in this case, the articulation of the *nostoi* in terms of
Greekness and barbarity appeared not in the context of the foundation of
Apollonia but only later, in the early fifth century, as a result of its territorial expansion and conquest. Thus a whole spectrum becomes apparent
(and the pattern will recur when we examine the *nostoi* in Italy): after six
or seven generations, about two centuries, the "chemistry" of the myth
metamorphoses. For Greeks sailing to Epirus, notably Ithacans, Corinthians, and Euboians, it starts as mediating perceptions and contacts with both
the land and its inhabitants. It is adopted by the latter and plays a role in the
relation of various ethnic royalties to each other (Thesprotians, Molossians,
Chaones) and to other Greeks. The landscape itself becomes punctuated
with sites associated with Odysseus's travels and actions: a city is founded,
an oracle established. However, with time (and with more recent Greek
colonists) the robe of Nessos is exposed to a different light, and myth as
justification emerges.

It is perhaps ironic that Epirus seems to have been responsible for the
dissemination of whole "ethnic" patterns. Not only did Greeks in antiquity
(followed by some modern scholars) consider ("barbarian"?) Epirus the
original home of the Hellenes, and not only was it also the origin of the
name "Graikoi," by which the Greeks are known in the west to this day, but
the mythological "fractal" of *nostos* articulation seems to have been exported
to Italy, where Nostoi operated as they did in Epirus—both as progenitors
and founders and eventually expressing (as in Rome) the sets of contrasts
Greek-Trojan and Greek-barbarian.

FIVE

Pithekoussai, Odysseus, and the Etruscans

A boy of about twelve died on Pithekoussai, in the Bay of Naples, around the year 720 B.C., and the new future that his parents, part of the first generation of colonists to this the oldest Greek colony in the western Mediterranean, may have been hoping for was marred by their personal tragedy. They accorded him an adult burial, placing in his tomb vases of the kind used in the *symposion* (kraters for wine mixing, rare on Pithekoussai)[1] and in particular a small inscribed cup. The vases were smashed on purpose, as was common on Pithekoussai; the parents seem to have been expressing sadness at the wasted potential of their dead son: he would neither grow up to drink in adult company nor experience the powers of Aphrodite.[2] Young adolescent deaths were relatively uncommon, a fact expressed in the relative rarity of such burials, particularly in Pithekoussai,[3] and the parents may have felt the loss particularly severely.[4]

The cup (probably a Rhodian kotyle) bears a verse inscription in three retrograde lines (one either prose or iambic trimeter, two hexameters), with the words and phrases separated, implying its use in the *symposion*:[5] "I am[6]

1. Ridgway 1992: 57.
2. For an interpretation of the burial in terms of the *symposion* see Murray 1994.
3. Cf. Ridgway 1992: 51–52, 67–77. See Buchner and Ridgway 1993: 301–691 (inhumation burials nos. 244–723).
4. Golden 1988: 155 on the different attitude to the more frequent infant deaths. Cf. Morris 1987: 62.
5. Buchner and Russo 1955; Cantarella 1968: 41; Ridgway 1992: 55–57; Murray 1994 (contra Danek 1994–95). On the meter of the first line and a comparison with the text of the *Iliad*, see comments by C. F. Russo in Buchner and Ridgway 1993: 746–47; cf. Hansen 1976: 35–40. For an overview see Powell 1991: 163–67; Robb 1994: 45–48.
6. The first line seems comparable to inscribed titles of ownership found on drinking

the cup of Nestor, a joy to drink from [or "Nestor had a fine drinking cup"], but anyone drinking from this cup will immediately be struck with desire for lovely-crowned Aphrodite." Not only is this one of the earliest inscriptions in the Archaic Greek alphabet in our possession and one of the very few pieces of original poetry from the eighth century[7] but it exhibits maturity, sophistication, and literary savoir faire. It jokingly plays on the allusion to the famous cup of Nestor in the *Iliad* (perhaps alluded to also in the *Odyssey*),[8] a heavy, ornate metal affair, indicating acquaintance with details that include, in the *Iliad*, a digression on the venerable cup of the old counselor. As Oswyn Murray observes, the first line is certainly intended to be poetic; it is not a mere reference to someone called Nestor.[9] If in fact that was the name of the owner of the cup, the joke, probably made in the manner of composing by taking turns during the banquet, was all the more poignant. It plays on the contrast between the Homeric hero and the contemporary drinker, between the heavy heroic cup and the delicate little kotyle, and between the aged counselor and the contemporary man in his prime, ready for the pleasures of Aphrodite.[10]

THE CUP OF NESTOR

The Iliadic details concerning the Pithekoussai Nestor cup are important, since Homeric stories could have been known in a variety of ways—bedtime stories, vase paintings, and so on.[11] But a Greek version of Lamb's *Shakespeare for Children* would have eliminated precisely such passages as Agamemnon's staff or Nestor's cup. Their effect lies only in precise recitation. With some exceptions, most scholars who have written about the inscription on the cup found at Pithekoussai agree that the allusion loses its point unless it refers to the cup in the *Iliad*.[12] But the implication, which may be uncomfortable for those who underestimate the role of memorization of entire passages, is

---

vessels; the restored word is $\epsilon[\mu]\iota$ or $\epsilon\iota[\mu]\iota$ (see Hansen 1976: 29–32; Powell 1991: 164; Murray 1994: 28).

7. Cf. Robb 1994: 31–32 on the Dipylon oinochoe and the Ithaca vase.

8. *Il.* 2.632–37; cf. *Od.* 3.51–53, 63.

9. Murray 1994: 28. The adjective εὔποτον is added to the standard ownership formula Νεστορός εἰμὶ ποτήριον. It is based on the Homeric ἡδυπότοιο Cf. Cantarella 1968: 44.

10. On the erotic aspect and in particular the possibility that the cup represents a hexameter incantation of the kind that was current from the Bronze Age on, see Faraone 1996. This possibility, however, does not constitute an alternative to the epic allusion implied in the name of Nestor but places the entire verse in a different context.

11. Cf. Snodgrass 1979.

12. See comments by C. F. Russo in Buchner and Ridgway 1993: 745–50; for a full bibliography see O. Vox, in Appendix 1, in Buchner and Ridgway 1993.

that the "cup of Nestor" at Pithekoussai indicates familiarity not just with the plot of the *Iliad* but with particular details of it. In my view it clearly assumes knowledge of Homer—not necessarily the Iliadic text as we have it but perhaps something rather close to it, known and recited along with a host of pre- and post-Iliadic poems including the various *nostoi* (chap. 1).

The verses are written in the alphabet of Euboian Chalkis.[13] The tomb is particularly rich and may indicate that the boy belonged to a family that was well-off, perhaps aristocratic. It seems fairly reasonable to infer that the cup's owner and the child's family were Euboian. However, emphasizing the fact that some of the graves have an unusual number of Near Eastern goods, David Ridgway tentatively says that "it may seem heretical to suggest that the Greek verses inscribed on the Nestor kotyle belonged to a family that was partly of non-Greek, Levantine extraction." His other alternative, that these goods suggest an affluent Euboian family, makes much better sense. The *owner*, in any case, is certainly Greek.[14]

It is also safe to infer that the allusion was meaningful to the family that buried the child but not to it alone. Since we are dealing here not with some private inscription that might point to an exceptional individual who knew some Homeric poetry but rather with a symposiac cup, the implication is one of the utmost importance. Because it is symposiac, this Nestor cup assumes the shared familiarity of the entire symposiac group, namely, the generation of the boy's parents, around 750 or perhaps a little earlier. Since the cup of Nestor figures in the *Iliad* and possibly in the *Odyssey*, it is safe to see in it also an implied knowledge of Odysseus, a major hero in both epics. This may be a point of some importance for the role of the hero as mediator between Greek colonists, the lands they inhabited, and the populations they encountered.

Several passages in Athenaeus that have not received sufficient attention illustrate the subsequent importance of the Homeric cup of Nestor, especially in Campania. Centuries after the Pithekoussai cup, the "real" cup of

13. Jeffrey 1990: 235–36; cf. Guarducci 1967: 226–27.
14. Ridgway 1992: 116. For a convenient description of the excavation see Ridgway 1992: chap. 4. He speaks of a possible partly Levantine origin for the family (1992: 111–18). The argument ("partly non-Greek" or the ambiguous "Levantine extraction") is somewhat speculative. Its reliance on settlement pattern (promontories and offshore islands) as "startlingly reminiscent" of Phoenician custom is blind to the fact that this is the consistent pattern for all maritime colonizations; the Crusaders' colonies of Acre or Atlit or the British Hong Kong could be similarly interpreted. The Semitic inscription on amphora 571 is not directly tied to the Rhodian kotyle (the Nestor cup), which need not have been brought there by Phoenicians passing through Rhodes. Without addressing the general question of Phoenicians (or Aramaeans) on Pithekoussai, the plain fact remains that the inscription on the cup is Euboian Greek.

Nestor apparently became the subject of symposiac discourse, with treatises on its precise shape and implications[15] and even attempts to re-create it.[16] Directly relevant is an "inscribed cup . . . dedicated to Artemis in Capua, in Campania; it was made of silver according to the pattern described in the Homeric poems, and had the letters stamped on it in letters of gold, and was said to be the cup which belonged to Nestor."[17] Athenaeus says that Promathidas of Heraclea studied this particular cup to argue a point about the Homeric Nestor's Cup. This cup, unlike the Pithekoussai cup, with its playful allusions and real symposiac function, was a dedication, claiming to copy rather than paraphrase. Its occurrence in Capua, the main Campanian city, with its Etruscan elite, may indicate that together with the *symposion* adopted from the Greeks of Pithekoussai and Kyme, the cup of Nestor itself, as a symposiac emblem, was adopted as well. Since we do not have a date for this dedication, this must remain a general suggestion.

Another indication, although less explicit, of familiarity with Homeric subjects may be seen in a seal impression on an amphora from the acropolis dump on Monte di Vico (Pithekoussai) that is contemporary with the Nestor cup. It shows two figures, probably Ajax carrying the body of Achilles. The image, from the same or a similar seal stone, is known from dedicatory votives in the Samian Heraion.[18] Achilles, however, does not die in the *Iliad*, and the scene must allude to one of the poems of the Trojan Cycle. This, too, is quite significant. As we shall observe, almost none of the applications of the *nostoi* in the west is derived from Homer himself; rather, they come from alternative versions. In Homer, for example, Menelaos returns home via Egypt and Libya, whereas in other versions (which also find cultic expressions) he reaches Italy and Sicily.[19] We may immediately conclude, therefore, that Euboian Greeks knew of additional Trojan stories when colonizing Pithekoussai and that such stories need not have been made up after the end of the eighth century. As we have seen, the Cycle and the *Iliad* and *Odyssey* imply each other.

By contrast, a narrative scene depicting a shipwreck (also contemporary with the Pithekoussai cup), with sailors drowning and being devoured by fish, may or may not be reflective of the *Odyssey*.[20] It is sufficiently generic to express what may have been a fate all too familiar to Greek explorer-

15. Ath. 11.461d, 781d; a work by Asclepiades of Myrleia *On Nestor's cup:* 487f–493d; cf. 433b–d.

16. Ath. 489b with 492a: "It is said that Dionysius of Thrace constructed Nestor's cup at Rhodes with silver contributed by his pupils."

17. Ath. 466e = 489c; 477b. See also Eust., *Il.* 11.635.

18. Ridgway 1992: 89–90; Ahlberg-Cornell 1992: 35–38 (with examples).

19. Malkin 1994a: chap. 2.

20. Brunnsåker 1962; Ridgway 1988b; Ahlberg-Cornell 1992: 27–28.

merchants (the ship seems to be a warship) and colonists. Hesiod, as we shall see, dislikes the sea but shows informed familiarity with its way of life (see chap. 6). The "painful gifts to Poseidon" (= drowned men) of Archilochos are similarly evoked by the Pithekoussai shipwreck scene.[21]

Above all, the Pithekoussai cup provides a way out of a familiar loop: does the *Odyssey* precede or reflect Greek colonization? On the one hand, one may regard Homer and the *Odyssey* in particular as reflective of the colonial experience. The passage in the ninth book in which Odysseus describes the offshore island opposite the land of the Cyclopes in colonial terms is an often-adduced example, although it could just as well reflect earlier migrations and settlements, for example, on the offshore islands and promontories of Asia Minor. On the other hand, if, as I have been suggesting, Greeks had Homer in their heads, say, in the third quarter of the eighth century, then the *Odyssey* would be less a reflection of colonization than a commonly recognized frame of reference that had long been familiar to the colonizing Greeks. The Nestor cup from Pithekoussai swings the pendulum rather decisively toward the latter approach.[22]

It is possible to argue that since the passages in the epics that contain detailed descriptions of objects (such as royal staff, cup, boar's-tusk helmet) are probably the earliest (since these objects having archaeological counterparts in the real Mycenaean world), the cup of Nestor need not have had a full surrounding *Iliad* and *Odyssey* to have been known to the Greek colonists of Pithekoussai. The Pithekoussai cup, however, is not isolated. If my reconstruction of the cult of Odysseus in Ithaca is accepted, then we have earlier (ninth-century), external evidence for awareness of particular episodes (not objects) in the *Odyssey*. Such points are bound to be argued over and over again, especially since it is always possible to dissect "Homer" into early and late bits and pieces. However, since for our purposes it is sufficient to show that some Homer did penetrate Italy at this time via the Euboian colonists and since the example we have is so early and so sophisticated, I think that it has been sufficiently substantiated.

ODYSSEUS AND THE ETRUSCANS

No Etruscan city faced the Greek settlers of Pithekoussai on the Italian mainland in the region of Campania, where Greeks also founded Kyme no later

21. Archil. 12.1 West; for other references regarding Greek attitudes to the sea, see West 1978: 618.

22. On whether the *Odyssey* may reflect some real colonization experiences, aside from its general protocolonial aspect, see appendix.

than the 720s. In fact, Etruria lies much farther north, with Latium in the middle. But Etruscans, very much like Greeks, were frequenting the coasts, trading, sometimes settling, and generally leaving behind them enough material evidence to imply close encounters with both native Campanians and Greeks during the eighth century. Hesiod (see chap. 6) says that Odysseus was the progenitor of those who ruled the Tyrsenoi (Etruscans), thus connecting the *nostos* of Odysseus with the ethnography of the most distinctive Italian civilization that Greeks encountered.[23] The Etruscans apparently adopted the hero just as they did other figures of Greek mythology. In the Etruscan language Odysseus's name is Utuse, a "transliteration" that clearly points to the identity of the Greeks responsible for introducing Odysseus: the Euboians.[24] We are concerned, therefore, with a double (Greek and Etruscan) "colonial situation" in Campania in which Odysseus, a mediating hero, may have functioned also as an ethnic definer.

Hesiod provides us with a typical Greek "ethnographic" model for regarding and defining Others: heroic genealogy. The sons that Odysseus had with Circe, he says, "ruled over the famous Tyrsenoi."[25] We have no idea how the Etruscans liked this notion or whether Greeks cared if they did. Even if Odysseus did not serve the Etruscan ethnic *self*-definition, we should still attempt to evaluate whether Odysseus's connection with the Etruscans was a one-sided Greek idea or whether the Etruscans too were susceptible to Odysseus in various ways. It is legitimate to inquire about Odysseus among the Etruscans as early as the second half of the eighth century for the following reasons: (1) Hesiod's text, written probably ca. 700 B.C.; (2) the manifest presence of Greek mythological motifs—Odysseus included—in early artifacts, notably painted vases, current among the Etruscans; (3) a context, archaeologically established, of close commercial and cultural contacts between Etruscans and the Euboians of Pithekoussai and Kyme during the second half of the eighth century and even earlier; (4) our knowledge, based on the Pithekoussai Nestor cup, that those Euboians knew some Homer; and (5) the Etruscan adoption of the Euboian alphabet in general and of the Euboian form of Odysseus's name, Utuse, in particular. I propose to ex-

23. On the advanced level of Etruscan city development, see Peroni 1988. By contrast, Latium in the eighth century seems to have been made up of villages grouped around sanctuaries. Only in the second half of the eighth century do centers emerge. Ampolo et al. 1980; Guidi 1985; Colonna 1988.

24. Cf. Cristofani 1972; 1978; 1979; 1983; Colonna 1980; Delpino 1989; De Simone 1968; 1970; Frederiksen 1979; Ridgway 1994b. By contrast, we have seen that the form "Olytteus" (eventually "Ulysses") may have had its origins in Corinth, arriving in Latium probably via Messapia.

25. On *Theogony* 1011–18 see chap. 6.

amine these reasons and then suggest a role for Odysseus in the Etruscan context.

Historians of the Etruscans mostly acknowledge the fact that the arrival of the Greeks, first as protocolonists in the first half of the eighth century and then through the Euboian colonies of Pithekoussai and Kyme during its second half, provided the Etruscans with unprecedented social, cultural, and political stimuli.[26] It is noteworthy, for example, that in the Etruscan orbit transition from Villanovan IIB to the Orientalizing period was contemporary with the first tombs on Pithekoussai.[27] Opinions vary to what extent some of these stimuli derived from the Phoenicians;[28] some, such as Michel Gras, prefer to regard the Etruscans themselves as an expansive, maritime power. Gras emphasizes not only the receptive aspects of Etruscan culture but also their own contacts with the Aegean world, notably Lemnos, where an Etruscan inscription from the early sixth century was discovered.[29] Indications of contact seem to be mounting.[30] For example, bronze helmets, probably from Tarquinia, were dedicated in Olympia and in Delphi in the first half of the eighth century.[31] During the second half one finds more varied dedications of Etruscan origins (spear tips, shields, fibulae, and various ornaments) in the sanctuaries of Dodona, Perachora, and Samos,[32] and it is now reported that two Etruscan fibulae were discovered in Chalkis.[33] It seems probable that Greeks (rather than Etruscan visitors) dedicated these, although it is not clear under what circumstances. It is possible that the helmets and shields in particular were war trophies, although there is little likelihood of hostile encounters between Greeks and Etruscans so early. It is more likely that they were prestige objects, perhaps acquired through guest-friendship relations. Whatever the occasion, it is clear that the Etruscans were part of the Greek experience throughout the eighth century. The dedications were seen on the mainland (and Samos) where they could be viewed by various Greek visitors to the pan-Hellenic and city sanctuaries.

26. See, e.g., Cristofani 1978: 33.
27. D'Agostino 1990: 77.
28. Cf. Frederiksen 1979: 283; Rathje 1979: 157.
29. See Gras 1985: chap. 11 and especially 630–31.
30. I am grateful to Bruno D'Agostino for the following observations. See now von Hase 1995; 1996; cf. *La presenza etrusca* 1994 with Ridgway 1994b.
31. Kilian (1977: 429–42) dates the helmets closer to 800; von Hase 1995: 253 with n. 24 places them in the first half of the eighth century.
32. Von Hase 1979; Herrmann 1983: 271 ff.
33. D'Agostino, personal communication.

One is justified, therefore, in seeing Greek contacts with Etruscans at least since the mid-eighth century, increasing in intensity over time. Veii, for example, contains Greek pottery, perhaps made by a resident Greek potter, ca. 750 B.C.[34] Greek vases originating mostly in Euboia[35] in both halves of the eighth century are found in burials along the Tyrrhenian coast, in Etruria, Latium, and Campania. These seem to indicate Greek maritime activity along the coast and, particularly, around the areas of the river mouths: the Picentino (Pontecagnano), the Volturno (Capua), and the Tiber (Veii).[36]

Today it is sometimes possible, thanks to the Mössbauer technique, to determine the origin of the clay from which pots were made and the temperature at which they were fired, and this allows imports to be distinguished from pots made locally.[37] At Veii, for example, Euboian imports can now be distinguished (in terms of firing at different temperatures) as produced in Euboian workshops different from those that produced otherwise indistinguishable vases discovered at Pithekoussai and Pontecagnano. Euboian Cycladic (mostly Chalkidian) pottery is found in various other Etruscan sites during the first half of the eighth century; these were soon copied.[38] Etruscan elites are evidenced at Pontecagnano (and later in Naples and Capua).[39] It has plausibly been argued that Pithekoussai was responsible for some of the exact and remarkable correspondences of material culture.[40] It seems to have had a particular impact on the Opicians (in Campania), where Middle Geometric and Late Geometric pottery—kotylai, Aetos 666 pottery, a few chevron cups and later Thapsos cups, and oinochoai—has been found in burials (especially in the Sarno valley).[41] In Kyme, the rich, aristocratic Fondo Artaico tomb, ca. 730–720, included an Etruscan shield covering the cauldron that contained the deceased's ashes. Fifty-two metal

34. Ridgway and Ridgway 1979, 113–27. On the downdating of the Pendant semicircle skyphoi, see Descoeudres and Kearsley 1983; Kearsley 1989: 126–28 with Holloway 1994: 46; von Hase 1995: 248–52. For a revised approach, see Ridgway 1992: 131 with Toms 1986.

35. D'Agostino 1985.

36. *La céramique grecque* 1982; Descoeudres and Kearsley 1983: 9–53; Ridgway, Boitani, and Deriu 1985: 139–50. The area is particularly rich in metal minerals (between Caere and Tarquinia and in western Etruria and in Populonia and the island of Elba).

37. D'Agostino 1990: 73, 84.

38. Cristofani 1978: 35–36; Boardman 1957: 9, 24–25. On local copies, see comments by A. M. Small in *Greece and Italy in the Classical world* 1979, 191.

39. Bartoloni 1989; D'Agostino and Gastaldi 1988. D'Agostino interprets the evidence from the grave to indicate that local populations in Campania included many Opicians (D'Agostino 1988).

40. Buchner 1979: 133.

41. D'Agostino 1979; 1982. The small number of chevron cups creates difficulties in determining the chronology (see the table in Ridgway 1992: 132).

objects, including gold, silver, and electrum, were also found. Either the tomb indicates significant Etruscan influence or, as Strøm argues, perhaps an Etruscan was actually buried there.[42] Clasps found in the tomb also illustrate Buchner's point that personal ornaments used by Greeks in Pithekoussai and Kyme in the second half of the eighth century "were *identical* to those used in Etruria and Latium."[43]

It could be argued that the Euboians were not necessarily the Greeks who introduced Odysseus to the Etruscans. The Ionian Greeks (Euboians included) are generally recognized to have had the most significant impact on Etruscan culture between the eighth and the sixth centuries. The best-known of them, the Phokaians,[44] were trading and colonizing in the western Mediterranean (Spain, Massalia, and Corsica) and the Adriatic before 600 B.C. After the conquest of their homeland by Persia in 545, more Phokaians arrived in the west, resulting in the famous battle of Alalia (Corsica) and the consequent abandonment of Corsica, perhaps the swelling of Massalia's population, the foundation of Elea in Italy, and a massacre of Phokaians by Etruscans that was compensated for by annual sacrifices.[45] The Phokaians were most probably responsible for disseminating Greek gods such as Artemis (Etruscan Artumes) and Apollo (Etruscan Apulu). Herakles (Etruscan Herkle) in particular became very popular among them.[46] However, Phokaia's western expansion seems to have had little to do with *nostoi* in general and that of Odysseus in particular. Moreover, the Phokaian story belongs mostly to the second half of the seventh century; since a vase painting with an unmistakable Odysseus scene is known from Etruscan Caere about the mid-seventh, it would seem that we should look for an earlier context in which the name of the hero (Etruscan Utuse) was adopted by the Etruscans.

Earlier than the Phokaians in terms of actual presence in Italy was the colony of Sybaris. Timaios says it was known for its friendly relations with the Etruscans,[47] but it is not quite clear when this started. There was apparently a land route, passing by way of Sybaris's colony Poseidonia, whose territory reached the mouth of the Sele. A late writer called it a partly Etruscanized

42. Buchner 1979: 130–31, 138; Frederiksen 1979: 290; Albore Livadie 1975; contra Strøm 1971: 47, 59 ff, 98 ff.; 1990: 90.

43. Buchner 1979: 133, contra Strøm 1990: 90. See Coldstream 1993: 90–95 on the possibility of mixed marriages. Coldstream's paper overlooks much of the earlier discussion; see Graham 1984.

44. Gras 1985: 627 and passim.

45. Hdt. 1.165–67 (see chap. 8).

46. Richardson 1964: 233; cf. Jourdain-Annequin 1989: 247, 361, 485; Torelli 1984: 16–23; Spivey and Stoddart 1990: 101.

47. Timaios *FGrH* 566 F 50.

settlement,[48] and its famous paintings have been judged identical with those of a south Etruscan group."[49] It would seem that Sybaris, again, is somewhat late to have been responsible for the Etruscans' familiarity with Odysseus. Its main links may have had more to do with the export from Miletus of dyed fabrics of which the Etruscans were particularly fond.[50]

Corinthian pottery was very popular among the Etruscans, especially around 625, and they were soon imitating it.[51] The exiled Corinthian aristocrat Demaratos is said to have migrated to Etruscan Tarquinii with three artists and fathered Tarquinius Priscus, later king of Rome.[52] Nobility and artisanry combined, Demaratos is a good example of another route of diffusion. But the last third of the seventh century seems not to have been the initial context for the Etruscan encounter with Odysseus: had that been the case the fifth-century Etruscan form of the hero's name would have followed the Corinthian (Olytteus) rather than the Euboian (Odysseus) orthography.

The most plausible context for the encounter of the Etruscans with Odysseus remains, therefore, the contact with the generation of Euboians that drank from the Pithekoussai Nestor cup, especially in the second half of the eighth century. Unlike the Phokaians, who flourished in the late seventh century, Euboians had practically abandoned their overseas trade and colonization after the end of the eighth century. The second half of the eighth century was the period of vigorous Euboian-Etruscan contact and acculturation, and the most expressive form of this contact was the adoption of the alphabet. The Etruscans learned their alphabet from the Euboians of Pithekoussai and Kyme.[53] By about 700 it had been absorbed and already influenced by the requirements of Etruscan phonetics. The alphabet seems to have been regarded as possessing intrinsic importance. The tablets of Marsiliana d'Albegna, for example, preserving a whole Greek alphabet series, were placed in a cauldron inside a tomb dating to about 675–650.[54] The alphabet's pattern of distribution, especially during the seventh century, indicates that it was introduced by Greeks or by Etruscans who knew the precise nature of Greek phonetics. In terms of Walter Burkert's ideas of how the North Semitic alphabet was disseminated among Greeks,[55] it seems rea-

48. Aristoxenos in Ath. 14.632a.
49. Pallottino 1974: 100, 122.
50. Heurgon 1973: 86; Rathje 1979: 145.
51. Hus 1976: 78; Strøm 1971: 11 (different theories).
52. Polyb. 6.11a.7; Pliny *HN* 35.43, 152; Dion. Hal. 3.46.3–5. Cf. Blakeway 1935; Musti 1987; Ridgway 1992: 143.
53. Guarducci 1964; 1967; Jeffrey 1993: 236 -37; Cristofani 1972; cf. Ridgway 1992: 141.
54. Cristofani 1979: 379; Jeffrey 1990: 236.
55. Burkert 1992: 28–33; cf. Powell 1991: 123–80.

sonable that in Italy too individual "teachers" were involved. They may have been like the individual craftsmen and potters who worked among the Etruscans and were probably responsible for the rapid dissemination of Greek-type vases. Such teachers, both craftsmen and script professionals, were probably also responsible for the spread of motifs from the Greek epics.

Among the Greek artists who, by the second quarter of the seventh century, had settled in Etruscan Caere, adapting their styles to the local taste, was the potter of the Aristonothos krater. The krater itself may indicate an adoption of the Greek lifestyle associated with the *symposion;* it is an elaborate affair and was probably used in much the same way as Greek ones. It is possible that there was a preference for more expensive metal kraters, but that should not rule out a symposiac function for this beautifully painted ceramic one. During a *symposion* the krater would have been placed in the middle, and drinkers would have drawn wine from it into their own cups. Their gaze would have fallen on whatever was on it (in this case, painted scenes and writing), and their conversation must sometimes have revolved around this. The scenes painted on the Aristonothos krater show naval warfare combined with the scene of Odysseus and his companions blinding the Cyclops Polyphemos. When compared with contemporary representations of the blinding of Polyphemos, it "agrees most closely with the *Odyssey*."[56] The same may be said today of the contemporary (650–625) painted pithos showing an enormous wine jug in the center of the scene and Odysseus with companions blinding a Polyphemos sitting on a chair.[57] In the Aristonothos krater there are also signs in Euboian characters.[58] We see, therefore, that by the second quarter of the seventh century writing, lifestyle, and epic content combined to illustrate the spread of the Odysseus motif among the Etruscans. Odysseus, shown on the krater in the most popular painted narrative scene from the *Odyssey*,[59] is thus shown to have been known to the Etruscans by the time the Aristonothos krater was made in Etruscan Caere, and it is probable, since it was adapted to suit an existing taste, that it implies prior knowledge of Odysseus.[60] It has also been claimed that the scene implies that an Etruscan prince saw himself as a descendant of Odysseus (with the naval scene indicating Etruscan "piratical" activity),[61] but such ideas must remain conjectural. The Euboian characters provide further

56. Ahlberg-Cornell 1992: 94–95. For other representations of scenes from the Homeric epics in Etruscan art, see Colonna 1980; Massa Pairault 1994: 19–23.

57. *A passion for antiquities* 1994: 182–86.

58. Jeffrey 1990: 239.

59. See Shapiro 1994: 49–54; cf. Ahlberg-Cornell 1992: 94–95; Touchefeu-Meynier 1968: 10 and in general for the diffusion of the *Odyssey* scenes; Buitron et al. 1992: 31–74.

60. Cf. Dench 1995: 39 and chap. 1 with nn. 31 and 32.

61. Massa-Pairault 1994: 19–20.

proof, if such were needed, for the identity of the agents of this cultural dissemination. It stands to reason, therefore, that the Etruscans already called Odysseus something like Utuse, even though our direct epigraphic evidence for this comes much later.

The symposiac association of the Aristonothos krater recalls the context of the Nestor cup from Pithekoussai. The custom of the *symposion,* apparent in the *Odyssey* (e.g., in the song of Demodokos),[62] seems evidenced materially among both Greeks and Etruscans during the second half of the eighth century.[63] Although some may argue whether the term *symposion* is apt as early as the eighth century, few would deny that the ensemble of its elements was present by that time.[64] The *symposion* may have also been the context for gift exchange and for the prestige goods discovered in Greek and Etruscan "princely tombs."[65] Such tombs, dating to the later eighth century, have been discovered in Euboian Kyme, Etruria, and Latium. Contemporary with these are the princely tombs in Euboian Eretria and at Paphos and Salamis in Cyprus, whose salient features are said to have been inspired by Homeric descriptions, notably that of Patroklos's funeral.[66] Similar influences may have affected the Etruscans.[67]

To the extent that one can speak of "Homeric society," the Etruscans of this period seem to fit the picture almost as well as the Greeks.[68] It is true that the idea of the banquet need not have reached the Etruscans via the Greeks and that the Etruscan "*symposion*" probably did not express a Greek social frame of reference. In the Near East the reclining banquet was well known, and it is possible that the Phoenicians were its cultural agents.[69] However, the close contacts between, especially, the Euboians of Kyme and the Etruscans, as well as the dissemination of undisputed Greek *symposion* paraphernalia[70] and the Etruscan borrowing of Greek names for vases,[71] should lead to the conclusion that Greek influence on the Etruscan symposiac gatherings was strongly felt.

62. Cf. Slater 1990.

63. This is the general conclusion of Rathje's study (1990).

64. Murray 1994; cf. Schmitt Pantel 1992: 46–48. On the funerary context of the Etruscan *symposion* see Murray 1988; cf. Bartoloni, Cataldi Dini, and Zevi 1982.

65. D'Agostino 1977b; cf. Holloway 1994: 156–60.

66. Coldstream 1977: 349–51 with Ridgway 1992: 138. See also chap. 3 with n. 54.

67. Ridgway 1992: 138.

68. Cf. Frederiksen 1979: 294; Ampolo 1980: 165–92.

69. Cf. Lichtenstein 1968; Grotanelli 1981; Dentzer 1982; Strøm 1984.

70. D'Agostino 1990: 76. D'Agostino emphasizes that Tomb 168 from S. Valentino, in addition to Greek drinking vessels, also contained the salient vessel of the symposium, a krater, but reserves judgment.

71. E.g., lekythos = *lechtum,* kylix = *kulichna,* askos = *aska.* See Colonna 1973–74.

The *symposion* of the second half of the eighth century was "Homeric" both in content and in form: as the songs of Phemios and Demodokos in the *Odyssey* illustrate, the subject of the poetry sung in symposia was often *nostoi*. Homer describes symposia, and the Greeks (and Etruscans) were reclining in Homeric-style symposia, drinking from cups with Homeric motifs expressed either in inscribed verse (as on the Pithekoussai Nestor cup) or in painted scenes such as the blinding of Polyphemos. Transport amphorae such as the one discovered at Pithekoussai with the seal showing Ajax carrying Achilles (ca. 700) must have been known to the Etruscans.[72] It would seem, therefore, that Odysseus in particular, believed by Greeks of ca. 700 to have been the progenitor of the Etruscans (see chap. 6) must have played a special role as a mediating hero in the encounter with a non-Greek aristocratic culture with similar customs, drinking from the same cups and probably entertaining each other. During the eighth and seventh centuries Greek and Etruscan elites underwent an intensive acculturation of ideas and customs.[73] To excise Odysseus from this context would call, I think, for special pleading.

Why would Odysseus have appealed to the Etruscans, and why, from the Greek point of view, was Odysseus chosen as the source of the ethnic definition of the Etruscans?

We have seen that in the last third of the eighth century the settlers of Pithekoussai were familiar with Homer. If we turn to the geographical context of cultural communication between the Euboians and the Etruscans we may also be able to assess why Odysseus may have been significant to the latter. The major issue, in my view, is the fact that Pithekoussai and Kyme faced Campania, separated from Etruria to the north by Latium. Both Etruscans and Greeks were newcomers to this area, which was a region of blending of various influences.[74] As Bruno d'Agostino has shown, the remoteness of Campania from Etruria indicates that Etruscan contacts with this area—like those of the Greeks—were by sea.[75] The Campania cities contained a mixture of local and Etruscan elites, heavily influenced by Greeks, especially from Pithekoussai and Kyme. By 650 the Etruscans were already a major influence in Campania.[76] Capua, for example, had seen unbroken development since the ninth century. The same Euboian pottery (Pithekoussai)

72. Ridgway 1992: 89–90.
73. D'Agostino 1977a.
74. Cf. Strøm 1990 (who emphasizes more the Near Eastern connections).
75. D'Agostino 1990.
76. Frederiksen 1984: 117–29.

recurs in several Etruscanized centers and especially in Capua. There are other examples of Etruscan influence, such as Nola and Pompeii (where Strabo mentions a period of Etruscan control),[77] although these may have been Greek foundations that had been "Italicized."[78]

The most significant Campanian site to demonstrate the acculturation of local Etruscan, and Greek cultures is Pontecagnano (Picentia), on the River Picentino. Its cemeteries show a sequence, as in Etruria, beginning in the ninth century. Particularly rich tombs of ca. 700 also seem to evidence links with coastal areas.[79] In the pottery types strong Euboian influence is evident. Imported pottery provides an interesting indication of circulation, whereas locally made Greek pottery and Greek decorations on local and hybrid shapes point to Euboian models. D'Agostino offers as an example skyphoi glazed in black all over that had largely disappeared in Greece but were still being produced in Euboia (Middle Geometric II) at the time that they remarkably appear in Pontecagnano. Such pots indicate direct and close contacts.[80]

In contrast to the conflicts of the sixth and fifth centuries (the Etruscan defeats in the wars with Kyme in 525–524, 506, and 504[81] and the intervention of Syracuse in 474), Greek-Etruscan relations during the eighth and seventh centuries seem to have been much more pacific. Even in the sixth century relations and points of contacts were varied and complex. Greeks inhabited, in small communities, Etruscan ports such as Gravisca and Pyrgi.[82] There was also a wide variety of Greek settlers: captives, traders, metics, craftsmen, aristocratic guest-friends, political exiles, and so on.[83]

To sum up the geographical context and its significance: Campania, facing Pithekoussai and Kyme, where neither Greeks nor Etruscans were the majority of the population, functioned as a meeting point of commercial and aristocratic elites. Because of its nature as a commercial and colonial frontier zone, Campania played a mediating role in Greek-Etruscan acculturation. The role of non-Greek and non-Etruscan local elites, such as at Pontecagnano, remains elusive, but one may suspect that it was rather significant. Neither Greek nor Etruscan presence seems to have constituted a territorial threat in the early period of the cultural encounter (second half of the eighth century), and it should come as no surprise that we do not find

77. Strabo 5.247. See Frederiksen 1979: 297.
78. Lomas 1993: 28–30.
79. See D'Agostino 1990 with previous references to his important work; cf. Frederiksen 1979: 279; Rathje 1979: 152 ff. with Pliny *HN* 3.5.70; Cuozzo 1994.
80. D'Agostino 1990: 78–80.
81. Dion. Hal. 7.6.1–2.
82. Ridgway and Serra 1990; Torelli 1977; 1990a.
83. Frederiksen 1979: 290.

the *nostoi* functioning as territorial charter myths. As if through a magnifying lens, Greek mythological discourse mediated and articulated the identities of the peoples encountered, not the annexation of their lands.

During the eighth and seventh centuries the Etruscans were rather similar to the Greeks in their position in Campania; they were also colonists, trading and sometimes settling. The colonial situation lent itself to the application of myth to the new lands and newly encountered peoples. Greek myths of origins and travel seeped into Etruscan culture, perhaps among guest-friends, together with the wine drunk at aristocratic symposia. It also reached the Etruscans with the other aspects of contact and adoption of Greek culture, through art, artisans, and alphabet teachers. In short, the same colonizing need, the same situation of strangers penetrating new lands, shared by both Etruscans and Greeks, enhanced the appeal of the Greek legends as meaningful and applicable.

Why, one may ask, did the Etruscans adopt the Greek Odysseus, whereas there is no evidence for the Greek adoption of Etruscan mythological discourse? This question applies to most Mediterranean cultures in many historical periods. Greek *nostoi*, the product of the Trojan War, provided the ethnography of the Mediterranean with a framework of identity. Romans, invading Franks in the early Middle Ages, Britons, Portuguese ("Lisbon," literally, means "the city of Ulysses/Odysseus"), and others have associated themselves with the Greek side of the mythological articulation. The Trojan Nostoi (whether Greek or Trojans) are but the most famous; the Greeks themselves also told of the ethnic origins of Cretans, Arkadians, Pelasgians, and so forth. What was so powerful about the *Greek* myths of origins ("Trojan origins" is itself a Greek myth) as to make so many cultures susceptible?

Perhaps the Greeks had more "authority." In his brilliant article "Origines Gentium," Elias Bickerman suggests that the success of Greek myths of origins depended on other nations' bowing to the "scientific" aspect of the Greek view of things. Everyone had myths, but Greek myths were also the result of "investigation." Bickerman claims that Greeks of the Classical period never paid much attention to what natives had to say about their own origins; what mattered was what the Greeks "knew."[84] Thucydides, for example, says that although the Sikans of Sicily claim to be autochthonous, "the truth" is that they were Iberians who migrated to Sicily.[85] Witness also the frustration of someone like Josephus in *Contra Apionem,* charging the Greeks with not having read the Jewish sources. Often, Greek myths of ori-

84. Bickerman 1952; cf. Dench 1995: 35.
85. Thuc. 6.2.2.

gins were regarded not as myths but as knowledge. It was the recognition that this knowledge was the result of scientific inquiry that made some non-Greek peoples bow to it. In a later period, probably in the sixth century, the Etruscans seem to have adopted the Greek "scientific" theory of their Lydian—not Odyssean—origins.[86] Was this also the situation during the Archaic period, before the rise of logography and history?

Obviously not, since Odysseus contradicts the Lydian-origins theory, but Homer may have been an "authority" too. Whether or not they had reached their final form as early as the second half of the eighth century, the *Iliad* and the *Odyssey* seem to have already been in existence by 700 B.C. They were great epics, sung, alluded to, and represented in paintings. They were something that no Etruscan could match. Both their power and beauty and their heroic and aristocratic terminology transcended the Greek sphere and were adopted by non-Greeks as well. The function of Greek myths of origins in their "scientific" guise in the Classical period was fulfilled in the early Archaic by the great epics. This may just be a case where, following Anthony Smith, "the fuller *ethnie* set the pace for the empty ones."[87] This is why Odysseus was brought to Italy, whether as progenitor (Hesiod) or, according to one of the *Odyssey* sequels, during his second travels after the first return. The Etruscans, a "people" being formed at the time of the encounter with Greek and Phoenician civilizations (some would see here a causal relationship), were probably also forming some ideas of who they were. It was probably in such contexts that they adopted the story of Utuse, Odysseus.[88]

Something similar to what later happened to the Romans apparently took place among the Etruscans. Since Rome was in the Etruscan orbit until the end of the sixth century, Greeks, who since Hesiod had considered Odysseus the progenitor of both the Latins and the Etruscans, extended the story and applied it specifically to Rome (see chap. 6). Erich Gruen suggests that the Romans adopted the Greek myth of Trojan origins because thus they could at once "belong" and remain distinct from "Greeks."[89] The suggestion is convincing but does not go far enough in the direction of understanding what specifically Romans were reacting to. I shall later explore the possibility of whether the later Roman insistence that Aeneas alone was

86. See chap. 6 with n. 12.

87. Smith 1986: 178 with Appadurai 1981.

88. Ridgway (1992: 138), citing Coldstream's idea that Greeks gave Cyprus in the late eighth century the "greatest gift" in the form of the Homeric epics, goes on to say that the Euboians had done the same for the Etruscans: "Could not the Nestor kotyle, the Ajax and Achilles seal impression and aspects of the burial rite at Pithekoussai have equally momentous implications for the circulation of the Homeric poems in the West?"

89. Gruen 1992: 21.

their founder was a reaction against the Etruscan-Greek version of their foundation, combining, as we shall see, Odysseus and Aeneas in Italy.

The origins *mentalité* of nations (if I may risk a generalization) is curiously susceptible to adopting the stranger's opinion. Perhaps this is no different from snobbery—one of the most underrated forces in social history. In a sense, this is a recognition of some inferiority; however, by appropriating the stranger's myth or cultural achievements one can stop resisting them and become stronger with them. Some Jews in antiquity claimed that the Greek philosophers had stolen their wisdom from the Hebrew sages, just as certain African Americans claim that the wisdom of the "West" is of African origin.[90] For both this is basically a way to accept and integrate the culture of the Other. The myth of the colonizer may be adopted by the colonized but with a twist. The Romans seem to have adopted an Etruscanized Greek myth but carved their independent niche by isolating Aeneas from Odysseus.

The adoption by Etruscans and Romans of the mythical foundation discourse of the Greeks is not unparalleled. In general, as Juliette de la Genière has observed,[91] the level and degree of acculturation often depend on the readiness of the particular culture. The Hellenization of the Sikels in Sicily, for example, eventually led to the Greek-style national rebellion of Douketios.[92] By contrast, the Messapians seem to have resisted Greek (especially Tarentine) political influences, although they did not reject Greek material culture. The Segestans (Elymians) in Sicily provide a Roman-type example: they were considered "Trojans" and adopted the outward forms of a Greek city (including Segesta's famous unfinished temple) but remained "barbarians" and fierce opponents of Greek attempts to colonize or expand.[93] The Elymians also approximate the model of non-Greek civilization that resists the first onslaught of Greek colonization but adopts the Greek origins discourse. Just as Odysseus "founded" Rome, other Nostoi were the founders of mostly non-Greek cities. Epeios, Diomedes, and Philoktetes, for example, were associated with cities such as Lagaria, Chōne, Makalla, Krimissa, and Segesta (see chaps. 7 and 8). Their *nostoi* are obviously non-Homeric, since Nestor says that these heroes reached Thessaly and Argos.[94] The adaptation of such non-Greek Nostos foundation stories to sites that existed before the Greek colonial foundations disproves Jean Bérard's thesis that such associations reflect old Mycenaean memories.[95] The association with the Nostoi

90. E.g., James 1992 (1954).
91. La Genière 1978.
92. Adamesteanu 1962; Malkin 1987a: 85–86.
93. Lacroix 1965b: 55–72; Mele 1993–94.
94. *Od.* 3.181, 190.
95. La Genière 1978: 274.

ennobled non-Greeks on Greek terms without involving submission to Greek political rule and may have smoothed the way for political alliances.

Paradoxically, because Greek colonies such as Kroton or Kyme had identifiable and historical founders with secure and recognized dates, non-Greeks could claim a "Greek" antiquity greater than the Greeks themselves. As we shall see, Philoktetes or Diomedes belonged to the age of the Trojan War; Myskellos of Achaian Rhypai, who founded Kroton toward the end of the eighth century, was obviously of lesser antiquity and heroic status. Odysseus, although not a founder, had a presence in Italy and an association with the Etruscans, the Latins, and the hinterland peoples "earlier" than the colonists of Kyme. One may wonder whether such non-Greek appropriations of the Greek foundation discourse did not provoke the Greek colonies themselves to invent parallel, "ancient" founders. Kroton worshipped also an "ancient" eponymous hero, a companion of Herakles; Taras turned to another eponym, in addition to Phalanthos. I once suggested that such eponyms were a response to the challenge of the greater antiquity of the mother cities in Greece; I should now add that the non-Greek neighbors of Greek colonies may have provided the immediate stimulus. Both Greeks and non-Greeks entered, therefore, a kind of competition for ennobled Greek origins, especially within the Trojan discourse.

A significant hiatus separates the early and the later, mostly late-Classical and Hellenistic sources that link Odysseus with the Etruscans. When we hear of him again, Odysseus is no longer primarily connected with Campania, viewed through the eyes of Greek protocolonists as progenitor of the Tyrsenoi, although he may still be vaguely linked with Pithekoussai[96] or portrayed as having landed in Kyme after his stay with Circe.[97] Odysseus became Etruscanized, connected with particular Etruscan sites and accorded a founder-hero worship (on a Greek model) as the founder of Etruscan Cortona.

We have seen that the Etruscan Utuse (Odysseus) appears, without a clear context, in inscriptions from the fifth century and that Odysseus's story, observed in vase paintings, must have been familiar to Etruscans as early as the mid-seventh. Aside from visual representations, the first source to provide an Etruscan *story* is Theopompus.[98] Playing on the theme of the unfaithful Penelope, who causes Odysseus to depart a second time from Ithaca, Theopompus has Odysseus sail to Tyrrhenia and found the city of Gortynaia

96. Lycoph. *Alex.* 688–93 with schol. on 688.
97. Ps.-Scymn. 225–41.
98. *FGrH* 115 F 354 = schol. Lycoph. *Alex.* 806.

(Cortona, above Lake Trasimene). Odysseus dies there and is worshipped by its people. This seems compatible with the fragment of the Aristotelian *Constitution of the Ithakesians*,[99] discussed above (chap. 4), where Odysseus departs for Italy after his first return to Ithaca. Another fragment,[100] in a context of epitaphs for the heroes who participated in the Trojan War, preserves two epigrams about Odysseus's burial in Tyrrhenia. Lycophron, who knows the Italian-Etruscan stories of Odysseus but conflates various traditions, follows the *Telegony* in having his Odysseus die in Ithaca at the hands of Telegonos, his son by Circe. However, Odysseus's ashes seem to reach Gortynaia: "Perge, hill of the Tyrrhenians (Monte Perge, near Cortona?), shall receive his ashes in the land of Gortyn."[101]

The most important point here is the clear implication of cult. The moment our literary source refers to cult practices it ceases to be strictly literary. In other words, we must judge it according to different criteria from those applied to ancient erudites referring to each other. Cult points to a living reality, even though this reality remains for the most part unknown and elusive. We have no idea when the cult to Odysseus began, nor can we be clear about its function. In Epirus and Aitolia Odysseus's "tomb" served prophetic and oracular purposes. By contrast, in Etruscan Cortona he seems to have functioned in terms of a Greek colonizing model of a city founder. The cult, quite obviously, was a founder's cult, providing a symbol of common orientation, collective identity, and a perception of "beginning."[102] In Italy and Sicily in particular founder's cults had special prominence and seem to have provided the conceptual framework for imitation by other peoples, such as the Etruscans and, later, the Romans. By the fifth century B.C. it seems that identity and ethnic origins could be perceived mostly in Greek terms.

By the Hellenistic era some traditions seem to have enlarged the role of Odysseus from the founder of Cortona to a leader of the entire Etruscan migration and settlement in Italy. Possibly Timaios and certainly Lycophron speak of Odysseus in such terms. Lycophron probably draws on one of the contradictory traditions about the Etruscans' origins to bring in Odysseus. According to Hellanikos[103] a certain Nanas led Pelasgians from Thessaly, sailed to the River Spines (at the head of the Adriatic), and went on to take Kroton (probably Etruscan Cortona). Probably because Odysseus was independently identified as a founder of Cortona and as a cult recipient there, Lycophron identifies this Nanas with *nanos,* "short in stature," namely,

---

99. Arist. frg. 507 (Rose) = Plut. *Quaest. Graec.* 14.
100. Ps.-Aristotle *Peplos:* 640 Rose 12, 13.
101. Lycoph. *Alex.* 795, 807; Phillips 1953: 65.
102. Malkin 1987a: pt. 2.
103. *FGrH* 4 F 323a; Theopompos *FGrH* 115 F 354.

Odysseus.[104] The "*nanos* who in his wanderings explored all the nooks of sea and land," says Lycophron, would join Aeneas with a friendly army.[105]

In the later period, when Hellenizing influences were powerful and ubiquitous, a direct Etruscan disposition for accepting Odysseus is evident. Although coming to us from Greek sources, it no doubt built on the early Greek association of Odysseus with the Etruscans but has changed character, appearing more "indigenized": Odysseus is not just a progenitor and his sons no longer merely rule the Tyrsenoi. The indigenization follows—how not?—a Greek frame of reference. Now, in very real Greek terms of colonization, Odysseus becomes an Etruscan founder and the recipient of a founder's cult.

CONCLUSION

Facing the Bay of Naples and the Campanian mainland, Pithekoussai sets the scene for one of the first voices to be heard from mid-eighth-century Greece. This voice, with its sad burial context and merry symposiac verses, belongs to the first generation of the earliest Greek settlers in the western Mediterranean. The inscription on the Nestor cup testifies to the lifestyle of the Euboians on Pithekoussai and to what they had in their heads: a famous figure from the *Iliad* (Nestor) and the detailed description of his cup. A scene of Achilles carrying the body of Ajax further indicates familiarity with the subject matter not just of the *Iliad* but also of the Trojan Cycle. Odysseus, a prominent figure in the *Iliad*, the *Odyssey*, and the Cycle, was almost certainly familiar as well.

It is perhaps significant that for generations to follow the Nestor cup had particular significance in Campania. Euboian Pithekoussai and Kyme on the Campanian mainland, a frontier zone where both Greeks and Etruscans were maritime newcomers, also set the context for Greek-Etruscan acculturation. This is probably where the Euboian alphabet, the *symposion*, and Greek myths were transmitted. The archaeological context of contacts between Euboians and Etruscans, the awareness of the Homeric epics among the Euboians, the Etruscan adoption of the Euboian alphabet and particularly of the Euboian form of the name of Odysseus, Odyssean motifs in art among the Etruscans, and the explicit lines of Hesiod about Odysseus as the father of those who ruled the Etruscans have opened the way for the discussion of Odysseus and the Etruscans.

Since the first half of the eighth century Greek influence on the emerging Etruscan civilization was widely felt, although one may no longer view

104. Lycoph. *Alex.* 1242–45. On Odysseus's being short, see *Il.* 3.193; *Od.* 6.230.
105. Phillips 1953: 60–61; Horsfall 1979b: 381; Dury-Moyaers 1981: 65–72; Poucet 1983: 148–49.

influences on Etruscans as purely Greek or one-sided; Phoenicians played their role, and the Etruscans themselves ventured out. Greek culture penetrated in a variety of ways, including the import of material goods, local manufacture and imitation, individual immigration of Greek artisans (Aristonothos) and aristocrats (Demaratos), direct contact with the colonies of Pithekoussai and Kyme, guest-friendship relationships and similar symposiac lifestyles, and alphabet learning. The Etruscans seem to have shared with the Greeks aspects of 'Homeric society" that may have included *nostoi,* as they do in the *Odyssey.*

I have suggested that the "colonial" situation in Campania, common to both Greeks and Etruscans, induced the borrowing by Etruscans of Greek myths as meaningful and applicable. The application was not of a territorial charter myth, because at the time neither Greeks nor Etruscans posed a territorial threat to the local populations or to each other. Greek mythological discourse mediated and articulated not the annexation of lands but the ethnographic identities of the peoples encountered.

We find no Etruscan counterpart of Odysseus/Utuse among the Greeks. It appears that the Greeks were not prone to adopting myths of the Etruscans (or Opicians) as "explanations" of what they were finding in Italy. In considering why the Etruscans were susceptible, I have extended Bickerman's hypothesis about the Classical period, when Greek ethnographic myths had the authority of scientific inquiry, to the Archaic period, substituting "Homer" for "scientific authority." The Homeric epics not only were attractive aesthetically and socially but provided a "full past." In Appadurai's terms, the Etruscans came to share Greek conventions about the sources, origins, or guarantor of pasts and "how closely any past must be interdependent with other 'pasts' to ensure minimal credibility."[106] It was the *nostos* frame of reference, with its genealogical flexibility and heroic ethos, that provided such interdependence. Whether the Etruscans accepted Odysseus as their progenitor so early is open to question, but absorb him they certainly did, perhaps in conjunction with the Trojan Nostos Aeneas, who was said to have come with Odysseus to Italy.

The Etruscans of later periods seem to have fully integrated the myth of *their* Odysseus/Utuse: the hero became more Etruscanized, connected with particular Etruscan sites, and accorded a founder-hero worship as the founder of Etruscan Cortona. In some sources, apparently smoothing out the contradiction between the autochthonous image of the Etruscans and the sixth-century Greek idea that they had immigrated from Lydia, Odysseus becomes a leader of the entire Etruscan migration to Italy.

106. Appadurai 1981: 203. See also Introduction.

As we will see in the next chapter, the Romans too and many others in Italy illustrate the tendency of ethnic groups to explain their "imagined community" in terms of foreigners' opinions about their origins. This kind of explanation allowed non-Greeks to join and, paradoxically, sometimes claim a "Greek" antiquity greater than that of most Greek colonies in Italy. By contrast, by choosing the "Trojan side," later Romans could both join and distinguish themselves from Greeks.

SIX

Odysseus and Italy:
A Peripheral Vision of Ethnicity

The Etruscans have just provided us with the first Italic context of an Odyssean articulation of ethnic identity. The source that spells out that articulation is a passage in Hesiod's *Theogony* in which Odysseus appears as the progenitor of other Italic peoples, notably the Latins. A concept that I shall call peripheral ethnicity will emerge that has direct implications for the role of Odysseus in the foundation of Rome.

The passage in question will be seen as an element of the earliest pattern of the application of Nostos genealogies to non-Greek peoples, probably earlier than such peoples were ready to adopt them for themselves. Without mentioning either cities or Greeks, the verses seem to describe a non-Greek, protocolonist horizon that is probably a reflection of Euboian images current a generation or two before Hesiod. The poet, active when Euboian colonial activity was at its height, employs this *proto*colonial perspective because he is speaking of "ancient times." The main figure is thus the protocolonist hero Odysseus, who like Herakles explores and leaves descendants behind but does not settle. His Italian sons, Latinos and Agrios, eponyms of the Latins and the wild hinterland peoples, are characteristic of a maritime perspective (sea to shore) of the protocolonial explorers and the Euboian colonies of Pithekoussai and Kyme, filtered to Hesiod through the Euboians of Chalkis.

In terms of specific ethnicity, it is crucial that these verses do not refer to the ethnography of direct contact—to the peoples living immediately across from Pithekoussai and Kyme on the mainland. These peoples, among them the aristocratic elites of the Etruscans or the local elites of places such as Pontecagnano, "immediately" (between 770 and 700?) became too familiar (and therefore distinct and differentiated) for a general appellation. Rather, the Latins and the Agrioi ("Wild Ones") denote a peripheral vision, a glimpse of what lies beyond the range of direct contact through commerce and colonization. Thus the Latins, more distant and amorphous, could be given a general name and an eponymous ancestor, Latinos.

This is not exceptional. As we have seen, it was the ethnographic periphery rather than the peoples with whom Greek colonists came into immediate contact that usually acquired a Nostos genealogy. Odysseus in particular was well suited to the Beyond and the "wild." This kind of Nostos genealogical ethnography should be distinguished from other kinds of Grecocentric ethnographies: first, it does not belong to the genre of making foreign peoples originally "Cretans," "Arkadians," "Pelasgians," and so on;[1] second, it is very different from attempts by western Greeks, mostly in the later Classical period, to attach Nostos origins to *themselves*. Rather, what we have here is the view from Greece itself (in the modern, geographical sense), apparently from Euboia, based on the reports of aristocratic kinsmen from Pithekoussai and Kyme. Hesiod would certainly have heard such reports at Chalkis, where he sang at the funeral of Amphidamas.

Perhaps it is because the Greek pattern was consistent in providing non-Greeks with whom contacts were *less close* a Nostos genealogy that, paradoxically, such genealogies became popular particularly among non-Greek peoples. Because they did not come under direct control of the various Greek colonies, the extension to them of Greek "ethnic" myths was apparently not, at least during the first generations of colonization, interpreted as threatening territorial expansion. Jean Bérard, arguing for reflections of a Mycenaean past, has observed that most *nostoi* are not associated with the centers of Greek colonies. The itineraries of Diomedes (see chap. 8), for example, are mostly associated with the realms of the "immediate beyond."[2] Juliette de la Genière makes an excellent point by emphasizing the non-Greek aspect of Nostos identifications and claims that, in contrast with other regions, where evidence for contacts during the Mycenaean period is quite clear (e.g., at Scoglio del Tonno near Taras or at Sicilian Thapsos), the regions associated with Greek Nostoi lack precisely such evidence. Thus the myths cannot be taken as dim reflections of Mycenaean contacts but instead constitute a phenomenon of Archaic colonization.[3]

---

1. Bérard 1957: chap. 11; Briquel 1984: Poucet 1985: 187.

2. See Bérard 1957: 368–74; Van Compernolle 1988: 111–13; Braccesi 1988: 137–38.

3. La Genière 1978. It has also been suggested (Terrosi Zanco 1965: Van Compernolle 1988: 115–22) that the Greek *nostoi* reflect immigrations of Balkanic peoples into, especially, Apulia. The idea is not unattractive, as it attributes to non-Greek immigrants a need similar to that of Greeks: to articulate their presence in a new land. That this should have happened—or at least come down to us—via Greek myths may constitute a fascinating example of appropriation. However, this must remain a theory, since we do not have substantial evidence for those migrations en masse.

HESIOD AND ODYSSEUS

The closing verses of Hesiod's *Theogony* read as follows:

And Circe the daughter of Helios, Hyperion's son, loved steadfast Odysseus and bare Agrios and Latinos who was faultless and strong; also she brought forth Telegonos by the will of golden Aphrodite. And they ruled over the famous Tyrsenoi, very far off in the recess of the holy islands. And the bright goddess Calypso was joined to Odysseus in sweet love, and bare him Nausithoös and Nausinoös.[4]

The authenticity of these verses has been much debated, and a negative verdict has been pronounced by Hesiod's most prominent commentator, Martin West, who relegates them to the Hesiodic tradition of the *Catalogue of Women* of the mid-sixth century. West's opinion has proven very influential,[5] and if it is accepted we may not regard the verses as representing a Greek view of about 700. His case rests particularly on historical considerations external to the text. By removing these I wish to contribute, beyond providing greater confidence in the text as such, to an insight into a proto- and early colonial outlook on the *nostoi*, colonization, and ethnicity. The debate, I am sure, will continue, with varying views concerning also matters of language. For the moment, I shall concentrate on West's case, which relies on a set of assumptions concerning what it was impossible or unlikely for Hesiod to have known, either personally or in terms of his contemporary historical context.

Written in the first person and abounding in biographical details, Hesiod's work is considered by many as truly personal. Several scholars suggest, however, that Hesiod is a poetic *persona*, representing poetic voices perhaps belonging to a genre of "wisdom literature"—that the "autobiography," including a brother (Perses) and a fictional father who immigrated from Kyme to Askra, is all a mask, an invention intended to enhance points made in the poems. Richard Martin, for example, accepting that the ancient "life" tradition of Hesiod the poet is "already operative in the *Works and Days*," considers the position of the "immigrant" a device to enhance the observation through the eyes of the *metanastēs* (wanderer, migrant).[6] There are many problems with the persona theory beyond its irrefutability. The biographical details seem irregular and unconventional: Hesiod addresses a brother, the father does not play a conventional wisdom-literature role, the local Boiotian aspect is stressed, the specific maritime distance to Chalkis is spelled out, and so on. Although there seem to be topoi and parallels, the

4. Hes. *Theog.* 1011–18, Evelyn-White, LCL.
5. See Wiseman 1995: 46.
6. Martin 1992a: 14; cf. Griffith 1983.

overlap is often only general and motif-oriented. Such topoi are known to originate in real persons as well.

Without pretending to settle the issue, I want to point out that even a mask can solidify, sometimes as a writer stamps his personality on the persona in order to create great poetry, perhaps adding his own biographical details to "stock" wisdom poems. If this is what happened, it seems to have taken place rather early, as the *Works and Days* seem to indicate. If not, we could still regard the *Theogony* historically as representing an "authentic" mask of its own period. Moreover, if we accept Richard Janko's language dating of the *Theogony* and the *Works and Days* the context is, once again, around 700. I shall therefore continue to call the poet "Hesiod." For my purposes, even if he was, say, a poet masquerading as someone who had won a poetry prize in Chalkis (as Hesiod says he did), this is unlikely to have happened (or to have been invented) after the decline of the Euboian city in the seventh century.

What did (or could) Hesiod know of the west? What could he have learned about it? Unlike Archilochos, he represents himself as having had no first-hand experience. Archilochos, that true-to-life hardy mid-seventh-century poet-soldier and colonist, roamed the Mediterranean from Siris to Thrace and settled in Thasos. Hesiod was the opposite of the voyager and feared the sea; once in his life he made a sea voyage of some sixty-five meters, crossing the narrow channel separating Chalkis in Euboia from Aulis in Boiotia. But this does not mean that he could not exhibit knowledge about the sea and seafaring—which must imply, for his audience as well, some knowledge about the places people would sail to. Throughout the long passage in the *Works and Days* that deals with the sea, seamanship, and maritime trade, the poetry is very knowledgeable. The passage shows the poet sensitive and sensibly aware of the implied irony in the mention of the "daring" crossing of the Euboia channel. Moreover, Ralph Rosen has beautifully shown that the sailing passage, shifting between the literal and the metaphorical, is also a metaphor for poetic prowess and motivation.[7] This capacity for a metaphoric level obviously enhances the informed maritime aspect of the passage with which we are concerned here.

The sailing passage is of the utmost importance in providing us a feel for the significance of the sea for late-eighth-century Greeks. It is full of references to danger, both to property and to life. Hesiod is not exceptional: "For I say that there is no other thing that is worse than the sea is for breaking a man," says Alkinoös in the *Odyssey*[8]—this from the king of the best mariners. Archilochos too reveals the same sad, almost mournful attitude,

7. Rosen 1990.   8. *Od.* 8.138–39.

speaking, for example, of the "painful gifts to Poseidon," apparently the bodies of his dead companions drowned by storm. Personal attitudes (and metaphoric uses) aside, Hesiod, with remarkable condensed artistry, makes the sea a dominant motif. He manages to speak of his father's migration and his own passage to Euboian Chalkis and to offer an abundance of practical and obviously knowledgeable advice about seamanship and trade.

Hesiod's father is represented as an experienced sailor "who used to sail on shipboard because he lacked sufficient livelihood." Hesiod's own knowledge of seamanship, albeit theoretical, therefore has a good explanation.[9] In implied contrast to himself, his father "came to this very place crossing over a great stretch of sea: he left Aeolian Kyme." In other words, both the father's livelihood and the personal voyage overseas made Hesiod well aware of the sea, its routes, and what seamanship implied. Living a short distance from Euboia, home of the two major colonizing Greek states of the eighth century, Hesiod could have been well informed also by his neighbors. Even if only a persona, the "poet" would have belonged to a world in which Euboian information concerning maritime affairs and distant lands would have been proverbial. It is wrong, therefore, to consider the poet parochial, as West does when he attributes to Hesiod (in his opinion a real person) the outlook of a modern Greek villager who cannot give the English tourist directions to a place fifty miles away.

Hesiod was a poet famous for his métier and the winner of a major prize in the funeral competition of a Euboian noble. He had "crossed over to Chalkis, to the games of the wise Amphidamas, where the sons of the great-hearted hero proclaimed and appointed prizes."[10] His prize was the first, a tripod, which he dedicated to the Muses at Mt. Helikon upon his return. It is inconceivable that such a poet would have refrained from talking to his Euboian noble hosts. If Amphidamas is the Euboian who died in the Lelantine War, ca. 705 B.C.,[11] then our context becomes even more precise. These Euboian nobles belonged to a particular milieu, one that, for about a generation, buried its dead in princely tombs with ritual reminiscent of Homeric descriptions of the funeral of Patroklos. The same aristocrats, about the same time and possibly even from the same families, were similarly buried in Italian Kyme (a colony of Chalkis).[12] As we have seen (chap. 5), they also knew enough Homer to allude in the Pithekoussai burial, to the cup of Nestor.

These Euboians of Kyme and Pithekoussai had also introduced elements of their culture—vases and luxury ornaments, gift exchange, the *symposion*,

9. Hes. *Op.* 634; cf. West 1978: ad loc.
10. Hes. *Op.* 654, Evelyn-White, LCL.
11. Plut. *Mor.* 153F.
12. Coldstream 1977: 349–52; Malkin 1987a: 263–66.

Homeric motifs, the alphabet, and stories—to the Etruscans. By 700 these contacts had been developing for at least seventy years. Are we to believe that a poet active around this time was ignorant of all this? Hesiod knew nothing of the Etruscans, claims West, because the Greeks felt their impact only in the sixth century. This is patently wrong. Moreover, Hesiod's idea of the Etruscans seems earlier than other Greek notions. By the sixth century an alternative "Lydian" model for the origins of the Etruscans had emerged that was diametrically opposed to the notion expressed in the *Theogony* (another model mentioned by Dionysius of Halicarnassus, that the Etruscans were autochthonous, apparently did not develop before the fourth century). It was the Lydian model, which probably emerged before the Persian conquest of Lydia in the mid-sixth century, that eventually took hold.[13] Thus the sixth-century "Hesiodic" poet postulated by West would have been contemporary with the Lydian model. It seems, therefore, that the verses in question precede these alternative explanations of the origins of the Etruscans and must not be summarily detached from the *Theogony*.[14]

Hesiod, in sum, is represented as familiar with the sea and the implications of seamanship and in contact with some Euboian aristocratic families. Such a poet must have heard of Pithekoussai and Kyme and of the various local elites with whom their colonists came into contact, especially the Etruscans. His vision of Italy passes through (apparently Euboian) filters of time (the geography is that of protocolonization, not that of contemporary Euboian cities), his own distance from Italy, the distance of the peoples described from the Euboian centers of colonization (Etruria and Latium as peripheral to Campania), and oral reports. No accuracy needs to be expected in all this. What matters is the poet's articulation of ethnicity through Odysseus.

Latinos is almost unanimously identified in modern scholarship as the ancestor of the Latins.[15] He may have had an independent cultic existence

13. Hdt. 1.94; cf. Tac. Ann. 4.55. See Asheri 1988 on Hdt. 1.94 arguing against Xanthos the Lydian as the source (contra Scullard 1966: esp. 227). For a full discussion see Briquel 1991b: 25–26, 31–32; cf. Briquel 1993 and 1984 on the Pelasgian construct of ethnicity.

14. Wiseman 1995: 46 adopts West's view but still bases an argument on the geographical ignorance of a "Boeotian poet," which seems strange if the Boeotian Hesiod is denied a role altogether.

15. West 1966: ad loc.; cf. Gruen 1992: 10. Aristotle, in the fourth century, wrote of Greek (Achaian) Nostoi who landed in "Latinion" in the country of the Opicians and settled there because their ships had been burned. Dion Hal. 1.72.3–4. In the Hellenistic era this Greek-Latin aspect made Rome a πόλις Ἑλληνίς. Heraclid. *Pont.* ap. Plut. Camillus 22.2.

aside from the erudite-eponymous aspect that renders him suspect a priori.[16] The term "Latin" is first attested, independently, in an Etruscan graffito (*"mi tites latines"*) on a small amphora found in a tomb of the end of the seventh century at Veii and Greek pottery of the mid-eighth century is found in Latium.[17] An as yet unpublished grave stele of ca. 600–550 in the J. Paul Getty Museum, inscribed in an alphabet consistent with that of Euboian colonies in the west, bears the name "Latinos."[18] In late traditions "Latinus" retains some Greek component: he is variously referred to as a son of Telemachos, of Odysseus and Circe, or of Herakles.[19]

Latinos and Agrios go together with the Tyrsenoi (= Etruscans) because, I think, they were viewed from a particularly Euboian "ethnic" perspective. By emphasizing ethnography and *origines gentium* rather than cities or locations, it seems that all "Italic" peoples, Latins included, were subsumed under the general name "Tyrsenoi," probably introduced in the course of contacts between Greeks and Etruscans during the first half of the eighth century. We are told independently that this was the case.[20] Hesiod therefore did not confuse the more powerful Etruscans with the Latins[21] but used "Tyrsenoi" as a general term for all the Italic peoples encountered. This is also the reason the verses do not provide an Etruscan genealogy: the term "Etruscans" was a general one, comprehending both Etruscans and others.

It is the maritime perspective of Italy, as it was reiterated for Hesiod in mainland Greece, that also explains the "holy islands": "And they ruled over the famous Tyrsenoi, very far off in the recess of the holy islands." West and others are correct that Hesiod's geography is fuzzy here. It is also true that mainlands may appear at first sight to be islands, but this explains very little. The maritime perspective in the world of protocolonization and settlement means, quite simply, that one sees the mainland and its inhabitants from the sea. The promontory of "Circe's mountain" (Mt. Circeo) may have seemed or, in fact, been an island,[22] which would savage some of Hesiod's geogra-

16. Grandazzi (1988) argues for an independent Latinos cult in the centers of the Latin League, Lanuvium and Alba.

17. Gianni 1996: 133 n. 113; cf. Palm 1952: 57, no. 8 pl. 5; Dury Moyaers 1981: 42. "Latines" is taken to be the ethnic designation of a foreigner living at Veii: Colonna (1974: 316) notes that from the second half of the sixth century "Latinie" as an ethnic is well attested in Etruria.

18. Jameson and Malkin n.d.

19. Plut. *Rom.* 2.3; Serv. ad *Aen.* 1.273; Hyg. *Fab.* 127; Dion. Hal. 1.44.3; Ps.-Scylax 8; cf. Gruen 1992: 16.

20. Dion. Hal. 1.29.1–2; cf. Gruen 1992: 9; Mastrocinque 1993: 176 with n. 727.

21. Thus Alföldi 1965: 189.

22. See Theophr. *Hist. Pl.* 5.8.3, who says that this is the belief of the natives, who point out the grave of Odysseus's companion, Elpenor; cf. Pliny *HN* 15.119; Cic. *Nat. D.*

phy here. But even if this was not the case, what seems to matter is that Hesiod projects an ideal situation of "colonizing sites" from a Greek point of view. It is no accident that offshore islands and promontories were also the recurrent pattern in Greek colonization.[23] The island just off the land of the Cyclopes in the *Odyssey*, a potential colonizing site, is similarly in an ideal (Greek) position, since the Cyclopes have no ships. Hesiod should not be expected to provide a portolan of Italy; rather, he expresses poetically the Greek notion of rule from the safety of an island (hence the expression "in the recess," namely, the "undisturbed part").[24] Hesiod does not say that the Tyrsenoi inhabited the islands; instead, he says only that from those islands Latinos and Agrios ruled the Tyrsenoi. By analogy, one could say "and the British ruled the Chinese from the island (Hong Kong)" without implying that all Chinese were island dwellers or that the rule was effective or far-reaching.

"Agrios" supports this approach. No one knows exactly what is meant by the "Wild One." Various theories have been put forward, mostly in terms of syncretism or translation of local Latin divinities such as Faunus, Silvanus, or the king of Alba Longa, Silvius.[25] Such theories are attractive and perhaps plausible, but I wonder whether there might not be another explanation. Agrios, obviously meant as an eponymous ethnic appellation, may be just what the name implies: the "wild people,"[26] the kind of people Odysseus is afraid of encountering in a foreign land.[27] Consider, for example, the name of the Greek colony Thera; in spite of attempts to call it Kalliste, "the most beautiful," it was its forbidding aspect as a wild place, where wild animals roamed, that eventually won out as its name. Similarly, we find names given to colonizing sites in terms of their "emptiness" of human habitation: Monkey Island, Snake Island, Deer Island, Quail Island, Bear Island, and so on.[28]

3.48; cf. *CIL* 10.6422; Ps.-Scylax 8; Arist. *Vent.* 973b; Ps.-Arist. *Mir. Ausc.* 78, 835b33; Ps.-Scymn. 224–25; Strabo 5.232; Varro ap. Serv. ad *Aen.* 3.386.

23. Winter 1971: 12–29.

24. West 1966: ad loc.

25. Altheim 1938: 214–16; Alföldi 1965: 238–39; 1979: 24 ff.; cf. Durante 1951: 216; Dury-Moyaers 1981: 43–44, n. 58, n. 59; Mastrocinque 1993: 179; Wiseman 1995: 47–48. Hartmann 1917 arbitrarily links Agrios with Thrace. Wilamowitz-Möllendorf 1899: 610–11 has the right hunch about "Der wilde Agrios."

26. Cf. Antonetti 1987: 67.

27. *Od.* 6.121, where ὑβρίσται and ἄγριοι are contrasted, as often, with δίκαιοι and θεουδεῖς. In *Od.* 1.198–99, for example, Athena mentions the possibility that Odysseus is captive among "rough and savage men" (*chalepoi, agrioi*) and in 9.215 Odysseus envisages the possibility of meeting an *agrios;* cf. 13.201–2 with Vidal-Naquet 1986: 33 n. 40.

28. I have examined this elsewhere: Malkin 1994a: 96–97.

Who were the "Wild Ones"? Ethnographically, I suspect that what lies behind "Agrios" is the "badlands" of the hinterland peoples. We are concerned, again, with a maritime and settlement perspective: first there were the Latins, and farther inland, say, along the Tiber, one might encounter the "Wild Ones." "Latins" (a real ethnic name in contrast to the descriptive "Agrioi") were better known: they lived north of the area of close contact, Campania, and probably mediated the commerce into the hinterland from the mouth of the Tiber (the midpoint between Pithekoussai and Elba, the source of its iron ore). Perhaps this is hinted at by the words "Latinos who was faultless and strong," leaving Agrios unqualified. Throughout the history of the Greek cities in Italy and that of early Rome, raiding and invasion by the mountain (Apennines) peoples (e.g., the "Samnites") constituted a serious problem, and by the fifth century some of the Greek cities, such as Kyme, had ceased being Greek. There is no hard evidence for this interpretation of Agrios as the eponym of these frightening, "badlands" peoples, but it seems the most likely explanation in that it adopts a Greek perspective and conforms to the pattern of place-naming in the world of Greek colonization. To claim, rather, that Agrios is a "translation" of a local name or term is far-fetched. That a Roman poet (Ovid) of the first century used an *agr-* compound to "translate" Faunus (*agrestis*),[29] for example, is no evidence; if anything, this would have been a Roman adjusting to Greek lore and not reflecting a translation of Silvanus/Faunus/Silvius by Hesiod several centuries earlier.[30] In this way we should also interpret what Nonnus says about Faunus's being the son of Circe.[31]

The point is that Greek colonists did not usually translate local names but adopted or rejected them as the case might be. Abdera, for example, seems to have retained its Semitic root (which has to do with "servant" or "slave," ABD) rather than being translated into "Douleia."[32] The Greek colony of Lindioi in Sicily failed to retain its new name and came to be known as Gela, after the local river. Later aitiological stories connected the name with the Greek verb *gelao,* "to laugh," which only illustrates that rather than being changed or translated place-names had explanations invented for them in Greek.[33] A more fruitful approach, which takes into account the ideas of Altheim and others about the similarity in meaning between Greek and Latin

29. Ov. *Fasti* 2.193, 3.315, with Altheim 1938: 214–16; Durante 1951; Alföldi 1965: 238–39; Cornell 1975: 31; Dury-Moyaers 1981: 43–44, n. 58, n. 59.

30. See West 1966: ad loc. for other "Latin" interpretations; cf. for another refutation Weinstock 1959: 170. For a similar view accepting Silvius = Agrios = king of Alba Longa as a non-Greek, local identification, see Mastrocinque 1993: 179.

31. Dionys. 12.328; cf. *Silvanus lar agrestis CIL* 6.646.

32. On Abdera's name, see Graham 1992: 44–45.

33. Thuc. 6.4.3; for discussion and references see Malkin 1987a: 52–54.

names but observes them from a different angle, is to ask how non-Greeks might have reacted when faced with Greek names and myths that perhaps evoked "similarities" in their own culture, a common pattern of syncretism.

Mastrocinque claims that Circe is the key to the Latins' attraction to the story of Odysseus.[34] She hardly has an independent existence in Greek mythology apart from Odysseus, and the mention of her, even when his name is missing, implies an association with the *Odyssey*. A mistress of transformation from human to animal and back, she assumed a special role in rituals associated with the deer/fawn and especially the wolf. The *lupi* (wolves) of ritual were connected with Circe, and the Luperci, naked wolves, evoked Odysseus's companions. The Lupercalia, a Latin festival, underwent "internal Hellenization" once the myth of Odysseus and Circe became familiar. We have evidence for its familiarity from vase paintings from the seventh century on, but it was probably circulating as early as the eighth. That, says Mastrocinque, is also the reason Circe is the mother of so many local figures. She is the wife of Picus;[35] in Virgil[36] Latinos is the son of Faunus and Marcia, who is identified with Circe,[37] Hyginus makes him son of Telegonos and Circe.[38] Perhaps this is why Telegonos, son of Odysseus and Circe, was also considered the founder of Tusculum,[39] whose denarii of the gens Mamilia are quite explicit.[40] The progenitor of the Marsi was also a son of Circe.[41] Circe is associated with ethnic territorial myths explaining why the Daunians are "no longer" at some place and are "now" elsewhere; Parthenius says that Kalchos, king of the Daunians, who was in love with Circe, was transformed into a pig after the arrival of Odysseus. His subjects were liberated on condition that they abandon the island of the sorceress.[42]

It is very difficult to assess Mastrocinque's thesis, since it relies on very late and disparate sources. Its attractiveness lies in identifying a non-Greek interest, a local chord struck by Greek myth. The myth of Romulus and Remus, the twins suckled by a wolf, would fall into this pattern of a wolf-associated Circe (and her consort, Odysseus). Hence, perhaps, the tenacity

34. Mastrocinque 1993.
35. Val. Fl. 7.232; Verg. *Aen.* 7.187–91; Ov. *Met.* 14.308–404.
36. Verg. *Aen.* 7.47.
37. Serv. ad *Aen.* 12.164; Lactant. *Div. Inst.* 1.21.23.
38. Hyg. *Fab.* 127.
39. Livy 1.49.9; Dion. Hal. 4.45; Festus *Gloss. Lat.* s.v. "Mamiliorum"; Hor. *Carm.* 3.29.8; Ov. *Fasti* 3.92.
40. Crawford no. 362; cf. Wiseman 1995: 50.
41. Pliny *HN* 7.15 = Solin. 2.27; 25.11; Gell. 16.11.
42. Parth. *Erot. Path.* 12.1–3.

with which Odysseus was associated with Rome's foundation even in the third century B.C., if that is the date assigned by Xenagoras, who says that Rhomos, Anteias, and Ardeias (all eponymous heroes of Latin cities: Rome, Antium, and Ardea) were the sons of Odysseus and Circe.[43]

If accepted as authentically Hesiod, the *Theogony* passage constitutes the earliest attestation of the localization of Circe in the west and specifically in Italy. In the *Odyssey* her island, Aiaia, where Eos (Dawn) has her home, has been argued to signify the far east. This is an inference from a description that seems to place Circe at the "edge of the earth." However, when Homer wishes to specify directions he does so straightforwardly. Circe is the sister of Aiëtes and the daughter of Helios, the sun. Since the sun rises in the east and sets in the west, distinguishing between the two becomes almost meaningless, since the sun exists in both and Dawn may set out from its opposite, the site of Night ("west").[44] Moreover, Aiëtes seems to have been located in the east (Colchis)[45] as early as Eumelos,[46] and if his sister lived "at the other end" this would place her in the west. Odysseus makes the ambiguity of Aiaia explicit in spite of the anachronistic application of "east" and "west" concepts: "we do not know where the darkness is nor the sunrise, nor where the Sun who shines upon people rises, nor where he sets."[47] The point here, however, is not the deliberately impossible geography of the *Odyssey* but how Hesiod and the Archaic poetic, "Hesiodizing" tradition represented it.

A fragment of the *Catalogue of Women* that comes from a scholion on the *Argonautica* reads:[48] "Apollonius, following Hesiod, says [φησί] that Circe came to the island over against Tyrrhenia on the chariot of the sun. And he called it [εἶπεν] Hesperian, because it lies toward the west." It is clear that the subject of "he says" is Apollonius; however, "and he called it Hesperian" may signify Hesiod,[49] a point that will prove important later. That "Circe came to the island over against Tyrrhenia on the chariot of the sun" is cer-

---

43. Xenagoras *FGrH* 240 F 29; cf. Cornell 1975: 20–21; Solmsen 1986: 98; Gruen 1992: 19; Wiseman 1995: 50.

44. Cf. *Od.* 10.190–92.

45. Meuli 1921: 112–14.

46. Davies *EGF* F 2; cf. Mimnermos West 1971 fr. 11–11a; Hdt. 1.2.7.

47. *Od.* 10.190–92. See also Heubeck in Heubeck and Hoekstra 1989 on *Odyssey* 10.135–39, where it is taken as self-evident that "east" is meant; the needless insistence on the terms "east" and "west" makes for a confused commentary on 10.190–92. Wiseman (1995: 45) rightly says that Homer "was probably concerned not so much to identify its location as to emphasize that Circe was the daughter of Helios, the Sun." He also suggests (1995: 47) that a local cult may be responsible for the "otherwise puzzling location of Circe in the west" (cf. Mastrocinque 1993, not cited by Wiseman).

48. *Catalogue of Women* 46 Merkelbach and West 1967 = Schol. Ap. Rhod. 3.311.

49. The tense may change (φησί-εἶπεν) simply because the scholiast has the text of Apollonius open before him: "he says" (i.e., the text says) and "he called" (i.e., Apollo-

tainly regarded by the scholiast as Hesiodic, and most would agree that this is perhaps the earliest explicit reference to Mt. Circeo.[50] It is also compatible with the *Theogony,* in which a situation across from the mainland seems to be envisioned. So too is the name "Tyrrhenia," the general name of the regions facing the Greeks on the Bay of Naples. It is probable that the verse in Ps.-Scymnus[51] in which Odysseus arrives at Kyme after the episode with Circe belongs to the same tradition. This is another corroboration of the "Etruscan" aspect of Odysseus, whose association with Circe is self-evident.

Against this background the various localizations of the Sirens in Campania (the Bay of Naples) become meaningful. The *Catalogue of Women*[52] names the island of the Sirens (who "charmed even the winds") "Anthemoissa" (flowery) and provides some individual names. Collectively the Sirens were identified on the Athenaion promontory, or Sirenoussa, opposite Capri, where there was a sanctuary to Athena established by Odysseus.[53] There was also a temple to the Sirens and some small deserted offshore islands called the "Sirens" (today I Galli).[54] Strabo[55] mentions a sanctuary of the Sirens that Odysseus founded on the "Sirens Promontory" (= Sorrento). Individual Sirens were identified with particular cities, notably Parthenope with Naples.[56] Keukosia was localized near Poseidonia.[57] In some accounts the Sirens episode is compared to passing through the clashing rocks; once Odysseus had passed by them, they committed suicide by throwing themselves into the Tyrrhenian Sea.[58]

Finally, the quoted passage, in which goddesses are having sons by mortal men, connects Odysseus with Scheria/Phaiakia and Italy. Calypso's sons seem particularly baffling: How can Odysseus be the father of Nausithoös, who in Homer is the leader of the Phaiakians, the founder of Scheria? In terms of the *Odyssey* this is, of course, impossible. Odysseus was hosted by

---

nius did, when he was writing it). In contrast, as, for example, the editor of the Budé series takes it, "he" may signify Hesiod, whom the scholiast is paraphrasing.

50. See n. 21; a temple of Circe at Mt. Circeo: according to *Mir. Ausc.* 78, poisonous herbs grow there.

51. Ps.-Scymn. 225–241.

52. *Catalogue of Women* 47 (= Schol. Ap. Rhod. 4.892).

53. Strabo 5.247 with *Mir. Ausc.* 103, which speaks of regular sacrifices there. Cf. Breglia 1996.

54. Strabo 5.247; cf. 1.22, 23, 6.258.

55. Strabo 5.247, 1.14. See also *Mir. Ausc.* 110; Ptolemy 3.1.79. Eust., *Od.* 1709; Verg. *Aen.* 864; Mela 2.4.9; Pliny *HN* 3.62; Solin. 2.22.

56. Strabo 1.26 with Raviola 1990.

57. See Lycoph. *Alex.* 722 with schol.; Strabo 6.252.

58. Apollod. *Epit.* 7.19; Hyg. *Fab.* 125, 141; Lycoph. *Alex.* 711–16.

Alkinoös, the king who ruled Scheria after Nausithoös. Although in the *Odyssey* he went to bed with both Calypso and Circe, Odysseus is not represented as having had children with either. These traditions, therefore, seem to be an elaboration on the *Odyssey* and must not be judged in its context. In a later tradition, for example, the Ausones of central Italy are made the descendants of Odysseus and Calypso.[59] Telegonos may be relevant here. It is curious how readily the line about Telegonos is rejected as spurious, in contrast to the others, whereas, in fact, it is this line that provides a context for the rest (in spite of the fact that it scans badly). All these children, not just Telegonos, seem to belong to the post-*Odyssey* tales about Odysseus. To reiterate: by "post-*Odyssey*" I mean not composed later but concerning what happened to Odysseus after his return to Ithaca. As we have seen, such tales are alluded to in the *Odyssey* itself and seem to be evidenced independently at least for the seventh century.

In the *Odyssey* Odysseus spends seven years on the island of Calypso, his last stop before he reaches Scheria. No six-year-old Nausithoös could have become Scheria's founder and died in time to be replaced by Alkinoös. However, mythic time operates differently from calendar time, especially outside the framework of the *Odyssey* (which is rather consistent in its internal time reckoning). A sense of "first and after," Odysseus with Calypso "first," the land of the Phaiakians "later," could be sufficient for allowing Nausithoös to be Scheria's founder. To such a development may also belong a fragment of Hellanikos that makes Phaiax, the eponymous hero of the Phaiakians, a son of Poseidon and Corcyra, the eponymous heroine of the island identified with Homeric Scheria.[60] Thus, in non-*Odyssey* versions there may have been another motive for the help so readily given Odysseus by the Phaiakians: he was the father of their founder (Phaiakia was a young state, even in the *Odyssey*). Nausithoös and Nausinoös may, however, be just names without committing one of them to Scheria's founder; ship-related names such as *Nausi*kaa or *Nausi*thoös are particularly apt for the Phaiakians.[61]

Thus the geography of western colonization becomes specific in translating the mythic itineraries of Odysseus into colonial topography. Both Circe and the Sirens seem to have been closely associated with the Bay of Naples, which also happens to be the area of the earliest Greek colonization (Pithekoussai, Kyme) in Italy. One observation may be significant: whereas the geography of the *Odyssey* seems to have been identified with areas just facing

59. Ps.-Scymn. 229.
60. Hellanikos *FGrH* 4 F 17, 30.
61. Cf. Hainsworth in Heubeck, West, and Hainsworth 1988 on 8.111–17.

the earliest Greek colonies (Pithekoussai and Kyme facing Campania), the ethnography stemming from the *Odyssey* (Odysseus as progenitor) relates to peripheral ethnicity: Etruria, Latium, and the badlands of the wild peoples. Hesiod, if he was the first to localize Circe in the west, was writing after almost a century of protocolonial and colonial contacts. The process of grafting mythic scenes onto colonial topography seems to have been gradual and particular but may have started rather early. By the sixth century Italy and the western Mediterranean were full of such associations. To this context of the west may also belong other poetic representations, foremost among them the work of Stesichoros of Himera.

STESICHOROS AND THE WEST

The extant fragments of Stesichoros, the early sixth-century poet from Sicilian Himera,[62] do not mention Odysseus in Italy. However, Stesichoros does tell of Aeneas's going "to the west," and the association of Odysseus with Aeneas made explicit by Hellanikos in the fifth century, as well as the plausibility of Hellanikos's having drawn on a variety of sources including Stesichoros's celebrated *Ilioupersis,* justifies a brief discussion of the question. Moreover, if Stesichoros implies the arrival of Odysseus in Italy, this has further bearing on Hesiod's Odysseus in the region implying Italy, especially since Hesiod turns to Odysseus immediately after mentioning Aeneas's birth as if it were a natural association.[63]

The *Ilioupersis* is quoted by the artist who created the Capitoline *Iliad* tablets (*tabula Iliaca Capitolina*) at the end of the first century B.C.[64] This series of reliefs depicting scenes relevant to Aeneas and the Trojan origins of the Iulii family follows motifs from the *Iliad,* the *Aithiopis,* and the *Little Iliad,* as well as illustrating, explicitly, "The Destruction of Troy according to Stesichoros." One relief shows Aeneas accepting the *hiera sacra* (sacred relics); another shows him carrying his father Anchises and another Aeneas, Anchises, and Misenus boarding a ship, with an inscription specifying that Anchises "and his family and followers" (literally, "his own") are departing "for the west" (εἰς τὴν Ἑσπερίαν).

Horsfall, in particular, has challenged the authenticity of the Stesichoros fragment, judging it propaganda influenced by contemporary Latin poetry (an acceptable point in itself).[65] His approach is detailed and thorough—

62. See West 1971: 302–6; Burnett 1988: 135–47; cf. Malkin 1994a: 209.
63. West 1966 on *Theogony* 1008.
64. Sadurska 1964: 24–37.
65. *FGrH* 840 F 6 b; Horsfall 1979a: esp. 35–43; cf. 1979b: 375–76; Perret 1942: 84–89, 110–15, 306–9.

so much so, in fact, as to lose sight of the only fact that seems to matter, the explicit attribution to Stesichoros.[66] One of his lines of argument, comparing what is shown in a tablet with what is known from texts and fragments, is flawed: artistic conventions often overpower or simply disregard texts. For example, Horsfall is bothered by what is *not* depicted, comparing the scenes with the known fragments of Stesichoros; this is an argument from silence (as he admits) that is basically irrelevant. At the same time, he considers it of "crucial importance" that the artist depicts Menelaos drawing his sword on Helen, "contradicting" Stesichoros,[67] but this had been the artistic convention about the meeting of these two since the Archaic period.[68] In short, it is dangerous to confound iconographic and literary criteria.

The *words* are a different matter, even if they do not conform to what the modern critic sees in the figurative reliefs. The mention of Stesichoros could serve no obvious propaganda purpose, especially since the quotation chosen is so vague—saying nothing of either Italy or Rome. In fact, this vagueness supports its authenticity; a forger would have had free rein. Moreover, aside from Stesichoros, there were many other more explicit "authorities" (Dionysius of Halicarnassus counts forty-six different versions) to draw from.[69] To the arguments in support of authenticity I would add the following: a man of Sicilian Himera, Stesichoros was fascinated with the *far* west (beyond Italy and Sicily); his *Geryoneis,* for example, takes Herakles all the way to Spain, and in later sources "Hesperia" refers to Spain rather than Italy.[70] This far-western significance of the term "Hesperia," as well as the various far-western concerns of Stesichoros, were well known in the first century B.C.; a reader of an isolated verse of Stesichoros in that period could therefore have understood Aeneas as going to Spain, not Italy. Still, the artist who quoted the poet adhered to his text, probably because Stesichoros—in the lost verses of the *Ilioupersis*—was in addition explicit about Aeneas's going to Hesperia, meaning Italy, and this was well known. Therefore, in spite of its vagueness, this text was selected because it lent authority to this self-serving (and rather mediocre) piece of flattering art.

The idea of Hesperia as west=Italy reminds us that the Hesiodic fragment just discussed speaks of Circe's making her home in the land facing

66. See Gruen's (1992: 14) criticism with Galinsky 1969a: 106–13; Dury-Moyaers 1981: 49–53.

67. Horsfall 1979a: 38.

68. Pipili 1987: 30–31; L. Kahil (with N. Icard), in *Lexicon Icongraphicum Mythologiae Classicae* 4(1): esp. 539–63.

69. Galinsky 1969a: 107.

70. On *Hesperia ultima* as Spain, see Hor. *Carm.* 1.36.4; Serv. *ad Aen.* 1.530. On Hesperia as Spain, see Suidas. s.v. Ἰσπανία; cf. Wikén 1937: 40. For a review of Greek mythological perceptions of the far west, see Grilli 1990.

Tyrrhenia (Italy) and that the scholiast says that it was called Hesperia. It is noteworthy too that Dionysius of Halicarnassos, possibly paraphrasing Hellanikos, says that "Hesperia" was an ancient name for Italy.[71] It is often claimed that "Hesperia" in the sense of "west" is not attested before Apollonius, thus casting doubt on the Stesichoros fragment.[72] Horsfall rests much of his argument on this issue,[73] but it is another dangerous argument from silence. *Hesper*-related words in the sense of "west" existed well before Apollonius of Rhodes. *Hesperios* in the *Odyssey*[74] means "a man of the west." The Hesperides, Daughters of the Night, are mentioned three times in the *Theogony*. The name of one of them, Hesperethousa, is attributed by two scholiasts to Hesiod, and she may be the same as Arethousa of Syracuse.[75] The place where the sun sets and night emerges is Hesperia, the place of "sleeping" and, sometimes, the kingdom of the dead.[76] What concerns us here, however, is the straightforward meaning of "west": in the *Catalogue of Women* "Ogygia . . . is toward the west" ($\pi\rho\grave{o}\varsigma$ $\dot{\epsilon}\sigma\pi\acute{\epsilon}\rho\alpha\nu$);[77] the Argive lands "toward the west" in the Peloponnese and the "western part" of Sicily are called *hespera* by Herodotus and Thucydides.[78] Stesichoros had a particularly western interest and, unlike Sophocles, who, in the *Laokoön*, has his Aeneas flee to Ida, can be expected to have had Aeneas go west.[79] There is also a parallel in Teucer of Cyzicus, who mentions Hesperia when speaking of another Trojan Nostos, Helenos, as "sailing toward the west."[80] I therefore consider it very probable that the poet did in fact use "Hesperia" as a substantive.

Nostoi sailing westward, localized in Italy, would have been a common motif by the time of Stesichoros of Himera. I am in agreement with those who see no good reason for Greeks in the sixth and fifth centuries to have paid special attention to Aeneas and the foundation of Rome. At the same time, however, there is no need to suppose that Stesichoros sang the Trojan legend of Roman origins or wrote a *Little Aeneid*.[81] But one need not focus on

71. *FGrH* 4 F 111.17 (which Jacoby adds to Hellanikos's fragment in his "uncertain print category"); cf. Dion. Hal. 1.28.3.

72. Cf. Galinsky 1969a: 106; Gruen 1992: 14.

73. Horsfall 1979: 39.

74. *Od.* 8.29.

75. Hes. *Theog.* 215, 275, 518; Merkelbach and West 1967: fr. 360; cf. Pind. *Pyth.* 3.69; Wikén 1937: 29.

76. Ἑσπέρα, "sleeping, west": Eur. *Or.* 260; Thuc. 6.2; Hdt. 1.82; 8.130. ἑσπέρος, "western, the region of sleeping": Aesch. *PV* 348; Soph. *Aj.* 805; ἑσπέρος θεός, "Hades, god of the west" *OT* 171.

77. Schol. *Od.* 1.85.

78. Hdt. 1.82.1; Thuc. 6.2.2.

79. Dury-Moyaers 1981: 50.

80. Teucer *FGrH* 274 F 1.

81. Sadurska 1964: 23.

Rome in order to associate the Greek Odysseus with the Trojan Aeneas in Italy, just as in Epirus Helenos was linked with Neoptolemos or, in Africa, Antenor with Menelaos. Thus it is reasonable to assume that the pattern of both Greek and Trojan Nostoi, together or separately (chap. 4), was already current in Italy. As we have seen, there is nothing in the extant fragment about Odysseus (although he appears in an *Iliad* tablet), and the Roman artist would have had no particular interest in him. It seems reasonable to assume, however, that, rather than speaking of Aeneas in isolation, the Sicilian poet was following a more ancient association that connected the two. This may be hinted in the *Theogony* as well: Aphrodite "joined in sweet love with the hero Anchises and gave birth to Aeneas. . . . And Circe made love to Odysseus and gave birth to Agrios and Latinos." West, in spite of his reservations, is too good a literary scholar to have missed this obvious association of Aeneas and Odysseus in the *Theogony*.[82] The poet first mentions Aeneas, then turns to Odysseus, implying an Italian localization.

The earlier traditions that seem to be reflected in the closing lines of the *Theogony* become quite explicit in Hellanikos, who must have known the work of Stesichoros:

> The author of the *Priestesses at Argos* and of what happened in the days of each of them says that Aeneas came to Italy from the lands of the Molossians with Odysseus[83] and became the founder of the city, which he named after Rhome, one of the Trojan women. He says that this woman, growing weary with wandering, stirred up the other Trojan women and together with them set fire to the ships. And Damastes of Sigeion and some others agree with him.[84]

Hellanikos here seems to be following some of the non-*Odyssey* traditions about the Epirote wanderings of Odysseus that I have discussed above. He may also be following traditions about Trojans settling in Italy and Sicily: for example, Hekataios knows that Capua was founded by a Trojan, Kapys,[85] and Thucydides has Trojans, together with Greeks, going to western Sicily.[86]

82. Hes. *Theog.* 1009–13 with West 1966 ad loc.
83. Now the commonly accepted reading ($\mu\epsilon\tau'$ 'Οδυσσέα) rather than "after Odysseus" ($\mu\epsilon\tau'$ 'Οδυσσέως). See Dury-Moyaers 1981: 52 n. 128. For the opposite view see Boyancé 1943: 289. "With" is also implied by Lycoph. *Alex.* 1242–45. The chronographic aspect of the *Priestesses* provides further argument in support of the generally accepted reading "with Odysseus" instead of "after Odysseus," since we would not expect an "after" clause to be in the same chronological rubric.
84. Dion. Hal. 1.72.2 = *FGrH* 4 F 84; Damastes *FGrH* 5 F 3.
85. *FGrH* 1 F 62.
86. Thuc. 6.2.3 and chap. 7.

Aeneas's arrival in Italy from the Epirote land of the Molossians places it well within the *nostoi*. During the fifth century, the Molossians had expanded their influence at the expense of the Thesprotians and, in particular, taken control of Zeus's oracle at Dodona. Pindar was their guest-friend, and that Hellanikos mentions them rather than the Thesprotians, who loom large in the sources from the eighth through the sixth century (*Odyssey, Thesprotis, Telegony*), seems to reflect this Zeitgeist.

It may be irrelevant to point out that in Homer Poseidon prophesies that Aeneas and his sons will rule over Trojans, since most Greek *nostoi* (e.g., those of Diomedes and Menelaos) do not conform to what is related in Homer.[87] This is especially significant because, by being linked with Aeneas,[88] Odysseus's arrival in Italy follows the pattern that we have already observed of coupling a Greek and a Trojan. Both Epirotes and Makedonians continued, for centuries, to regard this coupling as natural and flattering. A diametrically opposed attitude has been observed, also in Epirus, on the part of the Greek newcomers, the people of Adriatic Apollonia, at the beginning of the fifth century. Their expansion and conquests found an artistic expression in juxtaposing Greeks and Trojans in terms of "Greeks and barbarians" (chap. 4). It is in this Epirote context, as I have suggested, that both the honorific and the derogatory aspect of the Nostos coupling (Neoptolemos/ Helenos, Odysseus/Aeneas, and so on) were born and exported to Italy.

Hellanikos, we are told, was keenly interested in the west.[89] He calculated, for example, the chronology of the Sikel migration, obviously with an interest in the history of Greek colonization in Sicily.[90] It seems clear that he was also interested in Odysseus, since he wrote about places associated with Odysseus in several of his works. Stephanus of Byzantium says that "Hellanikos, in the first book of the *Priestesses,* writes: Phaiax was the son of Poseidon and of Corcyra the Asopid, after whom the island was called Corcyra, its earliest name being Drepane or Scheria." Hellanikos is speaking here of the eponymous hero of the land of the Phaiakians, identified with Corcyra. The fragment has an obvious connection with Odysseus that makes it evident that Odysseus played a part in Hellanikos's chronographical project of

---

87. *Il.* 20.307–8; cf. *Homeric Hymn to Aphrodite* 196–97. Of course, for antiquarians in the Hellenistic period it became important to harmonize the contradiction, for example, by saying that Rome was the New Troy.

88. I see no reason to second-guess the text and to claim that Aeneas only met Odysseus in Italy (Solmsen 1986: 95). I agree, however, with Solmsen's criticism of Prinz 1979: 155–56.

89. Dion. Hal. 1.28.3 = *FGrH* 4 F 4; cf. Vanotti 1994.

90. Dion. Hal. 1.22.3 = *FGrH* 4 F 79b. Hellanikos's interests were wide-ranging; he also wrote a book entitled *Foundations of Peoples and Cities* (κτίσεις ἐθνῶν καὶ πόλεων, or ἐθνῶν ὀνομασίαι) (see *FGrH* 4 F 70 with Jacoby's commentary).

the *Priestesses,* "of what happened in the days of each of them." In a different context Dionysius cites him, for example, for what happened "in the
twenty-sixth year of the priestess Alkyone."[91] Strabo, disagreeing with Hellanikos's identification of Kephallonia with Doulchion, thus provides another corroboration of the interest in Odysseus.[92] He also mentions the Cyclopes[93] and, with a notorious Athenian bias, says (perhaps in the *Atthis*) that
Telemachos married Nausikaa and Andokides was descended from them.[94]

It is against this background that doubts about Hellanikos's authorship
of the *Priestesses* fragment concerning Odysseus and Aeneas in Italy seem as-
tonishing.[95] Dionysius, who quotes the "author of the *Priestesses*" with regard
to Odysseus and Aeneas, also quotes him with regard to the priestess Alkyone, here mentioning Hellanikos's name. Stephanus of Byzantium does the
same. Still, there are those who raise doubts. Hellanikos's *Troïka*[96] takes Aeneas to Pallene in Chalkidike, and his cult at Thracian Aineia is evidenced
from the fifth- or early fourth-century coinage and is described by Livy.[97]
Did Hellanikos have Aeneas stop and settle in Pallene, whereas in the *Priestesses* he proceeds to Italy? The difference between the *Troïka* (Aeneas in
Chalkidike) and the *Priestesses* (Aeneas in Rome) is often stressed, but it is
of little significance.[98] The two works are clearly different in kind. It is unnecessary to assume that the *Troïka* was written when Hellanikos was young
and the *Priestesses* when he was older, experienced, and had "expanded his
horizons" in order to account for the "contradiction."[99] Even if Hellanikos
were to have written the two works simultaneously there would be no in-
consistency. In fact, on the *Troïka* side, Hellanikos does not say that Aeneas
stopped at Pallene, although some scholars are ready to assume so.[100] What
is more important, however, is the nature of the *Priestesses.* Unlike the *Troïka,*
a narrative work, the *Priestesses* was a chronography, very much in the an-
nalistic style, except that events were grouped not by year but in terms of the

91. Dion. Hal. 1.22.3 = *FGrH* 4 F 79b.
92. *FGrH* 4 F 144 = Strabo 10.214. Pearson (1939: 193) thinks that this fragment
belongs to the *Troïka,* which is possible. However, because of the explicit reference to the
Priestesses with regard to Phaiakia (i.e., with a "geographic explanation" of sites associated
with Odysseus), I think this fragment too belongs in that work.
93. *FGrH* 4 F 88 = Schol. Hes. *Theog.* 139.
94. *FGrH* 4 F 156; cf. Arist. fr. 506 Rose.
95. See the sober discussion of Vanotti 1995: 17–35.
96. *FGrH* 4 F 31 = Dion. Hal. 1.47.
97. Livy 3.1.8 with Head 1911: 214; Kraay 1976: 142; cf. Malkin 1987a: 196.
98. Cf. Dury-Moyaers 1981: 54; Solmsen 1986: 101; Gruen 1992: 18 n. 56 contra
Perret 1942: 367–78 and others.
99. Solmsen 1986: 101–2; cf. Dury-Moyaers 1981: 53–54.
100. Gruen (1992: 17): "apparently as final destination."

tenures of the priestesses of the goddess Hera at Argos (a dating system well-known also to Thucydides).[101] Because of its chronographic nature, it is not in conflict with the *Troïka*. Gruen, who sensibly rejects some elements of Horsfall's critique, nonetheless remains skeptical: the account, he says, is a patchwork of tradition, and that Hellanikos assembled it is a "dubious proposition."[102] However, since it has been conclusively shown that Hellanikos was the author of the *Priestesses* and since the nature of this chronological work was, by definition, a patchwork, I see no more room for skepticism in this case.

The burning of the ships, the third major element in the Hellanikos fragment,[103] was a very common motif both in Aeneas stories and in other *nostoi;* sometimes the ships were Greek, sometimes Trojan.[104] Ships were supposed to have been burned, for example, in locations such as Pallene, Daunia, Apulia, and Sicily. It is this recurrence of the motif, its expected presence as a topos in many *nostoi,* that is of vital importance. As Dionysius of Halicarnassus concludes his quote from Hellanikos, "Damastes of Sigeion and some others agree with him."[105] Damastes was a pupil of Hellanikos,[106] and thus the tradition about Odysseus's arrival in Italy with Aeneas seems secure. However, because it is possible to distinguish different elements in the fragment of Hellanikos, the ship-burning being the third, it has been argued that Damastes agreed with his master only on the final point (the ships) and not about Odysseus in Italy.[107] However, this is stretching text criticism too thin. I fail to see a good reason that Dionysius of Halicarnassus would have cared about substantiating a topos, the one element in the story that was expected there in any case. It is much more likely that he felt it necessary to bring in Damastes and the others to support the entire Hellanikos quotation, which—for his purposes—included the founding of Rome. Nor did Dionysius need Damastes for the arrival of Odysseus in Italy or his association with the Latins. Hellanikos, in contrast to others, went beyond the Hesiodic ethnic identification (Latins) to reach a particular city, Rome. It is that story—

101. Thuc. 5.20; 2.2.1; 5.19.1 with Gomme 1945: 3–8.
102. Gruen 1992: 18 contra (believing in Hellanikos as the author) Galinsky 1969a: 103–6; Dury-Moyaers 1981: 53–56; Solmsen 1986; Poucet 1989: 238–40; Gabba 1991: 12.
103. Cf. Solmsen 1986: 94, who claims there are four components: the foundation of Rome by Odysseus, the foundation of Rome by Aeneas, Rhome as eponym, and the burning of the ships.
104. Dury-Moyaers 1981: 56; Gruen 1992: 11 n. 21.
105. Dion. Hal. 1.72.2 = Damastes *FGrH* 5 F 3.
106. Dion. Hal. *Thuc.* 5.330; Suidas s.v. Δαμάστης.
107. Thus Horsfall 1979b: 382.

belonging to the framework of Odysseus's arrival—that concerned Dionysius and for which he felt the need for a footnote.

Throughout the various discussions one encounters the use of arguments
from silence, as well as the doubt (already dispelled for the Etruscans)
about what Greeks could have known of Rome. Unless placed in a particularly rich and complete context, this kind of argument is always a dubious
proposition. Erich Gruen, for example, claims that "nothing in the epic
cycle suggests western movement by Aeneas or his offspring."[108] But we do
not have "the epic cycle"; all we have are some fragments and concise plot
summaries by Proclus. Moreover, most of our information about important
Greek (not Trojan) Nostoi in the west takes the form of snippets of information, literary and archaeological, and Aeneas, after all, was not an important Greek hero like Diomedes. In short, we may draw no substantial
conclusions from what does not exist in an epic cycle that we cannot read.

In contrast to this faulty argument from silence, some of the discussions
of Aeneas in Italy are disturbingly negligent of the positive evidence we can
draw from the Greek Nostos context aside from Aeneas. I am referring to a
nostos genre that often includes as a matter of course a Trojan traveling with
his Greek captor. Whether supporting the idea of Aeneas in Italy or rejecting it, scholars seem strangely uncomfortable with the idea that Odysseus
was associated with this "mortal enemy."[109] But why not? What better than
to be so associated after the total defeat of that enemy? Many prominent Trojans who did not die or escape were forced to accompany the victors on their
returns. Sparing the life of a man (unlike that of a woman) was exceptional
and assumed a special relationship. This may be hinted at in the *Odyssey*,
where the "sons of the Trojans" arbitrate between Aias and Odysseus regarding who should get the weapons of the dead Achilles.[110] Antenor was allowed to accompany Menelaos,[111] and, similarly, the Trojan seer (an exception, again) Helenos is coupled with the son of Achilles, Neoptolemos, and
becomes a city founder in Epirus. A Trojan companion of Philoktetes, Aigesthes, is said to have continued to Sicily, where he founded Segesta.[112] In
short, Odysseus *together* with Aeneas in both Epirus and Italy falls neatly into

108. Gruen 1992: 12 n. 30.
109. Restated by Gruen (1992: 17) as "the old antagonists" and by Wiseman (1995:
50) as "unnatural association."
110. *Od.* 11.547. The line was rejected by Aristarchus in antiquity; see Heubeck in
Heubeck and Hoekstra 1989: ad loc.
111. His story too, is full of contradictions: did the Antenoridai end up in Libya,
Venice, or both? See Malkin 1994a: 52–57, 64–66; Braccesi 1984; 1987.
112. Strabo 6.254; cf. Steph. Byz. s.v. Χώνη.

this pattern. The "unnatural association"[113] of the two belongs rather to a later date, and their being together actually supports the antiquity of the Hellanikos tradition.

It is important to emphasize that Trojan fugitives settled lands that the Greek Nostoi only passed through. In terms of the *nostos* this was only natural: Menelaos did not wish to remain in Libya, and the captive Antenoridai did not wish to go with him to Sparta. This concept of a Trojan settlement resulting from a Greek *nostos* was, therefore, a Greek one by the time Hellanikos was writing; it is explicitly evidenced by Pindar's fifth *Pythian*. Moreover, such ideas did not belong to the province of poetry alone. Why is it acceptable that Thucydides (and probably his predecessor Antiochus) thought that Trojans *together with* Greek Phokaians settled in western Sicily and founded Segesta[114] but unacceptable that Hellanikos considered something very similar (Odysseus with Aeneas) for Rome? I find such an approach misguided. Just as fifth-century Greeks knew about Segesta, they could also have known about Rome.

Or perhaps they could not? The Hellanikos fragment is often doubted on the grounds that Aeneas's association with Italy and Rome is too early. Were Greeks aware of Rome as early as the fifth century? Tim Cornell provides an apt example when he speaks of Rome in terms of "mere passing reference to obscure and far-away places, which they [Greeks] knew little beyond the mere name and probably cared less." Similarly, Erich Gruen speaks of Rome as being "previously just in the margins of their consciousness."[115] Even if Rome was considered "minor," one may point out that in Epirus, for example, Odysseus is credited with the founding of Bouneima: this was rather a minor place whose Greekness is uncertain. In other words, barbarian foundations by Nostoi need not have been "major" to have been noticed and associated with them.

A more general objection to this approach is also at hand. Any attempt to represent "the Greeks" and what "they" were "not interested in" may be misguided. Such generalization ignores the living realities of varied, close, and numerous contacts between Greeks (of all kinds) and the various cities of Campania, Latium, and Etruria not just during the fifth century but ever since the eighth. Few would claim today that "Greeks," say, Euboians, Corinthians, Samians, Phokaians, and others, "cared little." Orga-

---

113. Wiseman (1995: 50) in particular is led astray by this misconception to see it as implying that Hellanikos conflated two traditions.

114. Thuc. 6.2.3; Antiochus *FGrH* 555 F 6; cf. Plut. *Nic.* 1.3; Paus. 5.25.6. See also Galinsky 1969a: 76–78.

115. Cornell 1975: 23; cf. 1995: 64; Gruen 1992: 10.

nized colonies, individual merchants and agents coming and going from Greek cities of various origins, small resident merchant communities in Italian cities (Gravisca, Pyrgi), high-ranking settlers (the seventh-century Corinthian Demaratos, father of a Roman king), artisans such as the "best-born bastard" Aristonothos of Caere, and numerous others who worked for and among Etruscans, slaves and freedmen, gift-exchangers and partici-pants in symposia, the princely tombs in Kyme, Campania, and Latium (e.g., Praeneste), and so forth, are crucial. The varieties of types of contacts as well as of those who made them cover a wide spectrum.

More specifically, it is no longer permissible to assume that the "Greeks" whose awareness of, for example, Caere, Veii, and Pontecagnano is readily acknowledged should have been unaware of Veii's neighbor, Rome. The city, or "village," on the river that controls the inland route on the coastal point between Elba and Pithekoussai would not have been ignored.[116] A dis-covery near Rome (Osteria del'Osa) of what may be a Greek inscription on a pot dating to the early eighth century should serve as a reminder of very early, protocolonial Euboian contacts.[117] Perhaps we will discover one day that by the sixth century there was a resident Greek community of mer-chants, analogous to Gravisca or Pyrgi, on the Aventine that could have influenced contacts and transmitted religious ideas. In any case, the Phoka-ian connection with Rome and the Latins, especially through Massalia, is well attested; Massalia's Artemis of Ephesos was exported to Rome and in-fluenced the cult of Diana on the Aventine during the reign of Servius Tul-lius, son-in-law of Demaratos's son.[118] Later, the Massaliote treasury at Del-phi housed dedications from Rome.[119] Nearby, in the temple of Ceres, Liber, and Libera, the priestess came from Velia (a colony of the Phokaians, like Massalia) or Naples (founded from Kyme).[120] The Greek cult of the Dios-kouroi arrived in Rome by 484, probably via Taras, and was probably con-flated with the Penates.[121] A contemporary of Aristonothos (ca. 650 B.C.), a Greek named Kleiklos, had his name inscribed on a Corinthian vase that was discovered in one of the tombs at the Esquiline cemetery.[122] Finally, Eu-boian pottery fragments keep surfacing in Rome.[123] The evidence, there-

116. See Wiseman (1995: 35–39), who aptly remarks (p. 43) that "there was hardly a time or a place in which Rome was not of interest to Greeks."

117. Bietti-Sestieri 1992: 184–85. The writing as it appears in figures 8 and 9 is not clear enough to be certain, however. Cf. Holloway 1994: 112.

118. Just. 43.3.4; 5.3; Strabo 4.180; cf. Ampolo 1970; Malkin 1990d: 45.

119. Gras 1987; see Malkin 1990d: 45 n. 11 for more references.

120. Cic. *Balb.* 55.

121. Galinsky 1969b: 11.

122. *SEG* 31.875; see Wiseman 1989: 131; 1995: 37.

123. La Rocca 1982.

fore, that we gather from the nonhistoriographical or antiquarian perspective (which, as it happens, is what we have most of) points unequivocally to a reality of familiarity and contact during the seventh and sixth centuries and, a fortiori, by the fifth ("before Herodotus was born," as Wiseman aptly puts it).[124]

When ordinary knowledge translates into erudite subjects is, of course, a tricky question. By the fifth century, however, even from a historiographical perspective, we may allow Greek knowledge of Rome, although this does not mean that someone like Hellanikos was necessarily keenly interested in Roman history. The framework of Hellanikos's *Priestesses* was no different from that of other Greek historiography, logography, and genealogography. It was, in our terms, "Hellenocentric."[125] Although the heart of Dionysius's paraphrase of Hellanikos is Aeneas and the founding of Rome, we may assume that in the fifth century Odysseus, not Aeneas, was Hellanikos's focus. Some of the rationalizing and ordering that characterize genealogical works such as the *Catalogue of Women* are also observable in the work of the early historians. Genealogy was an independent genre long before the rise of the Greek historical spirit.[126] The interest that attached Odysseus to the Latins or the Etruscans was not historiographical, and neither was the Etruscan interest in absorbing Greek myths and stories. When logographs and historians began working, they had some background of nonerudite knowledge to draw from. A broad spectrum of concerns and interests must, therefore, be recognized. The minimum conclusion, in any case, is that the a priori assumption that in Hellanikos's day "Greeks" knew something about Rome must be fairly well established.

We also have circumstantial, event-oriented evidence for Greek awareness of Rome precisely in a context of political use of Greek myth. Shortly before 509, when the Spartan Dorieus set his sights on the Carthaginian emporia in North Africa, Rome signed its first treaty with Carthage.[127] This was supposedly its first international act upon its liberation from the Etruscans and the establishment of the Roman republic. There is, of course, no certainty with regard to anything in early Roman history; material evidence for Etruscan "influence" on Rome down to the mid-fifth century is, however, quite acceptable. Greeks were in close contact with Etruscan local elites, whether in Veii (Rome's neighbor) or in non-Etruscan cities such as those of Campania. They would have heard about Rome from their Etruscan contacts as well. The last generation of the sixth century had seen a series of

124. Wiseman 1989: 132.
125. Cf. Cornell 1995: 65.
126. Henige 1984 (1974); West 1985: 1–30.
127. Polyb. 3.22–23 with Walbank 1957–79, vol. 1: 339–46.

wars waged by the Etruscans against the Greeks of Kyme; later, in 474 Hieron of Syracuse rushed to the aid of Kyme and defeated the Etruscans yet again. In Sicily the conflict with Carthage, the Etruscans' ally, developed from a Sicilian-Phoenician defense against Dorieus ca. 509 to a Carthaginian offensive in 480, six years before the battle of Kyme. The Roman treaty with Carthage of 509 has been assessed, correctly, in this general Mediterranean context, and, again, it is untenable that Greeks—especially at a time of pan-Hellenic enmity toward the Etruscans (but not yet, as in 509, toward Carthage)—were not aware of a Latin city, a neighbor of a familiar Etruscan city (Veii), and striking deals with Carthage. For Hellanikos, a contemporary of Herodotus, all these events were his métier.

On the Roman side what perhaps happened was the pursuit of communal identity in some reaction to the Etruscan influence.[128] By the end of the sixth century, aside from its own foundation myth of the Twins, the air was also buzzing with Greek foundation stories (genealogical and eponymic), mostly surrounding the figures of Herakles and—especially in Italy—the Nostoi. I have suggested above that it is perhaps worth pursuing the notion that the facile adoption by the Etruscans of both "Greeks" and "Trojans," both Odysseus and Aeneas, is precisely what the new Romans were reacting to. Some insistence on Aeneas (instead of "Aeneas and Odysseus") may have begun as early as the mid-fifth century. Greeks such as Hellanikos, keenly interested in the west but probably oblivious to what its indigenous peoples had to say about themselves, continued to speak of a joint arrival in Italy of Aeneas and Odysseus.

The response to Jacques Perret's denial of any role for Aeneas before the third century has concentrated, in part, on the archaeological evidence, which seemed to confirm that Perret was misguided. The terra-cotta statuettes of Aeneas from Veii were dated to the sixth or fifth century. Then the pendulum swung again, with the revision of the dates to the fourth century or possibly later (though not as late as Perret might have wished).[129] Modern discussion of this topic has been basically Romanocentric. Thus Galinsky, for example, suggests that the Etruscans worshipped Aeneas and the Romans, once liberated, reacted against him.[130] An argument for a reverse

128. I am avoiding the notorious question of whether the Etruscans were "expelled." Archaeologically their influence is apparent in Rome until the middle of the fifth century.
129. See the review of the scholarship by Poucet 1989: 228–34; on the statuettes, see Cornell 1975: 78; 1995: 66; Torelli 1984: 227–81; cf. Schauenburg 1960; Brommer 1960: 273–74.
130. Galinsky 1969a: 142. According to Galinsky, the Etruscans could accept Aeneas but the post-450 Romans could not because they accepted the Latin chronology of

process may be offered. Since there does not seem to be any basis for Etruscan worship of Aeneas before the fourth century and Aeneas was not a major figure, we should perhaps look for the more likely figure to have stimulated the articulation of ethnic or city origins in Greek terms. A more plausible reconstruction is that Odysseus was adopted by the Etruscans (regardless of the Romans) and Aeneas came to be associated with him, just as Helenos, for example, was associated with Neoptolemos. When Etruscan rule (or just significant Etruscan influence) diminished in Rome, Odysseus, loosely associated in Greek terms as progenitor and possibly also as founder of cities, was rejected by Rome in the fourth century as too closely identified with the Etruscans. Here Galinsky has the right idea but the wrong personages: rather than rejecting Aeneas in favor of Romulus,[131] the Romans may have rejected Odysseus in favor of Aeneas.

The Roman reaction, paradoxically, was itself cast in Greek terms. It was in line with a major development in fifth-century Greece of distinguishing Trojans from Greeks in terms of a Greek-barbarian dichotomy. I have pointed out the expression of this dichotomy in Greek tragedy and historiography brought about especially by the Persian Wars (Trojans = Persians = Barbarians). In addition, I have suggested that in the colonial world the first expression of this relevant to Odysseus may be found in early fifth-century Epirus: to commemorate their conquests and expansion, the colonists of the relatively young Apollonia set up a monument at Olympia showing pairs of fighting heroes, a Greek and a Trojan, signifying by this a Greek-barbarian contrast. Since in Epirus, as we have seen, the *nostos* of Odysseus was particularly salient, it is not impossible that notions of transfer of the hero with Aeneas from Epirus to Italy (Hellanikos) came to imply, in the early fifth century, also the equation of "Greek-Trojan" with "Greek-barbarian." This new fifth-century (Greek) attitude, combined with the specification of Odysseus not merely as an ethnic progenitor but also as associated with Rome's foundation, may well have helped prompt the Roman reaction in terms of Roman self-definition: they were not Etruscan/Greek (Odysseus) but Trojan (Aeneas). Gruen is quite right to suggest that thus the Romans could hold the stick at both ends: they both participated in the major ethnic-constitutive myth of the west (the *nostos*) and retained their own particular identity.

LATE TRADITIONS AND CONTEXTS

Greek interest in Rome grew significantly during the fourth and, especially, the third century. Versions about various founders and the city's foundation

---

Rome's foundation in the eighth century. Aeneas is relegated to the background because of his Etruscan associations.

131. Cf. Cornell 1975; Bremmer 1987; Poucet 1989: 246-52.

multiplied, and one must not confound them as belonging to a single tradition. One can sympathize with Dionysius or Plutarch, whose amused exasperation at the numerous versions and variations of Rome's origins is clearly felt. In itself this variety illustrates how the erudite speculation in the Hellenistic period proliferated; most of it was Hellenocentric, and none of it expressed a sacred foundation story commemorated in a ritual or a sacred text. The tale was basically Greek, one of many in which Aeneas (sometimes) became attached to the framework of the major story, that of Odysseus.[132] It is only the modern preoccupation of national "imagined communities" that assumes the need to gloss over variants and reach consensus about one's ethnic origins.[133] Such consensus is apparent today in the deliberate investment in numerous curricula of modern secondary education and national holidays: Ernest Gellner, for example, sees in this a salient feature of Industrial Age nationalism.[134] It is a far cry from the forty-six versions known to Dionysius of Halicarnassus about Aeneas or the thirty-odd versions of Rome's foundations known to us.

In his introduction to the *Life of Romulus,* Plutarch mentions a variety of eponymic stories, such as the one about Rhome, now identified as the daughter of Telephos (a son of Herakles) or (in another version) a granddaughter of Telemachos, the one about Rhomanos, son of Odysseus and Circe, the one about Rhomos, sent from Troy by Diomedes, and so on. Others bring Herakles, as often, into the picture.[135] Companions of Odysseus such as Drakon, Baios, and Misenos fulfill, as do the various helmsmen of Menelaos,[136] various secondary functions of founding or naming.[137] Lycophron has Aeneas joined, in Italy, by Nanos—as we have seen, a probable reference to Odysseus, who was short in stature.[138] He thus seems to refer to the tradition reflected in Hellanikos's fragment; however, the lateness of the source and its nature add little weight to the argument.[139] Gruen is correct in stating that Odysseus still had a place in the story of Rome's origins valid

132. Dury-Moyaers 1981: 47; cf. Galinsky 1969b: 10.

133. Anderson 1983 with Renan 1882.

134. Gellner 1983: 35–38.

135. Dion. Hal. 1.72.5.

136. On Pharos, see Hekataios *FGrH* 1 F 307; on Kinados, see Paus. 3.22.10; on Phrontis (Sounion), see discussion in Abramson 1981.

137. Strabo 1.2.18; 5.4.6; cf., for example, Solmsen 1986: 99.

138. Lycoph. *Alex.* 805–6; cf. Dion. Hal. 1.28.3; Theopompus *FGrH* 115 F 354; cf. chap. 5 nn. 104 and 105.

139. See Schur 1921: 137–43; Phillips 1953: 60–61; Dury-Moyaers 1981: 65–72. The identification is not affected by doubts raised about Nanas the Etruscan founder (Horsfall 1979b: 381) or about the Timaian origins of Lycophron (Pearson 1987: 85; Poucet 1983: 148–49).

in the third century. By this time, however, so much of Greek attention had become "erudite" as to render it of little significance for the subject at hand, which is not Rome per se but the place of Odysseus in Italy.

The Hellenistic erudites actually make it possible to sharpen some lines of demarcation. We have noticed, so far, several types of Greek "interest" in Odysseus in Italy and the origins of nations. It is misleading to talk of "Greek interest," "what the Greeks knew," and so on, without distinguishing the sources of mental activity that give rise to such interests. Polybius speaks of three categories of study of the remote past: genealogies, city foundations, and ethnic relationships.[140] To this should be added the reality of cult accorded to founders—not a historiographical point but a significant reflection of what Greeks could care about with regard to origins. In most Greek colonies the identity of the founder, such as that of Antiphemos of Gela, is commemoratively and annually present in the life of the community. It serves as a focus of "national" identity by means of ritual acts involving the entire community. From this reality Greeks could project historiographical images onto others. Once foundation stories began to be told (the earliest is that of Rhodes, in the *Iliad*), they were provided with the Greek historiographical model of colony foundation: a precise date, foundation ex nihilo, and an identifiable founder.[141] Aside from this we know of poetic traditions, interested neither in cult nor in investigating what really happened, such as the work of Stesichoros or the poets to whom Thucydides refers when he speaks, for example, of the Cyclopes in Sicily.[142] Such poets could serve as "sources" for those engaged in yet another type of mental activity, deliberate research, such as Hekataios, Herodotus, or Timaios (the erudite poetry of Lycophron may be subsumed here). Included among the poets but constituting a separate, "research-oriented" activity was genealogical poetry, where we find ethnographic genealogy as in the last lines of the *Theogony* and in the *Catalogue of Women*.

THE "RIGHT TIME"

A major problem running through the whole discussion of Odysseus and Aeneas in Italy has been the unnecessary insistence on establishing the singular, exclusive, and most likely historical context for the role of either hero or assuming that one legend "eclipsed" another, as if legends were mutually exclusive.

---

140. Polyb. 9.1.4; cf. 12.26d.2 with ref. to Timaios; 34.1.3–5 = Strabo 10.465 (on Eudoxus and Ephorus, see Dion. Hal. *Pomp.* 4.4 (Theopompus).
141. Cf. Polyb. 9.1.4; cf. 12.26d.2 with Cornell 1975: 2.
142. Thuc. 6.2.1.

The beginning of the fourth century B.C. was a "right time" for the linking of the Aeneas legend with the foundation of Rome, perhaps even for the association of the hero with Odysseus. Equally appropriate was the historical context of Pyrrhus's invasion of Italy, when the Epirote king asked for Greek support against the "Trojan colonists."[143] Above I have suggested another appropriate time, in Roman terms, after the diminishing influence of the Etruscans and the explicit expression of the Trojans as *barbarians* opposed to Greeks. The mid-third century, with the rise of Roman interest in Greek Sicily and the interest in Rome of Sikeliote historians such as Timaios or Alkimos, is certainly an acceptable context as well.[144] Yet another is the first century, when the Roman *familiae troianae*, such as the Iulii, also provide an excellent context for interest in Aeneas.

But all this does not mean that what may seem to us the most appropriate time was also the earliest occasion for the use of mythological justification. By analogy, the most appropriate time in Jewish history for the application of the divine promise to Abraham of the Land of Israel as a relevant political myth is the twentieth century A.D. One can easily conceive of someone a few centuries hence arguing forcefully that the relevant verses in *Genesis* were interpolated during the third quarter of the twentieth century by nationalist religious Jews to support irredentist claims that the earlier pragmatic, secular, and socialist-oriented Zionists had never taken too seriously. However, we know for a fact that the same divine charter has been variously "used" for the past twenty-five hundred years, at least since the Persian permission to rebuild the temple in Jerusalem.

For our purposes a more secure scenario would involve all the categories of evidence operating at once—for example, evidence for a *cult* of Odysseus (which we may have in the Greek colony of Taras)[145] overlapping with Greek genealogical and historiographical works and with clear evidence for native adoption of both story and cult. But we do not have all this evidence. What we have been able to do for Odysseus in Italy is assess the sources in their historical and archaeological context, arriving at the conclusion that from the second half of the eighth century down to the fifth Odysseus was "in Italy," not so much serving (for Greeks) as a civilizing hero such as Herakles, who fought monsters and received local charters for future colonies (Kroton, Eryx), as providing a *Greek* ethnographic aspect to the land and its inhabitants, the Latins and the wild peoples of the periphery. These inhabitants, notably the Etruscans, seemed to have accepted Odysseus-Utuse, although we cannot be sure in exactly what capacity. I have suggested that the

143. Paus. 1.12.1.
144. See Gruen 1992: 15.
145. Among the Laertidai. *Mir. Ausc.* 106.

Greek idea of Odysseus as progenitor was adopted, perhaps not too seriously, by the Etruscans and that was why, with the rise of Roman self-identity sharpened against Etruscan culture, Aeneas was preferred over Odysseus.

CONCLUSION

The image of Odysseus as progenitor of "Agrios and Latinos who was fault-less and strong," rulers of "the famous Tyrsenoi, very far off in the recess of the holy islands," conforms to a peripheral vision of Italic peoples as seen from the area of the Bay of Naples. It was the ethnographic periphery rather than the peoples with whom Greek colonists came into an immediate con-tact that usually acquired a Nostos genealogy. Hence, for example, we find Odysseus's descendants not in Campania but farther north, in Latium. A similar pattern will become evident when we consider the figures of Nestor, Epeios, Philoktetes, and Diomedes. Only in later periods (mostly Classical and Hellenistic) will Greek colonies attach Nostoi to themselves (rather than to native populations). Sometimes we will even find these later Greeks us-ing the Archaic Nostos attachments of non-Greeks as a casus belli against native populations. The whole phenomenon was new and should be as-sessed within the time frame beginning in the eighth century. Thus *nostoi* should not be seen as dim reflections of Bronze Age connections, since Nos-tos attachments do not overlap with areas where Mycenaean material evi-dence has surfaced.

In the first two centuries of Greek colonization, when the *nostoi* were ap-plied mostly to the non-Greek periphery rather than to the Greek commu-nities themselves, the Italiote (Greek) communities seem to have encour-aged such attachments, especially when they constituted no territorial threat. Perhaps the *nostoi* served as mediating myths of acculturation and contact. There is also the possibility that individual Greeks, whether through *xenia* relationships or as residents (individuals or small communities of migrants) among Latins and Etruscans, stimulated the Nostos attachments.

The ancient Greek world has left us with an overabundance of poetic and erudite expressions of genealogical ethnicity, from India to the far west. In addition, entire nongenealogical ethnographies were developed, such as the Cretan origins of the Iapygians in southern Italy. What is common to most genealogical ethnicities and ethnographies is their Greek frame of ref-erence and terminology. Paradoxically, because of this, the Greekness of the perspective often becomes diluted, for if everyone is Greek then no one is. In the Archaic period, having the same "Greek" heroes sire genealogies of Indians, Persians, Etruscans, Epirote Molossians, and so on, apparently seemed natural to many, although perhaps not to non-Greek peoples who were supposed to have descended, say, from Herakles. By the fifth century, when ethnic categories became more comprehensive and sharpened by the experience of the wars with Phoenician and Persian barbarians, the Greek origins of others, rather than being denied, seem to have become a source for a feeling of superiority. By the Hellenistic era certain "representatives" of ancient Near Eastern cultures, such as Josephus, Manetho, or Philon of Byblos, strongly protested against the Hellenocentric perspective.

Greek poetic and erudite speculations articulating genealogical ethnicities may be rewarding in themselves, but they become historically significant when ideas achieve material force—when identifications of genealogical ethnicities come to *function* historically, whether for Greeks or for others. Thus in contrast to the great centralized powers in the Near East and Asia Minor, where Greek ethnographic-heroic genealogies (such as Perseus = Persians) were often disregarded, in the western Mediterranean *nostoi* seem to have had a warmer and earlier welcome. They functioned historically both for Greeks and for native populations. When, for example, centuries after Hesiod, the Romans asserted their non-Greek individuality, they did so within the framework of a Greek myth. Odysseus, in the *Theogony*, is the earliest of the Nostoi to have functioned in this way in Italy.

Examining the arguments about what was possible that are used to dismiss the relevant verses in the *Theogony*, I have concluded that Hesiod knew about the sea, the Etruscans, and the Euboian colonies. Internal "editorial" considerations regarding the composition of the *Theogony* are too doubtful and too often rely on thematic interpretation; they are usually raised in conjunction with external historical criteria of "what could have been known" that, in this case, are shown to be worthless. The verses imply a Euboian maritime perspective on western Italy and its ethnography. They seem to reflect protocolonial and early colonial perspectives deriving from Euboian maritime exploration, trade, and colonization of Pithekoussai and Kyme in the Bay of Naples. The blanket appellation of all peoples as "Etruscans" is thus easily understood (and confirmed by later sources), since the prominent coastal and maritime culture encountered by protocolonists and the settlers of Pithekoussai was Etruscan.

The passage in Hesiod is thus an element in the earliest pattern of the (Greek) application of Nostos genealogies to non-Greek peoples: Etruscans, Latins, and, as suggested here, the "wild" mountain and hinterland peoples that for centuries had harried the coastal settlements. "Agrios" provides another case of peripheral ethnography, denoting a ferocious quality (as felt by those coming from the sea) rather than being an ethnic appellation such as "Latins." Several Odysseus-related figures may have played a role in the native readiness to adopt Greek Nostoi. I have examined the interesting thesis that Circe was particularly apt for adoption by native populations as the mistress of transformation (especially into wolves). She may represent a case in which a Greek myth struck a local chord. Together with the Sirens, she is certainly associated with early localizations of *Odyssey* scenes, especially in the area of the Bay of Naples (Pithekoussai and Kyme again).

Discussion of a fragment of the *Ilioupersis* of Stesichoros (sixth-century) that takes Aeneas to the west and of one from Hellanikos (fifth-century) that links Odysseus and Aeneas in the foundation of Rome has yielded the conclusion that both are authentic. The pairing of Odysseus and Aeneas was the norm for Greek-Trojan *nostoi* before the mid-fifth century. Hellanikos had a Trojan Nostos (Aeneas) found Rome just as Hekataios before him had told of Kapys founding Capua and Thucydides of Trojans (Aigesthes implied), with Greeks, founding Segesta in Sicily. There is therefore nothing "too early" about such a notion in Greek historiographical traditions. Furthermore, Rome was not too obscure for Greek attention. Even minor places such as Epirote Bouneima could be ascribed to Greek or Trojan Nostoi, and in any case there was nothing obscure or marginal about Rome by that time. Greeks were aware of Rome at least as early as 509 B.C., when Rome entered into an alliance with Carthage and Dorieus was threatening Carthaginian interests in North Africa and Sicily. Perhaps Rome was "marginal" in the sense that no Greek *Aeneid* was written, but it was not unknown.

In general, Trojan Nostoi could have been more easily perceived as permanent founders in that they were not really "Nostoi": unlike the Greeks, they had no home to return to. Thus, for example, Antenor preferred to stay in Libya, and Menelaos proceeded to Sparta. With time, this quality came to play an independent role: I have suggested that the Roman insistence on Aeneas (without Odysseus) may have begun in the fifth century as a reaction not so much against Greeks but against Etruscans, who had accepted Odysseus and Aeneas as a *pair*. The fifth century was also the context, as we have seen in the case of Apollonia in Epirus, when the Greek-Trojan difference began to be understood especially as a Greek-barbarian dichotomy. These aspects overlapped to create, in later centuries, the Roman insistence on the Roman-Greek *difference* inherent in the use of the *same* Greek myth.

SEVEN

The Other Nostoi:
Nestor, Epeios, Philoktetes, Trojan Siris

The Nostoi discussed in the next two chapters mostly do not share Odysseus's protocolonial aspect of ethnic articulations of entire peoples and lands. Overlapping with Odysseus in his function as a hero of colonization, these Nostoi played a role only in relation to particular sites. They were first attached to the periphery of the Greek colonies, to the frontier areas between colonies, and to non-Greek communities. Heroes of mediation, convergence, and acculturation, they would come to serve different political purposes over the centuries and would eventually be appropriated by some of the Greek city-states in Italy and used to justify war and annexation.

The end of the Trojan War seemed to most Greeks to have produced worldwide movement and turbulence reflected not only in the Nostoi in the west but also in mass migrations eastward to the Aegean and Asia Minor. Thus, according to one popular version, the "Ionian migration" originated in the turmoil in Achaia following the return of the heroes from Troy. We shall see that such notions of migrations and colonization have had their influence on ideas about the arrival of both Greek and Trojan Nostoi in the west.

It seems that at least by the eighth century the origins of some Greek cities in Asia Minor (and Cyprus) had begun to be explained in terms of *nostoi*.[1] Mimnermos, a man of Kolophon, Siris's mother city, and a poet active around the mid-seventh century, provides one of the earliest extant Nostos foundation stories.[2] It is the first to tell of Neleus, the leader of the

---

1. Sakellariou 1958; Vanschoowinkel 1991.

2. On whether foundation stories (*ktiseis*) were a separate genre, see Dougherty 1994, who argues against it. It is disturbing to find (p. 40) that when arguing against the implication of the most explicit reference for such poetry, the title of Xenophanes's *Ktisis of*

Ionian migration, and the foundation of Kolophon from Pylos under the leadership of Andraimon, son of Kodros.[3] In addition to this Pylian version of the Ionian migration to Asia Minor there was a rich Achaian version[4] that in the case of the Achaian and Ionian colonies in the west could easily have been amalgamated with it. Pylos, homeland of the wise counselor Nestor, thus becomes important both for Ionian colonization in the east and for Achaian colonization in the west. Specifically, it appears that the Nostos foundation story current among the Achaian and Ionian colonists at the heel of Italy[5] was invoked at the particular juncture of the foundation of Metapontion in the face of a challenge from the Dorian/Spartan colony of Taras.

NESTOR AND THE MEN OF PYLOS

Metapontion was founded by the Achaians about the first quarter of the seventh century, probably in order to prevent Taras's expansion toward Sybaris.[6] We are now dealing with historical, not Homeric, Achaians, who came from the northwestern Peloponnese.[7] It seems, however, that the overlapping of the name "Achaians" at some point suggested the use of *nostoi* to strengthen territorial claims not in relation to native populations but with regard to the Spartan colony of Taras. Metapontion thus "became" much older than Taras (founded 706 B.C.; it was declared a foundation of Nestor and his people from Pylos, who were diverted to the heel of Italy on their way home. A cult was accorded to the Neleidai (Neleus was Nestor's father) at Metapontion. Thus, aside from what was probably a founder's cult accorded the historical founder of the city (whose name is unknown), Metapontion also worshipped its heroic, Nostos founders.[8] The phenomenon is far from unique: Taras too worshipped an eponymous hero aside from its founder Phalanthos, and the same was true of both Achaian Kroton (founded by Myskellos of Rhypai) and Abdera.[9] This duality of founder's cults probably provided the city with

---

Kolophon (Diogenes Laertius 9.20), she omits from her quotation of Diogenes the last two words, which describe it as a poem 2,000 verses long.

3. Mimnermos F 9, 10 West (= Strabo 14.1.3); cf. Paus. 7.3.5. See Schmid 1948: 13–14; Sakellariou 1958: 146–72; Prinz 1979: 323–30; Vanschoowinkel 1991: 374–75.

4. Vanschoowinkel 1991: 375–76; for the more familiar Athenian version, see 377–85.

5. Bérard 1957: 327 rejects the Siris connection.

6. Strabo 6.264–65, citing Antiochos.

7. On the confusion between Homeric and historical Achaians, see Ronconi 1974–75: 46–47; 1975–76: 158–61; Lombardo 1986: 56 n.3.

8. On Pylians with Nestor, see Strabo 6.264; cf. Vell. Pat. 1.1 (Epeios, separated by storm from Nestor); Solin. 2.10. On the cult, see Giannelli 1963: 89; on the founder's cult in colonies, see Malkin 1987a: pt. 2.

9. On Kroton, see chap. 5; on Taras, see Malkin 1994a: 133–39.

a sense of great antiquity. It could present itself as just as old as any Greek polis in the older Greek world, in spite of the fact that it was clearly a new colony with identifiable origins, founder, and date. In the case of Metapontion it seems that this self-enhancement helped to bolster its claim to the site it occupied in relation to another Greek state. Thus the Pylian *nostos* of Nestor functions quite differently from that of Odysseus. It is addressed by Greek settlers to themselves and to other Greeks. It defines no ethnography, nor does it mediate an unfamiliar landscape as Odysseus and the *Odyssey* do. It serves an internal function, the articulation of a link with the land.

Why Pylos and Nestor? The Pylian myth of origins, as we shall see in the case of Epeios, was rather prominent. Ciaceri has suggested that Metapontion may have been influenced by its neighbor Siris, the only Ionian colony in the region, whose mother city was Kolophon in Asia Minor.[10] This seems convincing, especially since Siris may have wanted to strengthen its commonalities with its numerous Achaian neighbors. Resorting to this myth of origins made Siris (originating in Asia Minor) and the Greeks of the northwestern Peloponnese basically from the "same" place.

The *nostos* framework of Nestor and the Pylians in Italy also articulated the explanation of the origins of a non-Greek city, Etruscan Pisa. Another group of Pylians was supposed to have founded it, whereas others went to Metapontion.[11] Strabo, our source here, seems to force the synchronization of the foundation of the Greek and Etruscan cities. There was apparently an independent tradition concerning Pisa; Cato speaks of a pre-Etruscan city there whose inhabitants spoke Greek,[12] and Hellanikos links the same region with the Etruscan-Pelasgian migration that eventually founded Cortona.[13] All these confused "versions" seem to signify that at some point either Greeks or Etruscans or both adopted the Pylian *nostos* framework. This functioned as another articulation of the ethnic origins of non-Greeks in Greek terms such as we have seen in the northwest, but here there is a significant difference: in the cases of Pisa and Cortona the story revolves around the foundation of a city rather than the progenitor of a nation. It is less ethnographic and more political and "Greek." By contrast, we find Greek ethnography operating also in the familiar pattern of making everyone Greek. Among the various speculations on the eponym of Metapontion, Metabos, a Boiotian element emerges: the Messapians were originally Boiotians. Messapos, the eponym, gave the name to Mt. Messapion on the Boiotian

10. Ciaceri 1926–40, vol. 1: 116–17.
11. Strabo 5.222 with Pliny *HN* 3.50 = 8.1; Solin. 2.7; Just. 20.1.11.; cf. Musti 1988: 125 n. 2; Briquel 1991b: 249–57.
12. Cato *HR Rel.* frg. 45 (= Serv. ad *Aen.* 2.179).
13. Hellanikos *FGrH* 4 F 4 = Dion. Hal. 1.28.3.

shore opposite Euboia.[14] These Boiotians adhere to the familiar Pelasgian-Arkadian-Cretan model of explaining foreign ethnography in terms of mass migrations during the heroic age, mostly before the Trojan War.[15]

EPEIOS, LAGARIA, AND METAPONTION

Unlike Nestor's, a *nostos* whose end is Italian, is that of Epeios, one of Nestor's men. Epeios, we recall, was the artisan who built the Trojan horse. A late source (Justin) claims that Epeios was the founder of Metapontion, where, in the temple of Athena, he had dedicated the tools with which the Trojan horse had been built.[16] It seems, however, that Epeios originally had very little to do with Metapontion[17] but instead functioned as the founder of a non-Greek city. He is the first of the Nostoi in eastern Italy discussed here to have functioned in a manner diametrically opposed to that of Odysseus.

The sources are late, and we cannot be sure of the antiquity of the observed associations. The likelihood of early connections depends on the overall picture of the Italian Nostoi and on certain historical events known to be associated with them in the Archaic period. Lycophron has Cassandra prophesy that Epeios will be the founder of Lagaria, where he will dedicate his tools in Athena's temple (thus repeating the story about Metapontion).[18] The Aristotelian author of *De Mirabilibus Auscultationibus* says that Epeios was invited to Lagaria in a dream in which he was ordered to deposit his tools in the temple of Athena, called Hellenia, near Metapontion.[19] Strabo simply says that Lagaria is a foundation of Epeios and the Phokians,[20] although he is probably confusing Phokaians (from Asia Minor) with Phokians here and the site should be regarded as a Hellenized native place.[21]

It is the obscurity of Lagaria, of which we know nothing aside from its probable location between Siris and Metapontion, that is intriguing.[22] It was probably small, overshadowed by but for a time independent of Metapon-

14. Strabo 9.405 = 2.13; cf. Steph. Byz. s.v. Μεσσάπιον, Βοιωτία. On Metabos, see Bérard 1957: 333; Giannelli 1963: 80–86.

15. Bérard 1957: chap. 11; Briquel 1984.

16. Just. 20.2.1 with Vell. Pat. 1.1, where the name, Epeios, is restored in the corrupt manuscript.

17. Cf. the contradictory version about the founder Daulios: Ephoros *FGrH* 70 F 141 (= Strabo 6.265) with Musti 1988: 147 n. 34.3.

18. Lycoph. *Alex.* 930, 946–50.

19. *Mir. Ausc.* 108.

20. Strabo 6.263 = 1.14.

21. Bérard 1957: 337, 341; cf. Thuc. 6.2.3, where the "Phokians" who settled in Sicily together with Trojans all became barbarian Elymians. See also Giannelli 1963: 70–73.

22. Bérard 1957: 336, contra Dunbabin 1948a: 35 n. 2; Giannelli 1963: 75–79, 107–8. See La Genière 1990: 405–8; 1991a.

tion. Its proximity probably facilitated the transfer of Epeios's legend to Metapontion. In my view this also explains the cult title of Athena; the manuscript says that she was the Hellenic ('Ελληνίας, "Greek") Athena. The emendation (which occurs twice) rests on a reference in the Byzantine *Etymologicum Magnum* that speaks of both Eilenia polis and Eilenia Athena and her *hieron* (sanctuary).[23] But nothing is said of Lagaria, and "Eilenia polis" may be something entirely different. Tzetzes's commentary on Lycophron,[24] which also mentions Eilenia, omits Epeios entirely and mentions Philoktetes instead.[25] The more likely explanation preserves the text intact, with no need for a double emendation: if Lagaria was not a Greek city, it was very "native" of it to call its Athena a "Hellenic" goddess. Lagaria thus became more "Greek" than Greek Metapontion.

It is precisely this quality that makes some of the Nostoi in southeastern Italy so markedly different from Odysseus. It was the minor, non-Greek cities, such as Lagaria with its Epeios, that attached themselves to the Nostoi. They were in the immediate orbit of the great colonies but, for a while at least, not subdued by them. I believe, with Bérard,[26] that eventually Lagaria was annexed by Metapontion and its central sanctuary of Athena (or the goddess identified with her) became a peripheral sanctuary of Metapontion. The Pylian-Nestorian origin of the one and the Epeios legend of the other (both "Pylian") probably facilitated the process. What started as a claim to independent existence, relying on its "own" (paradoxically, Greek) foundation story, ended up with a complete overlap of the Nestor foundation story of Metapontion and the Epeios one of Lagaria.[27]

PHILOKTETES

A hero who performed a similar but more complex function was Philoktetes. Both Epeios and Philoktetes were relatively minor heroes in the Homeric epics; poetically, however, their role seems to be identified with the final victory, the immediate cause for the fall of Troy, and, consequently, with the beginning of the return voyages. They are at the point where war ends and wanderings begin. Epeios built the Trojan horse; Philoktetes was in charge of Herakles's bow and arrows, without which victory would never have been

23. *Etym. Magn.* 298.25.
24. Tzetz. ad Lycoph. *Alex.* 947.
25. Giannelli (1963: 75–79, 107–8) tries to get out of the difficulty by saying that Philoktetes replaced Epeios at the sanctuary.
26. Bérard 1957: 334–36; cf. 184–85.
27. Schol. ad *Il.* 23.665 has Epeios's mother named Lagaria.

achieved.[28] Both the tools of Epeios and the bow and arrows of Herakles be-
came tangible sacred objects (*hiera*) in the colonial region of the heel of
Italy.[29] In Homer Philoktetes returns to his Thessalian kingdom;[30] by contrast, in his western *nostos* he reaches Italy and dedicates the arrows of
Herakles in a temple of Apollo Alaios, perhaps as a god of "wanderings."
   Philoktetes is somewhat atypical in another respect: he is the ailing hero,
having been bitten by a snake and abandoned on the barbarian island of
Lemnos[31] for almost ten years before Odysseus came to pick him up along
with the weapons of Herakles. Eventually he would be particularly well
suited to Kroton, the city that boasted of its numerous Olympic victors and
its reputation for health,[32] but first, he was well suited to living among barbarians and serving as a hero of acculturation.

Strabo, following Apollodorus's commentary on the *Catalogue of Ships*,[33] says
that Philoktetes came to the region of Kroton and colonized Cape Krimissa[34] and, in the hinterland, the city of Chōne; some of his companions
went on to found Segesta in Sicily under the leadership of the Trojan Aigesthes.[35] Turning to an unnamed source, Strabo adds that Philoktetes came
to Italy after his successful return (as in Homer), since he had to leave his
Magnesian city Meliboia[36] because of civil strife; he then founded Petelia,
the "mother city" of all the "Leukanians" or "Chōnes."[37]
   The Aristotelian *De Mirabilibus Auscultationibus* and Lycophron seem to
draw partly on the same source in their versions of the Italian Philoktetes.

28. Cf. *Little Iliad* (Proclus's summary, Bernabé 1987); Soph. *Phil.* 1439.

29. Cf. Musti 1991: 23; on Philoktetes as a literary "hero of margins" see Gills 1992.

30. *Od.* 3.190; *Il.* 2.716 ff.

31. *Il.* 2.722–23; cf. the summaries of Proclus of the *Kypria* and the *Little Iliad* (Bernabé 1987) and Sophocles's *Philoktetes*. On Lemnians as *agriophonoi* (wild-spoken), see
Od. 8.294.

32. Maddoli 1980a emphasizes this quality of the hero; see also Giangiulio 1991: 52
with Mele 1984: 41; Maddoli 1984.

33. *FGrH* 244 F 167.

34. On the possible confusion between "settle" and "inhabit," see Giangiulio 1991:
44–45 with Casevitz 1985: 77–80. I see no reason here to reject the meaning of "founded"
merely because confusion was possible.

35. Strabo 6.254 = 1.3; cf. Steph. Byz. s.v. Χώνη.; Nenci 1991.

36. *Il.* 2.717.

37. Strabo loc. cit. The reading τῶν Χώνων is based on the foundation of Chōne,
named also by Strabo. See Maddoli 1979: 141 and cf. Verg. *Aen.* 3.402; Serv. *ad loc.;* Sil.
Ital. 12.433; Solin. 2.10. See also the survey by Giannelli 1963: 162–67 and the discussion of Siris's Trojan origins below.

In Lycophron's *Alexandra*,[38] Cassandra prophesies that Philoktetes will be received by the small city Krimissa in the land of the Oinotrians; his tomb will be near the Krathis River by the sanctuary of Apollo Alaios, at the mouth of the River Nauaithos;[39] there he will be killed by the Pellenian Ausonians while helping the Lindians (colonists from Rhodes), blown there by the north wind, "to dwell in a strange and alien soil" (ξένη ἐποικήσοντας ὀθνείαν χθόνα). In Makalla the natives (*enchorioi*) will build a great sanctuary upon his grave and honor him like a god with libations and sacrifices.

The Aristotelian author says that the people of Sybaris have a cult to Philoktetes. Upon his return from Troy the hero went and colonized Makalla in the region of Kroton and dedicated Herakles's bow and arrows in the sanctuary of Apollo Alaios; the arrows were seized by the Krotoniates "during their time of power" and deposited in their own temple of Apollo. In the same region Philoktetes has his tomb, having been killed near the River Sybaris while fighting the local barbarians alongside of the Rhodians who had come there with Tlepolemos.[40]

The sources imply a rather late date, probably in consequence of the war between Kroton and Sybaris in 510 B.C. when the cult of Philoktetes and the *hiera* of Herakles became a bone of contention between the two. Philoktetes was taken over by Kroton and transferred either to Kroton or to the Sybarite territory that it had just won. In the later fifth century (at the earliest), Thourioi, which had replaced Sybaris, challenged Kroton, claiming Philoktetes and the sacred relics for itself; Justin even makes Philoktetes the founder of Thourioi, where there was, in the Roman period, a monument erected in his memory. The arrows of Herakles were similarly pointed out in the temple of Apollo there.[41] Although both Sybaris and Kroton claimed the sacred arrows of Herakles, neither seems to have had them originally. Rather, they had belonged to the minor, probably native towns of the frontier zone separating them.

Philoktetes mattered, sometimes simultaneously and always differently, to the protocolonists sailing past Cape Krimissa, the non-Greek frontier communities, the small groups of Greeks who settled among them, and finally the major colonies of Kroton and Sybaris. The discussion of the history of the cult today is polarized, with Domenico Musti arguing for a transfer of

38. Lycoph. 911–13, 919–29.

39. A river near Kroton, another location for the burning of ships by Trojan women: Strabo 262.

40. *Mir. Ausc.* 108; cf. Tzetz. ad Lycoph. *Alex.* 911 citing Euphorion, an Alexandrian erudite of the third century, who says that Philoktetes founded the temple of Apollo Alaios between Kroton and Thourioi. I am skeptical about the reality of Rhodian colonization (sharing Bérard's view), but see Maddoli 1979: 151–59.

41. Justin 20.1.16; cf. Giangiulio 1991: 46.

Philoktetes from Kroton to Sybaris and others, such as Gianfranco Maddoli and Maurizio Giangiulio, seeing things the other way around.[42]

Philologically, it has been demonstrated that the relevant texts may indicate a move of Philoktetes (the sacred relics and even his tomb/hero-shrine) to Sybaris; the subject-antecedents of the relevant verbs and pronouns are sufficiently elusive to yield this meaning. According to Musti's reading, Kroton did this at the height of its power ($\kappa\alpha\tau$᾽ $\epsilon\pi\iota\kappa\rho\acute{\alpha}\tau\epsilon\iota\alpha\nu$), probably after it had won, against all odds, its war against powerful Sybaris in 510 B.C. Musti's interpretation is just possible, but the motive attributed to Kroton seems doubtful. Kroton, which according to Musti cared little for its own heroic ("Mycenaean") past,[43] transferred Philoktetes to Sybaris as a kind of "compensation" (*risarcimento*) of the divinity (Apollo) of the hostile city, a god whom it also honored.[44] Most readers, however, read the texts more straightforwardly in the opposite direction, from Sybaris to Kroton. Mele, for example, thinks that Philoktetes was a hero of Sybaris who was violently stolen by Kroton during its *epikrateia* (dominance).[45] According to this view it was Kroton, at the height of its power, that appropriated Philoktetes. In my view this interpretation is correct but only partial. The evidence does not point to any worship of Philoktetes in Sybaris itself; rather, he seems to have been the hero of the land in between Kroton and Sybaris and of its natives. Another Greek hero seems to support this: Herakles and the heroic antiquity he had given Kroton.

By the middle of the fifth century we have evidence that Kroton had become rather enamored of its heroic origins. Its coinage portrayed Herakles with the explicit legend, in deliberately archaizing forms, "OIKIMTAM," "founder."[46] Thus Herakles seems to have overshadowed the city's historical founder, Myskellos of Achaian Rhypai, perhaps much as, at Taras, Phalanthos was overshadowed by the eponymous "Taras."[47] This was clearly a late development, since Kroton's earliest coinage (sixth-century) bears the symbol of the tripod of the Delphic oracle that prophesied to Myskellos.[48] It is reasonable to assume that the context for the beginning of the emphasis on Herakles may be found toward the end of the sixth century, when Philoktetes, Herakles's trusted companion, would have been of paramount importance.

42. Maddoli 1980a; 1980b; Giangiulio 1991.
43. Musti 1991: 23.
44. Musti 1991: 28.
45. Mele 1984: 36.
46. Lacroix 1965b: 76–79; Giangiulio 1989: 71.
47. Malkin 1994a: 133–39.
48. See Head 1911: 97; cf. 98; Kraay 1976: 181; Giangiulio 1989: 70–74; Malkin 1987a: 43–47.

We should remember what Kroton must have been going through just before the war. Having been threatened with annihilation by the wealthy and powerful Sybaris, it expressed its relief and vengeance proportionally. Some thirty years earlier (the date is an estimate) Kroton had been faced with a similar situation, before its war with Lokroi (although then its odds were more favorable). Both cities had turned to Sparta; it was probably then that Kroton claimed Sparta as a mother city and localized the *nostos* of Sparta's Homeric king, Menelaos, at the temple of Hera at nearby Cape Lakinion.[49] Dorieus the Spartan, on his way to reclaim a legacy of his ancestor Herakles at Eryx in Sicily, apparently came to Kroton's aid against Sybaris ca. 510 B.C. This rare use of an explicit charter myth probably did not leave the victorious Krotoniates unaffected, especially since Herakles was closely associated with a similar myth of the eponymous Kroton.

In western Sicily Herakles, returning to Greece with the cattle of Geryon, was challenged by the lord of the land, the eponymous Eryx. It was agreed that Herakles would either lose the cattle or win the land. Having won, Herakles left the country in the safekeeping of its inhabitants until one of his descendants should return to reclaim it.[50] Traveling in Italy with the same cattle, Herakles accidentally killed Kroton; he erected a tomb and prophesied to the inhabitants that one day a city would rise named after the man he had killed.[51] Unlike the Herakleid myth in Sicily, the Krotoniate myth is less a charter myth than a "myth of origins." The idea, expressed in Kroton's coinage, that Herakles was a founder was obviously an extension of the notion of "beginning" to that of "foundation," although Herakles did not actually "found" the state. In both myths Herakles creates a precedent, a constitutive act; in both he makes a kind of pact with the indigenous people, prophesying (or legitimating) future Greek colonization.

Probably compensating for the inferiority most colonials came to feel in the Classical period with regard to the "epic" mother cities of mainland Greece, this new pride in a past more ancient than the Trojan War may have been the context for the particular emphasis placed on Philoktetes. Like the eponym Kroton, he was another companion of Herakles, the one he seems to have trusted most.[52] But Philoktetes was chosen for another reason as well: to win a war. Greek recipes for winning wars include stealing a Palladion, building a Trojan horse, or bringing Philoktetes from Lemnos with the bow and arrows of Herakles.[53] I am suggesting that Kroton brought the

49. Its defeat by Lokroi does not change its attitude just before the war. See, for a fuller discussion, Malkin 1994a: 62–64.
50. I discuss this at length in Malkin 1994a: 203–19.
51. Diod. 4.27.7; cf. Lacroix 1965b: 77; Giangiulio 1989: 73–74.
52. Lacroix 1965a: 9–11.
53. See Faraone 1992: passim and chap. 6.

victory talismans, the *hiera* of Herakles, from the countryside separating it from Sybaris. This was the land "in between," the frontier, and it was the land where Philoktetes had founded cities, at (Cape) Krimissa, Petelia, Chōne, and Makalla.[54] The Iamidai, professional seers, were probably involved in this ritual transfer. Perhaps they had prophesied that victory would be Kroton's if, as before the Trojan War, it had the bow and arrows of Herakles? Herodotus, preoccupied here with Dorieus, is silent about this, but in discussing what Kroton and Sybaris had to say about Dorieus he provides us with the precious information that the Iamidai, having just deserted Sybaris, were handsomely compensated following Kroton's victory.[55]

The thanks offering to the gods following Kroton's victory was not to install Philoktetes and the sacred relics in a temple of Apollo at Sybaris as Musti suggests. We are not quite in the dark here, since we are informed of a substantial Krotoniate offering: this was the dedication of a *temenos* to Athena (not to Apollo) by the River Krathis (Sybaris). Seeking to prove that he had aided Kroton, the Sybarites claimed that it was Dorieus who established it; the Krotoniates denied his involvement. But that is beside the point, since no one denied that the precinct was established and that this was a consequence of Kroton's victory.

Kroton's war against Sybaris was a consequence of its expansion in the Cape Krimissa region, settled mostly by non-Greeks. The tradition in the Aristotelian *De Mirabilibis Auscultationibus* that Philoktetes died fighting barbarians by the River Sybaris may have arisen following Kroton's appropriation of the hero from these barbarians. Reclaiming sacred relics brought by a Greek hero to a "barbarian" land in the heroic age seems to have served as a justification for colonial expansion at their expense. In Sicilian Gela, for example, one of its two founders, Antiphemos of Rhodian Lindos, conquered and pillaged the native city of Omphake and brought back to Gela a statue "made by Daidalos."[56] The myth of Daidalos in Sicily provides a fascinating set of mythological precedents centered especially around Minos, the king of Crete, who pursued Daidalos to Sicily and was murdered there by Kokalos, the Sicilian king, at the capital city Kamikos. In the seventh century Antiphemos reconnected with a relic, evidence for ancient presence of a Greek hero. The "recovery" of Daidalos's statue, because of its connection with a victory over a native city, is what lends the relic its significance as implied justification of the conquest. With Philoktetes's relics, their recovery apparently served a double purpose: justification of penetration into the hinterland in relation to non-Greeks (as with Antiphemos) and a claim in inter-Greek rivalry.

54. Musti 1991: 23, 26; cf. Maddoli 1980a: 144–46.
55. Hdt. 5.44–45. On the Iamidai in Kroton, see Giangiulio 1989: 178–79.
56. Paus. 8.46.2; cf. Dunbabin 1948a: 112, 318.

This type of legitimation is quite familiar from parallel conquest and colonization practices in which the remains of the heroes themselves served the purpose. Kimon, for example, discovered the bones of Theseus on the island of Skyros when he conquered it. The Dolopians who had treacherously murdered Theseus were now punished and the sacred remains of the hero transferred to Athens.[57] Hagnon, the Athenian founder of Amphipolis, brought the bones of the hero Rhesos to the city, thus instituting an ancient heroic cult in a new colony. The foundation oracle of Amphipolis makes it explicit that this was a "condition" for the success of the colony.[58]

In our case it is important to note that the statue of Daidalos or the arrows of Herakles were connected not strictly with the founding of the colony but rather with its subsequent expansion and history. No justifying charter oracle—of the kind Dorieus used when going to Sicily to reclaim a legacy of Herakles—exists for either Kroton, Sybaris, or Gela. In contrast to these major Greek colonies, Sicilian Omphake and Italian Krimissa, Chōne, Makalla, and Petelia were all minor, peripheral sites. The use of cult and heroic precedent is applied not to the centers of the new colonies at the time of their foundation but to the territorial expansion toward the frontier in later generations. The growing territorial challenge and ambition are now articulated in more expressive terms of mythological justification. As in the world of the Spartan Mediterranean, the pattern of (territorial) challenge and (mythological) response is also apparent, although less explicitly, with the *nostoi* in southeastern Italy.

Whereas the proportions between challenge and response seem similar, the challenges themselves were not. There is one major difference, in particular, in the application of the charter myth by the contemporary Dorieus and by the Krotoniates. In the Spartan world charter myths could be used a priori, to justify setting out to colonize; with Daidalos or Philoktetes mythological justifications more often had to do with a situation of territorial expansion from an existing colony. Also, no divine or heroic "promised land" (such as Sparta itself, according to Tyrtaios,[59] or Eryx in Sicily) is implied here. Rather, the natives, who appeared to possess sacred objects that were not "rightly theirs," were being punished. The "repossession" of the objects, whether a statue by Daidalos or the arrows of Herakles or the bones of Theseus, implies Greek legitimation. A Greek heroic "precedent" had been es-

57. Plut. *Kim.* 8; *Thes.* 35–36; Paus. 3.3.7. Cf. Aristid. 3.409 with schol. (p. 688 Dindorf); schol. Aristoph. *Plut.* 627b; Walker 1995: 55–61.

58. Polyaen. *Strat.* 6.53; cf. Marsyas *FGrH* 135 F 7; Parke and Wormell 1956, vol. 2: 133; Malkin 1987a: 81–84. For the Spartan examples see Malkin 1994a: 26–30. On the heroic transfer of relics in general, see Pfister 1909–12: 188 ff.

59. Tyrtaios fr. Ia (Prato).

tablished; "now" the new colonists redeemed the objects and brought what had been started to its conclusion, Greek territorial appropriation and the reinstallation of the *hiera*.

Why was Philoktetes, during the seventh and sixth centuries, sacred not in the Greek centers but rather in the non-Greek frontier zones? The answer may reveal a more complex reality than first envisaged. First, a closer observation of the sites involved: Cape Krimissa is probably Punta dell'Alice, some forty kilometers north of Kroton;[60] most of the other sites seem to be in its orbit.[61] Cirò, at the top of a hill a few kilometers to the south, in the interior,[62] could be Chōne; Petelia, which may be identical to Makalla,[63] may be the site of Strongoli, north of Kroton.[64] All of these sites are minor, peripheral, or hinterland places, and none is mentioned in the sources as a Greek colony.[65] The Chōnes were clearly not Greeks, and we are therefore concerned here with indigenous sites, located in the frontier zones between the areas of Kroton and Sybaris. It seems reasonable that these cities could for a while escape direct Greek domination precisely because of this geopolitical situation. However, they probably did not escape acculturation, including the absorption of Greek *nostoi;* Greek material culture certainly reached them.[66]

The situation was probably more complex than one of Greek versus native; we should be looking for individual Greek families or small Greek communities living among the indigenous people. Several entries in Strabo seem to support this. First, when discussing the lands of both Kroton and Sybaris, Strabo says that the River Neaithos, north of Kroton, was one of the numerous locations where the Trojan women supposedly burned the Greek ships, forcing both Greeks and Trojans to settle in Italy. Several other Achaian groups,[67] he says, came later, "and thus rose many *katoikiai* most of which took their names from the Trojans." Second, when speaking of Sybaris's enormous territory, Strabo says that at the time of the war with Kroton it

60. Dunbabin 1948a: 159; Giangiulio 1989: 229–30.

61. Lacroix 1965a: 8.

62. Giangiulio 1989: 44; 224–26.

63. Bérard 1957: 347. On Makalla, see also Steph. Byz. s.v. Μάκαλλα. Cf. *Etym. Magn.* 574.16; schol. ad Thuc. 1.12.

64. Dunbabin 1948a: 161; Giangiulio 1989: 229.

65. Krimissa is mentioned as a landmark in the foundation oracle to Myskellos. Diod. 8.17.1

66. La Genière and Sabbione 1983–84; Giangiulio 1989: 43–45 (epigraphic evidence), 224–28 (material culture); cf. Giangiulio 1991: 52.

67. Strabo 6.262 stresses the kinship relations κατὰ τὸ ὁμόφυλος.

222 THE RETURNS OF ODYSSEUS

ruled four tribes (*ethnē*) and twenty-five subject cities.[68] The frontier region
that concerns us may have been part of this. Third, in another context we
hear of a specific identity attributed to Greek settlers. As we have seen,
Strabo says that Lagaria is a foundation of Epeios and the Phokians,[69] and
Pisa was, according to some versions, a Phokian city, founded by Epeios.[70]

We also hear of Lindians,[71] similar to the "Rhodians" on the Traeis at
Sybaris.[72] The Rhodian connection seems to be a conflation of various traditions. Tlepolemos appears in the earliest foundation story in Greek literature, in the Homeric *Catalogue of Ships,* as the founder of Rhodes. At the
other end of the chronological spectrum, we find Strabo, writing at the time
of Augustus, apparently believing in what we would call "Bronze Age colonization" by Rhodians of the entire western Mediterranean, including the
Balearics and Spain. In fact, the notion of colonizing Rhodians seems much
more aptly applied to Rhodian Gela between the seventh and the fifth century. Perhaps because Philoktetes was connected with the foundation story
of the Elymian city of Segesta,[73] he was also perceived in conjunction with
otherwise unattested "Rhodians" in Italy. Again, the Rhodians seem similar
to the "Phokians" of Epeios and may be an extrapolation from the presence
of Greeks outside the framework of the organized colonies. Finally, the "Pellenian Ausonians" (perhaps from Achaian Pellene),[74] enemies of Philoktetes who supported the "Lindians" (Lycophron), are particularly important. Bérard thinks that they are exactly the same as the "barbarians" in
Ps.-Aristotle, but the specificity of their name, belonging to the Achaian orbit (to which Kroton also belongs), seems indicative of a distinct tradition.
These may be Achaian Greeks living among the "Philoktetes communities"
that were taken over by Kroton.

All this is frustratingly elusive, but the implications of the possibility of
Greek presence in noncolonial small communities perhaps analogous to
Gravisca, Pyrgi, and even Amphipolis before its official foundation[75] are
quite significant for the notions of acculturation and the mythological colonial discourse. The indications in Strabo seem to point to the settlement of
small groups of Greeks among non-Greeks on the periphery of both Kro-

68. Strabo 6.263.

69. Ibid.; cf. schol. ad *Il.* 23.665; Epeios's mother, named Lagaria, is connected with
Phokis.

70. Serv. ad Verg. *Aen.* 10.179.

71. Lycoph. *Alex.* 923; *Mir. Ausc.* 107.

72. Strabo 14.654.

73. Krimissa is the name of the river of Segesta, another typical mixture of Greek and
Trojan elements. Nenci 1987: 927 with n. 22; cf. 1991.

74. Lycoph. *Alex.* with Giangiulio 1991: 47–48.

75. Isaac 1986: 4–8.

ton and Sybaris.[76] These may have been among the twenty-five "subject cities." This point of contact may explain the means of "acculturation" (a term too often used too loosely). It may also explain how it was that the localization of the *nostoi* of Epeios and Philoktetes initially took place not in the great centers of Sybaris and Kroton but in the periphery. It seems that local interest developed as a response to a challenge posed by the major colonies, providing the minor sites a heroic antiquity greater than that of either. The indigenous peoples, learning all this from the settlers among them, eventually made these beliefs their own.

In the early phases of their history the great colonies would have had no reason to object to this indigenization of their heroes. On the contrary, Greek heroic associations would have constituted useful diplomacy, especially in an early period for which there is no evidence for any feeling of ethnic superiority (articulated in terms of heroic genealogies) in relation to barbarians. On the contrary, it appears that most non-Greeks were "explained" as originally having stemmed from the Greek orbit. As we have seen, the Iapygians, for example, were originally the Cretan men of Minos who came to southern Italy after the death of their king, who had pursued Daidalos to Sicily. A diplomatic example may be adduced: it was claimed, for example, that Taras flattered the Samnites on its frontier by calling them "Pitanatai" (after one of the Spartan villages) and minting coins for them.[77] This was "exactly as some centuries later the Roman Senate called the Aedui in Gaul 'brothers and relations.'"[78]

Heroic origins are therefore seen as answering, simultaneously, the needs of various distinct groups: the Greek settlers among the native communities who may be credited with the initial association with Philoktetes and the native populations that adopted this as part and parcel of their self-image. Both would have found such origins encouraging in relation to the ever-growing threat of the expansive major colonies, which, counterintuitively to the modern observer, cared little about attributing such origins to themselves. Their land was theirs in any case, and aside from the general Delphic charter of their colonization no specific charter myth was needed, at least initially, to justify the possession of their own sites. (Herakles as founder of Kroton would come later). Neither Sybaris nor Kroton would find reason to resist indigenization; rather, Philoktetes associations could mediate and ameliorate interrelationships. By the end of the sixth century, however, the tables would turn, and Philoktetes would need redemption and vindication.

---

76. Cf. Dunbabin 1948a: 160: "It is probable that the region received settlers from Greece, who never formed a colony but were in time absorbed by Kroton."
77. Strabo 5.240; Head 1911: 27; Wuilleumier 1939: 81; cf. Salmon 1967: 71 n. 6.
78. Bickerman 1952: 74; cf. Pearson 1975: 181; 1987: 64–65.

The robe of Nessos, a gift to ensure love, had been exposed to the sun and burned its wearers.

Both Epeios and, especially, Philoktetes were connected with real cult sites that became viable places of worship for the major colonies. Most important of these was the temple of Apollo Alaios on Cape Krimissa, excavated by Paolo Orsi.[79] The epithet "Alaios" was interpreted in antiquity as connected with "wanderings," namely, the sanctuary where the wanderings of Philoktetes came to an end.[80] The etymology may be wrong, but the association seems to express a poetical truth authentically connected with the site, perhaps evoking a powerful image of the end of migration that would have been particularly close to the hearts of the unorganized Greek migrants. What must have enhanced all this was the "in-between" situation of Cape Krimissa and its related Philoktetes cities. Being in the frontier zone between Kroton and Sybaris, where local communities had some freedom and self-identification, the temple of Apollo Alaios was a kind of peripheral sanctuary, situated outside of the city centers and possibly independent, serving probably for both colonies. It was not theirs to begin with; nor did it serve as an expression of a "border" decided upon by either one of them, in the vein of the argument that underlies François de Polignac's *La naissance de la cité grecque*. Rather, because of its liminal—yet independent—situation it could serve as a point of mediation between natives, the Greeks living among them, and the Greeks of the major colonies.[81] In time, with growth and expansion, the peripheral siting in relation to both Kroton and Sybaris came to express a territorial challenge, thus enhancing its mythological significance. Finally, when things came to a head between the two major Greek cities, the "in-between" position was destroyed and Kroton appropriated Philoktetes.

The foundation oracle of Kroton, which mentions "sacred Krimissa," provides directions for sailing along the Corinthian Gulf and Aitolian shore (Taphiassos, Aitolian Chalkis), the "sacred land of the Kouretes," and the Echinades Islands off Akarnania. The oracle then skips to the major landmarks in Italy: "I would not expect you to miss Cape Lakinion, nor sacred Krimissa, nor the river Aisaros." It has been claimed that the prophecy implies Krontoniate control of the cape;[82] since the epithet "sacred" is attached to Krimissa, either the oracle is a late concoction, reflecting the time of Krotoniate control, or it expresses Krotoniate territorial ambitions. This is one

79. Orsi 1932; Mertens 1984: 207–23; Giangiulio 1989: 230.
80. Euphorion ap. Tzetz. ad Lycoph. *Alex.* 911.
81. This is de Polignac's current approach to the study of "extra-urban" (the term not quite applicable, of course) sanctuaries. See de Polignac 1991; 1994.
82. Giangiulio 1991: 48; cf. Mele 1984: 36–37.

of the few foundation oracles at our disposal with some claim to authenticity, especially because of the rather dull list of place-names, which "looks an improbable invention for a forger; something more picturesque or more significant would be what one would have expected."[83] In that case, "ambition" may be the correct interpretation and does not contradict the fact that Kroton did not actually possess the cape and that local populations could develop there independently. However, since the oracle seems merely to pinpoint the site of the city of Kroton at the mouth of a river,[84] locating it *between* two capes (Lakinion and Krimissa), I see no special territorial significance here. "Sacred" is also the title of the land of the Kouretes, not necessarily implying the existence of the temple there.

At the same time, the oracle, if authentic, is highly significant in another way. Krimissa was a promontory and as such probably already known in the eighth century. Promontories in general attracted sacred sitings, often associated with Nostoi, such as the famous sanctuary of Menelaos's helmsman, Phrontis, at Sounion.[85] Promontories and capes constitute one of the few instances of the attribution of "inherent sacredness" to landmarks in the colonial world. Whereas major state sanctuaries were set up by founders according to rational criteria of town and country planning,[86] promontories were different. For example, the sanctuary of Hera at Cape Lakinion (much closer to Kroton than Krimissa) became a major state temple. Also, as the list of sacred promontories in the Mediterranean illustrates,[87] because of their prominence as natural landmarks, important for both sailors and land dwellers, promontories readily lent themselves both to syncretistic influences and to possible continuities of cult from the Mycenaean period on.[88] It was probably easy to imagine and identify them as the points of contact with heroic sailors, such as Menelaos's visit to the Heraion at Cape Lakinion. Odysseus too was associated, alternatively with Menelaos, as the founder of Hera's temple on the cape.[89] It is therefore much more likely that Apollo's

83. Parke and Wormell 1956, vol. 1: 70.
84. On the Aisaros and adjacent territory, see Giangiulio 1989: 216–19.
85. Abramson 1981.
86. Malkin 1987a: chap. 4.
87. Semple 1971 (1932): chap. 21.
88. Pugliese Carratelli 1962b.
89. With Cape Lakinion perceived to have been first an island: Ps.-Skyl. 13; Plin. *HN* 3.96; Iambl. *De Pyth. vita* 11.57. Another promontory is noteworthy: Skylletion, a city in Bruttium that was Hellenized by Kroton but also came under Lokrian rule (Bérard 1957: 160), is said to have been founded by the Athenians with the Nostos Menestheus, a well-known hero from the *Iliad* (*Il.* 2.552; 4.327; 12.231; on the founder, see Strabo 6.261). However, as in the case of Kalchas, Menestheus is more strongly connected with traditions making him a founder of a city in Asia Minor, Elaia (Steph. Byz. s.v. Ἐλαία with Head 1911: 480; Strabo 13.622; cf. 3.140). He is also said to have gone to Spain, where

temple was built on Cape Krimissa because the cape was sacred rather than the other way around. Its title "sacred" therefore means little in our context. It may well have been sacred to native populations and respected by Greek sailors long before the founding of Kroton.

An intricate symbiosis between colonists and natives seem to have been operating here. It was the Greek mythological discourse of the *nostoi* that articulated the constitutive "historical" picture of the identity (and possibly origins) of the peripheral native sites, centered around what came to be known as a Greek temple of Apollo on Cape Krimissa. Whether the Greeks "started it" may not be known, but it is clear that the Greek colonies did not start it for themselves; we do not hear of either Epeios or Philoktetes as their own founders. What seems to matter is the natives' *reception* of the discourse and its adoption as their own. The symbiosis, however, consists in the eventual Greek use of the same *nostoi* to legitimate their own expansion at the expense of the native communities that had previously appropriated them, perhaps as a point of pride and even "defense" against precisely such encroachment. What may originally have been a Greek, "Odyssean" articulation of the identity of local populations (e.g., the Chōnes), as was the case with the Thesprotians or the Etruscans, metamorphosed during the subsequent history of Greek presence into articulation of rivalry and "punishment," implied in the removal of the *hiera*. The attitude that developed in the sixth century toward the inhabitants as the object of conquest and annexation seems to be expressed in the association made by the Aristotelian source, articulating the natives as "barbarians," and Lycophron, who makes them a distinct group of Achaians.[90]

SIRIS

Philoktetes, we are told, was perhaps the founder of the mother city of the Chōnes, a point that seems to be underappreciated in discussions of the Tro-

---

he founded a city and an oracle, and another tradition makes him a ruler of Melos (Tzetz. ad Lycoph. *Alex.* 911; Apollod. *Epit.* 6.15b). The variety of traditions connected with Menestheus (Giannelli 1963: 175) makes his case difficult to understand. Unlike Odysseus and Diomedes, for example, he is not primarily associated with the west. What complicates matters are the contradictory traditions crediting Odysseus either with Skylletion's foundation or with the founding of Athena's temple (Serv. *ad Aen.* 3.553 with Solin 2.8, who says that Odysseus founded Athena's temple there). It is quite possible that a confusion between Skylla and Skylletion led to this erudite elaboration (Giannelli 1963: 176).

90. Cf. Bérard 1957: 349 with Giannelli 1963: 191, also for the possible confusion between the historical Achaians and the Homeric, "pan-Hellenic" ones; Giangiulio 1989: 163–66; Moscati Castelnuovo 1989: 50.

jan origins of Siris, a city in Chōnes country.[91] The identification of the non-Greeks at Siris with the Trojans/Chōnes signifies that the reconstructed ethnic past of the place regarded it in terms similar to the Greek perceptions of the Elymians in Sicily. In both cases we have a Greek Nostos, Philoktetes, who was responsible indirectly for the Trojan foundations. In Sicily it was the Trojan companion of Philoktetes, Aigesthes, who went farther and, together with Phokian Greek Nostoi, founded Elymian Segesta.[92] In Italy these were other Trojans, originating from the foundation of Petelia, the mother city of all Chōnes,[93] whose founder was Philoktetes. The history of Siris is so complicated, however, that it is difficult to determine the temporal context of the "Trojan origins" version and assess its significance. Siris had a relatively short life. We are told that it was founded at the beginning of the seventh century by Ionians of Kolophon fleeing the Lydians.[94] The Kolophonian ancestry is further supported by the cult of Kalchas, which existed in both the mother city and the colony.[95] Because Archilochos compares lovely Siris with hateful Thasos,[96] many date its Kolophonian foundation to the time of Gyges (680–652), who attacked Kolophon and other Ionian cities of Asia Minor.[97] The colony existed for a little more than a century; it was destroyed by a coalition of Italiote Achaian cities (Metapontion, Kroton, and Sybaris), possibly in the first half of the sixth century (the second half saw the war between Kroton and Lokroi and the destruction of Sybaris around 510). In the fifth century, before the battle of Salamis, Themistokles forced the Spartans not to return to the Peloponnese, threatening that the Athenians would abandon the field and resettle at Siris in Italy (he is said to have named his daughters Sybaris and Italia).[98] But the Athenians eventually returned home, and Siris was finally recolonized in 433 by a joint effort of Taras and Thourioi and renamed Herakleia.[99]

The site of Siris has not been decisively identified, although it seems most likely to have been on the hill of Policoro. Archaeologically, this poses a problem, since there is clear evidence of Greeks residing on Policoro before the time of Gyges. In fact, to judge from the cemeteries, Greeks and natives

91. Apollodorus *FGrH* 244 F 167 = Strabo 6.254; cf. Arist. *Pol.* 1329b17–22 (7.9.3); Lycoph. *Alex.* 983; cf. Moscati Castelnuovo 1989: 133 n. 7.
92. Cf. Mele 1993–94.
93. Strabo 6.254.
94. Strabo 6.264 calls them Ionians; Timaios *FGrH* 566 F 51 and Aristotle fr. 584 (Rose) speak particularly of Kolophonians.
95. Lycoph. *Alex.* 1047; cf. 426 with Strabo 6.284; Moscati Castelnuovo 1989: 51.
96. Archilochos fr. 22 West.
97. Hdt. 1.14.4; cf. Graham 1982: 172.
98. Hdt. 8.62; Plut. *Them.* 32.2.
99. See Graham 1982: 172–74; Moscati Castelnuovo 1989: 47–53.

resided there together, with no indication that natives were there prior to the Greeks.[100] Moscati Castelnuovo suggests, quite plausibly, that a distinction should be made between Polieion, the earlier phase at Policoro, and the Kolophonian colony of Siris. I would add the analogy of Massalia (Marseilles) and Kyrnos (Corsica). The Phokaian colony at Massalia was founded ca. 600 B.C., but the wave of refugees (this time from the Persians) that appeared in the western Mediterranean after 545 drastically altered the fate of both: Kyrnos became piratical and under pressure from Carthage and the Etruscans had to be abandoned; some Phokaians reached Massalia, which grew and prospered, and others founded a new Italian colony, Elea. Similarly to Massalia before the second wave of Phokaians, Siris may have been an "Ionian" foundation before the arrival of the Kolophonians; once this had happened (the analogy ends here) the city's character became predominantly and probably violently Greek. This seems to have been true also of the countryside. The nearby settlement of Incoronata, which also saw Greek and native coexistence between 700 and 640, was also abandoned.[101]

It appears, therefore, that violence against the local population—a mixture of both Greeks and non-Greeks—was an essential feature of Siris's foundation. This violence may be in the background of the myth of massacre and sacrilege that appears in connection with the foundation story and of the identification of the "former inhabitants" as Trojans. Aristotle and Timaios say that Trojan fugitives "held" Siris, and according to the Aristotelian *De Mirabilibus Auscultationibus* "in earlier times, when the Ionians held it, Siris was called Pleion; even before this time it was called Sigeion [the name of a city in the Troad colonized by Athenians] by the Trojans who possessed it."[102] Strabo, perhaps following Antiochus,[103] tells the story of sacrilege: when the Ionians captured the city from the Chōnes and renamed it Polieion, they committed such acts of violence that the statue of Athena Ilias (the Trojan Athena, brought over from Troy) shut its eyes. The story, of course, repeats the motif of the *Ilioupersis* (the destruction of Troy), in which suppliants, among whom was Cassandra, were torn away from Athena's altar. Lycophron tells a similar story but changes the roles: it is Achaians who massacre Ionians. His scholiasts say that the natives, descendants of the Trojans, helped the Achaians destroy the Ionian city. These Achaians are not the Homeric ones[104] but the Achaian cities of Metapontion, Sybaris, and

100. Graham 1982: 174; Moscati Castelnuovo 1989: 80; cf. Luraghi 1990.

101. Moscati Castelnuovo 1989: 82.

102. Aristotle fr. 584 Rose; Timaios *FGrH* 566 F 51 (= Athenae. 12.523d); *Mir. Ausc.* 106.

103. Strabo 6.264. On Antiochos as his source here, see Moscati Castelnuovo 1989: 51.

104. Ronconi 1974–75: 46–47; 1975–76: 158–61; Musti 1991: 18 n. 22; Lombardo 1991: 56 n. 3.

Kroton. The episode is therefore transposed by Lycophron to ca. 535 B.C.[105] Late moralizing tales attach a similar story to Sybaris: rebelling against their tyrant, Telys, the Sybarites massacred his followers by the altar of the goddess, and the statue (of Hera, this time) averted its gaze.[106] The story, not dissimilar to that of the massacre of Kylon's followers at Athens, justifies the "curse" and, in the case of Sybaris, its final destruction.

Violence against natives was common enough, but violence perceived as sacrilege was highly exceptional. We are told, time and again, of expulsions, annexations of native territories, and even the subjugation of natives as serfs. Hardly ever do we find implicit or explicit apologies or the idea that the act of possession in and of itself was hubristic. Now and again there are "tricks" such as the purchase of a clod of earth from the natives to justify the appropriation of the entire land.[107] Winning the heart of a local princess is another common motif. In the extreme world of Spartan colonization we find explicit charter myths that legitimate territorial ambitions and are told with complete disregard for the native point of view. Herakles acquired Eryx; Dorieus, his descendant, "returned" to implement his charter, and there is no apology or sign that his expedition was considered trespass. Moscati Castelnuovo argues that the Siris myth reflects the need to compensate for the initial crime of violence against natives. This is, of course, correct, but the question is why this reflection is so exceptional in the Greek world. In my view Siris was particularly aware of the sacrilegious aspects of its colonization because of its origins in Kolophon; the seventh-century Kolophonian poet Mimnermos (fl. 632–629)[108] speaks explicitly of hubris as implied in the act of colonization.

Mimnermos recounts a foundation story: colonists arrived by sea from Neleian Pylos and with hubris subdued the inhabitants and took over Kolophon; then they proceeded to conquer what was already a Greek (Aiolian) city, Smyrna.[109] Such awareness of the crime involved in taking over someone else's land is so rare in Greek literature that some modern editors of Mimnermos have emended his text.[110] Kolophon seems to have been keenly aware of its colonial position in Asia Minor, as Mimnermos and later Xeno-

105. Lycoph. *Alex.* 978–92 with scholia; cf. Justin 20.2.4; cf. Moscati Castelnuovo 1989: 125–9.

106. Heraclides Ponticus fr. 49 Wehrli (1953).

107. Malkin 1994a: 180.

108. Suidas s.v. "Mimnermos."

109. Mimnermos fr. 9 West; fr. 3 Gentili Prato; cf. Schmid 1947: 182–88.

110. Gentili and Prato, happily, do not emend ὕβριος ἡγεμονές; cf. Mimnermos fr. 10 West = Strabo 14.633, where Mimnermos gives the name of the founder, Andraimon; Vanschoowinkel 1991: 374–75. Schmid 1947: 182–88 offers several more examples of (often implied) hubris; cf. Dougherty 1994: 38.

phanes testify. The Kimmerian invasions of the seventh century, threatening the existence of the Greek cities there, as well as the Lydian pressure, probably brought out somber thoughts about the precarious colonial situation and a fresh regard for those who had paid the price for its success, the natives.[111] It was this attitude, I suggest, that the contemporary Kolophonians brought over to the west when they colonized Siris. This attitude found expression, according to this reconstruction, both in regarding the local population as Trojan and in retelling the story of the sacrilege that took place at Troy as if it were happening yet again.

If Siris was colonized at the expense of a mixed population of Greeks and natives, as it appears, this may account for the ethnic origins attributed to the former holders of the site. The ethnic mixture was articulated as "Trojan." Here I differ from Moscati Castelnuovo and others, such as Musti, who follow a simple formula of natives = Trojans.[112] Since the identification of Trojans as "barbarians" is clearly a later development (certainly later than Homer), one always feels unease with this formula. The case is far more interesting than that.

What is important about *difference* is not so much the distinction between discrete entities but difference *within* that which appears "the same." It is the need to point out a significant difference (mostly for political or social reasons) without giving up the advantages of sameness that highlight the finer lines of unity and separation. This is especially true when enmity and friendship are not far apart; Arabs and Jews are "cousins" (both descendants of Abraham), Roman and Greeks were "Trojans" and Greeks. To illustrate with an analogy from a different region, in the early fifth century B.C., Ezra led the return of the Jews to Israel, with the explicit charter of the Persian king to rebuild the temple in Jerusalem. He found in the land a mixture of Jewish, Moabite, Ammonite, and Samaritan populations that had never left and had not participated in the various transformations of the religion common among the exiles to Babylon. The newcomers found their self-perceptions and privileges were threatened by the residents, and rather than joyously rejoining them they redefined them as *am ha'aretz* (literally, "people of the land")—a term that meant, effectively, non-Jews. By contrast, the returnees were *zera kodesh* ("holy seed").[113] In this colonial situation, with Ezra as founder, they were articulated as the same yet different. The Samaritans, who were also "Jews" (having converted in previous genera-

111. Cf. Moggi 1983: 983. Mimnermos also wrote on the war between Smyrna and Gyges the Lydian. Paus. 9.29.4.

112. Lacroix 1965b: 72–74; Ronconi 1974–75: 53–64; Braccesi 1984: 51–67; Musti 1981.

113. *Ezra* 9.1–2; see Funkenstein 1993: 56.

tions), were denied this sharing and are considered "different" today (a tiny community still resides in the hills of Nablus and in a suburb of the Israeli city of Holon and celebrates its Passover with bloody sacrifices as prescribed in the Old Testament). The Trojan "*am ha'aretz*" in Italy, I suggest, were the mixed Greek and local inhabitants. The feeling of unease at what was done to them was enhanced precisely because of their apparent "sameness." Combined with the contemporary Kolophonian *mentalité*, as expressed in the verses of Mimnermos, the hubris was expressed metaphorically in the myth reduplicating the Trojan sacrilege against the colony of "Trojans" in Italy.

CONCLUSION

The most famous founder of cities among the Nostoi came from Pylos, Nestor's city, and led a migration of Ionians to Asia Minor. Pylos plays a founding role also in the western Mediterranean, where the Pylian Nostos framework articulated various ethnic origins of native populations and the foundation of various (mostly non-Greek) Italian cities. Thus Etruscan Pisa also became Pylian. Pylian origins were invoked among the Achaian colonies (perhaps because of the homonymity of the Homeric Achaians); in the case of Metapontion, founded by Nestor apparently to block the coastal expansion of the Spartan (Dorian) colony of Taras, this seems to have constituted a recourse to heroic "antiquity" in the face of the Tarentine challenge. The terms are those of an inter-Greek rivalry, not rivalry between Greek and "native."

Epeios is the first to indicate the pattern for the colonization role of the Nostoi, quite different from that of the protocolonial Odysseus. This role, perceived in terms of permanent settlements rather than open-ended ethnography, was first played in relation to non-Greek settlements. Epeios was first a founder of an obscure, non-Greek neighbor of Metapontion, where he deposited the tools with which he had built the Trojan horse in the temple of the Hellenic Athena—a name that, as suggested, hints at a claim to being more "Greek" than Metapontion. Lagaria is typical of the frontier cities, in the immediate orbit of the great colonies but at first not directly threatened by them. Its use of the Greek *nostos* seems to have expressed acculturation and contact, developing not a priori but consequent on the establishment of Metapontion. Eventually, however, it was annexed by Metapontion.

There may be a correlation, I have suggested, between the thematic role of the heroes in the epics and their presence in Italy: the device of Epeios and the talisman of Philoktetes had been responsible for ending the Trojan War and hence for the beginning of the return wanderings. The tools with which Epeios built the Trojan horse and the bow and arrows of Herakles entrusted to Philoktetes were displayed as sacred objects, *hiera,* and their tombs were variously pointed out among the peripheral cities. Philoktetes is predominant in the frontier regions of Kroton and Sybaris, where he founded several cities, and some of his companions went on to found Segesta in Sicily under the leadership of the Trojan Aigesthes. In the course of the war between Kroton and Sybaris the settlements of the frontier zone between them were crushed, and Kroton took control of both the territory and Philoktetes. Dorieus the Spartan had stopped in Kroton during the war on his way to Italy to reclaim the legacy of his ancestor Herakles. Whereas thirty years earlier, facing a war with Lokroi, Kroton had claimed Spartan origins and associated itself with another Nostos, Menelaos, now it adopted Herakles and Philoktetes. Unlike the Herakleid myth in Sicily, which articulated an a priori, irredentist charter, however, the Krotoniate myth was a myth of origins regarding what already existed, Kroton itself, and its newly won territories.

Kroton took Philoktetes's *hiera* as victory talismans from the frontier cities that the Nostos had founded. This ritual action, involving the justification of territorial expansion by a Greek colony long after its foundation, has been compared to the "return" of the bones of Rhesos to Amphipolis or of those of Theseus to Athens and especially to the retrieval of a statue made by Daidalos that the founder of Sicilian Gela discovered in his expansionist drive in the native city of Omphake. In these cases the "justification" involved is not of the initial act of colonization but of the expansion of the colonies either in relation to other Greek cities (Metapontion versus Taras) or in relation to a combination of native populations and other colonies (Sybaris, Krimissa).

The frontier and buffer situation around Cape Krimissa guaranteed the natives' independence for quite a long time. Archaeologically they show signs of Greek acculturation, and it has been suggested that the region was settled by individual Greek families or small Greek communities living among the indigenous population. A local interest apparently developed as a response to a status challenge posed by the major colonies: the minor settlements could take pride in heroic antiquity greater than that of either Kroton or Sybaris. They may well have had an awareness of having existed before the coming of the Greeks, an awareness that was later articulated in Greek terms of heroic priority. For their part, the colonies, whose civic pride centered around the cults to their own founders, did not seem to mind. However, when the claim to a heroic antiquity emerged, at least a century after their foundation, it was as a response to the heroic cities of the Greek mainland and in relation to developments in the local scene in southern Italy. Heroic origins are seen therefore as simultaneously answering the needs of various groups: native populations, the unorganized Greek settlers among them, and the colonies. By the end of the sixth century, when the situation changed, Philoktetes needed redemption and vindication through the conquest of another Greek city and the frontier territories of the natives in between. The temple of Apollo Alaios on Cape Krimissa, where Philoktetes's *hiera* were displayed until their transfer, seems to have served both Kroton and Sybaris, occupying land that was sacred because it was a promontory and denoted as such in Kroton's foundation oracle and representing the end of Nostos "wanderings."

Siris, founded at the beginning of the seventh century by Ionians from Kolophon—probably because of pressure on the mother city by the Lydian Gyges—had lasted just a little over a century when it was destroyed by the Italiote Achaian cities of Metapontion, Kroton, and Sybaris. The sources seem consistent in assigning it Trojan origins. It now seems that at Policoro, a probable site of Siris, Greeks and natives resided together, with no indication that natives were there prior to the Greeks. The Ionian colony was violently founded at the expense of this mixed population, and the violence is expressed in our sources in the same terms as the sacrilege that accompanied the final destruction of Troy. Awareness of violence in relation to natives is highly exceptional in the world of Greek colonization, and I have suggested that Siris was particularly aware of the sacrilegious aspects of its colonization because of its origins in Kolophon, whose own foundation is described by Mimnermos as hubris. The awareness of hubris was enhanced, in Italy, by the presence of Greeks at Siris. Ethnicity insists on difference, and in Italy the difference of the local population—not entirely different from the colonizing one—was articulated in terms of Trojan origins.

EIGHT

The Other Nostoi:
Diomedes

Compared with the few ships Odysseus had brought with him to Troy, the contingent that accompanied the Homeric Diomedes was enormous— eighty ships, with men from Argos, Tiryns, Hermione, Asine, Troizen, Eionai, Epidauros, Aigina, and Mases.[1] With impunity he had challenged and fought both Ares and Aphrodite on the fields of Troy and returned to Argos.[2] His return thus markedly contrasts with that of Odysseus, prolonged by many years because of the revenge of Poseidon. But an entirely different Diomedes, with multiple presences and roles, emerges in the west and especially in the Adriatic. In fact, no other Greek Nostos has such a wide variety of cultic, political, and ethnic functions. He was a hero of empty places but also the founder of numerous cities. He was very Greek, contrasting Greeks with barbarians, and yet he was mainly worshipped by non-Greeks. He was associated with maritime routes and the open spaces of the sea but also with magical territorial boundary markers. The colonial uses of his myth are attested from the seventh century down to the Roman (Republican) colonization. He was an Argive and Aitolian hero but also a hero of Daunians, Illyrians, Eneti, and Gauls. In modern scholarship he is often regarded as an amalgamation, a syncretism, of heroes common to Illyrians, indigenous

---

1. *Il.* 2.559 ff. He was with Odysseus in several episodes: persuading Philoktetes to come from Lemnos (Soph. *Phil.* 570 ff.; Hyg. *Fab.* 102); conspiring with Odysseus and killing Palamedes (Dict. Cret. 2.15; Paus. 10.31.1); negotiating for peace in Troy after the death of Paris (Dict. Cret. 5.4); hiding in the wooden horse (Hyg. *Fab.* 108); and stealing the Palladion (Verg. *Aen.* 2.163; Eust. ad Hom. p. 822).

2. *Od.* 3.180–82. For a convenient (not always complete) summary of Diomedes-related myths, see Vellay 1953, vol. 1: 189–201.

Italians, and colonizing Greeks. Since most of the sites in Italy whose founder he was were not Greek, it has been suggested, for example, that here a local hero was fused with the Greek one. However, the term "local," as we shall see, begs the question, especially in that Greeks were not the only ones moving, migrating, and settling.

The distribution of Diomedes associations in the west includes, aside from foundations attributed to the hero, ritual actions that he is supposed to have performed and cults accorded him. Given that a map of this distribution would encompass Corcyra, the Adriatic Islands of Diomedes (offshore islands facing the Gargano Promontory),[3] and numerous sites north of Iapygia (see map 6), it is not surprising that a non-Greek "origin" of Diomedes has been suggested. This origins approach takes Diomedes a step backward, beyond syncretism; here his Thracian connections and his role as a "Tamer of Horses" are considered highly significant. The Eneti (in the region of Venice), for example, sacrificed horses to Diomedes, and this is said to reflect his arrival in Italy before the Greeks. Terrosi Zanco, for example, places his arrival in the second millennium; Ugo Fantasia speaks of migration, especially across the Strait of Otranto, apparently between the tenth and the eighth (or even seventh) century. For lack of a better term, and following late authorities,[4] the migrant populations have been called "Illyrians." (We have encountered some of the archaeological evidence, mainly associated with Albania [chap. 2].) Some claim that Diomedes was their hero, linked with the sites of Illyrian colonization.[5]

The implications of this idea are intriguing. Did Greek colonists "choose" Diomedes from among their numerous possible Nostoi because they had already found "him" (or a hero very much like him) there—because he was already someone else's colonial hero? Was the syncretism, therefore, effected because of the similarity in colonial functions? In support of this hypothesis one may note the extraordinary number of sites that are associated with the hero, a number that sharply contrasts, for example, with that of the sites linked with Epeios and Philoktetes. What argues against it is that different temporal and political contexts, spanning almost five centuries, may be variously responsible for the distribution map, most of which comes down to us from late sources.[6]

It seems, instead, that in the earliest sources the *nostos* of Diomedes is distinctly Greek and nonterritorial. A paraphrase of the poet Mimnermos

3. Strabo 6.284.
4. Festus s.v. "Daunia"; Varro ap. Prob. in Verg. *Eclog.* 6.31.
5. See Terrosi Zanco 1965 on immigration in the second millennium and Fantasia 1972 on the possibility of Illyrian migration.
6. Cf. Lepore 1980: 114–17.

Map 6. Diomedes in the Adriatic and Italy (partly after Mastrocinque 1987).

(seventh-century) [7] has Diomedes's wife, Aigialeia, playing an unsuccessful Clytemnestra to Diomedes's Agamemnon.[8] This was Aphrodite's doing: the goddess finally had her revenge against the hero who had wounded her and driven her off the battlefield.[9] Escaping from his wife's conspiracy, Diomedes finds asylum as a suppliant at the altar of Hera and then flees with his companions to Italy. There he seeks refuge with Daunos, the king of Daunia (Apulia), who betrays and kills him. Some of the literary motifs are topical and familiar: murder in the court of a barbarian king was also the end of Theseus among the Dolopians and of Minos at the hands of the Sicilian king Kokalos. But that, in itself, is of little significance from a historical point of view, since what matters is not the truth of the story but the placement of Diomedes in Daunia in the seventh century. Nor should it cast doubt on the authenticity of the fragment. Such doubt is raised by editors of the fragments of Mimnermos, who place this one (without comment) among the *dubia et spuria*[10] (possibly because of the indirect character of the paraphrase). Support for its authenticity has been marshaled by Lepore[11] and, in an excellent and balanced analysis of the fragment, by Musti,[12] especially with regard to the actions attributed to Diomedes as the result of Aphrodite's anger (expressed, as one would expect in indirect speech, by the infinitives). Similarly, a fragment of Ibykos (also a scholiast's paraphrase of the sixth-century poet) places Diomedes on Diomedeia (one of the Tremiti Islands), where he is worshipped as if a god.[13]

Nothing in these (very partial) references to Diomedes points to anything colonial or territorial. Mimnermos brings Diomedes to Italy, Ibykos to an offshore island in the Adriatic. New colonial elements, for example, the foundations of cities in Italy, should be judged according to different crite-

---

7. Schol. Lycoph. *Alex.* 610 = Bergk; West fr. 22. Fantasia 1972: 127 claims that because of the epic vocabulary in *Mir. Ausc.* 109 on Diomedes in Italy (ἑλκεσίπεπλοι and βαθύκολποι) there must have been an epic poem about Diomedes that served as its source. This may lend support to the antiquity of the Italian tradition.

8. Cf. Dict. Cret. 6.2; Tzetz ad Lycoph. *Alex.* 609; Serv. ad *Aen.* 8.9.

9. Ares too, in another (late) story, punishes Diomedes. Returning from Troy, a storm throws the hero onto the shore of Lycia, where King Lykos intends to sacrifice him to Ares. However, the king's daughter, Kallirrhoe, pities Diomedes and arranges for his escape. See Stoll in Rocher *Lexikon* 1.1.1024.

10. West 1972: 90, but not Gentili and Prato 1979: 56–57 (fr. 17); cf. Giangiulio 1997.

11. Lepore 1980: 117.

12. Musti 1988: 189–91.

13. Schol. Pind. *Nem.* 10.12, 3.167–68; Drachmann Bergk fr. 38 = *PMG* fr. 13 (294) = Davies 1991: 294, with Pliny *HN* 3.151, a prominent monument of Diomedes; 10.127 now adds "tomb and shrine" (*tumulo atque delubro*); cf. 12.6, plane tree introduced to shade the tomb of Diomedes.

ria. One may therefore proceed cautiously and selectively to adduce later sources in order to enrich the context of these fragments, inasmuch as they constitute an elaboration of the same theme. King Daunos stands out; his relations with Diomedes have been variously developed. In one version of Lycophron's account, which seems closer to that of Mimnermos,[14] Diomedes reaches Italy via Corcyra and is killed for no apparent reason by King Daunos (as in Mimnermos). The grief-stricken companions then metamorphose into birds[15] and migrate to Diomedeia (mentioned by Ibykos). They seem to establish some kind of a bird *apoikia* (colony) there; Lycophron pays particular attention to the building of their walls, which he likens to the walls of Thebes.[16] An ethnic distinction between Greeks and barbarians now becomes evident, since the birds are friendly only to the Greeks and accept food from their table—a sign of hospitality and guest-friendship.[17] In Antoninus Liberalis the birds fly toward any Greek ship that enters the harbor but shy away from any Illyrian (it was the Illyrians, he says, who massacred Diomedes's companions). Aelian's story is heartwarmingly "Greek." His birds (herons) simply avoid the barbarians, but whenever a Greek ship puts in they "join wings like hands to welcome and embrace the newcomers." They may land in a Greek's lap "as if invited to dine." These transformed companions of Diomedes, "although they changed their original appearance to that of birds, yet retain their Greek nature and love of Greece."[18]

It is possible that Ibykos too had the birds on the island, although the story is not cited by the scholiast who paraphrases his work. It seems, however, that the birds' attitude toward barbarians is a rather late development, the result of a situation of long familiarity and uneven encounters. It expresses Greek weakness and fear of non-Greeks, generalized as "barbarians." It may belong to the fourth century, when Greeks were threatened by a new influx of peoples ("Lucanians"). A very similar story is told about Hadranon in Sicily in which dogs at the temple drive away non-Greeks but wag their tails at their Hellenic visitors.[19] Similar dog behavior is claimed also for Diomedes by the Aristotelian *De Mirabilibus Auscultationibus:*[20] in Daunia, he says, there is a temple of the Achaian Athena where bronze axes and other weapons were dedicated by Diomedes and his companions, and the temple dogs will not harm Greeks. All these temples seem to have ex-

14. Lycoph. *Alex.* 592–632. Lycophron combines two different versions; see Pearson 1987: 73–75.

15. Cf. Schol. Lycoph. 592.

16. Lycoph. *Alex.* 603–4.

17. Cf. Ov. *Met.* 14.498 ff.; Verg. *Aen.* 11.271 ff; Strabo 284.

18. Ael. *NA* 1.1, with Pollard 1977: 164; cf. Gagé 1972: 763–66.

19. Ciaceri 1911: 8 ff., 122 ff.; Bérard 1957: 358.

20. *Mir. ausc.* 109; Ael. *NA* 11.5.

isted in non-Greek places where most visitors were non-Greeks. The stories (apparently folk motifs) seem to express the insecurity of a Greek in a foreign land, where the presence of the Greek would be an exception. These are certainly not stories about the organized, political expression of territorial presence or even aspirations.

The emphasis on Greeks in general rather than on any particular Greeks denies the story a colonization character in the strict, polis-oriented sense of the word. A strong folklorist feature is that in later versions the birds distinguish not between Greeks and barbarians but between moral qualities.[21] To this Adriatic Diomedes may be added the version according to which Diomedes is not murdered by Daunos but disappears among the islands named after him, one of which is inhabited and the other deserted.[22] A story in Antoninus Liberalis has a friendly Daunos and Diomedes dying of old age in Italy. His companions (called Dorians) bury him on the island named after him and proceed to cultivate the lands given to them by the upright Daunos. After his death they are massacred by Illyrians, and Zeus, taking pity on them, changes them into birds on the Islands of Diomedes. This bird motif is current also in Latin literature and seems to have had independent popularity, especially because of the metamorphosis motif beloved of late poets and mythographers.[23] It is important to note that the bird city was no allegory for a human colony such as Aristophanes's *Birds*. It is a sailors' motif not unlike the Sirens (who are also portrayed as half-bird).[24] It seems to apply to places that Greeks might frequent, such as foreign temples or uninhabited or sparsely inhabited islands. The perspective is one of sailing in the Adriatic, often via Corcyra, with which Diomedes was also associated.

Timaios, the third-century Sicilian historian, and Lykos of Rhegion (said to have been Lycophron's adoptive father) are cited as placing Diomedes in Corcyra. We are told that in Corcyra Diomedes encountered the famous Colchian dragon (the guardian of the Golden Fleece), which was destroying the land, and killed it, having distracted it with the golden shield of Glaukos. Diomedes, greatly honored, set up a statue made from stones he had brought with him from Troy.[25] A second version in Lycophron[26] takes Diomedes di-

21. Strabo 6.284.

22. Ibid.

23. Verg. *Aen.* 11.271 ff; Ov. *Met.* 483 ff.; Juba ap. Pliny *HN* 10.126; Ael. *NA* 1.1; August. *De civ. D.* 28.16; Steph. Byz s.v. Διομήδεια; Dionys. Per. 483–85 = *GGM* 2 p. 132. Cf. Sil. 3.367; 16.369. Pliny (*HN* 4.112) has Diomedes stopping on his way to Iberia and founding Tyde (Tuy), named after his father. Gagé 1972: 762.

24. Buitron 1992: 108–35.

25. *FGrH* 566 F 53; *FGrH* 570 F 3 = Schol. Lycoph. *Alex.* 615; cf. Geffcken 1892: 5–9. See also Paus. 2.3.9; Apollod. 1.9.25 for the localization of the Argonauts' myth in Corcyra.

26. Cf. Pearson 1987: 74.

rectly from Argos to Italy; cheated by Daunos of lands promised him and with his companions turned into birds, Diomedes now goes to Corcyra, where he slays the serpent and receives divine cult after his death. In another source the grateful Corcyreans, delivered from the dragon, join Diomedes and attack Brentesion (Brindisi), one of the gateways to Italy from the Adriatic.[27] Justin says that Brentesion was founded by Aitolians led by Diomedes.[28] The Aitolians were expelled by the Apulians and told by an oracle that "those who reclaimed the territory would possess it forever" (*locum qui repetissent perpetuo possessuros*). They sent ambassadors to demand the return of the city, but the Apulians, "fulfilling" the oracle, killed them and buried them in the city so that they "would forever inhabit the place" (*perpetuam ibi sedem habituros*). Lycophron refers to this episode when he speaks of the Aitolian ambassadors who came to demand "the fields of Diomedes." The Daunians, in response, buried them alive: they "set up a memorial of the dead without funeral rites, roofed with piled stones, giving them the land which they desired to get, the land of the son [Diomedes].[29] In the fourth century Alexander the Molossian, an oracle in hand, based his claim to the city on this story.[30]

There was, it seems, some kind of Corcyrean association with Diomedes, although nothing similar to either that of Odysseus or the cult to the Phaiakian king Alkinoös. The Colchian serpent (Timaios, Lykos) is present in Corcyra apparently in conjunction with the late idea that Corcyra was partially settled by Colchians and with late Adriatic itineraries of the *Argo*.[31] Rather than searching for a specific, localized cult in Corcyra, it seems preferable to connect the island with a general context of a northwestern Greekness, and the key to this seems to be the Aitolian character of Diomedes.[32] To put it succinctly, what Ithaca was for the Epirote and Adriatic Odysseus, Aitolia was for Diomedes.

Both Argos (Homer) and Aitolia (later sources) claimed Diomedes.[33] His father, Tydeus, was a quintessential Aitolian, embodying some of their salient characteristics.[34] Some of the Italian *nostoi* make the Aitolian connection of

27. Heraclid. Pont. *FHG* 2. p. 220; Wehrli 1953: 102.
28. Justin 12.2.5–11 (alluded to also in Lycoph. *Alex.* 1056–66); cf. Ant. Lib. 37; Hyg. *Fab.* 175.
29. Lycoph. *Alex.* 1059.
30. Justin 12.2.7–11; cf. Strabo 6.256, 280; Livy 8.3, 17, 24; Arr. 3.6.7.
31. Ap. Rhod. 4.552 ff. with Vian in Vian and Delage 1981: 27–28; cf. Strabo 5.215–16; Lycoph. *Alex.* 619–29. Cf. chap. 2.
32. Giannelli 1963: 56; Musti 1988: 193; cf. Gagé 1972: 736.
33. Lepore 1980: 119 ff.; Musti 1988: 192–93; cf. Apollod. 1.8.5–6; Paus. 2.25.2; Ant. Lib. 37; Ov. *Her.* 9.153.
34. Antonetti 1990a: 49, 54, with Aesch. *Sept.* 375–96.

Diomedes explicit: in Antoninus Liberalis's versions[35] Diomedes returns to Argos and then, having to leave it because of his wife, goes to Kalydon in Aitolia to restore his grandfather Oineus to the throne.[36] Returning home, he is driven by a storm onto the shores of Daunia. In one of Lycophron's versions Diomedes, cheated by Daunos, curses the land with sterility: it will bear no fruit unless one of his Aitolian descendants tills it.[37] As we have just seen, when Aitolian ambassadors tried to claim the land they were buried alive. Strabo, recounting the sacrifice of a white horse to Diomedes among the Eneti, says that it takes place near two sacred precincts founded by the hero—one of Hera Argeia and the other, significantly, of Artemis Aitolis.[38] The goddess is associated with Aitolia (Kalydon) in the *Iliad*,[39] and her cults are attested in Aitolia (Kalydon) and in neighboring places such as Naupaktos, Patrai, Kephallonia, and Phokian Hyampolis.[40]

The Aitolian Artemis possibly also implies the motif of the transformation into birds of Diomedes's companions on Diomedeia. It has been suggested that birds and bird transformations seem to be a particularly Aitolian motif,[41] having possibly more to do with folklore than with religious practices and beliefs.[42] Antonetti renders "Aitolian" the metamorphosis of Aēdōn and Chelidonis into birds, but this does not seem to be textually attested, although the scene is portrayed in the early metopes of the Aitolian temple of Apollo at Thermon.[43] A far more explicit connection is the myth about Artemis's transforming the sisters of the Aitolian Meleagros into birds after his death. Here the goddess "settled them on the island of Leros,"[44] and therefore we have both an Aitolian context and a content of settling transformed Aitolians on an island similar to what happened to Diomedes's companions. Antonetti adds the bird presence and the magic egg in the myth of

35. Ant. Lib. 37.
36. Cf. Dict. Cret. 6.2.
37. Lycoph. *Alex.* 619–29; cf. Gagé 1972: 757–59, citing a parallel for using stones brought over by Portuguese ships to use as colonial markers in Brazil.
38. Strabo 5.215; cf. Artemis Aitolē in Naupaktos, Paus. 10.38.12; cf. Antonetti 1990a: 257. In the epos Diomedes was famous for the capture (together with Odysseus) of the white horses of the Thracian Rhesos (*Il.* 10.435–504), possibly another point of syncretism.
39. *Il.* 9.529 ff.
40. Paus. 7.18.8 (Kalydon); 4.31.7 (Naupaktos); 7.18.8 ff. (Patrai); Ant. Lib. 40 (Kephallonia); Paus. 10.35.7 (Hyampolis); cf. Mastrocinque 1987: 21–26.
41. Antonetti 1990a: 181.
42. Cf. Mihailov 1955: 190–91; Pollard 1977: 172–77; Bodson 1978: 93–119 (source collection and analysis).
43. Payne 1925–26; Antonetti 1990b.
44. Ant. Lib. 2.

Leda, daughter of the Aitolian Thestios.[45] The Aitolian mountain Pleuron is associated with the myth of Kombe, transformed into a bird to escape the violence of her children.[46]

What is the significance of the Aitolian Diomedes? There was no Aitolian colony, either in Iapygia/Messapia or in Daunia.[47] Diomedes seems to be associated rather with points of approach and contact—with offshore islands[48] and maritime routes. In Italy he was linked mostly with coastal, non-Greek sites. It would appear, therefore, that aside from the hypothetical "Illyrian" Diomedes the dissemination of the hero in the Adriatic had something to do with *trafics adriatiques* (to paraphrase the title of Michel Gras's book on the Etruscans). He began, perhaps, as a hero of brief, ad hoc encounters involving commerce, marriage, and hospitality.

"Aitolian" is a term that covers, somewhat ambiguously, a regional aspect of northwestern Greece. Musti is correct to emphasize a "Greekness" (*grecità*) of the northwest in which the elusive Aitolians must have played a part (one Aitolian visits Ithaca in the *Odyssey*).[49] This may explain why most Greek sailors used Diomedes only marginally; he was neither a pan-Hellenic Odysseus nor a Corinthian or Euboian hero but part of a regional, northwestern cultural *koinē*. Unlike Odysseus, who also belonged to this *koinē*, Diomedes had no Ithaca to serve as a common cult site whence non-Ithacan (mostly Euboian and Corinthian) ships would continue to the Ionian and Adriatic Seas. Moreover, Odysseus had an *Odyssey* that served as a powerful common framework of association and could translate the world of the unfamiliar into patterns of recognition in the course of the travels of the most famous hero. Diomedes had no *Odyssey*, but the range of applications of Diomedes in the Adriatic and the variety of those employing them was to prove greater.

The Diomedes of Mimnermos reaches Italy, but that is all he succeeds in doing: he arrives and is killed by Daunos. This is the story of an individual hero producing nothing beyond his persona. The Ibykos fragment does not even take Diomedes to Italy, and in a later period "Diomedeia" became a site in Daunia itself, a mark of localization of the Diomedes myth.[50] Perhaps Mimnermos said a little more; it seems likely that he would have said something regarding the relations between Diomedes and Daunos, possibly along

45. See discussion in Pestalozza 1957: 619–20.
46. Ov. *Met.* 7.382–83; Hesych. s.v. "komba"; cf. Ov. *Met.* 7.371–81.
47. As we have seen (chap. 2), the Aitolians are said to have colonized Bruttian Temesa but to have been expelled by the natives (Strabo 6.255), but Bruttium is not on the Adriatic.
48. Strabo 6.284.
49. *Od.* 14.379.
50. Steph. Byz. s.v. Διομήδεια.

the lines reported in later sources. As Menelaos did in Egypt,[51] Diomedes helps King Daunos win a war. In Lycophron, probably drawing on Timaios,[52] Diomedes founds Argyrippa (Arpi), or Argos Hippion ("equine Argos," a name suited to Diomedes).[53] As a reward, Daunos offers Diomedes a choice between land and spoils. Cheated of the land by his half-brother Alainos, who had his own plans for marrying the king's daughter, Diomedes curses the land with sterility unless his Aitolian descendants till it, as we have seen above. He sets up as boundary markers stones from the walls of Troy (originally established by Poseidon)[54] that he had used as ballast when he sailed away from the ruined city. Defying the hero's injunction that the boundary stones not be moved, Daunos tries to throw them away, but they miraculously return to their original spots.

The stones are a boundary-maker's dream. They can be neatly distinguished in the different versions: in the first they serve to make statues in Corcyra, and in the second they become Apulian territorial markers. But they are markers of frustration. Rather than serve as a monument of separation, as the altars of the Philaini brothers came to signify the border between Cyrenaica and Carthaginian lands,[55] the stones of Diomedes separate nothing. The curse of sterility, the stoning of the Aitolians, and possibly some real "magic" stones that were pointed out to travelers in Apulia are all signs of unrealized ambitions. These seem to belong not to the seventh century (Mimnermos) but to the centuries of Greek presence and contacts with the regions to the north of Iapygia, following a pattern of direct link between the explicitness of the charter myth and its failure to be realized. In a previous book I have argued for the existence of such a pattern, mostly in the Spartan world of colonization, for example, in the case of the Spartan Dorieus and his "irredentist" claim to Sicilian Eryx; he failed to realize the claim and paid for it with his life. Pearson is right to suggest a thematic comparison between Diomedes's story and Dorieus's title to the legacy of Herakles at Sicilian Eryx.[56] Like Dorieus, when Alexander the Molossian invaded Italy in the later fourth century (334–330) he demanded the realization of the Aitolian legacy. With a view to the population of Apulia and especially the city of Brentesion, Alexander presented himself as the heir of Diomedes,

51. Malkin 1994a: 48–50.
52. Pearson 1987: 74 with *FGrH* 566 F 55.
53. Argyrippa, where Diomedes had a temple, is mentioned by Polemon ap. schol. ad Pind. *Nem.* 10.12 = *FHG* 3 p. 122 fr. 23; Verg. *Aen.* 11.246 ff; Serv. ad loc. and ad 8.9; Pliny *HN* 3.104; App. *Hann.* 31; Justin 20.1.10; Solin. 2.10; Auson. *Epit.* 6; Steph. Byz. s.v. Ἀργύριππα; cf. Giannelli 1963: 55.
54. Lycoph. *Alex.* 617.
55. Malkin 1994a: 187–91.
56. Pearson 1987: 60, 74.

coming to undo the curse of sterility with which the hero had afflicted the land of Daunos.[57]

In the later traditions the perspective has shifted to the colonial world in Italy; it is still Greek in attitude but not in territorial realization. In contrast to the unoccupied territory of the magical boundary stones, the cities Diomedes is supposed to have founded were not Greek. Arpi/Argyrippa, just noted, is the first of the numerous non-Greek cities whose foundation is attributed to Diomedes. Strabo says[58] that Elpie,[59] the port of Argyrippa, and Canusium,[60] its neighbor, were both foundations of Diomedes. The name of the region, says Strabo, was the "Plains of Diomedes."[61] The hero also placed dedications at the temple of Athena Ilias (Trojan Athena) in Luceria, a Daunian city.[62] Strabo knew of several versions about Diomedes's end. According to one of them he also functioned as a culture hero, digging a canal through the plain to the sea, but he did not finish this work before he returned to his homeland.

A friendlier Daunos, similar to the historical King Hyblon in Sicily, who invited the Megarian colonists to establish Megara Hyblaia in his country,[63] appears, as we have seen, in Antoninus Liberalis. Diomedes helps King Daunos fight his Messapian neighbors to the south, and the king, true to his word, gives Diomedes his daughter and part of his kingdom, which Diomedes then distributes among his companions. Diomedes eventually dies of old age in Daunia, and his companions bury him on the island named for him. The barbarian Illyrians, who covet their Daunian land, massacre them on the spot while they are sacrificing to Diomedes. This is basically another thematic version of colonial failure, cast in more realistic terms. It is also true to the pattern of maritime direction of colonial expansion. The colonists seem to have their base on an offshore island from which, following a pact with a local ruler, they proceed to the richer mainland. They bury their founder (Diomedes) on the site of their initial settlement, which might be considered analogous in geographical position and political status to Ortygia in relation to Syracuse. However, another maritime people, the Illyrians, intervenes and massacres the colonists. It is not impossible that some memory of a failed colonization is here being enhanced and articulated in the

57. Justin 12.2.7–11 with Lycoph. *Alex.* 1056–66 and scholia; Aeschin. 3.242; cf. Fantasia 1972: 118–19; Briquel 1984: 511. All argue against an invention ex nihilo.

58. Strabo 6.283–84; 5.215.

59. Cf. Vitruvius *De arch.* 1.4.12.

60. Cf. Hor. *Sat.* 5.92; schol. ad Verg. *Aen.* 11.246.

61. Cf. Livy 25.12.5; cf. Festus *Ep.* 66.

62. Strabo 6.284.

63. Thuc. 6.4.2.

language of myth. This might explain the persistent Aitolian colonization theme even though no Aitolian colonization is reported.

To clarify some of the attitudes implied here, I propose an analogy. After the disastrous battle of Alalia in 560, the Phokaians abandoned their colony in Corsica. The captive crews of the forty Phokaian ships that had been destroyed by the Carthaginians and Etruscans were divided among the victors. The majority fell into the hands of the people of Agylla (Caere), who led them out of the city and stoned them to death. Consequently, any living thing, man or beast, that passed by the site of the stoning would become "distorted and crippled and palsied." The people of Agylla sent to Delphi, "desiring to heal the *hamartia* (offense)." Following the Pythia's command, the people of Agylla "to this day" sacrifice to the Phokaians as to heroes (ἐναγίζουσι), conducting games and horse races.[64] The story concerns another colonial failure and its results. The massacre of the colonists and the consequent affliction of the living may be compared to Diomedes's curse of sterility. Caere was not to become Greek (although there was a Greek community in its port, Pyrgi), and the "imbalance" is compensated for by honors to the Greek heroes. In this case we are certain of the historical kernel of the story. The analogy, like any analogy, is of course partial, and the involvement of Delphi places the whole episode in a context of ongoing relations between Greeks and Etruscans. However, it may reveal something about the way in which such a story may arise from actual events and colonial attempts, the relative weakness of colonists, and their reliance on the goodwill of a local king. It also conforms to a colonial schema of the transition from the relative safety of the island (Diomedeia, Corsica) to the greater risk on the mainland. Colonial motifs do not in themselves render suspicious any story in which they may appear. After all, they do arise from repeated patterns of settlement.

Such a motif is present in a fragment of Nicolaos of Damascus about the original colonization of the Phokians/Phokaians in Asia Minor.[65] The Phokians expelled the bastards born to them of the enslaved concubines whom they had won in their war with Orchomenos. The young men, whose status replicates that of the Spartan Partheniai and Epeunaktai,[66] went to Thorikos in Attica and joined the Ionians and many Peloponnesians. They first settled on an offshore island at the mouth of the River Hermos, withstood many attacks by barbarians, and then moved to a hill on the main-

64. Hdt. 1.167. Gras (1985: 425–76) proposes to distinguish between the people of Agylla and their leaders, comparing the lapidation with Ionian themes of stoning the tyrant and hence connecting this with Etruscan tyranny (Mezentius).

65. *FGrH* 90 F 51 with Paus. 7.2.4, 3.10; see Gras 1985: 436–37.

66. Malkin 1994a: 139–42.

land. Intervening in the conflict between the tyrant of Kyme, Mennes, and his brother, Onatias, they were victorious once again. The tyrant was delivered into the hands of the people and stoned to death. Onatias became king and rewarded the colonists with a significant part of Kyme's territory.[67]

The legend reveals the expectations of colonists and, probably, a range of options open to them. First, there are the menacing barbarians, resisting the first landfall of the colonists on the offshore island. Second, there is colonization by invitation, with the colonists supporting a part of the population—a familiar pattern in the histories of small colonial groups, such as that of the Spaniards with Cortez and their alliance with Indian peoples that wished to rebel against Aztec rule. This time, supposedly, the story is one of success (but not for the lapidated tyrant). Third, the Phokaians in Caere and the companions of Diomedes in Diomedeia and Daunia exemplify the other extreme of the range of colonial expectations: annihilation at the hands of barbarians and a curse laid upon the land.

Liberalis, a late mythographer, calls Diomedes's companions not Aitolians but "Dorians." The name "Dorians" may allude either to traditions about heroic Rhodian colonization (Elpie is said in a late source to have been a Rhodian colony founded in the heroic age)[68] or, perhaps more likely, to the closest neighbors of the Daunians, the Dorians of Taras, who also had their eye on Brentesion. Liberalis may have been influenced by Taras, where Diomedes's cult is implied in the cult to the "Tydeidai."[69] There was also a cult to Diomedes at Metapontion, Argyrippa, and Thourioi and perhaps already also at Sybaris.[70] Another suggestion is made by Braccesi, who claims a one-to-one connection between Diomedes and the propaganda of the Spartan Kleonymos, who came in 303/2 from the mother city to help Taras against the Lucanians and later occupied Corcyra.[71] Braccesi suggests an "allegory" with Diomedes, as if Kleonymos had been identified with Diomedes and become the source of some aspects of the Diomedes myth.

In general terms I agree that the fourth century, a time of trouble for Greek colonies facing new dangers from new "Italian" populations, may have been a time when stronger mythic associations were evoked, followed,

---

67. Cf. Sakellariou 1958: 235.

68. Vitruvius *De arch.* 1.4.12.

69. *Mir. Ausc.* 106. For a discussion of this passage, which seems to be an agglomeration of various cults rather than evidence for a single cult accorded to various heroic houses (Atreidai, Laertidai, and others), see Malkin 1994a: 60.

70. Polemon ap. schol. ad Pind. *Nem.* 10.12 = *FHG* 3 p. 122 fr. 23 with Giannelli 1963: 90–91; cf. Graf 1982: 161. I see little reason to stress the divine/heroic distinction in such cases; cf. Malkin 1987a: 193.

71. Braccesi 1994: 121–27. See Plut. *Pyrrh.* 26; Diod. 20.104; Livy 10.1. See Wuilleumier 1968 (1939): 94–96; Marasco 1981: 38–48; Cartledge and Spawforth 1989: 30.

perhaps, by the institution of a cult to Diomedes at Taras. The "Dorian" identification of Diomedes's companions may belong to this climate. However, to make a claim of deliberate identification between Kleonymos and Diomedes is a different matter. One needs to provide a context of comparisons in which such simple one-to-one relations exist. Agesilaos posing as a second Agamemnon or Alexander playing an Achilles could have served as starting points for such a comparison, but even in their case the historical figure does not *become* the mythic hero. Mythic associations, except, sometimes, when used deliberately as charter myths, do not emerge as a result of "propaganda"—itself a loaded term that requires substantiation.

Braccesi also discusses at a greater length an earlier, sweeping use of Diomedes as justification of Greek expansion in the Adriatic. The time is the early fourth century, and the person directly responsible for the dissemination of the cult of Diomedes is Dionysios I, tyrant of Syracuse,[72] who colonized the Adriatic and entered into alliances with Illyrians, Molossians, and Celts.[73] Diodorus attributes this Adriatic expansion to a wish to take control of Epirus and eventually rob Delphi—a motive justifiably suspect as a literary commonplace. Specifically, he says that Dionysios sought to make the Ionian strait (probably the Strait of Otranto) his own. He may have wished to strengthen his contacts with the Corinthian Gulf[74] or to create an empire to counterbalance Carthage and gain access to trade routes and mercenaries (Gauls).[75] By this time the Celts had overcome the Etruscans in the Po Valley, and the Etruscan city of Spina, which had been declining since the collapse of the Athenian empire, may have been overrun as well. A few years before 385 B.C. Dionysios colonized Lissos in Illyria, at the mouth of the Drilo River. He also supported the colony of Paros to Adriatic Pharos in 385 and warded off an Illyrian attack against it. He colonized the offshore Illyrian island of Issa and may have sent colonists also to Black Corcyra and Epirus. He entered into an alliance with the Illyrians and an exiled Molossian prince, Alketas, to reinstate Alketas, and the invasion was successful in part (the Spartans intervened and the Illyrians withdrew, but Alketas remained in power). In Italy Dionysios founded Ancona in Picenum, just south of the country of the Nones Celts (the Ager Gallicus), and may have recolonized Adria, thus reaching the Veneti (where he had a stud farm). This was the time when the Gauls first swept through Italy, reaching Iapygia and Rome, and Dionysios apparently turned to the Senones as a rich source of mercenaries.

Since Diomedes was obviously present in the Adriatic before the fourth century, Braccesi suggests that it was Corinth, Syracuse's mother city, that

72. Braccesi 1994: 85–110.
73. Cf. Caven 1990: 149–52.

74. Stroheker 1958: 120.
75. Caven 1990: 150.

had introduced him; the myth was then "revitalized" by Dionysios I in the hope of making the Adriatic a Syracusan lake.[76] Dionysios I, he claims, installed (or "revitalized") Diomedes in the Po Delta (Adria), on the Coneno promontory (Ancona), the Liburnidi Islands (an alternative to the Tremitis as the "Island of Diomedes"), the Sebenico promontory in Illyria (Issa), and the Gargano Promontory in Italy (colonies founded by Dionysios the younger), and at Timavum (Timauon) in Caput Adriae. The contacts with the Gauls of the north are a major component of his thesis. Siculus Flaccus, a writer on land surveying of unknown date (but probably not of the Republican period), speaks of Makedonians (in Libya), Phrygians, and Etruscans and of Diomedes "with the Gauls in Apulia." Braccesi suggests that Diomedes was therefore the "*archēgetēs* [founding leader] of the Gauls"[77] and that the occasion for this connection was Dionysios's hiring of Gallic mercenaries. It has also been suggested that the aitiological-eponymic tale of the Cyclops Polyphemos and Galatea, parents of Keltos (Celts, Gauls) and Illyrios (Illyrians), belongs to the court poetry of Dionysios.[78] Furthermore, claims Braccesi, Gauls are significantly identified with the legendary people of the north, the Hyperboreans: according to Stephanus of Byzantium, possibly drawing on Philistos (the Syracusan court historian of Dionysios I),[79] an eponymous Galeotes was the son of Apollo and Themisto, a daughter of Zabios, the king of the Hyperboreans.[80] The Adriatic is also the scene of the gifts of the Hyperboreans: Herodotus tells of their journey from the Hyperboreans through the Scythians "to the Adriatic Sea, which is the most westerly limit of their journey" (τὸ πρὸς ἑσπέρης ἑκαστάτω ἐπὶ τὸν Ἀδρίην), and then to the south (πρὸς μεσαμβρίην), "the people of Dodona being the first Greeks to receive them." Braccesi regards this as the "legend of the migration of the Hyperboreans, or their gifts," and sees as the point of contact the area just beyond the Celtic (Gallic) sphere, probably west of Adria.[81] This he connects with the area of Timauon (Timavo), "in the recess of the Adriatic," where Diomedes had a temple.[82] Hence, he claims, we have a convergence of Celts, Hyperboreans (= Celts), a temple of Diomedes, and a

76. A phrase of Ciaceri 1926–40: 409 ff. Braccesi does not here confront the implications of the "Rhodian" introduction of Diomedes (in the heroic period) for which he argued earlier (1977: 57–59).

77. Braccesi 1994: 93.

78. Timaios *FGrH* 566 F 69; App. *Ill.* 2; Braccesi 1994: 94; cf. Caven 1990: 153.

79. Philistos went to the Adriatic. Plut. *Dion.* 11. Cf. Braccesi 1994: 91; the language of Diod. 15.7.3 and Plutarch signifies that he was a fugitive, not an official. See Beaumont 1936: 202.

80. Steph. Byz. s.v. Γαλεῶται.

81. Braccesi 1977: 65.

82. Braccesi 1994: 99–101 with Strabo 5.214.

Syracusan presence. The myth of Diomedes therefore appears as a justification for the new Syracusan initiative in the Ionian and Adriatic Seas.[83]

The argument seems to rest on meager evidence and to attempt to cover
far too much ground. The emphasis on the fourth-century context is dis-
proportionate, since, as we have seen, the Diomedes Adriatic myth is attested by Mimnermos (seventh-century) and Ibykos (sixth-century) long
before the days of Dionysios I. Neither source is discussed,[84] and there is
nothing Corinthian in either. That Corinth started all this, perhaps by some
connection between the *Argonautica* and Phaiakia, is not only unverifiable
(as Braccesi freely admits) but also highly unlikely. The Argonautic itinerary
in the Adriatic is late, and Corinth's connection with Diomedes is summed
up in the story that Diomedes founded a temple to Athena Oxyderkes
there.[85] In the Corinthian-Ithacan-Corcyrean context it was, as we have
seen, the *Odyssey* and Odysseus that articulated Adriatic contacts.

There are other difficulties. Dionysios's wish "to make the Ionian strait
his own" (Diodorus) is compared with Strabo's statement that "Diomedes
had the domination over the Adriatic." Since "domination" (*dynasteia*) was
a term often associated with the Sicilian tyrants, Braccesi sees an overlap between "Dio-medes" and "Dio-nysios." He translates Strabo's phrase τῆς δὲ
τοῦ Διομήδους δυναστείας περὶ τὴν θάλατταν ταύτην as if it amounted to
an implicit connection with the maritime domination of Dionysios.[86] However, Strabo's περὶ seems to mean the "area by the sea," that is, the coastal
cities (which he goes on to enumerate), rather than the sea itself.

Siculus Flaccus's phrase "with the Gauls in Apulia" is the sole explicit basis for connecting Diomedes with the Gauls. The source is a chronological
mystery. The specification "in Apulia" needs further explanation, since if
Dionysios's interest was to use the Gauls as mercenaries he would not have
wanted them to overrun Apulia. It is more likely that the source connected
the invading Gauls with the local, Apulian hero (Diomedes is abundantly attested in Apulia) rather than seeing Diomedes as arriving with them. The
conclusion that he was their founding leader seems far-fetched. Finally, the
tradition about the gifts of the Hyperboreans is not a "legend of the *migration* [my emphasis] of the Hyperboreans," and the identification of the latter with the Gauls seems uncertain.[87]

---

83. Braccesi 1994: 104.

84. Cf. Beaumont's appendix, "Greek Cults in the Adriatic" (1936: 194–95), which
is not mentioned by Braccesi 1994; both sources and Beaumont are referred to in Braccesi 1977: 14, 57–59.

85. Paus. 2.24.2. This is not discussed by Braccesi.

86. Braccesi 1994: 89–90.

87. Nor is there any indication that Philistos was the source of Diodorus here, a point
made in passing.

What remains is a plausible context, especially with regard to the attested cult of Diomedes in the "recess of the Adriatic." This is Braccesi's best point, since cult has a stronger presence than ancient erudite speculations and the geographical context is in the general area of the periphery of Celtic influence (though not among the Gauls). His thesis forms a good starting point but must be severely limited to a single instance of the employment of myth. It does not explain "Diomedes in the Adriatic," nor does it say much about why he was readily accepted by non-Greeks. It does, however, add to the multifaceted uses of the *nostoi*, both as mediating between Greeks and non-Greeks and as illustrating how a Greek *nostos* that had an independent and earlier presence in mostly non-Greek Apulia could be "used" by Greeks in ad hoc political circumstances. The irony consists in an apparent Greek appropriation of a *Greek nostos* familiar or current among non-Greeks as an element of mediation in the fluctuating relations with such peoples.

In late, mostly Roman-influenced sources, Diomedes is credited with a series of city foundations in central and western Italy: Venusia, Venafrum, Beneventium, Equus Tuticus, Lanuvium, Salapia, Sipous, Elpie, Brentesion, and Garganum.[88] In one version Rome itself derives from his action: Diomedes sent the eponym Rhomos from Troy.[89] Spina too is sometimes regarded as his foundation.[90] It is impossible to determine the precise origins and cause of these surprisingly numerous identifications. The sheer number, unprecedented and unparalleled for any other Greek Nostos, seems to argue against a syncretism hypothesis unless one resorts to some "panethnic" hero along the lines of the Illyrian hypothesis. The number of Adriatic foundations has led to a search for a large context, a single cause, rather than a slow process of adoption by one non-Greek city after another of Diomedes as founder. One plausible explanation, distinguishing the aspect of city foundation from other aspects of Diomedes's "presence," points to a later, concentrated activity of war, expansion, and colonization. Here, however, we are dealing no longer with Greeks but with the Romans of the late fourth century.

Mythical actions such as fighting wars, associating with local princes and/or their daughters, digging canals, or slaying monsters are biography-oriented, and the death of the hero marks the end of their effects. In fact,

88. Strabo 6.283–84; Pliny *HN* 3.20; Justin 12.2; Solin. 2.10; Serv. ad *Aen.* 8.9; 11.246; Procop. *Goth.* 1.15; on Equus Tuticus, Serv. ad *Aen.* 8.9; on Venusia, Venafrum, schol. ad Verg. *Aen.* 9.246; on Lanuvium, App. *BCiv.* 2.20; cf. Musti 1987: 188. On Polidarios at Garganum see Lycoph. *Alex.* 1047 ff.; Strabo 6.284 with Giannelli 1963: 59.

89. Plut. *Rom.* 2.2. On Diomedes and Aeneas, see Dion. Hal. 12.22 (16).

90. Pliny *HN* 3.120.

he is a hero precisely because of his life-larger-than-life. By contrast, if it is anything more than an erudite guess, the association of a hero with a city's foundation carries with it a whole set of community connections. Founders could expect heroic cult and worship by an entire community. When there was no such cult (perhaps because no one had thought the particular hero deserved one), once the claim was made it carried with it the implication of impiety if it were not instituted. Conversely, once instituted, the cult could serve as a vindication of territorial claims and the new "foundations" of those who supported it. One is therefore fully justified in searching for the reason for the association in a political context and in terms of the deliberate initiative of an external force. The case becomes particularly strong here in view of the exceptional number of attributions of non-Greek cities to Diomedes and, especially, their geographical clusters. The foundation of non-Greek cities by Greek Nostoi is not unparalleled; we have observed, for example, that Epirote Bouneima adopted Odysseus as its founder. But in Apulia we are concerned with a huge number of sites, mostly not directly related to Greek colonization or Greek expansion but surprisingly fitting a different pattern of colonization: that of Rome.

We have come full circle. The Roman context of the late fourth century, of course, is not exclusive but simply the most recent of a fascinating multiplicity of contexts first attested for the seventh century. First we encounter a Diomedes associated with the Adriatic by Greeks, probably Aitolians, emphasizing a maritime perspective and empty offshore islands. Concurrently, Diomedes is a guest of the local king, Daunos, probably acting upon the land and setting a heroic precedent of presence but not of foundation or colonization. It is possible, however, that the Daunia failure, the massacre of the companions, and their metamorphosis may reflect a failed and feeble attempt to colonize. Like Epeios and Philoktetes, Diomedes was adopted by non-Greek communities and peoples. Various cult centers were associated with him either as his foundations or, more commonly, as places where he had made dedications in early periods when the distinction between non-Greeks and Greeks was not crucial and even Daunos himself could be considered "Greek" (an Arkadian). Non-Greek peoples living beyond the range of frequent contact, such as the Veneti and later the Gauls, found in Diomedes a ready-made mediator. With increasing tension and the adoption of sweeping distinctions between Greeks and barbarians, various Greeks seem to have used the indigenization of Diomedes against the indigenous peoples. Dionysios I and especially Alexander the Molossian provide the best examples. Finally, this Greek pattern of political application of the hero's presence seems to have been followed by Romans, using a Greek myth to articulate, mediate, and perhaps even justify their own expansion. The robe of Nessos stuck as strands of it were exposed to the sun in the fourth and third centuries. The gift turned poisonous and burned the recipients, but unlike Herakles they were consumed only partially. From the perspective of the *longue durée,* after the Romanization of Italy the hybridization of the Diomedes myth was fully integrated.

THE CULT OF DIOMEDES

The cultic dimension of the hero is possibly the most elusive and complicated. On the one hand, we hear of sacred relics (dedications made by Diomedes) associated with the hero, functioning as evidence for his precedent-setting visits. We also hear of temples and cults that he instituted. On the other, we learn of worship of Diomedes; Lycophron says, "a high god shall he be called by many, even by those who dwell by the cavernous plain of Io."[91]

Perhaps the most curious cult is the one involving horse sacrifice reported by Strabo for the Eneti.[92] According to one of the versions of his death, Diomedes had an apotheosis among the Eneti.[93] His presence there provides us with an interesting parallel to Menelaos's pairing with Antenor in Libya, since among the Eneti he would have been a neighbor of the Trojan companions of Antenor.[94] According to one tradition Diomedes helps the Trojans against Turnus.[95] Archaeological evidence points to horse sacrifice in Venetia, especially in the cemetery at Este, as early as the end of the ninth century and during the eighth; entire horses were buried.[96] It seems plausible that a syncretism was operating here, considering Diomedes's special connection with horses.[97] The temples supposedly founded by the hero in the area are a mystery. It is unlikely that they had anything to do with early sixth-century Phokaian penetration into the "head" of the Adriatic, since the epithets of the goddesses are explicitly Argive and Aitolian. It is more plausible that they were connected with Greek activity around Adria and Spina, but, again, it is not clear how. Possibly, because Diomedes was both an Argive (he found refuge at the altar of Argive Hera, according to Mimnermos) and an Aitolian (see above), the Greek view of the Venetian cult sites somehow made the association.

What is important here, however, is the cult activity itself, conducted by non-Greeks and identified *by Greeks* as directed to a Greek hero. Was it

91. Lycoph. *Alex.* 630–32. Lycophron plays on the etymology Io-Ionian. Cf. Aesch. *PV* 829–41.

92. Strabo 5.215; 6.284.

93. Strabo 5.215; 6.284.

94. Braccesi 1984.

95. Paus. 1.11; Serv. ad *Aen.* 8.9.

96. Mastrocinque 1987: 79–88 with fig. 48–9, p. 81.

97. Mastrocinque 1987: 84 argues, unconvincingly, against any particular horse characterization of the hero.

"really" Diomedes who was worshipped? There is no evidence in the Greek world for horse sacrifice to Diomedes; nor is there archaeological evidence that the small dedications of bronze horses in Venetia or the excavated horse sacrifices mentioned above (most numerous in the fifth century B.C.) were associated with him. The connection seems at best tenuous and late.

Diomedes may have reached the Eneti, who were not colonized by Greeks, via the mouth of the River Timauon (Timavo).[98] This area seems to have been more closely linked with maritime activity, probably involving Greeks, Umbrians, Etruscans, and others,[99] and the river itself is likely to have served also as a way into the interior. The temple of Diomedes, named "Timauon," was on the harbor, with fountains of salt water pouring into the sea; the natives, says Strabo, believed that this was the source of the sea itself.[100] To the south, in the region of Ancona in the land of the Umbrians, we also hear of a cult and a temple to Diomedes.[101] Whether the Diomedes cult reached this area from the south (Daunia) or, perhaps more probable, from the sea is impossible to say. Nor can we say anything definite about the date of these associations before the Hellenistic era. It seems, however, that we may still admit that Diomedes functioned, probably quite late, as a hero of "convergence," a mediator between cultures.

At the other geographical extreme, in southeastern Italy, we hear of cult explicitly or implicitly accorded Diomedes by Greeks. As we have seen, at Taras his cult is implied as one of the Tydeidai (his father was Tydeus); he is also said to have had a cult at Metapontion and Thourioi. Everyone seems to agree, however, that the Greek cults are apparently late and derivative. This contrasts with the relatively strong cultic presence (distinguished from traditions about the foundations of cities) in non-Greek areas from just below the Gargano Promontory northward. Diomedes's was mainly an Adriatic, coastal, and specifically western Apulian cult.[102]

At the same time, since the earliest reference to a *cult* of Diomedes belongs to the sixth century (Ibykos) and applies to the Tremiti Islands, one may be correct in assuming that Greek Adriatic voyages, especially those of northwestern Greeks (Aitolians), were responsible for the introduction of Diomedes to Italy, where he was, in all probability, syncretized with some local hero-god. This also seems compatible with the non-Greek, Apulian geography of this cult. The Tremiti Islands are offshore of the Gargano Promontory, where two important sites of Diomedes are located. I find this explanation, based on points of contact and perhaps even attempted colo-

98. Strabo 5.214.

99. On the archaeology of the region, see Maselli Scotti 1983: 209–11.

100. Strabo 5.214, citing also Polybios and Poseidonius.

101. Ps.-Skylax 16 *GGM* 1 p. 24.

102. Cf. Bérard 1957: 374; Beaumont 1936: 194–95, 200–202.

nization, much preferable to assuming the spread of the cult northward from the Greek colonies in the south. It is also preferable to the "Rhodian hypothesis," according to which the cult was initiated by Rhodians who sailed the Adriatic in late Mycenaean times and founded Elpie.[103] Rhodian colonization in the Adriatic is highly suspect, and the traditions about it are rather late and sometimes aitiological.[104] I suggest, therefore, that the cult of Diomedes may have started as a Greek (Aitolian) cult not in but through the Adriatic, reaching non-Greek Apulia and thence spreading to the north and, somewhat marginally, to the Greek south.

The Apulian dimension may explain the silence of Herodotus concerning Diomedes. Herodotus speaks about the Cretan migration into Iapygia following the death of Minos in Sicily.[105] He is aware, therefore, of aspects of heroic ethnography of the South Italian colonial world. But Daunia lies outside his interests, and the early Adriatic attracted his attention only from a Phokaian point of view. The only ethnic names used by the early historians are "Iapygians" and "Messapians"[106]—again, disregarding the areas to the north where Diomedes's cultic presence was felt.

CONCLUSION

Every conceivable function of Nostoi is attributable to Diomedes in Italy. Diomedes associations are so widespread in the Adriatic that many have sought a single explanation for them. We have examined several such hypotheses: that Diomedes was an amalgamation of Greek and Illyrian heroes of migrations, that he was a result of syncretism with a native heroic entity, that it was Dionysios I of Syracuse who promoted him to justify his Adriatic claims, and that Roman colonization was responsible for his image as a city founder. Aside from the fact that there is hardly any evidence for any of these hypotheses, the search for a single explanation for all the associations is itself misguided. Rather, I have suggested that diverse functions and site identifications, sometimes feeding upon each other, developed differently over the centuries and that Diomedes first arrived in the west not as Illyrian or native but as a Greek Nostos as early as the seventh century.

In the earliest sources, the *nostos* of Diomedes is distinctly Greek and non-territorial, articulating a maritime perspective and initial contacts with local populations without any implication of colonization. Mimnermos tells why

103. Vitruvius *De arch.* 1.4.12; Giannelli 1963: 53–61; Braccesi 1977: 57–59; Ciaceri 1926–40, vol. 1: 387.
104. Bérard 1957: 374–75; Musti 1988: 191–92.
105. Hdt. 7. 169–70.
106. Hdt. 3.138, 4.99, 7.170; Thuc. 7.33 with Musti 1988: 191.

Diomedes fled Argos and how he found shelter in Italy with King Daunos, who then murdered him. Ibykos places Diomedes on one of the Tremiti Islands, where he was worshipped as a god. Motifs of this tradition (of which we have only fragments) are developed in later sources, reflecting the consequences of centuries following Greek colonization when the Greek-barbarian distinction became comprehensive and, especially in southern Italy, responsive to a sense of existential threat from non-Greeks. The various versions of the metamorphosis of Diomedes's companions into birds friendly to Greeks and hostile to barbarians belong to this context. Ironically, the view of barbarians on the verge of decolonization was not too dissimilar from the perspective of the protocolonists centuries earlier.

The Greek viewpoint is apparent in the connection with Corcyra, where Diomedes killed the Colchian dragon and erected a statue made from stones salvaged from the walls of Troy. Corcyra is also reported as the place from which Diomedes, as an Aitolian, had set out to conquer Brentesion. The Aitolian aspect of the hero reflects a generalized northwestern association that may preserve the memory of some failed attempt at Aitolian colonization. Because Diomedes, from a Greek point of view, belonged to a regional northwestern *koinē,* he was relatively marginal; he had neither Ithaca nor the *Odyssey* nor Euboians and Corinthians dedicating tripods in his honor behind him. Territorially, the Diomedes of Mimnermos and the traditions that elaborate on his story achieves nothing. The stones from Troy that in Corcyra served to erect a statue now become magical boundary markers that fly back to their positions each time they are removed. A fantasy of colonial frustration, the stones vindicate what real Greeks failed to achieve. The revenge of the weak, as often, consists in curses (here, sterility), unattainable metamorphosis (birds), and a territory assigned forever but with no one to realize its possession. I have suggested that the story is analogous to the stoning of the Phokaians near Etruscan Caere after the battle of Alalia: there too the land was cursed, and the Delphic compensation, while laying blame on the native population and providing a religious solution, nonetheless sanctioned the situation in which Caere and Agylla were not to be Greek. A more realistic pattern seems to be preserved in the story of colonization by invitation, in which King Daunos is friendly, but here again, on the death of their founder the colonists are massacred.

The cult of Diomedes is another matter. The later fourth century, when Greek colonies were facing new dangers from new "Italian" populations, may have been the context in which stronger mythic associations were invoked; it was perhaps then that the cult of Diomedes was instituted by Taras and possibly also Metapontion. In other words, the cult may have reached the Greek south later than the hero's ritual and mythological presence in the north; the Greek hero may have reached the Greek colonies via non-Greeks.

The most remarkable aspect of the Diomedes cult is the story about horses' being sacrificed to him by the Eneti of the far north. An examination of the archaeological evidence provides no explicit link with Diomedes, but it seems plausible that, given his connection with horses, a syncretism (probably rather late) evoked the identification (by Greeks) of the hero worshipped as Diomedes. Diomedes may have reached the Eneti via the mouth of the River Timauon, which seems to have functioned as a point of contact for seafarers, not only Greeks but also Umbrians, Etruscans, and others. For the most part his cult was Adriatic, coastal, and specifically western Apulian. Its first attestation is in fact Greek: Ibykos (sixth-century) speaks of a cult to Diomedes in the Tremiti Islands, opposite the Gargano Promontory.[107] The cult then spread, as in the north, via a point of contact, Tremiti-Gargano. The Greek colonies in the south seem to have endorsed the cult, rather marginally, later than the non-Greeks of Apulia.

Diomedes provides us an excellent opportunity to evaluate scholarly theories about the uses of *nostoi* as legitimation or justification. I have argued again against the tendency to look for one-to-one correspondences such as Kleonymos's presenting himself as Diomedes. When justification is explicit, as in the case of Alexander the Molossian, we may proceed to ask about the choice of theme, its various elements, and local adaptability. When an implied justification is suggested, however, it is insufficient merely to state the issue; the evidence for it must be investigated in detail. In general, we have

107. There were other Nostos cults associated with this promontory. Timaios and Strabo speak of cults to Podaleirios (a son of Asklepios) and Kalchas in the region of Mt. Gargano (Timaios *FGrH* 566 F 56a = Tzetz. ad Lycoph. *Alex.* 1050; Strabo 6.284; cf. Giannelli 1963: 59). Strabo says that the oracular *heroön* of Kalchas was on top of Drion, a nearby hill; consultants would sacrifice a black ram and receive inspiration while sleeping wrapped in its skin. Podaleirios's shrine was in the valley, where a flowing stream served as a cure against herd diseases. Bérard justifiably rejects the Rhodian "origins" of Podaleirios's cult, since the Rhodian origins of Elpie, as we have seen, are too legendary (Bérard 1957: 377). By contrast, he offers convincing examples of a Daunian Kalchos (Parth. *Erot.* 12; Pliny *HN* 3.104) (distinguished from the Greek prophet, whose tomb was known in Asia Minor), which provides a homonymous syncretism. Kalchas as Nostos is said to have gone to Kolophon with Podaleirios, where he died (Apollod. *Epit.* 6.2; schol. ad *Il.* 2.135; Tzetz. ad Lycoph. *Alex.* 427; 980; cf. Strabo 14.643). Kalchas is also said to have had a tomb near Siris (Lycoph. *Alex.* 978–80), which complicates matters somewhat. Possibly, as Giannelli suggests, this is because of the reputed Kolophonian origins of Siris (chap. 7) (Giannelli 1963: 108–12). On the whole it seems that we are concerned here with cults that may be considered Nostos cults only incidentally. The Nostos aspect is identified for Asia Minor, not Italy. These cults seem to have been a rural affair, especially connected with areas of grazing and transhumance (Bérard 1957: 378). They are, again, "peripheral," but to such an extent that their relevance to Greeks or as intermediaries between Greeks and native populations is difficult to discern.

seen that implied justifications such as the modern claim that Dionysios I used Diomedes for his Adriatic policies proceed by pointing out a likely historical context, a perpetrator, and a motive and correlating these with a synoptic map of points identified with the hero. However, given that the map is not synchronic, that not all of the rest is made explicit in the sources, and that Diomedes's Adriatic connections begin as early as the seventh century, the case remains elusive. Braccesi's claim that the Gauls in the "recess of the Adriatic" may have been approached in the early fourth century as mercenaries via localizations of Diomedes in the north may deserve serious consideration, but it cannot be the basis for a sweeping, pan-Adriatic "appropriate time" for the "revitalization" of Diomedes. The hero clearly entered the region in diverse ways, was relevant to (sometimes) unrelated peoples, and functioned differently. The case of Dionysios I, appropriately pruned, is a further example of the multifaceted uses of the *nostoi*, both as mediating between Greeks and non-Greeks and as illustrating how a Greek *nostos* with an independent and earlier presence in mostly non-Greek Apulia could be used by Greeks in ad hoc political circumstances. The irony, I suggest, consists in the apparent Greek appropriation of a Greek *nostos* formerly current among non-Greeks for use against native populations.

In later sources Diomedes's role as founder of (non-Greek) cities is surprisingly widespread. Diomedes was the founder of Argos Hippion (Arpi/ Argyrippa) and Canusium (= "Plains of Diomedes"). He was said to have made dedications at the temple of Athena Ilias (Trojan Athena) in Luceria, a Daunian city. In mostly Roman-influenced sources, he is credited with a series of city foundations in central and western Italy and even linked with the foundation of Rome. A hypothesis about an "appropriate time" for this has been examined: that it was Roman colonization of the late fourth and early third centuries that was responsible for the dissemination of Diomedes as city founder. Because the idea of the hero as founder carries with it associations that constitute a living reality (sometimes expressed through cult) for the whole city, it is appropriate to seek an explanation for it in terms of the deliberate initiative of an external force. That this was a use of a Greek *nostos* turned against Daunians not by Greeks but by Romans makes the robe of Nessos truly one of many colors.

APPENDIX: HOMERIC ISSUES

NOSTOI, EPISODES, AND THE QUESTION OF TRANSMISSION

The issue of transmitting detailed stories (not story "patterns" or narrative "structures" but the stories themselves, including "textual" details) is related to the debate about orality and memorization. The possibility that entire episodes could be memorized by singers implies the possibility of the conveyance of epic without the *aide-mémoire* of writing, the adoption of which is usually attributed to the eighth century (but see below). Memorization, accorded little importance by Parry and Lord, has been observed among bards in various societies. In a synthesis of the case for memorization, Rosalind Thomas claims that the process of composition of bards is not necessarily an ad hoc affair, an improvisation or composition-in-performance; both rehearsals and straightforward memorization have been observed.[1] Even among the Yugoslav bards, accuracy has been observed in repeated performances. It is true that although the bard may claim that he is repeating an earlier poem word for word, his concept of verbatim repetition is very different from our own,[2] but there is also constancy in the flux of improvisation. With regard to Homer, one often-cited example is the distinctiveness of the speech of Achilles in the *Iliad*, which indicates conscious elaboration on that particular hero and scene rather than interchangeable, improvised oral units.[3]

Oral comparativists have observed that many oral poems are not long. In ancient Greece, most of the Cycle epics were considerably shorter than the

---

1. Finnegan 1977: 80–86; Vansina 1985: 12.
2. Parry 1979 (1966): 436.
3. Thomas 1992: 36, but see Martin 1989: chap. 4.

Iliad and the *Odyssey* (*Kypria:* eleven books; *Aithiopis:* five; *Little Iliad:* four; *Ilioupersis:* two; *Telegony:* two). Again, the sheer length of the *Iliad* and the *Odyssey* juxtaposes them as exceptional.[4] Combining the notions of rehearsal and memorization, Thomas, for example, sees "no reason to doubt that the final Homeric poet of the *Iliad* could have worked on the grand structure over the period of many years."[5] Without taking a stand on that issue, and acknowledging, with Morris,[6] that memorization is exceptional compared with composition-in-performance, I still wish to emphasize the possibility that short *nostoi*, particularly powerful episodes, and even alternative *Odysseys* could have been disseminated either before or alongside of the exceptionally monumental *Odyssey*.

If performed oral poems were relatively short, episodic, and scene-oriented as the bards in the *Odyssey* seem to imply, the case for memorization becomes even likelier. It should seem an acceptable claim that, for example, the scene of Odysseus's landing in Ithaca, that "first moment" of the accomplishment of his return, was such a memorized episode. Jensen provides a balanced oralist view of memorization and its relationship to creative improvisation: "My point is that oral composition takes place through a constant dependence on both memory and creative power, that some epic traditions as such are capable of more precise transmission than others, that within a tradition some singers have more capacity for memorization than others, and that within one poem some passages are transmitted with greater care than others."[7]

The most influential article to have come out of the oralist perspective, an article that has also stamped the discussion of the historical Homeric society and its relation to the Homeric epics, was published by Adam Parry in 1966. Simply put, his answer to the question he poses in the title of his article "Have We Homer's *Iliad*?" is affirmative. He considers the poem of such high quality and so complex and coherent that it could not have been transmitted orally without fundamental change.[8] What underlies Parry's thesis is the assumption that transmission through memorization is so prone to alteration as to render the concept of "original" worthless. In one example

4. Jensen (1980: 46) calculates that on the average of 9.73 lines per minute the *Iliad* would take 26.9 hours to recite and the *Odyssey* 20.7.

5. Thomas 1992: 39; cf. Vansina 1985: 12, 37, examining traditions about officials as oral archives.

6. Morris 1986: 84. Verbal reproduction and accuracy matter little where they do not respond to any cultural demands, he claims. He is probably right; we are not dealing here with Etruscan-type ritual texts, where not the slightest mistake in recitation was permitted.

7. Jensen 1980: 45.

8. To this should be added the problem of characterization; Martin 1992: 226 and passim.

he shows a rate of change of 26 percent within just a few repetitions. This is impressive; an orally transmitted *Iliad* could not have suffered such a change rate. Therefore, concludes Parry, what we have must be Homer's original, *fixed within a short time of its composition.*

Parry's argument is a response to Kirk's view that the *Iliad* was transmitted orally through memorization between six and three generations before its fixation. Perhaps it should be remarked that some of the changes observed by Parry were rather slight; a scholar focusing on text may not tolerate such changes, but they do not signify, in and of themselves, that an *Odyssey* would have been fundamentally altered within three generations. And yet, if we consider the *Odyssey* a masterpiece Parry's argument is convincing: the distance between composition and fixity does need to be relatively short.

Parry thus approaches Lord's hypothesis that, for the same reason, Homer's must have been orally dictated texts. Lord regarded literacy as dealing a death blow to orality, a position that has since been revised by many, including Parry. However, since writing is the most efficient mode of fixation, Lord's thesis (imagining someone like himself taking dictation from the master) still seemed convincing. By contrast, Gregory Nagy has been promoting an alternative model that emphasizes the role of oral diffusion as promoting the fixation of the Homeric epics. Text fixation is a process, not an event, claims Nagy,[9] relying on Richard Martin's notion of the force of *mythos* and the conventions of performance as providing an oral explanation for the monumentality of the epics.[10] Nagy's recent formulation of text fixation is the "process whereby each composition-in-performance becomes progressively less changeable in the course of diffusion."[11] According to this criterion, the wider the diffusion the fewer the opportunities for recomposition. Nagy closely links diffusion with the concept of pan-Hellenism, relying on certain formulations of this concept by Anthony Snodgrass regarding the eighth century.[12] He also appeals to "tradition" as the way out of the aporia of fluidity versus "rigidity," but with him too the concept remains rather vague.[13] "Themes," another factor of fixity, are for him "basic units of content." If the return of Odysseus to Ithaca is such a unit, I find the argument compatible with what I have said regarding narrative themes above.

9. Nagy 1992: 51.
10. Martin 1989: esp. 10, 12 (on the distinction between *mythos* and *epos,* applying Searle's concept of speech act), 231, 85 (on the idea that "Homer composes like his heroes"); cf. Nagy 1990.
11. Nagy 1995: 165.
12. Nagy 1990: 54.
13. 1992: 25. On fluidity versus rigidity, see 1996: 107–10.

For Nagy, following especially Svenbro,[14] writing is not an *aide-mémoire* for oral composition, since the idea of a "transcript" (instead of speaking texts) is not earlier in his opinion than the sixth century. This too is arguable, especially with regard to proprietary inscriptions, but is beside the point at this stage. Writing was used as "an *equivalent* to performance not as a *means* for performance," says Nagy, and this may be the case.[15]

Nagy's case has its difficulties. Since he accepts Ian Morris's reasonable claim that oral poetry reflects the society of its audience and since that society is no later than an eighth-century one, what happens to the *Iliad* and the *Odyssey* until the sixth century? To avoid claims that the poems reflect a sixth-century society (which obviously they do not), Nagy postulates a distinction between "dynamic" and "static" phases of poetic dissemination. "The static phase could easily have lasted two centuries or so, spanning the time stretching from the later part of the eighth century, a point which we may call the formative stage in line with Ian Morris's observations, all the way to the second half of the sixth, a point that we may call a *definitive stage.*" However, the distinction between the static and the dynamic begins to seem somewhat arbitrary. Although Nagy insists on the relativity of the term "text," in claiming a static phase he comes rather close to the notion of a truly fixed text. What about Parry's claim (accepted by Morris) that the rate of change would be such as to alter the poems dramatically? Nagy's diffusionist-evolutionary model is supposed to replace "dictation" as contributing to fixity, but I still do not see lateral diffusion as resolving the essential difficulty Parry has raised. Parry's case for implied rapid change applies even to the lifetime of a single poet and is therefore not fully answered by the diffusionist-evolutionary model.[16]

WRITING DOWN HOMER

Writing down a text of Homer—for whatever reason—must remain for us the best conceivable means of fixing and preserving the *Iliad* and the *Odyssey*. Thus the adoption of alphabetic writing by Greeks establishes a kind of a time limit, at least for the availability of the means of this kind of text fixation. The role of the introduction of alphabetic writing looms large in Homeric scholarship, beyond the issue of its date. The "alphabetic revolution," namely, not only the adoption of the North Semitic letters but also the conversion of some of them into vowels (in contrast with their Semitic syllabic-consonant value), is seen as in need of special explanation.[17] The

14. Svenbro 1988: 33–52.
15. Nagy 1992: 35.
16. Reformulated and developed in Nagy 1996, the problem remains.
17. Robb 1994: 8.

Etruscans, for example, who received their alphabet from the Euboian Greeks, used it in the Semitic way. Was there any special Greek reason for adopting the alphabet that required that it be radically altered?

In 1952 Wade-Gery suggested[18] that the alphabet was adopted in order to record hexameter verse—hence the conversion of some letters into vowels. This attractive idea was adopted with qualifications by Richard Janko[19] and with much elaboration and enthusiasm by Kevin Robb and Barry Powell.[20] Robb claims that it was the need to inscribe hexameter dedications that was the motive force behind the revolution. In contrast, Powell follows Wade-Gery in claiming that the alphabet was adopted in order to write down, specifically, the epics of Homer. I address the validity of these theories only to the extent that they bear upon the question of the *terminus ante quem* for the *Odyssey* and the issue of reflection and impact.

The first and most crucial point is whether we can be sure about the date of the adoption of the alphabet. Greek was written in the Bronze Age in Linear B; when we next find Greek written it appears in Northwestern Semitic letters as short inscriptions, the earliest of which dates to around 775–750.[21] Ultimately, all arguments are based on finds of inscriptions; Robb argues from the hexameter-dedicatory aspects of eighth-century inscriptions and stresses their "Homeric" character. Powell concurs but directs his conclusions to Homer himself. Such inscriptions can, however, be counted on the fingers of one hand; there is always the possibility that most of what was written, perhaps on perishable wooden tablets and papyrus, simply disappeared. Herodotus says, for example, that early Ionians used leather scrolls, just like the Phoenicians.[22] The example of the hiatus (ca. 1025–725) in the use of the Cypriote syllabary is also a good example of the persistence of unforgotten yet unattested forms.[23] For example, the mundane use of writing, such as listing the contents of a ship's cargo, was probably familiar from the Near Easterners who taught Greeks how to write, and we may simply have no record of such matters. The fifth-century Akhikar inscription (ca. 475), an Aramaean palimpsest recording Ionian ships in Egypt, is a reminder of such needs.[24] Similarly, Alan Johnston's claim that proprietary inscriptions (identifying objects as belonging to someone) were the primary motivation

18. Wade-Gery 1952: 11–14; see Powell 1991: 109 n. 82 for other supporters of this view.

19. Janko 1982: 277 n. 3.

20. Powell 1991a; 1991b; Robb 1994.

21. Popham, Sackett, and Themelis 1980: 89–93; Bietti Sestieri 1992: 184–85, fig. 8.9 (a) (b).

22. Hdt. 5.58; cf. Janko 1990.

23. Cf. Ruijgh 1995: 38.

24. Yardeni 1994.

for the adoption of the alphabet is equally based on eighth-century sherds with letter markings.[25] We are obviously arguing from what we have, and what we have is very little and selective.

Powell stresses some of the unique aspects of the adoption of the alphabet by the Greeks to argue that it was achieved at a stroke. It is curious to find his own succinct summary of these aspects in a volume assembling the papers of a conference on writing in which some of the specialists on Near Eastern writing argue the opposite. Some claim that the consonant-syllabary aspect of Near Eastern writing systems is a misleading concept. Among the possible agents of the transmission of the alphabet, the Aramaeans are credited with the beginning of the vowel revolution, although this too is debatable.[26] From a different angle, Naveh has argued for a lengthy evolution of vowels,[27] and Xella claims that in general (aside from the Aramaean) syllabaries too can have some alphabetic value.[28] Isserlin demonstrates how Greek (especially Homeric-formulaic Greek) could be read without vowels. If any of these claims is acceptable, one of the implied needs to revolutionize the alphabet in order to write Greek, especially in hexameter, dissolves, and the process of adoption can be perceived in terms of an evolutionary model.

Powell impressively insists on the "single-stroke" model because of, among other things, the arbitrariness in the choice of which five signs were to represent vowels, the splitting of the Phoenician WAW into a consonant, digamma, and a vocalic, the confused reassignment of names and values of four Phoenician sibilants, and a new orthographic convention, the boustrophedon, that was different from contemporary Phoenician line-by-line retrograde writing.[29] Except for the last, these points are a question of assessing probabilities. Isserlin, for example, argues that at some point, *after* a long evolution of adoption, some "adapter" (Powell's term) gave the diffusion of the alphabet a further push "in its improved, vocalized form."[30] The boustrophedon form of writing has been used to argue the exact opposite of what Powell is claiming. Naveh claims that the alphabet was introduced into Greece as early as the beginning of the eleventh century. His detailed studies[31] are based on paleographic arguments; concerning boustrophedon, he claims that this form of writing was practiced in the Near East in the

25. Johnston 1979; 1983; cf. Jeffery 1982; Robb 1994: 59–60.

26. Segert 1963, contra Wachter 1989: 74; see also Knauf 1987. On the role of the Aramaeans as mediators (distinguished from Phoenicians), see Boardman 1990.

27. Naveh 1987: 181.

28. Xella 1991: 83–85 (a special addendum: "Alphabets or syllabaries?").

29. Powell 1991b: 359, argued more fully in Powell 1991a.

30. Isserlin 1991: 289.

31. Naveh 1987 with references to his previous work; cf. McCarter 1975; Sass 1990: 94–98.

twelfth and eleventh centuries, but by the eighth century (when most Hellenists claim that the adoption took place) the Near Eastern teachers of the Greeks had been practicing a systematic right-to-left linear script.[32] He concludes that the Greeks got the idea of boustrophedon at the time of the actual adoption of the Near Eastern alphabet, about the eleventh century. He makes similar arguments regarding eighth-century cursive writing in Phoenician, contrasted with the Greek lapidary style, extinct among Phoenicians after ca. 1050. Many of Naveh's arguments suffer from the same fault as those of his opponents: heavy reliance on an argument from silence. Naveh charges Hellenists with relying on the scraps from the eighth century without seriously considering the possibility that much could have been written on perishable materials before that time. At the same time, he cannot produce any hard evidence for his paleographic arguments.

Without some external control, paleography can be a dangerous field. "Much of the basic chronology of alphabetic development in the Levant remains founded on hypothetical evolutionary schemes and suggested dating may vary by a century or more."[33] For example, the mid-ninth-century bilingual Assyrian-Aramaean inscription on a statue from Tell Fekheriye is written in an Aramaean style of the eleventh century, but its content as well as the iconography of the statue are ninth-century. Amadasi Guzzo adduces this example to claim that in the "periphery" a more conservative style persisted, which might explain some of the Greek paleographic oddities.[34]

Building a context for alphabetic adoption by Greeks is often discussed. Powell correctly emphasizes the Euboian position in the eighth century, "between east and west," although he may be exaggerating the importance of Al Mina.[35] However, that context too is currently undergoing some serious revision: the Euboians at home (Lefkandi) and abroad (especially in Chalkidike) seem to have been active, trading and colonizing, as early as the tenth century, thus further fragmenting generalized images of the Greek Dark Age.[36] In other words, if our assessment of the adoption of the alphabet depends to some extent on the Euboians, they could have served as agents long before the eighth century.

32. Naveh 1987: 53, 178.
33. Isserlin 1991: 286, following Sass 1988.
34. Amadasi Guzzo 1991: 300, 305–7, concluding (in fact, similarly to Powell) that the adoption took place ca. 800.
35. Graham 1986, contra Boardman 1990.
36. Vokotopoulou n.d.; Snodgrass 1994; cf. Papadopoulos 1996. The tenth-century Protogeometric Euboian sherd recently discovered in a very secure archaeological context of the eleventh century by Günther Kopcke (chap. 2) may necessitate some revisions (or at least extensions) of our Euboian chronology.

Beyond all these considerations, if we are to adhere to Parry's criterion of a short time between the creation and the fixation of the epic, the crucial "Homeric" point remains the date. In spite of the comfortable consensus among classicists,[37] we must remember that Semiticists tend to date the adoption earlier than the eighth century; arguments range from the ninth to the fifteenth.[38] In general, Near Eastern scholars are somewhat more tolerant of Naveh's ideas. Although he is arguing in the face of a lack of hard, datable evidence, a single inscribed sherd could tilt the entire trend of scholarship in his direction; such things have been known to happen. It is noteworthy that the two prominent Semiticists (Lipinski and Sass) who have challenged Naveh still consider the latest time of adoption of the Greek alphabet as the ninth century,[39] and a recent claim for adoption ca. 1000 has been made by Ruijgh.[40] On the Greek side, the ninth century has also been advocated by Buchner, the excavator of Euboian Pithekoussai.[41]

The single conclusion I wish to draw from all this is that linking the composition of Homer's epics to the introduction of writing does not necessarily place that composition in the eighth century; the ninth century would do as well, and even the tenth is not inconceivable. "Homer" could have written (or dictated) the *Iliad* and the *Odyssey* before the eighth century without violating Parry's principle that the fixation must have taken place close to the time of composition.

Whether the adoption of the alphabet was the culmination of a process of evolution, the result of a sudden flash of recognition of options, or even an invention prompted by the wish to write down Homer we cannot tell. I would side with Isserlin's sensible position that the process was evolutionary and that Greeks initially adopted the alphabet in the way their teachers used it and then, at some point, a reform took place. This reform either made it possible for Greeks to record hexameter verse or was motivated by the need to do so; here I prefer Powell's idea (the need to write down Homer) over Robb's (the need to write down hexameter dedications).

I am inclined to accept some of Powell's ideas (perhaps pushing their time frame earlier than he does) because of a Near Eastern angle. It may be possible to suggest that the very idea of writing down a great epic could also have come from the Near East, where epic poetry was being written long before the Greeks had thought of using the alphabet to write down the Homeric epics. The Gilgamesh epic is, of course, the most familiar, but closer to the region of Greek-Phoenician acculturation oral Ugarit epics were be-

37. Jeffery 1982; cf. Coldstream 1982: 272; Burkert 1992: 27.
38. The latter is Bernal's (1987) position.
39. Lipinski 1988; Sass 1990.
40. Ruijgh 1995.
41. Buchner 1982: 296.

ing written down as early as the fourteenth century along the coast of Syria opposite Cyprus (Ras Shamra).[42] It is arguable how long the Ugarit epics had been remembered, but they were not isolated in the context of Near Eastern poetic and sacred writings during the period between the fourteenth and the eighth centuries. This took place between 1370 and 1350, when Niqmadu II, king of Ugarit, decided to establish an archive of cultic and mythological texts not in Akkadian but in the local language and in alphabetic script. These are the general areas (including Cyprus) of rencontre of Greeks, Aramaeans, and Phoenicians. I would argue, therefore, that along with the alphabet the Greeks adopted the knowledge that texts could serve to record poetry.

If Walter Burkert is correct in suggesting that the idea of *teaching* the alphabet came with the teachers themselves and if these Near Eastern teachers were used to teaching writing following models of *written* epics, then the idea of writing down Greek epic itself may have come to the Greeks with the teachers of the alphabet.[43] Moreover, the tradition that long written texts were epic ones and thus could be used for learning may also explain how Homer became a textbook (a fact that Burkert considers strange).[44] The Duris vase (ca. 490) shows what looks like a teaching scene: a person holding a book with a readable hexameter, the first verse of a song of Troy, but since it concerns Tiryns it does not belong to either the *Iliad* or the *Odyssey*.[45]

The Near Eastern evidence of written epic and other poetry as early as the third millennium B.C. is still in need of reassessment by classicists, who, as Cooper has pointed out, have not yet recognized how much they have to learn from Near Eastern studies about the development of epic tradition.[46] On the whole, specialists in Near Eastern cultures seem to regard the Serbo-Croat analogies of Parry and Lord as idiosyncratic.[47] It seems clear, for example, that texts were used as *aides-mémoire* for poetry that contained characteristic "oral" formulae and repetitions.[48] There are two versions of the Gilgamesh epic, for example, separated by about a thousand years. Thus what appears oral is known to have been transmitted in written form.[49] The

---

42. Cf. Xella 1991 with Lemaire 1978.

43. Burkert 1992: 25–33; cf. Lemaire 1978; E. Reiner in Rölling 1978: 157, 159–75 (on Akkadian epics); H. G. Güterbock in Rölling 1978: 232–43 (on Hittite); W. Rölling in Rölling 1978: 260–67 (on Ugarit); Gadd 1956; Elman 1975; Drijvers and MacDonald 1995.

44. Burkert 1987: 56.

45. Jensen 1980: 57; Shapiro 1993: 95.

46. Cooper 1992: 107.

47. Izre'el 1992: 155–56.

48. See Vanstiphout 1992: 263.

49. Alster 1992: 24, 29, 62; cf. Goody 1987: 96–109.

variability—with learning by heart[50] from fixed texts—implies that the Parry principle (a deliberate creation fixed almost immediately) can coexist with the tradition of singing shorter, oral episodes.

A similar case could be made for the Anatolian coast, where fragments of an epic whose first line is in Hittite and then in Luwian speak of "men who came from WILUSA," which Watkins and others regard as Luwian for Ilion (= Troy).[51] A recent find at Troy (as yet unpublished) of a seal inscribed in Luwian (eleventh-century) may be connected with this.[52] This seems to open the way for the extraordinary possibility that the idea of a written epic about Troy arrived in the Greek world from outside texts, the latest of which belongs to the eleventh century.

Ian Morris has argued, on the basis of the oral nature of the *Iliad* and the *Odyssey* and comparative material, that the poems reflect the society of their audience. He both adheres to Parry's criterion of the relationship between flux and fixity and accepts the Wade-Gery/Powell thesis. However, the compatibility of the two is problematic. The combination of the two theses, seemingly relevant to two different issues, in fact implies that everything was happening at once: the monumental Homeric poems would have had to acquire their powerful, idiosyncratic reputation almost immediately for that reputation to have inspired the adoption and modification of the Phoenician alphabet in order to preserve them. Isserlin's reconstruction of the process through which the alphabet was adopted—an evolution followed by a significant reform—may allow us to retain Morris's claim that "it seems very probable—indeed, almost certain—that the institutions and modes of thought in the poems were ultimately derived from the world in which Homer and his audience lived."[53] However, we must now become less confident with regard to the time frame of that world. It is no longer *necessarily* the eighth century, as Morris argues. If we shift the context of the adoption of the alphabet to a period earlier than the eighth century (and hence the possibility of a written Homer in the ninth century or even earlier, pace Naveh and Bernal), what does this imply regarding the social world reflected in the poems?

THE *LONGUE DURÉE* AND THE EIGHTH CENTURY

Just as Parry has argued that there cannot have been a long separation between the time of composition of Homer's epics and the time of fixation,

50. Van der Ploeg 1947.
51. Watkins 1995.
52. Mannsperger 1996.
53. Morris 1986: 82.

Morris (who agrees with him) makes a similar argument for the relationship of the epics to historical society.[54] Because oral poetry changes, the society of its audience needs to be close to it in time. Oral poetry needs a receptive audience that shares its collective representations and social assumptions. This observation seems to have become acceptable among readers of Homer.[55] Much as Parry relies on empirical data to determine the rate of change in bardic poetry, Morris relies on comparative anthropological analogies, although these are obviously less prone to measurement and quantification. Essentially I am quite happy with Morris's general argument. The issue that remains open for me is identifying those collective representations and social assumptions, especially with regard to some *longue durée* perspective. Morris claims that it had to be the eighth century; others, such as Walter Donlan, prefer the ninth.[56]

Morris has demonstrated that the eighth century is at least some kind of a *terminus ante quem* for the monumental epics. He thus joins others, such as Richard Janko, who, on linguistic grounds, pinpoints the dates of the composition of the *Iliad* and the *Odyssey*.[57] Morris's thesis, of course, does not imply that with the fixation of the *Iliad* and *Odyssey* the curtain has fallen on the lively performance of oral poems. Alternative *"Iliads"* and *"Odysseys,"* especially short epics or popular epic-episodes, were and probably continued to be performed. In his critique of Finley, who claimed that the world of Odysseus properly belongs to the tenth and ninth centuries, Morris brilliantly demonstrates that it is wrong to deny the eighth century the possibility of being the temporal context for that world.[58] The issue of "reflection" remains this: Homer sings about a distant, heroic age and uses two essential devices to create coherence—distancing and exaggeration, on the one hand, and exclusion on the other. He exaggerates the magnificence of the material world, and he excludes bread from the lands of fantasy and (inconsistently) iron from that of reality and places that reality in a limited geographical frame that excludes Ionia.

Morris's case is less successful, however, in demonstrating salient or exclusively eighth-century features in the *Iliad* and the *Odyssey*. If we accept the premise that the world of Odysseus was that of the audience of the oral poet and date it to the eighth century, must we also assume that world was

54. Morris 1986; see review by Raaflaub 1991.
55. Redfield 1975: 36–37; Vidal Naquet 1986; Morris 1986; Donlan 1993: 159.
56. Donlan 1985; 1989; Dickinson 1986; cf. Whitley 1991: 192 with Qviller 1981; Crielaard 1995b.
57. Morris (1986: 93) accepts Janko's (1982: 228–31) language analysis—that the *Iliad* was composed between 750 and 725 B.C., the *Odyssey* between 743 and 713.
58. Finley can hardly be said to argue the case fully, and his somewhat offhand presentation has long been in need of serious revision.

radically different from that of fifty or one hundred years earlier? Were the collective representations and social assumptions of a century earlier "extinct"[59] by the eighth century? Were the "cultural values" of the eighth century entirely different from those of the ninth?[60] How long, for example, did assumptions about the position of women in society persist? Morris, along with Marcel Detienne and others, mentions the examples of the Tiv and the Gonga in Nigeria, whose oral (genealogical) traditions have been shown to have changed significantly and often while those who recited genealogies to substantiate territorial claims before British colonial officials insisted that they were telling the same tales. It was, however, precisely the colonial rule that accelerated the change and demanded a translation of one system of remembrance into another. No comparable intervention took place in Greece between the ninth and the eighth century.[61]

Although Morris rightly comments that oral societies have the mistaken image of themselves as living in a perpetual present, from the perspective of the Braudelian *longue durée* such a self-image may correspond to a reality of relatively little social change. Only in his conclusion does Morris, following Finley,[62] address the claim that things actually changed little between the tenth and the eighth century, arguing that "it is in this sense only that Homer can tell us about the Dark Age." (It is unclear what is meant here by "only.") He goes on to say that "trying to find tenth- and ninth-century societies in the *Iliad* and the *Odyssey* is just as misguided as looking for the Mycenaeans." The equation is surprising: the Mycenaean world, with its palace-and-scribe economy, was obviously different both from the Dark Age and from the eighth century, but how different is the eighth century *as it is reflected in Homer*, according to Morris, from the ninth? (I limit myself here to the ninth century because there is less chance of significant change between the ninth and the eighth centuries than between the tenth and the eighth and because for my purposes here the ninth century is quite sufficient.) Rather than being the "spirit of the times," a Zeitgeist may sometimes reflect the concerns of an earlier generation.[63] In other words, mid-eighth-century audiences could have regarded the Zeitgeist of a grandparents' generation as their own; even in our own time, the recognition of change is often much slower than change itself.

59. Morris 1986: 86.
60. Morris (1988: 87), quoting Ong (1982: 46–48): "Oral tradition reflects a society's present cultural values rather than idle curiosity about the past."
61. Morris 1986: 87; Goody and Watt 1968: 31–33. See also Detienne 1986: 36; cf. Henige 1984 (1974): esp. 39–40, 85–90, 100–102.
62. Finley 1978: 154; cf. Donlan 1993: 157.
63. Cf. Yavetz 1976.

We claim to know, in general terms, that the later eighth century was different from the Dark Age: this was the period of the so-called Greek Renaissance. The salient features of this Renaissance are the adoption of the alphabet, the dissemination of the Homeric epics, the rise of the polis, the appearance of free-standing temples, colonization, and the rise of Delphi and Olympia in particular and of pan-Hellenism in general. This Renaissance image stands out in relief against that of the Dark Age current in scholarship in the early seventies. However, in recent years the Dark Age has rapidly become fragmented and de-stereotyped,[64] and even if we preserve the salient features of the "eighth-century Renaissance," can these be said to be particularly those of the *Iliad* and the *Odyssey*? To the best of my knowledge, the most that modern scholarship has been able to show (and Ian Morris has done this magnificently) is that the relationship between what is there (historically) and what is not there is the same for the Dark Age and for the eighth century. Morris[65] examines Finley's list of Homeric eighth-century exclusions—Dorians, Ionians, iron weapons, cavalry, and polis life— and establishes that except for the polis all of them would have been equally present in the tenth and the ninth century. In other words, these deliberate exclusions cannot decide the case.

With regard to the supposed lack of polis life, current scholarship seems to be revising its view of state formation in the eighth century, with each scholar discovering in Homer some "embryonic" polis and/or political community (especially on Ithaca).[66] Morris, in line with recent revised views, stresses the "polis in the making" aspect of Ithaca,[67] which could belong to the eighth century. The assembly in Ithaca, as he points out, demonstrates certain aspects of such a community: it had the ability to fine Halitherses, send the suitors into exile, and enter into an alliance with the Thesprotians.[68] For example, to the chagrin of Telemachos it chooses not to interfere with what the suitors present as an affair of the *basileis* ("kings," princes) alone. The entire scene in the second book of the *Odyssey* is constructed as a transition from the public to the private: when wondering why it was convened, the possibility of war—a community affair—is envisaged, but once it is made clear that Telemachos has a quarrel with the suitors the assembly becomes silent. Similarly, when the father of Antinoös had made a private arrangement with Taphian pirates to raid the Thesprotians, it was the

64. E.g., Donlan 1985; 1989; Morgan 1990; Thomas 1993.
65. 1988: 96–104.
66. See Scully 1990: 100–105; Raaflaub 1994; cf. Donlan 1989; Donlan and Thomas 1993: 68.
67. Morris 1986: 101–4.
68. *Od.* 2.192–93; 16.381–82, 424–30.

people of Ithaca who found this offensive (chap. 4). But is all this eighth-century? For those expecting reflection of a polis, it is perhaps too little (hence the notion of a backwater Ithaca with a polis only in the making); for those who observe Ithaca through Dark Age lenses, it may seem too advanced in terms of a political community. But Ithaca is also exceptional in the Homeric epics: it is nothing like Pylos, Sparta, or even Phaiakia, where the authority of king and council is preeminent. In fact, there is no council in Ithaca, the demos is surprisingly felt, and there are far too many *basileis*.

Similarly, the distinction between Dark Age migrations and eighth-century colonization is also becoming blurred in certain aspects: the Dark Age had more material wealth, more new settlements, and a tighter social organization than used to be thought.[69] At the same time, what may be seen as direct awareness of colonization in the *Odyssey*—the prospecting for an empty, offshore island in the ninth book (facing the land of the Cyclopes) and the foundation of Scheria by the Phaiakians (bk. 6)—could, says Morris, equally fit either eighth-century colonization or late eleventh- or tenth-century settlement in Ionia.[70] As I have been arguing, to the degree that the *Odyssey* reflects experiences of sailing in the western Mediterranean (west, that is, of Greece), it is more reflective of protocolonization than of colonization.

In arguing for the eighth century Morris claims to be able to trace the motivation behind the fixation of the *Iliad* and the *Odyssey:* an aristocratic ideology reacting to changing eighth-century circumstances by recalling the "old" virtues and expunging, so to speak, temporary elements that were particularly salient. This hypothesis, however, explains one deficiency by means of another. One can equally locate an ideological, aristocratic interest in tenth-century Ionia: an aristocracy living in a new country and keenly interested in what it has left behind, consolidating an image of an aristocratic heroic ethos and particularly receptive of the exclusion of Ionia from Homeric geography precisely because more than anyone it knew the novelty of its situation.

All these considerations do not exclude the eighth century as the social context for Homer's world but instead open the possibility for a ninth- or even a tenth-century context as well. Morris has advanced us a long way beyond Finley's *World of Odysseus* in his critique of its cursory dating, in establishing guidelines for the discussion of "Homeric society" and what a historian or an archaeologist may do with the Homeric texts, in placing this discussion in a comparative anthropological context, and in suggesting that behind the epics is some aristocratic ideology. My main argument regard-

69. Ithaca itself still has land available for cultivation. *Od.* 24.206–7.
70. Morris 1986: 98–100, following Finley 1978: 156.

ing his thesis has been to assess the possibility of shifting the time frame of the composition-fixation-reception relationship to the ninth century instead of the eighth. I have done this for the purpose of appreciating some points in the book, such as the historical role of Ithaca and the dedications made to Odysseus and the general protocolonization aspect of the *Odyssey*. Thus the epic may appear either as a "reflection" of ninth-century reality concerning captains of sailor-traders sailing the Ionian Sea or, at least, as evoking for Euboian, Corinthian, and even Ithacan traders and protocolonists Nostos associations pertinent to their experiences.

BIBLIOGRAPHY

Abramson, H. 1981. A hero shrine for Phrontis at Sounion? *California Studies in Classical Antiquity* 12: 1–19.

Acquaro, E., et al., eds. 1988. *Momenti precoloniali nel Mediterraneo antico.* Rome: Consiglio Nazionale delle Ricerche.

Adamesteanu, D. 1962. L'ellenizzazione della Sicilia e il momento di Ducezio. *Kokalos* 8: 1167–88.

———. 1974. *La Basilicata antica: Storia e monumenti.* Cava dei Tirreni: Di Maure Editore.

———. 1990. Greeks and natives in Basilicata. In Descoeudres 1990, 143–50.

Ahlberg, G. 1971a. *Fighting on land and sea in Greek Geometric art.* Stockholm: Svenska Institutet i Athen.

———. 1971b. *Prothesis and ekphora in Greek Geometric art.* Studies in Mediterranean Archaeology 32. Göteborg: Paul Aströms Forlag.

Ahlberg-Cornell, G. 1992. *Myth and epos in early Greek art: Representation and interpretation.* Jonsered: Paul Aströms Forlag.

Albore Livadie, C. 1975. Remarques sur un group de tombes de Cumes. In *Contribution à l'étude de la société et de la colonisation eubéenne,* 53–58. Cahiers du Centre Jean Bérard 2. Naples.

Alcock, S., and R. Osborne, eds. 1994. *Placing the gods: Sanctuaries and sacred space in ancient Greece.* Oxford: Clarendon Press.

Alföldi, A. 1965. *Early Rome and the Latins.* Ann Arbor: University of Michigan Press.

———. 1979. *Die trojanischen Urahnen der Römer.* 2d ed. Rome: L'Erma di Bretschneider.

Allen, T. W. 1924. *Homer: The origins and the transmission.* Oxford: Clarendon Press.

Alster, B. 1992. Interaction of oral and written poetry in early Sumerian literature. In Vogelzang and Vanstiphout 1992, 23–69.

Altheim, F. 1938. *A history of Roman religion.* London: Methuen.

Alther-Charon, A., and C. Bérard. 1978. Eretrie: L'organisation de l'espace et la formation d'une cité grecque. In *L'archéologie aujourd'hui*, ed. A. Schnapp, 229–40.
Paris: Hachette.

Alty, J. H. M. 1982. Dorians and Ionians. *JHS* 102: 1–14.

Aly, W. 1957. *Strabon von Amaseia: Untersuchungen über Text, Aufbau und Quellen der Geographica*. Strabonis Geographica 4. Bonn.

Alzinger, W. 1981–82. Grabungen Aegira. *JÖAI* 53: 8–15.

Alzinger, W. et al. 1985. Aegira-Hyperesia und die Siedlung Phelloë in Achaia (I).
Klio 67: 389–451.

Amadasi Guzzo, M. G. 1991. "The shadow line": Réflexions sur l'introduction de
l'alphabet en Grèce. In Baurain, Bonnet, and Krings 1991, 293–311.

Amandry, P. 1949. Le monument commémoratif de la victoire des Tarentins sur les
Peucétiens. *BCH* 73: 447–63.

———. 1984. Le culte des nymphes et de Pan à l'Antre corycien. In *L'Antre corycien 2*, 395–425. BCH suppl. 9.

———. 1987. Trépieds de Delphes et du Peloponnèse. *BCH* 111: 79–131.

Ampolo, C. 1970. L'Artemide di Marsiglia e la Diana dell' Aventino. *PP* 130–33:
200–210.

———. 1980. La fondazione della città nel Lazio. In Ampolo et al. 1980, 165–92.

———. 1990. Storiografia greca e presenze egee in Italia: Una messa a punto. *PP* 45:
358–70.

Ampolo, C. et al. 1980. *La formazione della città nel Lazio (Seminario tenuto a Roma 24–
26 giugno 1977)*. Dialoghi di Archeologia, n.s., 2.

Anamali, S. Les Illyriens et les villes de l'Illyrie du Sud dans les inscriptions de la Grèce.
In *Modes des contacts* 1983, 219–25.

Anderson, B. 1983. *Imagined communities*. London and New York: Verso.

Andreiou, I. 1993. Ambracie, une ville ancienne se reconstitue peu à peu par les
recherches. In Cabanes 1993, 91–110.

Antonaccio, C. 1993. The archaeology of ancestors. In Dougherty and Kurke 1993,
46–70.

———. 1995. *An archaeology of ancestors*. Lanham, Md.: Rowman and Littlefield.

Antonetti, C. 1987. AGRAIOI et AGRIOI, montagnards et bergers: Un prototype di-
achronique de sauvagerie. *DHA* 13: 199–236.

———. 1990a. *Les Etoliens: Image et religion*. Annales Littéraires de l'Université de Besançon 405.

———. 1990b. Il santuario apollineo di Termo in Etolia. In *Mélanges Pierre Lévêque*,
vol. 4, 1–27. Paris.

———. 1996. I Panhellenes dalla Grecia arcaica al tardo impero: L'unità irrealiz-
zabile. *Rivista di Antichità* 5(1): 9–14.

Appadurai, A. 1981. The past as a scarce resource. *Man* 16: 201–19.

Arend, W. 1933. *Die typischen Scenen bei Homer*. Berlin: Weidmann.

Arnold, I. R. 1960. Agonistic festivals in Italy and Sicily. *AJA* 64: 241–51.

Ashcroft, B, G. Griffiths, and H. Tiffin, eds. 1995. *The post-colonial studies reader*. London: Routledge.

Asheri, D. 1988. *Erodoto, le storie. Libro 1: La Lidia e la Persia*. Fondazione Lorenzo
Valla: Arnoldo Montadori Editore.

————. 1990. *Erodoto, le storie. Libro 3: La Persia.* Fondazione Lorenzo Valla: Arnoldo Montadori Editore.

————. 1995. Ferecide ateniese e le origini arcadiche degli Enotri. In *Festschrift E. Lepore.*

Attwood, B. 1989. *The making of the aborigines.* Sidney, Wellington, and London: Allen and Unwin.

Austin, M. M. 1970. *Greece and Egypt in the Archaic Age.* PCPS suppl. 2.

Austin, N. 1975. *Archery at the dark side of the moon: Poetic problems in Homer's* Odyssey. Berkeley: University of California Press.

Bacon, H. 1961. *Barbarians in Greek tragedy.* New Haven: Yale University Press.

Bakhuizen, S. C. 1987. The continent and the sea: Notes on Greek activities in Ionic and Adriatic waters. In Cabanes 1987b, 185–94.

Ballabriga, A. 1986. *Le soleil et le Tartare: L'image mythique du monde en Grèce archaïque.* Paris: Ecole des Hautes Etudes en Sciences Sociales.

————. 1989. La prophétie de Tirésias. *Métis* 4: 291–304.

Banks, M. 1996. *Ethnicity: Anthropological constructions.* London: Routledge.

Banton, M. 1977. *The idea of race.* London: Tavistock.

————. 1981. The direction and speed of ethnic change. In Keyes 1981a, 32–52.

Barker, G., and R. Hodges, eds. 1981. *Archaeology and Italian society.* 2 vols. British Archaeological Reports International Series 102.

Barnavi, E. 1984. Mythes et réalité historique: Le cas de la loi salique. *Histoire, Economie, Société* 3: 323–37.

————. 1995. The United States of Europe: The history of an idea. In *The challenges of the new Europe: Proceedings of the inaugural conference, Morris Curiel Center for International Studies,* 39–51. Tel Aviv.

Barnett, R. D. 1969. Ezekiel and Tyre. *Eretz Israel* 9: 6–13.

Barth, F., ed. 1969. *Ethnic groups and boundaries: The social organization of cultural difference.* Boston: Little, Brown.

Bartoloni, G. 1989. *La cultura villanoviana.* Rome: La Nuova Italia Scientifica.

Bartoloni, G., M. Cataldi Dini, and F. Zevi. 1982. Aspetti dell'ideologia funeraria nella necropoli di Castel di Decima. In Vernant and Gnoli 1982, 257–73.

Baslez, M.-F., and F. Briquel-Chatonnet. 1991. De l'oral à l'écrit: Le bilinguisme des Phéniciens en Grèce. In Baurain, Bonnet, and Krings 1991, 371–86.

Batović, S. 1983. In *L'Adriatico tra Mediterraneo e penisola balcanica nell'antichità: Atti del congresso internazionale di studi SE Europeo, Lecce-Matera 1973,* 67–85. Taranto: Istituto per la Storia e l'Archeologia della Magna Grecia.

Baurain, C. 1991. Minos et la thalassocratie minoenne. In *Thalassa: L'Egée préhistorique et la mer,* 255–70. Liège: Université de Liège.

Baurain, Cl., C. Bonnet, and V. Krings, eds. 1991. *Phoinikeia grammata: Lire et ecrire en Méditerranée (Actes du Colloque de Liège, 15–18 novembre 1989).* Namur.

Beaumont, R. L. 1936. Greek influence in the Adriatic before the fourth century B.C. *JHS* 56: 159–204.

Beloch, K. J. 1890. *Campanien.* Breslau: Morgenstein.

Benton, S. 1934–35a. Excavations in Ithaca III. *BSA* 35: 45–73.

————. 1934–35b. The evolution of the tripod-lebes. *BSA* 35: 74–130.

————. 1938–39. Excavations in Ithaca III: The cave at Polis II. *BSA* 39: 1–51.

———. 1949. Second thoughts on "Mycenaean" pottery in Ithaca. *BSA* 44: 307–12.

———. 1953. Further excavations at Aetos. *BSA* 48: 255–361.

Bérard, C. 1970. *Eretria: Fouilles et recherches. Vol. 3. L'héroôn à la porte de l'ouest.* Berne: Francke.

———. 1978. Topographie et urbanisme de l'Eretrie archaïque: L'héroôn. In *Eretria: Fouilles et recherches,* vol. 6, 89–96. Berne: Francke.

———. 1982. Récuperer la mort du prince: Héroïsation et formation de la cité. In Vernant and Gnoli 1982, 89–105.

———. 1983. L'héroïsation et la formation de la cité: Un conflit idéologique. In *Architecture et société de l'archaïsme grec à la fin de la république romaine,* 43–59. Rome: Ecole française de Rome.

Bérard, J. 1952. Le nom des Grecs en Latin. *REA* 54: 5–12.

———. 1957. *La colonisation grecque de l'Italie méridionale et de la Sicile dans l'antiquité: Histoire et légende.* 2d ed. Paris: Presses Universitaires de France.

Bérard, V. 1927–29. *Les navigations d'Ulysse.* Paris: A. Colin.

Bernabé, A. 1987. *Poetarum epicorum graecorum: Testimonia et fragmenta.* Pt. 1. Leipzig: Teubner.

Bernal, M. 1987. On the transmission of the alphabet to the Aegean before 1400 B.C. *BASO* 267: 11–19.

Bernstein, M. A. 1994. *Foregone conclusions: Against apocalyptic history.* Berkeley and Los Angeles: University of California Press.

Bhabha, H., ed. 1990. *Nation and narration.* London: Routledge.

Biancofiore, F. 1967. *La civiltà micenea nell'Italia meridionale.* 2d ed. Rome: Edizioni dell'Ateneo.

———. 1990. *Bibliografia topografica della colonizzazione greca in Italia e nelle isole tirreniche,* ed. G. Nenci and G. Vallet, vol. 8, 405–8. Pisa and Rome.

Bickerman, E. J. 1952. Origines gentium. *CPh* 47: 65–81.

Bietti Sestieri, A. M. 1988. The Mycenaean connection and its impact on the central Mediterranean societies. *Dialoghi di Archeologia,* n.s., 6: 23–51.

———. 1992. *The Iron Age community of Osteria del'Osa.* Cambridge: Cambridge University Press.

Blakeway, A. 1933. Prolgomena to the study of Greek commerce with Italy, Sicily, and France in the eighth and seventh centuries B.C. *BSA* 33: 170–208.

———. 1935. "Demaratus": A study in some aspects of the earliest Hellenization of Latium and Etruria. *JRS* 25: 129–49.

Blome, P. 1984. Lefkandi und Homer. *WJA* 10: 9–22.

Blume, F., K. Lachmann, and A. Rudorff. 1967 (1848). *Die Schriften der römischen Feldmesser.* 2 vols. Hildesheim: Olms.

Boardman, J. 1957. Early Euboean pottery and trade. *BSA* 52: 1–29.

———. 1980. *The Greeks overseas: Their early colonies and trade.* New York: Thames and Hudson.

———. 1983. Symbol and story in geometric art. In *Ancient Greek art and iconography,* ed. W. Moon, 15–36. Madison: University of Wisconsin Press.

———. 1990. Al Mina and history. *OJA* 9: 169–90.

Boardman, J., and C. E. Vaphopoulou-Richardson, 1986. eds. *Chios: A conference at the Homereion in Chios 1984.* Oxford: Clarendon Press.

Bodson, L. 1978. *Hiera Zoia: Contribution à l'étude de la place de l'animal dans la religion grecque ancienne.* Brussels: Palais des Académies.

Bohannan, L. 1952. A genealogical charter. *Africa* 22: 301–15.

Bologna, C. 1978. Il linguaggio del silenzio: L'alterità linguistica nelle religioni del mondo classico. *Studi Storico Religiosi* 2: 305–42.

Bonfante, L. 1981. *Out of Etruria: Etruscan influence north and south.* British Archaeological Reports International Series 103.

Borgeaud, P. 1979. *Recherches sur le dieu Pan.* Rome: Institut Suisse de Rome.

Boyancé, P. 1943. Les origines de la legende troyenne à Rome. *REA* 45: 275–90.

Braccesi, L. 1977. *Grecità Adriatica: Un capitolo della colonizzazione greca in Occidente.* 2d ed. Bologna: Patron.

———. 1984. *La leggenda di Antenore: Da Troia a Padova.* Padua: Signum.

———. 1987. Antenoridi, Veneti e Libyi. *Quaderni di Archeologia della Libia* 12: 7–14.

———. 1988. Indizi per una frequentazione micenea dell'Adriatico. In Acquaro et al. 1988, 133–45.

———. 1994. *Grecità di frontiera.* Padua: Esedra.

Bradford, E. 1963. *Ulysses found.* London: Hodder and Stoughton.

Braun, T. F. G. R. 1982. The Greeks in the Near East. *CAH²* 3.2: 1–31.

Breglia, L. 1996. *Dalla Magna Grecia a Cos.* Naples.

Bremmer, J. 1987. Romulus, Remus, and the foundation of Rome. In Bremmer and Horsfall 1987, 25–48.

Bremmer, J. N., and N. M. Horsfall, eds. 1987. *Roman myth and mythology.* University of London, Institute of Classical Studies, Bulletin suppl. 52.

Brinkman, J. A. 1989. Akkadian words for Ionia and Ionian. In *Daidalikon: Studies in Memory of R. V. Schoder, S.J.,* ed. R. F. Sutton, 53–71. Wauconda, Ill.: Bolchazy-Carducci.

Briquel, D. 1974. Le problème des Dauniens. *MEFRA* 86: 7–40.

———. 1984. *Les Pélasges en Italie: Recherches sur l'histoire de la legende.* Rome and Paris: Ecole Française de Rome.

———. 1990. Le regard des Grecs sur l'Italie indigène. In *Crise et transformation* 1990, 165–88.

———. 1991a. L'écriture étrusque: D'après les inscriptions du VIIᵉ s. av. J.-C. In Baurain, Bonnet, and Krings 1991, 615–31.

———. 1991b. *L'origine lydienne des Etrusques: Histoire de la doctrine dans l'antiquité.* Rome and Paris: Ecole Française de Rome.

———. 1993. *Les Tyrrhenes, peuple des tours: Denys d'Halicarnasse et l'autochthonie des Etrusques.* Rome and Paris: Ecole Française de Rome.

Brommer, F. 1960. *Vasenlisten zur Griechischen Heldensage.* 2d ed. Marburg: N. G. Elwert.

———. 1982–83. Zur Schreibweise des Namens Odysseus. *Zeitschrift für Vergleichende Sprachforschung* 96: 88–92.

———. 1983. *Odysseus: Die Taten und Leiden des Helden in antiker Kunst und Literatur.* Darmstadt: Wissenschaftliche Buchgesellschaft.

Brown, P. 1985. This thing of darkness I acknowledge mine: *The Tempest* and the discourse of colonialism. In *Political Shakespeare,* ed. J. Dollimore and A. Sinfield, 48–71. Manchester: Manchester University Press.

Brunsåker, S. 1962. The Pithecusan shipwreck. *Opuscula Romana* 4: 165–242.

Buchner, G. 1978. Testimonianze epigrafiche semitiche del VIII secolo a Pithekoussai. *PP* 179: 130–42.

———. 1979. Early Orientalizing: Aspects of the Euboian connection. In Ridgway and Ridgway 1979, 129–44.

———. 1982. Die Kolonie Pithekoussai und der nordwestsemitische Raum. In Niemeyer 1982, 277–98.

Buchner, G., D. Morelli, and G. Nenci. 1952. Fonti per la storia di Naples antica. *PP* 7: 370- 419.

Buchner, G., and D. Ridgway. 1993. *Pithekoussai I: La necropoli, Tombe 1–723*. Monumenti Antichi, n.s., 4. Rome.

Buchner, G., and C. F. Russo. 1955. La coppa di Nestore e un'iscrizione metrica da Pithecusa dell'VIII secolo av.Cr. *Rendi. Linc.* 10: 215–34.

Buitron, D. et al. 1992. *The* Odyssey *and ancient art*. Annandale-on-Hudson: Edith C. Blum Art Institute, Bard College.

Burkert, W. 1985. *Greek religion*. Translated by J. Raffan. Oxford: Blackwell.

———. 1987. The making of Homer in the sixth century B.C.: Rhapsodes versus Stesichoros. In *Papers on the Amasis painter and his world*, 43–62. Malibu: J. Paul Getty Museum.

———. 1988. The meaning and function of the temple in Classical Greece. In *Temple in society*, ed. M. V. Fox, 27–48. Winona Lake: Eisenbrauns.

———. 1991. Oriental symposia: Contrasts and parallels. In Slater 1991, 7–24.

———. 1992. *The Orientalizing revolution: Near Eastern influence on Greek culture in the early Archaic age*. Cambridge: Harvard University Press.

Burnett, A. 1988. Jocasta in the west: The Lille Stesichorus. *Classical Antiquity* 7: 107–54.

Burzachechi, M. 1967. Gli studi di epigrafia greca relativi alla Magna Grecia dal 1952 al 1967. In *Acts of the fifth international congress of Greek and Latin epigraphy*, 125–34.

———. 1979. Gli Eubei e l'introduzione dell'alfabeto greci in Occidente. In *Gli Eubei in Occidente* 1979, 209–20.

Buxton, R. 1994. *Imaginary Greece: The contexts of mythology*. Cambridge: Cambridge University Press.

Cabanes, P. 1979. Frontière et recontres de civilisations dans la Grèce du Nord-Ouest. *Ktema* 4: 183–99.

———. 1980. Sociétés et institutions dans les monarchies de Grèce septentrionale au IVe s. *REG* 93: 324–51 (*Iliria* 2 [1981]: 55–94).

———. 1987a. Les habitants des régions situées au Nord-Ouest de la Grèce étaient-ils des étrangers aux yeux des gens de Grèce centrale et méridionale? In *L'étranger dans le monde grec: Actes du colloque organisé par l'Institut d'Etudes Anciennes, Nancy, mai 1987*, ed. R. Lonis, 89–111.

———, ed. 1987b. *L'Illyrie méridionale et l'Epire dans l'antiquité*. Clermont-Ferrand: Adosa.

———. 1988. *Les Illyriens de Bardylis à Genthios (iv–ii avant J.C.)*. Paris: SEDES.

———, ed. 1993. *l'Illyrie méridionale et l'Epire dans l'antiquité 2*. Clermont-Ferrand: Adosa.

Calame, C. 1977. La légende du Cyclops dans le folklore européen: Un jeu de transformations narratives. *Etudes de Lettres*, pt. 2, 45–79.

Calder, W. M., III, and J. Cobet. 1990. *Heinrich Schliemann nach Hundert Jahren*. Frankfurt am Main.

Calder, W. M., III, and D. A. Traill, eds. 1986. *Myth, scandal, and history: The Heinrich Schliemann controversy and the first edition of the Mycenaean diary*. Detroit: Wayne State University Press.

Calligas, P. G. 1982. "Κέρκυρα, ἀποικισμός καὶ ἔπος." In *Grecia, Italia e Sicilia* 1984, 57–68.

———. 1988. Hero-cult in early Iron Age Greece. In Hägg, Marinatos, and Nordquist 1988, 229–34.

Cantarella, R. 1967. Omero in occidente e le origini dell'omerologia. *Letteratura e arte figurate nella Magna Grecia: Atti del sesto convegno di studi sulla Magna Grecia. Taranto, 1966,* 37–65. Naples.

———. 1968. He Megale Hellas. In *La città e il suo territorio: Atti del settimo convegno di studi sulla Magna Grecia,* 11–28. Naples.

Carter, J. B., and S. P. Morris, eds. 1995. *The ages of Homer: A tribute to Emily Vermeule*. Austin: University of Texas Press.

Carter, J. C. 1984. Crotone. *Crotone: Atti del ventitreesimo convegno di studi sulla Magna Grecia,* 169–77. Naples.

———. 1990. Metapontum: Land, wealth, and population. In Descoeudres 1990, 405–41.

Cartledge, P. 1993. *The Greeks: A portrait of self and others*. New York: Oxford University Press.

Cartledge, P., and A. Spawforth. 1989. *Hellenistic and Roman Sparta: A tale of two cities*. London: Routledge.

Casevitz, M. 1985. *Le vocabulaire de la colonisation en grec ancien: Les familles de κτίζω et de οἰκέω-οἰκίζω*. Paris: Klienksieck.

———. 1986. Sur quelques désignations d'autels. *Bulletin de Liaison de la Société des Amis de la Bibliothèque Salomon Reinach,* n.s., 6: 57–63.

Casson, L. 1971. *Ships and seamanship in the ancient world*. Princeton: Princeton University Press.

Castagnoli, F. 1982. La leggenda di Enea nel Lazio. *StudRom* 30: 1–15.

Catling, R. W. V., and I. S. Lemos. 1990. *Lefkandi II.1, the Protogeometric building at Toumba: The pottery*. London: Thames and Hudson.

Catling, R. W. V., and D. G. J. Shipley. 1989. Messapian Zeus: An early sixth-century inscribed cup from Laconia. *BSA* 84: 187–200.

Caven, B. 1990. *Dionysius I: War lord of Sicily*. New Haven and London: Yale University Press.

Cawkwell, G. L. 1992. Early colonization. *CQ* 42: 289–303.

Cazzaniga, I. 1971. Il estesione alla Sicilia della espressione Magna Grecia in Strabone. *PP* 26: 26–31.

Ceka, N. 1983. Processi di transformazione nell'Illiria del Sud durante il periodo arcaico. In *Modes des contacts* 1983, 203–18.

La céramique grecque au viiie siècle en Italie centrale et méridionale. 1982. Cahiers du Centre Jean Bérard 3. Naples.

Certeau, M. de. 1990. *L'invention du quotidien*. Paris: Gallimard.

Charneux, P. 1966. Premières remarques sur la liste argienne de théarodoques. *BCH* 90: 156–239, 710–14.

Chiapelli, A., M. J. B. Benson, and R. L. Fredi, eds. 1976. *First images of America: The impact of the New World on the Old*. Berkeley: University of California Press.

Chirassi, I. 1964. *Miti e culti arcaici di Artemis nel Peloponneso e Grecia centrale*. Trieste.

Ciaceri, E. 1901. *L'Alessandra di Licofrone*. Catania. (Reissued by M. Gigante, Naples, 1982.)

———. 1911. *Culti e miti nella storia dell'antica Sicilia*. Catania.

———. 1926–40. *Storia della Magna Grecia*. 3 vols. 2d ed. Rome.

Clay, J. 1980. Goat island: *Od.* 9.116–141. *CQ* 74: 262–64.

———. 1983. *The wrath of Athena: Gods and men in the* Odyssey. Princeton: Princeton University Press.

Clogg, R. 1986. *A short history of modern Greece*. Cambridge: Cambridge University Press.

Coldstream, J. N. 1968. *Greek Geometric pottery*. London: Methuen.

———. 1976. Hero cults in the age of Homer. *JHS* 96: 8–17.

———. 1977. *Geometric Greece*. London: E. Benn.

———. 1982. Greeks and Phoenicians in the Aegean. In Niemeyer 1982, 261–72.

———. 1983. Gift exchange in the eighth century B.C. In Hägg 1983, 201–6.

———. 1985. Greek temples why and where? In *Greek religion and society*, ed. J. V. Muir and P. E. Easterling, 67–69. Cambridge: Cambridge University Press.

———. 1991. The Geometric style: Birth of the picture. In *Looking at Greek vases*, ed. T. Rasmussen and N. Spivey, 37–56. Cambridge: Cambridge University Press.

———. 1993. Mixed marriages at the frontiers of the early Greek world. *OJA* 12(1): 89–107.

———. 1994. Prospectors and pioneers: Pithekoussai, Kyme, and Central Italy. In Tsetskhladze and De Angelis 1994, 47–60.

———. 1995. Euboean Geometric imports from the acropolis of Pithekoussai. *BSA* 90: 251–67.

Colonna, G. 1973–74. Nomi etruschi di vasi. *ArchClass* 25–26: 132–50.

———. 1974a. Ceramica geometrica dell'Italia meridionale nell'area Etrusca. In *Aspetti e problemi dell'Etruria interna: Atti del ottavo convegno nazionale di studi etruschi, Orvieto 1972*, 297–302. Florence: L. S. Olschki.

———. 1974b. Preistoria e protoistoria di Roma e del Lazio. In *Popoli e civiltà dell'Italia antica II*, ed. A. Radimili et al. Rome: Biblioteca di Storia Patria.

———. 1980. Riflessi dell'epos greco nell'arte degli Etruschi. In *L'epos greco in occidente: Atti del diciannovesimo convegno di studi sulla Magna Grecia, Taranto, 7–12 ottobre 1979*, 303–20. Taranto: Istituto per la Storia e l'Archeologia della Magna Grecia.

———. 1988. I Latini e gli altri popoli del Lazio. In Pugliese Carratelli 1988, 411–530.

———. 1994. L'Etruschità della Campania meridionale alla luce delle iscrizioni. In *La presenza etrusca* 1994, 343–78.

Condurachi, E. 1970. Dodone et ses rapports avec le monde balkanique. In *Adriatica praehistorica et antiqua: Miscellanea G. Novak dicata*, 325–33. Zagreb: Sveuciliste.

Connor, R. 1993. The Ionian era of Athenian civic identity. *PAPhS* 137: 194–206.

Contribution à l'étude de la société et de la colonisation eubéenne. 1975. Cahiers du Centre Jean Bérard 2. Naples.

Cooper, J. S. 1992. Babbling on: Recovering Mesopotamian orality. In Vogelzang and Vanstiphout 1992, 103–22.

Coppola, A. 1990. Diomede in età augustea: Appunti sull'Iullo Antonio. *Hesperia* 1: 125–38.

Cordano, F. 1974. Il culto di Artemis a Rhegium. *PP* 29: 86–90.

Cornell, T. J. 1975. Aeneas and the twins: The development of the Roman foundation legend. *PCPS* 201: 1–32.

———. 1977. Aeneas' arrival in Italy. *LCM* 2: 77–83.

———. 1995. *The beginnings of Rome: Italy and Rome from the Bronze Age to the Punic Wars (c. 1000–264 B.C.).* London and New York: Routledge.

Coulson, W. D. E. 1986. *The Dark Age pottery of Messenia.* Göteborg: Paul Aströms Forlag.

———. 1990. *The Greek Dark Ages: A review of the evidence and suggestions for further research.* Athens.

———. 1991. The "Protogeometric" from Polis reconsidered. *BSA* 86: 43–64.

Coulton, J. 1993. The Toumba building: Its architecture. In Popham, Calligas, and Sackett 1993, 33–70.

Courbin, P. 1995. Un fragment de cratère protoargien. *BCH* 79: 1–47.

Crielaard, J.-P. 1991–92. How the West was won: Euboeans vs. Phoenicians. *Hamburger Beiträge zur Archäologie* 18–19: 235–49.

———. 1994. Ναυσικλειτὴ Εὔβοια: Socio-economic aspects of Euboian trade and colonization. In Αρχείον Ευβοικών Μελετών 30/1992–1993, 45–53. Athens: Society for Euboian Studies.

———, ed. 1995a. *Homeric questions.* Amsterdam: J. C. Gieben.

———. 1995b. Homer, history, and archaeology: Some remarks on the date of the Homeric world. In Crielaard 1995a, 201–88.

———. 1996. The Euboeans overseas: Long-distance contacts and colonization as status activities in early Iron Age Greece. Ph.D. diss., University of Amsterdam.

Crise et transformation des sociétés archaïques de l'Italie antique au Ve siècle av. J.-C. 1990. Rome: Ecole Française de Rome.

Cristofani, M. 1972. Sull'origine e la diffusione dell'alfabeto etrusco. *ANRW* 1: 466–89.

———. 1978. *L'arte degli Etruschi: Produzione e consumo.* Turin: Einaudi.

———. 1979. Recent advances in Etruscan epigraphy and language. In Ridgway and Ridgway 1979, 373–412.

———. 1983. I greci in Etruria. In *Modes des contacts* 1983, 239–55.

Cross, G. N. 1930. *Epirus: A study in Greek constitutional development.* Cambridge: Cambridge University Press.

Cuozzo, M. 1994. Patterns of organization and funerary customs in the cemetery of Pontecagnano (Salerno) during the Orientalizing period. *JEA* 2: 263–96.

D'Agostino, B. 1968. Pontecagnano: Tombe orientalizzanti in Contrada S. Antonio. *Not. Scav.* 1968: 78–205.

———. 1977a. Grecs et "indigènes" sur la côte tyrrhenienne au vii siècle: La transmission des idéologies entre élites sociales. *Annales ESC* 32: 3–20.

————. 1977b. Tombe "principesche" dell'orientalizzante antico da Pontecagnano. *MAL*, ser. misc., 2.

————. 1979. Le necropoli protostoriche della valle del Sarno: La ceramica di tipo greco. *AION (archeol.)* 1: 59–75.

————. 1982. La ceramica greca o di tradizione greca nell'VIII secolo in Italia Meridionale. In *La céramique grecque* 1982, 55–67.

————. 1985. I paesi greci di provenienza dei coloni e le loro relazioni con il Mediterraneo Occidentale. In *Magna Grecia: Prolegomeni*, ed. G. Pugliese Caratelli, 209–44. Milan.

————. 1988. Le genti della Campania antica. In Pugliese Carratelli 1988, 531–89.

————. 1990. Relations between Campania, southern Etruria, and the Aegean in the eighth century. In Descoeudres 1990, 73–85.

D'Agostino, B., and P. Gastaldi, eds. 1988. *Pontecagnano II: La necropoli del Picentino 1, le tombe della Prima Età del Ferro*. Naples: Istituto Universitario Orientale.

Dakaris, S. P. 1964. Ὀι γενεαλογικοί μῦθοι τῶν Μολοσσῶν. Athens: Archeologike Hetaireia.

————. 1986. Iliada kai Odyssei: Mythos kai historia. In *Praktika tou IV Synedriou gia tin Odysseia, Ithaki [September 9–15, 1984]*. Ithaca: I. F. Kostopulou.

D'Andria, F. 1979. Salento arcaica: Le nuove documentazioni archeologica. In *Salento arcaica: Atti del colloquio internazionale, Lecce 1979*, 15–28. Galantina.

————. 1982. Il Salento nel VIII e VII sec. A.C.: Nuovi dati archeologici. *ASAA* 60: 101–16.

————. 1983. Greci ed indigeni in Iapygia. In *Modes des contacts* 1983, 287–97.

————. 1985. Documenti del commercio arcaico tra Ionio ed Adriatico. In *Magna Grecia, Epiro e Macedonia: Atti del ventiquattresimo convegno di studi sulla Magna Grecia, Taranto, 5–10 ottobre 1984*, 321–76. Taranto.

————. 1987. Problèmes du commerce archaïque entre la mer Ionienne et l'Adriatique. In Cabanes 1987b, 35–38.

————. 1988. Messapi e Peuceti. In *Italia, omnia terrarum alumna*, ed. G. Pugliese Carratelli, 653–715. Milan.

————. 1989. Il Salento e le sue radici indigene: Le origine Messapiche. In *Salento Porta d'Italia*, ed. S. Moscati. Galantina: Congedo.

————. ed. 1990a. *Archeologia dei Messapi: Catalogo della mostra, Lecce, Museo Provinciale "Sigismondo Castromediano" 7 ottobre 1990–7 gennaio 1991*. Bari: Edipuglia.

————. 1990b. Greek influence in the Adriatic: Fifty years after Beaumont. In Descoeudres 1990, 281–90.

————. 1991. Insediamenti e territorio: L'età storica. In *I Messapi* 1991, 393–478.

————. 1996. Corinto e lo'Occidente: La costa adriatica. In *Magna Grecia e Corinto: Atti del trentaquattresimo convegno di studi sulla Magna Grecia, Taranto, 7–11 ottobre 1994*. Naples: Istituto per la Storia e l'Archeologia della Magna Grecia.

Danek, G., 1994–95. Der Nestorbecher von Ischia, epische Zitiertechnik und das Symposion. *WS* 107–108: 29–44.

Dascalakis, A. P. 1965. *The Hellenism of the ancient Macedonians*. Thessalonica: Institute for Balkan Studies.

Dauge, Y.-A. 1981. *Le barbare: Recherches sur la conception romaine de la barbarie et de la civilisation*. Latomus 176. Brussels.

Daverio Rocchi, G. 1981. *Gli insediamenti in villagi nella Grecia del V e del IV sec. a. C.* Milan: Istituto Lombardo di Scienze e Lettere.

Davies, J. K. 1992. The reliability of the oral tradition. In Emlyn-Jones, Hardwick, and Purkis 1992, 211–25.

Davies, M. 1991. *Poetarum melicorum graecorum fragmenta.* Oxford: Oxford University Press.

Davis, J. 1989. The social relations of the production of history. In Tonkin, McDonald, and Chapman 1989, 104–20.

De Caro, S., and A. Greco. 1981. *Campania.* Bari: Laterza.

De Franciscis, A. 1972. *Stato e società in Locri Epizefiri.* Naples: Libreria Scientifica Editrice.

Dehl, H. C. 1984. *Die korinthische Keramik des 8 und frühen 7 Jahrhunderts v. Chr. in Italien.* Mitteilungen des Deutschen Archäologisches Institut Athen 11. Berlin: Mann.

De Juliis, E. 1988. *Gli Iapigi: Storia e civiltà della Puglia preromana.* Milan: Longansei.

Dekoulakou, I. 1984. Κεραμεική 8ου καί αἰ. π.Χ. ἀπό τάφους τῆς ᾽Αχαίας καί τῆς Αἰτωλίας, in *Grecia, Italia e Sicilia* 1984, 219–36.

Delage, E. 1930. *La géographie dans les Argonautiques d'Apollonios de Rhodes.* Bordeaux: Feret.

Delpino, F. 1989. L'ellenizzazione dell'Etruria villanoviana: Sui rapporti tra Grecia ed Etruria fra IX e VIII sec. a. C. In *Secondo congresso internazionale etrusco, 1985,* 105–16. Rome: G. Bretschneider.

Dench, E. 1995. *From barbarians to new men: Greek, Roman, and modern perceptions of peoples of the central Apennines.* Oxford: Clarendon Press.

Dening, G. 1981. *Islands and beaches: Discourse on a silent land, Marquesas 1774–1880.* Honolulu: University Press of Hawaii.

Denlaux, E. 1980–81. Civitate donati: Naples, Heraclée, Cûmes. *Ktema* 6: 133–41.

Dentzer, J.-M. 1982. *Le motif du banquet couché dans le Proche-Orient et le monde grec du vii au iv siècle avant J.-C.* Paris.

Desborough, V. R. d'A. 1952. *Protogeometric pottery.* Oxford: Clarendon Press.

———. 1972. *The Greek Dark Ages.* London: Benn.

Descoeudres, J-P., ed. 1990. *Greek colonists and native populations: Proceedings of the first Australian Congress of Classical Archaeology Held in Honour of Emeritus Professor A. D. Trendall, Sydney, 9–14 July, 1985.* Oxford: Clarendon Press.

Descoeudres, J.-P., and R. Kearsley. 1983. Greek pottery at Veii: Another look. *BSA* 79: 9–53.

De Sensi Sestito, G. 1984. *La Calabria in età arcaica e classica: Storia/economia/società.* Rome: Gangemi.

De Simone, C. 1968. *Die griechischen Entlehnungen im Etruskischen.* Vol. 1. Wiesbaden: O. Harrassowitz.

———. 1970. *Die griechischen Entlehnungen im Etruskischen.* Vol. 2. Wiesbaden: O. Harrassowitz.

———. 1989. La lingua Messapica. In Moscati 1989, 107–19.

Detienne, M. 1967. *Les maîtres de verité dans la Grèce archaïque.* Paris: François Maspero.

———. 1986. *The creation of mythology.* Chicago and London: University of Chicago Press.

De Vos, G., and L. Romanucci-Ross, eds. 1975. *Ethnic identity: Cultural continuities and change.* Palo Alto: Mayfield.

Dickinson, O. 1986. Homer, the poet of the Dark Age. *GR* 33: 20–37.

Diller, A. 1952. *The tradition of the minor Greek geographers.* Lancaster, Pa.: Lancaster Press.

Dion, R. 1969. *Les anthropophages de l'Odyssée: Cyclopes et Lestrygones.* Paris: J. Vrin.

———. 1977. *Aspects politiques de la géographie antique.* Paris: Les Belles Lettres.

Doherty, L. E. 1991. The internal and implied audiences of the *Odyssey. Arethusa* 24: 145–76.

Donlan, W. 1980. *The aristocratic ideal in ancient Greece: Attitudes of superiority from Homer to the end of the fifth century B.C.* Lawrence, KS: Coronado Press.

———. 1982. Reciprocities in Homer. *CW* 75: 137–75.

———. 1985. The social groups of Dark Age Greece. *CPhil.* 80: 293–308.

———. 1989. The pre-state community in Greece. *SO* 64: 5–29.

———. 1993. Duelling with gifts in the *Iliad:* As the audience saw it. *Colby Quarterly* 19: 155–72.

Donlan, W., and C. G. Thomas. 1993. The village community of ancient Greece: Neolithic, Bronze, and Dark Ages. *Studi Miceni ed Egeo-Anatolici* 31: 61–71.

Dörpfeld, W. 1927. *Alt-Ithaka: Ein Beitrag zur homerische Frage.* Munich: R. Uhde.

Dougherty, C. 1993. *The poetics of colonization: From city to text in ancient Greece.* New York and Oxford: Oxford University Press.

———. 1994. Archaic Greek foundation poetry: Questions of genre and occasion. *JHS* 114: 35–46.

Dougherty, C., and L. Kurke, eds. 1993. *Cultural poetics in Archaic Greece: Cult, performance, politics.* Cambridge: Cambridge University Press.

Drews, R. 1973. *Greek accounts of eastern history.* Cambridge: Harvard University Press.

Drijvers, J. W., and A. A. MacDonald. 1995. *Centres of learning: Learning and location in pre-modern Europe and the Near East.* Leiden: Brill.

Dubuisson, M. 1984. Le latin est-il une langue barbare? *Ktema* 9: 55–68.

Dunbabin, T. J. 1948a. The early history of Corinth. *JHS* 68: 59–69.

———. 1948b. Minos and Daidalos in Sicily. *BSR* 16: 1–18.

———. 1948c. *The western Greeks: The history of Sicily and South Italy from the foundation of the Greek colonies to 480 B.C.* Oxford: Clarendon Press.

Durante, M. 1951. Ἄγριον ἠδὲ Λατῖνον. *PP* 6: 216–17.

Dury-Moyaers, G. 1981. *Enée et Lavinium.* Latomus 174. Brussels.

Duval, P.-M. 1943. L'histoire et la légende de la colonisation grecque en occident. *RA,* ser. 6, 19: 126–32.

Ebner, P. 1964. L'Athenaion, santuario estramurano di Velia. *PP* 19: 72–76.

Edwards, M. W. 1975. Type-scenes and Homeric hospitality. *TAPhA* 105: 51–72.

———. 1990. Neoanalysis and beyond. *CA* 9: 311–25.

Ellinger, P. 1993. *La légende nationale phocidienne: Artemis, les situations extrêmes et les récits de guerre d'anéantissement.* BCH suppl. 27. Paris.

Elman, Y. 1975. Authoritative oral tradition in Neo-Assyrian circles. *Journal of the Ancient Near East Society of Columbia University* 7: 19–32.

Emlyn-Jones, C. 1986. True and lying tales in the *Odyssey. GR* 33: 1–10.

Emlyn-Jones, C., L. Hardwick, and J. Purkis. 1992. *Homer: Readings and images.* London: Duckworth.

Erbse, H. 1972. *Beiträge zum Verständnis der* Odyssee. Berlin and New York: de Gruyter.

Ermeti, A. L. 1976. La nave geometrica di Pithecusa. *ArchClass* 28: 206–15.

Ernout, A. 1962. Latin *graecus, graius, graecia*. *RPh* 36: 209–16.

Euchen Odyssei. 1995. ΕΥΧΗΝ ΟΔΥΣΣΕΙ: ΚΕΝΤΡΟ ΟΔΥΣΣΕΙΑΚΩΝ ΣΠΟΥΔΩΝ (Proceedings of the Conference on the *Odyssey,* Ithaca, September 3–8, 1993), Ithaca.

Fabre, P. 1981. Les Grecs et la connaissance de l'Occident. Ph.D. diss., Université de Lille III.

Fantasia, U. 1972. Le leggende di fondazioni di Brindisi e alcuni aspetti della presenza greca nell'Adriatico. *ASNP,* ser. 3, 2: 115–39.

Faraone, C. 1992. *Talismans and Trojan horses: Guardian statues in ancient Greek myth and ritual.* New York: Oxford University Press.

———. 1996. Taking the "Nestor's cup inscription" seriously: Erotic magic and conditional curses in the earliest inscribed hexameters. *Classical Antiquity* 15: 77–112.

Farina, A. 1961. *Senofane di Colofone, Ione di Chio.* Naples: Libreria Scientifica Editrice.

Farnell, L. R. 1921. *Greek hero cults and ideas of immortality.* Oxford: Clarendon Press.

Felsch, R. C. S. 1983. Zur Chronologie und zum Stil geometrischer Bronzen aus Kalapodi. In Hägg 1983, 123–29.

Felsch, R. C. S., and H. Kienast. 1975. Ein Heiligtum in Phokis. *AAA* 8: 1–24.

Fenik, B. 1974. *Studies in the* Odyssey. Hermes Einzelschriften 30. Wiesbaden.

Ferguson, J, 1989. *Among the gods: An archaeological exploration of ancient Greek religion.* London: Routledge.

Ferron, J. 1966. Les relations de Carthage avec l'Etrurie. *Latomus* 25: 689–709.

Finkelberg, M. 1990. A creative oral poet and the muse. *AJPh* 111: 293–303.

———. 1995. Odysseus and the genus "hero". *GR* 42: 1–14.

———. n.d. *The birth of fiction in ancient Greece.* Oxford. In press.

Finley, M. I. 1978. *Homer's* Odyssey. Cambridge: Harvard University Press.

———. 1979. *The world of Odysseus.* 2d ed. London: Chatto and Windus.

Finnegan, R. 1977 (1992). *Oral poetry: Its nature, significance, and social context.* Cambridge: Cambridge University Press.

Fittschen, K. 1969. *Untersuchungen zum Beginn der Sagendarstellung bei den Griechen.* Berlin.

Foley, J. M. 1981. *Oral traditional literature: A Festschrift for Albert Bates Lord.* Columbus, Ohio: Slavica.

———. 1988. *The theory of oral composition: History and methodology.* Bloomington: Indiana University Press.

Ford, A. 1992. *Homer: The poetry of the past.* Ithaca: Cornell University Press.

Fornara, C. W. 1983. *The nature of history in ancient Greece and Rome.* Berkeley, Los Angeles, and London: University of California Press.

Fortin, M. 1980. Fondation de villes grecques à Chypre: Légendes et découvertes archéologiques. In *Mélanges d'études anciennes offertes à Maurice Lebel,* 25–44. Quebec.

Frame, D. 1978. *The myth of return in early Greek epic.* New Haven: Yale University Press.

Franklin, W. 1979. *Discoverers, explorers, settlers: The diligent writers of early America.* Chicago and London: University of Chicago Press.

Frederiksen, M. W. 1979. The Etruscans in Campania. In Ridgway and Ridgway 1979, 276–311.

———. 1984. *Campania.* Edited by N. Purcell. London.

Funke, P. 1991a. Zur Ausbildung städtischer Siedlungszentren in Aitolien. In *Stuttgarter Kolloquium zur Historischen Geographie des Altertums*, ed. E. Olshausen and H. Sonnabend, 313–32. Bonn: R. Habelt.

———. 1991b. Strabone, la geografia storica et la struttura etnica della Grecia nordoccidentale. In Prontera 1991, 174–91.

———. 1997. Polisgenese und Urbanisierung in Aitolien im 5. und 4. Jh.v.Chr. In *Acts of the Copenhagen Polis Centre*, ed. M. H. Hansen, vol. 4, 145–88. Copenhagen: Royal Danish Academy of Science and Letters.

Funkenstein, A. 1993. *Perceptions of Jewish history*. Berkeley: University of California Press.

Gabba, E. 1976. Sulla valorizzazione politica della leggenda delle origini troiane di Rome fra III e II secolo a.C. In Sordi 1976, 84–101.

———. 1991. *Dionysius and the history of Archaic Rome*. Berkeley: University of California Press.

Gabrini, G. 1978. Un iscrizione aramaica a Ischia. *PP* 179: 143–50.

Gadd, C. J. 1956. *Teachers and students in the oldest schools*. London.

Gagé, J. 1972. Les traditions "diomédiques" dans l'Italie ancienne, de l'Apulie à l'Etrurie méridionale, et quelques-unes des origines de la légende de Mézence. *MEFRA* 84: 734–88.

Galinsky, G. K. 1969a. *Aeneas, Sicily, and Rome*. Princeton: Princeton University Press.

———. 1969b. "Troiae qui primus ab oris . . ." (*Aen.* 1.1). *Latomus* 28: 3–18.

Gallet de Santerre, H. 1958. *Delos primitive et archaïque*. Paris: Boccard.

Gauthier, P. 1972. *Symbola: Les étrangers et la justice dans les cités grecques*. Paris.

Geertz, C. 1963. The integrative revolution: Primoridal sentiments and civil politics in the new states. In *Old societies and new states*, ed. C. Geertz. Glencoe: Free Press.

———. 1973. *The interpretation of cultures*. New York: Basic Books.

Geffcken, J. 1892. *Timaios Geographie des Westens*. Philogische Untersuchungen 13. Berlin.

Gell, W. 1807. *The geography and antiquities of Ithaca*. London.

Gellner, E. 1983. *Nations and nationalism*. Ithaca: Cornell University Press.

Gentili, B. 1988. *Poetry and its public in ancient Greece: From Homer to the fifth century*. Baltimore and London: Johns Hopkins University Press.

Gentili, B., and C. Prato. 1979. *Poetarum elegiacorum testimonia et fragmenta*. Leipzig: Teubner.

Germain, G. 1954. *Genèse de l'*Odyssée*: La fantastique et la sacré*. Paris: PUF.

Ghinatti, F. 1974. Riti e feste della Magna Grecia. *Critica Storica* 2: 533–76.

Giangiulio, M. 1989. *Richerche su Crotone arcaica*. Pisa: Scuola Normale Superiore di Pisa.

———. 1991. Filottete tra Sibari e Crotone: Osservazioni sulla tradizione letteraria. In La Genière 1991c, 37–54.

———. 1997. Immagini coloniali dell'altro: Il mondo indigeno tra marginalità e integrazione. In *Mito e storia in Magna Grecia: Atti del trentaseesimo convegno di studi sulla Magna Grecia, Taranto 4–8 ottobre 1996*. Taranto: Istituto per la Storia e l'Archeologia della Magna Grecia.

Giannelli, G. 1963. *Culti e miti della Magna grecia: Contributo alla storia più antica delle colonie greche in occidente*. 2d ed. Florence: Sansoni.

Gianni, G. B. 1996. *Oggetti iscritti di epoca orientalizante in Etruria.* Florence: L. S. Olschki.

Gierth, L. 1971. Griechische Gründungsgeschichten als Zeugnisse historischen Denkens vor dem Einsetzen der Geschichtsschreibung. Ph.D. diss., Freiburg i. Br.

Gigante, M. 1990. L'antro itacese delle ninfe: Dalla realtà alla simbolo. In O Ομέρικος Οίκος: Από τα Πρακτικά του Συνεδρίου γιά την Οδυσσείαν [September 11–14, 1987, Ithaca], 127–47. Ithaca: ΚΕΝΤΡΟ ΟΔΥΣΣΕΙΑΚΩΝ ΣΠΟΥΔΩΝ.

Gills, E. 1992. Le destin d'Héraclès et de Philoctète dans *Les Trachiniennes* et le *Philoctète* de Sophocles: Une mise en parallèle. *Studi e Materiali di Storia delle Religioni* 58: 41–57.

Gjerstad, E. 1944. The colonization of Cyprus in Greek legend. *Opuscula Archaeologica* 3: 107–23.

Glazer, N., and D. Moynihan. 1975a. Introduction. In Glazer and Moynihan 1975, 1–26.

———, eds. 1975b. *Ethnicity: Theory and experience,* Cambridge: Harvard University Press.

Glen, J. 1971. The Polyphemos folktale and Homer's Kyklopeia. *TAPhA* 102: 133–81.

Gli Eubei in occidente: Atti del diciottesimo convegno di studi sulla Magna Grecia, Taranto, 8–12 ottobre 1978. 1979. Taranto: Istituto per la Storia e l'Archeologia della Magna Grecia.

Goekoop, A. E. H. *Ithaque la grande.* Athens.

Golden, M. 1988. Did the ancients care when their children died? *GR* 35: 152–63.

Gomme, A. W. 1945. *A historical commentary on Thucydides.* Vol. 1. Oxford: Clarendon Press.

Goody, J. 1987. *The interface between the written and the oral.* Cambridge: Cambridge University Press.

Goody, J., and I. Watt. 1968. The consequences of literacy. In *Literacy in traditional societies,* ed. J. Goody, 27–68. Cambridge: Cambridge University Press.

Graf, F. 1982. Culti e credenze religiose della Magna Grecia. In *Megale Hellas, nome e immagine: Atti del ventunesimo convegno di studi sulla Magna Grecia, Taranto, 2–5 ottobre 1981,* 157–85. Taranto: Istituto per la Storia e l'Archeologia della Magna Grecia.

———. 1993. *Greek mythology: An introduction.* Translated by T. Marier. Baltimore: Johns Hopkins University Press.

Graham, A. J. 1971. Patterns in early Greek colonization. *JHS* 91: 35–47.

———. 1982. The colonial expansion of Greece: The western Greeks. In *CAH²* 3(3): 83–195.

———. 1983. *Colony and mother city in ancient Greece.* 2d ed. Chicago: Ares.

———. 1984. Religion, women, and Greek colonisation. *Atti del Centro Richerche e Documentazione sull'Antichità Classica* 9 (n.s. 1): 293–314.

———. 1986. Al Mina and history. *DHA* 12: 51–65.

———. 1990. Pre-colonial contacts: Questions and problems. In Descoeudres 1990, 45–60.

———. 1992. Abdera and Teos. *JHS* 112: 44–73.

———. 1995. The *Odyssey,* history and women. In *The distaff side,* ed. B. Cohen, 3–16. Oxford: Oxford University Press.

Grandazzi, A. 1988. Le roi Latinos: Analyse d'une figure légendaire. *CRAI* 1988: 481–95.

Gras, M. 1983. Vin et société à Rome et dans le Latium à l'époque archaïque. In *Modes des contacts* 1983, 1067–75.

———. 1985. *Trafics tyrrhéniens archaïques*. Paris and Rome.

———. 1987. Le temple de Diane sur l'Aventine. *REA* 99: 47–61.

———. 1995. La Méditerranée occidentale, milieu d'échanges: Un regard historiographique. In *Les Grecs et l'Occident: Actes du colloque de la villa "Kerylos" (1991)*, 109–21. Collection de l'Ecole Française de Rome 208.

Grecia, Italia e Sicilia: Atti del convegno internazionale Grecia, Italia e Sicilia nell'VIII e VII secolo a.C., Atene, 15–20 ottobre 1979. 1984. ASAA 60.

Greco, E. 1970. In margine a Strabone. *PP* 25: 416–20.

———. 1980. *Magna Grecia*. Rome and Bari: Laterza.

———. 1989. La città. In *Un secolo di richerche* 1989, 305–28.

———. 1992. *Archeologia della Magna Grecia*. Rome and Bari: Laterza.

Greco, E., A. Pontrandolfo, and A. Rouveret. 1983. La rappresentazione del barbaro in ambiente magno-greco. In *Modes des contacts* 1983, 1051–66.

Grecs et barbares: Entretiens sur l'antiquité classique 8. 1962. Ed. O. Reverdin. Vandoevres-Genève: Fondation Hardt.

Greece and Italy in the Classical world: Acts of the Eleventh International Congress of Classical Archaeology, 1978. 1979. London: National Organizing Committee.

Green, J. R. 1994. *Theatre in ancient Greek society*. London and New York: Routledge.

Greenblatt, S. 1991. *Marvelous possessions: The wonder of the new world*. Chicago: University of Chicago Press.

Griffin, J. 1977. The Epic Cycle and the uniqueness of Homer. *JHS* 97: 39–53.

———. 1987. *The Odyssey*. Cambridge: Cambridge University Press.

———. 1992 (1986). Heroic and unheroic ideas in Homer. In Emlyn-Jones, Hardwick, and Purkis 1992, 21–31.

Griffith, M. 1983. Personality in Hesiod. *Classical Antiquity* 2: 37–41.

Grilli, A. 1990. Il mito dell'estremo occidente nella letteratura greca. In *La Magna Grecia e il lontano occidente: Atti del ventinovesimo convegno di studi sulla Magna Grecia, Taranto, 6–11 ottobre 1989*. Taranto: Istituto per la Storia e l'Archeologia della Magna Grecia.

Grotanelli, C. 1981. L'ideologia del banchetto e l'ospite ambiguo. *Dialoghi di Archeologia*, n.s., 3: 122–54.

Gruen, E. S. 1984. *Studies in Greek culture and Roman policy*. Leiden: Brill.

———. 1992. *Culture and national identity in Republican Rome*. Ithaca: Cornell University Press.

Guarducci, M. 1967. *Epigrafia Greca*. Vol. 1. Rome: Istituto Poligrafico dello Stato.

Guenée, B. 1978. Les généalogies entre l'histoire et la politique: La fierté d'être Capétien, en France, au Moyen Age. *Annales ESC* 33: 450–77.

Guidi, A. 1985. An application of the rank-size rule to protohistoric settlements in the middle Tyrrhenian area. In *Papers in Italian archaeology*, ed. C. Malon and S. Stoddart, 217–42. British Archaeological Reports International Series 245.

Guzzo, P. G. 1982. *Le città scomparse della Magna Grecia*. Rome: Newton Compton.

Haarmann, H. 1986. *Language in ethnicity: A view of basic ecological relations*. Berlin, New York, and Amsterdam: Mouton de Gruyter.

Hack, R. K. 1929. Homer and the cult of heroes. *TAPhA* 60: 57–74.

Hackens, T., N. D. Holloway, and R. R. Holloway. 1983. *The crossroads of the Mediterranean.* Louvain and Providence, R.I.: Brown University Center for Old World Archaeology and Art.

Hackman, O. 1904. *Die Polyphemsage in der Volksüberlieferung.* Helsinki: Frenckellska Tryckeri Aktebolaget.

Hadzisteliou-Price, T. 1973. Hero cult and Homer. *Historia* 22: 129–44.

———. 1979. Hero cult in the age of Homer and earlier. In *Arktouros: Studies presented to B. M. W. Knox on the occasion of his 65th birthday,* ed. G. Bowersock and W. Burkert, 219–28. Berlin and New York: de Gruyter.

Hägg, R., ed. 1983. *The Greek renaissance of the eighth century B.C.: Tradition and innovation.* Stockholm: Svenska Institutet i Athen.

———, ed. 1993. *Ancient Greek cult practice from the archaeological evidence (Proceedings of the Swedish Institute Seminar, Athens, October 1993).* Stockholm: P. Astroms.

Hägg, R., N. Marinatos, and G. Nordquist, eds. 1988. *Early Greek cult practice: Proceedings of the Fifth International Symposium at the Swedish Institute at Athens, 26–29 June, 1986.* Stockholm: Svenska Institutet i Athen.

Haider, P. W. 1996. Griechen im Vorderen Orient und in Ägypten bis ca. 590 v. Chr. In *Wege zur Genese griechischer Identität,* ed. C. Ulf, 59–115. Berlin: Akademie Verlag.

Hainsworth, J. B. 1970. The criticism of an oral Homer. *JHS* 90: 90–98.

———. 1991. *The idea of epic.* Berkeley: University of California Press.

Hall, C. C. ed. 1910. *Narratives of early Maryland 1633–1694.* New York: Scribner.

Hall, E. 1989. *Inventing the barbarian: Greek self-definition through tragedy.* Oxford: Clarendon Press.

Hall, J. 1994. Discourse and praxis: The detection and construction of ethnicity in the archaeological record. Paper delivered at the conference "Culture and Ethnicity in the Hellenistic East: Issues, Problems, and Approaches," Ann Arbor, Mich., March 1994.

———. 1997. *Ethnic identity in Greek antiquity.* Cambridge: Cambridge University Press.

———. 1995. The role of language in Greek ethnicities. *PCPS* 41: 83–100.

Halliday, W. R. 1975 (1928). *The Greek questions of Plutarch.* New York: Arno Press.

Halverson, J. 1992 (1985). Social order in the *Odyssey.* in Emlyn-Jones, Hardwick, and Purkis 1992, 177–90 (= *Hermes* 120 [1985]: 129–45).

Hammond, N. G. L. 1967. *Epirus.* Oxford: Clarendon Press.

———. 1982a. Illyris, Epirus, and Macedonia, in *CAH²* 3.3, 261–87.

———. 1982b. Illyris, Epirus, and Macedonia in the early Iron Age. In *CAH²* 3.1, 619–56.

———. 1989. *The Macedonian state: The origins, institutions, and history.* Oxford: Clarendon Press.

———. 1994. Literary evidence for Macedonian speech. *Historia* 43: 131–42.

Hansen, F. 1976. The story of the sailor who went inland. In *Folklore today,* ed. L. Degh, 221–30. Bloomington: Indiana University Press.

———. 1977. Odysseus' last journey. *QUCC* 24: 27–48.

Hansen, P. A. 1976. Pithecusan humour: The interpretation of "Nestor's cup" reconsidered. *Glotta* 54: 25–43.

———. 1983. *Carmina epigraphica graeca.* Berlin: de Gruyter.

Harding, A. 1984. *The Mycenaeans and Europe*. London: Academic Press.

Harrell, S. 1995. Languages defining ethnicity in Southwest China. In Romanucci-Ross and de Vos 1995, 97–114.

Hartmann, A. 1917. *Untersuchungen über die Sagen vom Tod des Odysseus*. Munich: Beck.

Hartog, F. 1988. *The mirror of Herodotus: The representation of the other in the writing of history*. Berkeley: University of California Press.

———. 1996. *La mémoire d'Ulysse*. Paris: Gallimard.

Hase, F.-W. von. 1995. Ägäische, griechische, und vorderorientalische Einflüsse auf das tyrrhenische Mittelitalien. In *Beitäge zur Urnenfelderzeit nördlich und südlich der Alpen*, 239–86. Römisch-Germanisches Zentralmuseum Monographien 35.

———. 1996. Présences étrusques et italiques dans les sanctuaires grecs (VIIIᵉ–VIIᵉ siècle av. J.-C. In *Les plus religieux des hommes: État de la recherche sur la religion étrusque. Actes du Colloque Paris 1992, XIIᵉᵐᵉˢ Rencontres de l'École du Louvre, Paris, 1994*, 293–323. Paris.

Havelock, E. 1963. *Preface to Plato*. Cambridge: Belknap Press.

———. 1982. *The literate revolution in Greece and its cultural consequences*. Princeton: Princeton University Press.

———. 1986. *The Muse learns to write*. New Haven: Yale University Press.

Head, B. V. 1911. *Historia numorum*. 2d ed. Oxford: Clarendon Press.

Hedreen, G. 1991. The cult of Achilles in the Euxine. *Hesperia* 60: 313–30.

Heikell, R. 1982. *Greek waters pilot*. Huntingdon: Imray.

Henige, D. P. 1984 (1974). *The chronology of oral tradition: Quest for a chimera*. Oxford: Clarendon Press.

Herman, G. 1987. *Ritualized friendship and the Greek city*. Cambridge: Cambridge University Press.

Herring, E. 1991. Socio-political change in the South Italian Iron Age and Classical periods: An application of the peer polity interaction model. *Accordia Research Papers* 2: 33–54.

Herring, E., R. Whitehouse, and J. Wilkins, eds. 1991. *The archaeology of power: Proceedings of the Fourth International Conference on Italian Archaeology*. London.

Herrmann, H. V. 1979. *Olympische Forschungen*. Vol. 11. *Die Kessel der orientalisierenden Zeit*, pt. 2. Berlin: de Gruyter.

———. 1980. Pelops in Olympia. In *Stele: Festschrift Nikolaos Kontoleon*, 59–74. Athens.

———. 1983. Altitalisches und Etruskisches in Olympia: Neue Funde und Forschungen. *ASAA* 45: 271–94.

Herzfeld, M. 1982. *Ours once more: Folklore, ideology, and the making of modern Greece*. Austin: University of Texas Press.

———. 1987. *Anthropology through the looking glass: Critical ethnography in the margins of Europe*. Cambridge: Cambridge University Press.

Heubeck, A., and A. Hoekstra. 1989. *A commentary on Homer's* Odyssey. Vol. 2. *Books 9–16*. Oxford: Clarendon Press.

Heubeck, A., S. West, and J. B. Hainsworth. 1988. *A commentary on Homer's* Odyssey. Vol. 1. *Introduction and books 1–8*. Oxford: Clarendon Press.

Heurgon, J. 1942. *Recherches sur l'histoire, la religion et la civilisation de la Capoue préromaine des origines à la deuxième guerre punique*. Paris: Boccard.

———. 1973. *The rise of Rome*. London: Batsford.

Heurtley, W. A., and H. L. Lorimer. 1932–33. Excavations in Ithaca. *BSA* 1932–33: 22–65.

Hiller, S. 1976. Der Becher des Nestor. *Antike Welt* 7(1): 22–31.

———. 1991. Die archäologische Erforschung des griechischen Siedlungsbereiches im 8.Jh. v. Chr. In Latacz 1991, 61–88.

Hobsbawm, E. 1990. *Nations and nationalism since 1780: Programme, myth, reality.* Cambridge: Cambridge University Press.

Holloway, R. R. 1994. *The archaeology of early Rome and Latium.* London: Routledge.

Holoka, J. P. 1991. Homer, oral poetry theory, and comparative literature: Major trends and controversies in twentieth-century criticism. In Latacz 1991, 456–81.

Hope Simpson, R., and J. F. Lazenby. 1970. *The catalogue of the ships in Homer's* Iliad. Oxford: Clarendon Press.

Hornblower, S. 1991. *A commentary on Thucydides.* Vol. 1. *Books 1–3.* Oxford: Clarendon Press.

Horowitz, D. L. Ethnic identity. In Glazer and Moynihan 1975, 111–40.

Horsfall, N. M. 1979a. Some problems in the Aeneas legend. *CQ* 29: 372–90.

———. 1979b. Stesichoros at Bovillae? *JHS* 79: 26–48.

———. 1987. The Aeneas legend from Homer to Virgil. In Bremmer and Horsfall 1987, 12–24.

Hugh-Jones, S. 1989. Wāribi and the White men: History and myth in northwest Amazonia. In Tonkin, McDonald, and Chapman 1989, 53–70.

Hus, A. 1976. *Les siècles d'or d'histoire étrusque (675–475 avant J.-C.).* Latomus 146. Brussels.

Huxley, G. L. 1959. Homerica 2: Eugammon. *GRBS* 2: 23–28.

———. 1969. *Greek epic poetry from Eumelos to Panyasis.* London: Faber.

Isaac, B. H. 1986. *The Greek settlements in Thrace until the Macedonian conquest.* Leiden: Brill.

Isajiw, W. 1974. Definitions of ethnicity. *Ethnicity* 1: 111–24.

Isler, H.-P. 1973. Zur Hermeneutik früher griechischer Bilder. In *Zur griechische Kunst: Hansjoerg Bloesch zum 60. Geburtstag,* 34–41. AntK suppl. 9.

Isserlin, J. B. S. 1991. The transfer of the alphabet to the Greeks: The state of documentation. In Baurain, Bonnet, and Krings 1991, 283–91.

Izre'el, S. 1992. The study of oral poetry: Reflections of a neophyte. In Vogelzang and Vanstiphout 1992, 155–225.

James, G. M. G. 1992 (1954). *Stolen legacy: Greek philosophy is stolen Egyptian philosophy.* Trenton: Africa World Press.

Jameson, M., and I. Malkin. 1998. The gravestone of Latinos of Rhegion. Athenaeum, forthcoming.

Janko, R. 1982. *Homer, Hesiod, and the Homeric Hymns: Diachronic development in epic tradition.* Cambridge: Cambridge University Press.

———. 1990. The *Iliad* and its editors: Dictation and redaction. *Classical Antiquity* 9: 326–34.

Janni, P. 1984. *La mappa e il periplo: Cartografia antica e spazio odologico.* Rome: Bretschneider.

Jeffery, L. H. 1982. Greek alphabetic writing. *CAH²* 3.1, 819–33.

———. 1990. *The local scripts of Archaic Greece: A study of the Greek alphabet and its development from the eighth to the fifth centuries B.C.* Rev. ed. with supplement by A. W. Johnston. Oxford: Clarendon Press.

Jensen, M. S. 1980. *The Homeric question and the oral-formulaic theory.* Copenhagen: Museum Tusculanum.

Jobst, W. 1970. *Die Höhle im griechischen Theater des 5. und 4. Jahrhunderts v. Christ.* Vienna: Bohlau.

Johannowsky, W. 1983. *Materiali di età arcaica della Campania.* (Monumenti Antichi della Magna Grecia.) Naples: G. Macchiaroli.

Johansen, K. F. 1967. *The Iliad in early Greek art.* Copenhagen: Munksgaard.

Johnston, A. W. 1979. *Trademarks on Greek vases.* Warminster: Aris and Phillips.

———. 1983. The extent and use of literacy: The archaeological evidence. In Hägg 1983, 63–68.

Jones, R. E 1980. Analyses of bronze and other base metal objects from the cemeteries. In Popham, Calligas, and Sackett 1993, 447–59.

Jones, R. E., and L. Vagnetti. 1988. Towards the identification of local Mycenaean pottery in Italy. In *Problems in Greek prehistory: Papers presented at the centenary conference of the British School of Archaeology at Athens, Manchester, April 1986,* ed. E. B. French and K. A. Wardle, 335–48. Bristol: Classical Press.

———. 1992. Traders and craftsmen in the central Mediterranean: Archaeological evidence and archeometric research (an addendum). *BSA* 87: 231–35.

Jordan, B. 1979. *Servants of the gods: A study in the religion, history, and literature of fifth-century Athens.* Hypomnetata 55. Göttingen: Vandelhoek and Ruprecht.

Jost, M. 1985. *Sanctuaires et cultes d'Arcadie.* Paris: J. Vrin.

Jouan, F. 1990. Les Corinthiens en Acarnanie et leurs prédécesseurs mythiques. In *Mythe et politique: Actes du colloque de Liège, 14–16 septembre 1989,* ed. A. Motte and F. Jouan, 155–66. Paris: Les Belles Lettres.

Jourdain-Annequin, C. 1989. *Héraclès aux portes du soir.* Annales Littéraires de l'Université de Besançon 402. Paris.

Just, R. 1989. Triumph of the ethnos. In Tonkin, McDonald, and Chapman 1989, 71–88.

Kallipolitis, V. G. 1984. Κεράμεικα Εὐρήματα ἀπό την Κέρκυρα. *ASAA* 44: 69–76.

Kannicht, R. 1982. Poetry and art: Homer and the monuments afresh. *Classical Antiquity* 1: 70–86.

Katz, M. 1991. *Penelope's renown: Meaning and indeterminacy in the* Odyssey. Princeton: Princeton University Press.

Kearns, E. 1989. *The heroes of Attica.* University of London, Institute of Classical Studies, Bulletin suppl. 57.

———. 1992. Between god and man: Status and function of heroes and their sanctuaries. In *Le sanctuaire grec,* 65–107.

Kearsley, R. 1989. *The pendant semi-circle skyphos.* BICS suppl. 44.

———. 1996. The Greek Geometric wares from Al Mina levels 10–8 and associated pottery. *MeditArch* 8: 7–81.

Kern, O. 1900. *Die Inschriften von Magnesia am Maeander.* Berlin: W. Spemann.

Keyes, C., ed. 1981a. *Ethnic change.* Seattle and London: University of Washington Press.

———. 1981b. The dialectics of ethnic change. In Keyes 1981a, 3–30.

Kilian, K. 1977. Zwei italische Kammhelme aus Griechenland. BCH suppl. 4: 429–42.

———. 1984. Magna Grecia, Epiro e Macedonia durante l'Età del Ferro. In *Magna Grecia, Epiro e Macedonia: Atti del ventiquattresima convegno di studi sulla Magna Grecia*, 237–88. Taranto.

———. 1990. Mycenaean colonization: Norm and variety. In Descoeudres 1990, 445–67.

Kirgin, B. 1990. The Greeks in central Dalmatia: Some new evidence. In Descoeudres 1990, 291–321.

Kirk, G. S. 1962. *The songs of Homer*. Cambridge: Cambridge University Press.

———. 1976. *Homer and the oral tradition*. Cambridge: Cambridge University Press.

Kleinberg, A. 1994. Historiography from the *Annales* to the present. *Encyclopedia Hebraica* 3 suppl., 321–29.

Knauf, E. A. 1987. Haben Aramäer den Griechen das Alphabet vermittelt? *WO* 18: 45–48.

Kontoleon, N. 1963. Οἱ ἀεινᾶυται τῆς Ἐρετρίας. *Archeologike Ephemeris*, 1–45.

Kopcke, G., and I. Tokumaru, eds. 1992. *Greece between East and West: Papers of the Meetings at the Institute of Fine Arts, New York University, March 15–16th, 1990*. Mainz: Verlag Philip von Zabern.

Korkuti, M. 1984. I rapporti fra le due coste dell'Adriatico meridionale nell'età del Bronzo e del Ferro. In *Magna Grecia, Epiro e Macedonia: Atti del ventiquattresimo convegno di studi sulla Magna Grecia*, 237–88. Taranto: Istituto per la Storia e l'Archeologia della Magna Grecia.

Kraay, C. M. 1976. *Archaic and Classical Greek coins*. London: Methuen.

Kretchmer, P. 1943. Die vorgriechischen Sprach- und Volksschichten. *Glotta* 30: 84–218.

Kyriakides, S. P. 1955. *The northern ethnological boundaries of Hellenism*. Thessaloniki.

Kyrieleis, H. 1990. Neue Ausgrabungen in Olympia. *Antike Welt* 21: 177–88.

———. 1992. Neue Ausgrabungen in Olympia. In *Proceedings of an International Symposium on the Olympic games*, ed. W. Coulson and H. Kyrieleis, 19–24. Athens.

Labarbe, J. 1991. Survie de l'oralité en Grèce archaïque. In Baurain, Bonnet, and Krings 1991, 499–531.

Lacroix, L. 1965a. La légende de Philoctète en Italie méridionale. *RBPh* 43: 5–21.

———. 1965b. *Monnaies et colonisation dans l'Occident grec*. Brussels: Palais des Académie.

La Genière, J. de. 1978. La colonisation grecque en Italie méridionale et en Sicile et l'acculturation des non-grecs. *RA* 1978 (2): 257–76.

———. 1979. The Iron Age in southern Italy and Etruria. In Ridgway and Ridgway 1979, 59–93.

———. 1990. *Bibliografia topografica della colonizzazione greca in Italia e nelle isole tirreniche*, ed. G. Nenci and G. Vallet, vol. 8, 405–8. Pisa and Rome.

———. 1991a. L'identification de Lagaria et ses problèmes. In La Genière 1991c, 55–66.

———. 1991b. Au pays de Philoctète, la montagne de Murge: Recherches dans les nécropoles. In La Genière 1991c, 75–116.

———, ed. 1991c. *Epeios et Philoctète en Italie: Données archéologiques et traditions légendaires*. Cahiers du Centre Jean Bérard 16. Naples: Centre Jean Bérard.

La Genière, J. de, and C. Sabbione. 1983–84. Indizi della Macalla di Filottete? (Le Murge di Strongoli). *Atti e Memorie della Società Magna Grecia*, n.s., 24–25: 163–92.

Lamberton, R. 1983. *Porphyry, On the cave of the nymphs: Translation and introductory essay.* Barrytown, N.Y.: Station Hill Press.

———. 1988. *Hesiod.* New Haven: Yale University Press.

Lamboley, J-J. 1987. Le Canal d'Otrante et les relations entre les deux rives de l'Adriatique. In Cabanes 1987b, 195–202.

———. 1996. *Recherches sur les Messapiens: IVᵉ–IIᵉ siècle avant J.-C.* Rome: École Française de Rome.

La Rocca, E. 1976. *Civiltà del Lazio primitivo.* Rome: Multigrafia.

———. 1977. Note sulle importazioni greche in territorio laziale nell'VIII secolo a.C. *PP* 32: 375–77.

———. 1982. Ceramica d'importazione greca nell'VIII secolo a.C. a Sant'Omobono: Un aspetto delle origini di Roma. In *La céramique grecque* 1982, 45–54.

Latacz, J., ed. 1991. *Zweihundert Jahre Homer-Forschung: Rückblick und Ausblick.* Stuttgart and Leipzig: Teubner.

Lattanzi, E. 1991. Recenti scoperte nei santuari di Hera Lacinia a Crotone e di Apollo Aleo a Cirò Marina. In La Genière 1991c, 67–74.

Lattimore, O. 1962. La civilisation mère de barbarie? *Annales ESC* 17: 95–108.

Leake, W.-M. 1967 (1835). *Travels in northern Greece.* 4 vols. Amsterdam: A. M. Hakkert.

Lemaire, A. 1978. Abécédaires et exercises d'écolier en épigraphie nord-ouest sémitique. *Journal Asiatique* 266: 221–35.

Lemos, I. S. 1992. Euboian enterprise in the eastern Mediterranean: Early imports at Lefkandi. *AJA* 16: 338–39.

———. 1997. Euboea and its Aegean koine. *AION (archeol).*

Lenclud, G. 1994. Qu'est-ce que la tradition?, in *Transcrire la mythologie*, ed. M. Detienne, 25–44. Paris: Albin Michel.

Lepore, E. 1962. *Richerche sull'antico Epiro.* Naples: Libreria Scientifica Editrice.

———. 1979. L'Italia dal "punto di vista" Ionico: Tra Ecateo ed Erodoto. In Φιλίας χάριν: *Miscellanea in honore di E. Manni.* 1342–44. Rome: Libreria Scientifica Editrice.

———. 1980. Diomede. In *L'epos greco in occidente: Atti del diciannovesimo convegno di studi sulla Magna Grecia, Taranto, 7–12 ottobre 1979*, 114–32. Taranto: Istituto per la Storia e l'Archeologia della Magna Grecia.

———, ed. 1984. *Recherches sur les cultes grecs et l'Occident.* Vol. 2. Cahiers du Centre Jean Bérard 9. Naples: Centre Jean Bérard.

Lepore, E., and R. Martin, eds. 1979. *Recherches sur les cultes grecs et l'Occident.* Vol. 1. Cahiers du Centre Jean Bérard 5. Naples.

Letteratura e arte figurate nella Magna Grecia: Atti del sesto convegno di studi sulla Magna Grecia, Taranto, 1966. 1967. Naples: Istituto per la Storia e l'Archeologia della Magna Grecia.

LeVine, R., and D. Campbell. 1972. *Ethnocentrism: Theories of conflict, ethnic attitudes, and group behavior.* New York: Wiley.

Lévy, E. 1984. Naissance du concept de barbare. *Ktema* 9: 5–14.

————. 1989. De quelques allusions à l'*Iliade* dans l'*Odyssée*. In *Architecture et poésie dans le monde grec: Hommages à Georges Roux*, ed. R. Etienne, M.-T. Le Dinaahet, and M. Yon, 123–31. Lyons and Paris: Maison de l'Orient/Boccard.

Lichtenstein, M. 1968. The banquet motifs in Kerett and in Proverbs 9. *Journal of the Ancient Near East Society* 1: 19–31.

Linders, T. 1989–90. The melting down of discarded metal offerings in Greek sanctuaries. *Scienze dell'Antichità* 3–4: 281–86.

Lipinski, E. 1988. Les Phéniciens et l'alphabet. *Oriens Antiquus* 27: 231–60.

Lomas, K. 1993. *Rome and the western Greeks, 350 B.C.–A.D. 200: Conquest and acculturation in southern Italy*. London and New York: Routledge.

Lombardo, M. 1986. Siris-Polieion: Fonti letterarie, documentazione archeologica e problemi storici. In *Siris-Polieion: Fonti letterarie e nuova documentazione archeologica (Incontro Studi-Policoro, 1984)*, 55–86. Galatina: Congedo.

————. 1991. I Messapi: Aspetti della problematica storica. In *I Messapi* 1991, 34–109.

————. 1992. *I Messapi e la Messapia nelle fonti letterarie greche e latine*. Galatina: Congedo.

Longo, O. 1983. Fra Ciclopi e leoni. *Belfagor* 38: 212–22.

Lonis, R. 1969. *Les usages de la guerre entre Grecs et barbares*. Paris: Les Belles Lettres.

Lo Porto, F. G. 1973. *Civiltà indigena e penetrazione greca nella Lucania orientale*. Rome: Academia Nazionale dei Lincei.

————. 1986. *Napoli antica*. Naples: G. Macchiaroli.

Lord, A. B. 1951. Composition by theme in Homer and South Slavic epos. *TAPhA* 82: 71–80.

————. 1953. Homer's originality: Oral dictated texts. *TAPhA* 84: 124–34.

————. 1960. *The singer of tales*. Cambridge: Harvard University Press.

————. 1981. Memory, fixity, and genre in oral traditional poetries. In Foley 1981, 451–61.

————. 1995. *The singer resumes the tale*. Ithaca: Cornell University Press.

Luce, J. V. 1975. *Homer and the Heroic Age*. London: Thames and Hudson.

Luraghi, N. 1990. La fondazione di Siri ionica: Problemi di cronologia. *Hesperia* 1: 9–18.

Maass, M. 1978. *Die geometrischen Dreifusse von Olympia*. Olympische Forschungen 10. Berlin.

McCarter, P. K. 1974. The early diffusion of the Greek alphabet. *BA* 37: 68.

————. 1975. *The antiquity of the Greek alphabet and the early Phoenician scripts*. Harvard Semitic Monograph 9. Missoula: Scholars Press.

Maddoli, G. 1980a. Filottete in "Italia." In *L'epos greco in occidente: Atti del diciannovesimo convegno di studi sulla Magna Grecia, Taranto, 7–12 ottobre 1979*, 133–67. Taranto: Istituto per la Storia e l'Archeologia della Magna Grecia.

————. 1980b. Filottete in "Italia." *Magna Graecia* 15(5–6): 1–15.

————. 1982. Megále Hellás: Genesi di un concetto e realtà storico-politiche. In *Megale Hellas* 1982, 9–30.

————. 1984. I culti di Crotone. *Crotone: Atti del ventitreesimo convegno di studi sulla Magna Grecia, Taranto, 7–10 ottobre 1983*, 313–40. Naples: Istituto per la Storia e l'Archeologia della Magna Grecia.

————. 1989. Religione e culti in Magna Grecia: Un secolo di studi. In *Un secolo di ricerche* 1989, 277–99.

Magna Grecia e il mondo miceneo: Atti del ventiduesimo convegno di studi sulla Magna Grecia. 1983. Naples: Istituto per la Storia e l'Archeologia della Magna Grecia.

Magou, E., S. Philippakis, and C. Rolley. 1986. Trépieds géométriques de bronze. *BCH* 110: 121–36.

Malcolm, E. C. 1985. Greek votive reliefs to Pan and the nymphs. Ph. diss., New York University.

Malkin, I. 1984. What were the sacred precincts of Brea (*IG³* no. 46)? *Chiron* 14: 43–48.

————. 1984–85. The origins of the colonists of Syracuse: Apollo of Delos. *Kokalos* 30–31: 53–55.

————. 1985. What's in a name? The eponymous founders of Greek colonies. *Athenaeum* 63: 114–30.

————. 1986. Apollo Archegetes and Sicily. *ASNP,* ser. 3, 16: 61–74.

————. 1987a. La place des dieux dans la cité des hommes. *RHR* 204: 331–52.

————. 1987b. *Religion and colonization in ancient Greece.* (Studies in Greek and Roman Religion 3.) Leiden: Brill.

————. 1989. Delphoi and the founding of social order in archaic Greece. *Metis* 4: 129–53.

————. 1990a. Lysander and Libys. *CQ,* n.s., 40: 541–45.

————. 1990b. Missionaires païens dans la Gaule grecque. In Malkin 1990c, 42–52.

————. 1990c. Territorialisation mythologique: Les "autels des Philènes" en Cyrénaïque. *DHA* 16: 219–29.

————, ed. 1990d. *La France et la Méditerranée.* Leiden: Brill.

————. 1991. What is an *aphidruma? Classical Antiquity* 10: 77–99.

————. 1993. Land ownership, territorial possession, hero cults, and scholarly theory. In Nomodeiktes: *Greek studies in honor of Martin Ostwald,* ed. R. M. Rosen and J. Farrell, 225–34. Ann Arbor: University of Michigan Press.

————. 1994a. Inside and outside: Colonization and the formation of the mother city. In *Apoikia: Studi in onore di G. Buchner,* 1–9. AION (*archeol*) 16.

————. 1994b. *Myth and territory in the Spartan Mediterranean.* Cambridge: Cambridge University Press.

————. 1996a. Nymphs. In *Oxford Classical dictionary,* 3d ed., ed. S. Hornblower and A. Spawforth. Oxford: Clarendon Press.

————. 1996b. Territorial domination and the Greek sanctuary. In *Power and religion in ancient Greece: Proceedings of the Uppsala Symposion 1993,* 75–82. Boreas 24.

————. ed. n.d. *A history of Greek colonization.* Leiden: Brill. In press.

Malkin, I., and A. Fichman. 1987. Homer, *Odyssey* iii 153–85: A maritime commentary. *MHR* 2: 250–58.

Malkin, I., and R. L. Hohlfelder, eds. 1988. *Mediterranean cities: Historical perspectives.* London: Cass.

Mallwitz, A. 1972. *Olympia und seine Bauten.* Munich: Prestal-Verlag.

Maltes, W. 1958. *Odysseus bei den Phäaken.* Mürzburg: Triltsch.

Manning, S. 1992. Archaeology and the world of Homer: Introduction to a past and present discipline. In Emlyn-Jones, Hardwick, and Purkis 1992, 117–42.

Mannsperger, B. 1996. Die neuen Ausgrabungen in Troia und ihr Einfluss auf die Homerforschung. In Η΄ ΔΙΕΘΝΕΣ ΣΥΝΕΔΡΙΟ ΓΙΑ ΤΗΝ ΟΔΥΣΣΕΙΑ, *Ithaca, 31 August–5 September 1996.* In press.

Mano, A. 1983. Problemi della colonizzazione ellenica nell'Illiria meridionale. In *Modes des contacts 1983.* 227–38.

Marasco, G. 1981. *Sparta agli inizi dell'età ellenistica: Il regno di Areo I (309/8–265/4 a.C.* Florence: CLUSF.

Marazzi, M. 1993. The early Aegean-Mycenaean presence in the Gulf of Naples. In Zerner 1993, 335–37.

March, J. R. 1989. Euripides' Bakchai: A reconstruction in the light of vase-paintings. *BISC* 36: 33–65.

Martelli, M. 1984. Prima di Aristonothos. *Prospettiva* 38: 2–15.

Martin, R. P. 1989. *The language of heroes: Speech and performance in the* Iliad. Ithaca and London: Cornell University Press.

———. 1992a. Hesiod's metanastic poetics. *Ramus* 21: 11–33.

———. 1992b. Review of *Der unbekannte Odysseus: Eine Interpretation der* Odyssee, by T. Reucher. *Classical Antiquity* 151–52.

———. 1993. Telemachus and the last hero song. *Colby Quarterly* 29: 222–40.

Martin, R., and H. Metzger. 1976. *La religion grecque.* Paris: Presses Universitaires de France.

Maselli Scotti, F. 1983. *Preistoria del caput Adriae.* Udine.

Massa Pairault, F.-H. 1994. *Iconologia e politica nell'Italia antica: Roma, Lazio, Etruria dal VII al I secolo a.C.* Milan: Longanesi.

Masson, O. 1995. Recherches récentes sur Heinrich Schliemann. *REG* 108: 593–600.

Mastrocinque, A. 1987. *Santuari e divinità dei Paleoveneti.* Padua: La Linea.

———. 1993. *Romolo: La fondazione di Roma tra storia e leggenda.* Este: Libreria Editrice Zielo.

Mayer, M. 1914. *Apulien vor und wärend der Hellenisierung mit besonderer Berücksichtigung der Keramik.* Leipzig and Berlin: Teubner.

Mazzei, M., ed. 1984. *La Daunia antica.* Milan: Electa.

Mazzei, M., and E. Lippolis. 1984. Dall'ellenizzazione all'età tardorepubblicana. In Mazzei 1984, 185–252.

Megale Hellas, nomi e immagine: Atti del ventiunesimo convegno di studi sulla Magna Grecia. 1982. Naples: Istituto per la Storia e l'Archeologia della Magna Grecia.

Mele, A. 1979. *Il commercio greco arcaico: Prexis ed emporie.* Cahiers du Centre Jean Bérard 4. Naples.

———. 1984. Crotone e la sua storia. In *Crotone: Atti del ventitreesimo convegno di studi sulla Magna Grecia, Taranto, 7–10 ottobre 1983,* 9–87. Naples: Istituto per la Storia e l'Archeologia della Magna Grecia.

———. 1993–94. Le origini degli Elymi nelle tradizioni di v secolo. *Kokalos* 39–40: 71–109.

Melissano, V. 1990. Otranto. In D'Andria 1990b, 19–48.

Merkelbach, R. 1969. *Untersuchungen zur Odyssee.* 2d ed. Munich: Beck.

Merkelbach, R., and M. West. 1967. *Fragmenta Hesiodica.* Oxford: Clarendon Press.

Mertens, D. 1984. I santuari di Capo Colonna e Crimisa: Aspetti dell'architettura crotoniate. In *Crotone, Atti del ventitreesimo convegno di studi sulla Magna Grecia,*

Taranto, 7–10 ottobre 1983, 207–28. Taranto: Istituto per la Storia e l'Archeologia della Magna Grecia.

———. 1985. Magna Grecia, Epiro e Macedonia: Notta introduttiva per l'architettura. *Magna Graecia* 20 (1–2): 12–15.

I Messapi: Atti del trentesimo convegno di studi sulla Magna Grecia, Taranto-Lecce, 4–9 ottobre 1990. 1991. Taranto.

Metzger, H. 1967. L'imagérie de la grande Grèce et les textes littéraires à l'époque classique. In *Letteratura e arte figurata nella Magna Grecia: Atti del settimo convegno di studi sulla Magna Grecia, Taranto, 1966*, 151–81. Naples.

Meuli, K. 1921. *Odyssee und Argonautica.* Berlin: Sackingen.

Mihailov, G. 1955. *La légende de Térée.* AUS 50(2).

Miller, M. C. 1995. Priam, king of Troy. In Carter and Morris 1995, 449–65.

Modes des contacts et processus de transformation dans les sociétés anciennes: Actes du colloque de Crotone (24–30 Mai 1981). 1983. Scuola Normale Superiore di Pisa, Collection de l'École Française de Rome 67.

Moggi, M. 1983. L'elemento indigeno nella tradizione letteraria sulle *Ktiseis.* In *Modes des contacts* 1983, 979–1002.

Mondi, R. 1983. The Homeric Cyclopes: Folktale, tradition, and theme. *TAPhA* 113: 17–38.

Morel, J.-P. 1975. L'expansion phocéenne en Occident: Dix années de recherches (1966–1975). *BCH* 99: 853–96.

———. 1983. Greek colonization in Italy and the West. In Hackens, Holloway, and Holloway 1983, 123–161.

Moret, J.-M. 1975. *L'Ilioupersis dans la céramique italiote.* Rome: Institut Suisse de Rome.

———. 1980. A proposito dei "Nostoi": Tradizione letteratura e tradizione figurata in Occidente. In *L'epos greco in occidente: Atti del diciannovesimo convegno di studi sulla Magna Grecia, Taranto, 7–12 ottobre 1979*, 185–228. Taranto: Istituto per la Storia e l'Archeologia della Magna Grecia.

Moretti, L. 1971. Problemi di storia tarantina. In *Taranto nella civiltà della Magna Grecia: Atti del decimo convegno di studi sulla Magna Grecia, Taranto, 1970*, 21–66. Naples: Istituto per la Storia e l'Archeologia della Magna Grecia.

Morgan, C. A. 1988. Corinth, the Corinthian Gulf, and western Greece during the eighth century B.C. *BSA* 83: 313–38.

———. 1990. *Athletes and oracles: The transformation of Olympia and Delphi in the 8th century B.C.* Cambridge: Cambridge University Press.

———. 1991. Ethnicity and early Greek states: Historical and material perspectives. *PCPS* 37: 131–63.

———. 1993. The Corinthian aristocracy and Corinthian cult during the eighth century. In *Peloponnesian sanctuaries and cult: Proceedings of the Swedish Institute Seminar, Athens, October 1993*, ed. R. Hägg. Stockholm. In press.

———. 1994. The creation of a sacral "landscape": Isthmia, Perachora, and the early Corinthian state. In Alcock and Osborne 1994, 106–43.

———. 1995. Problems and prospects in the study of Corinthian pottery production. In *Magna Grecia e Corinto: Atti del trentaquattresimo convegno di studi sulla Magna Grecia, Taranto, 7–11 ottobre 1994*, 313–44. Taranto: Istituto per la Storia e l'Archeologia della Magna Grecia.

————. 1996. Ritual and society in early Iron Age Corinthia. In *Ancient Greek cult practice from the archaeological evidence*, ed. R. Hägg. Stockholm and Athens. In press.

Morgan, C. A., and K. W. Arafat. 1995. In the footsteps of Aeneas: Excavations at Butrint, Albania 1991–2. *Dialogos: Hellenic Studies Review* 2: 25–40.

Morgan, C. A., and J. M. Hall. 1996. Achaian poleis and Achaian colonisation. In *Acts of the Copenhagen Polis Centre*, vol. 3, ed. M. H. Hansen, 164–232. Copenhagen: Royal Danish Academy of Science and Letters.

Morris, I. 1986. The use and abuse of Homer. *Classical Antiquity* 5: 81–138.

————. 1987. *Burial and ancient society: The rise of the Greek city-state*. Cambridge: Cambridge University Press.

————. 1988. Tomb cult and the Greek renaissance. *Antiquity* 62: 750–61.

Morris, S. P. 1992. *Daidalos and the origins of Greek art*. Princeton: Princeton University Press.

Morrison, J. S., and R. T. Williams. 1968. *Greek oared ships: 900–322 B.C.* Cambridge: Cambridge University Press.

Moscati, S. ed. 1989. *Salento Porta d'Italia: Atti del convegno internazionale (Lecce 27–30 novembre 1986)*. Galatina: Congedo.

Moscati Castelnuovo, L. 1989. *Siris: Tradizione storiografica e momenti della storia di una città della Magna Grecia*. Latomus 207. Brussels.

Mossé, C. 1980. Ithaque ou la naissance de la cité. *AION (archeol)* 2: 7–19.

Murnaghan, S. 1987. *Disguise and recognition in the Odyssey*. Princeton: Princeton University Press.

Murray, O. 1988. Death and the symposion. In *La parola, l'imagine, la tomba: Atti del Colloquio di Capri*, 239–58. AION (archeol) 10.

————. 1989. Omero e l'etnologia. *Magna Graecia* 9–10: 1–6. (Expanded in *Kokalos* 34–35: 1–13).

————, ed. 1990. *Sympotica: A symposium on the symposion*. Oxford: Clarendon Press.

————. 1994. Nestor's cup and the origins of the Greek symposium. In *Apoikia: Studi in onore di G. Buchner*, 47–54. AION(archeol) 16.

Murray, O., and M. Tecuşan, eds. 1995. *In vino veritas*. Rome and London: British School at Rome/American Academy in Rome.

Murray, W. C. 1982. The coastal sites of western Akarnania: A topographical-historical survey, Ph.D. diss. University of Pennsylvania.

Murray, W. M. 1987. Do modern winds equal ancient winds? *MHR* 2: 139–67.

Musti, D. 1970. Tendenze nella storiografia romana e greca. *QUCC* 10: 1–159.

————. 1981. "Una città simile a Troia": Città troiane da Siri a Lavinio. *ArchClass* 33: 1–26.

————, ed. 1985. *Le origini dei Greci: Dori e mondo egeo*. Rome: Laterza.

————. 1987. Etruria e Lazio arcaico nella tradizione (Demarato, Tarquinio, Mezenzio). In *Etruria e Lazio arcaico*. Quaderni del Centro di Studi per l'Archeologia Etrusco-Italica 15. Rome.

————. 1988. *Strabone e la Magna Grecia*. Padua: Editoriale Programma.

————. 1991. Lo sviluppo del mito di Filottete, da Cortone a Sabiri. In La Genière 1991c, 21–36.

Nagata, J. 1981. In defense of ethnic boundaries: The changing myths and charters of Malay identity. In Keyes 1981a, 87–116.

Nagler, M. 1988. Odysseus: The proem and the problem. *Classical Antiquity* 9: 335–56.

Nagy, G. 1979. *The best of the Achaeans: Concepts of the hero in Archaic Greek poetry*. Baltimore and London: Johns Hopkins University Press.

———. 1990. *Pindar's Homer: The Lyric possession of an epic past*. Baltimore: Johns Hopkins University Press.

———. 1992. Homeric questions. *TAPhA* 122: 17–60.

———. 1995. An evolutionary model for the making of Homeric poetry: Comparative perspectives. In Carter and Morris 1995, 163–81.

———. 1996. *Poetry as performance: Homer and beyond*. Cambridge: Cambridge University Press.

Napoli, M. 1978. *Città di Magna Grecia*. Naples.

Nava, M. 1990. Greek and Adriatic influences in Daunia in the early Iron Age. In Descoeudres 1990, 559–78.

Naveh, J. 1987. *Early history of the alphabet: An introduction to West Semitic epigraphy and palaeography*. Jerusalem: Magnes Press, Hebrew University.

Negbi, O. 1992. Early Phoenician presence in the Mediterranean islands: A reappraisal. *AJA* 96: 599–615.

Nenci, G. 1978. Per una definizione della Ἰαπυγία. *ASNP,* ser. 3, 8: 43–58.

———. 1987. Troiani e Focidesi nella Sicilia occidentale (Thuc. vi 2.3; Paus. v 25.6). *ASNP,* ser. 3, 17: 921–33.

———. 1990. L'Occidente barbarico. In *Hérodote et les peuples non-Grecs,* 301–82. Entretiens Hardt 35.

———. 1991. Filottete in Sicilia. In La Genière 1991c, 131–36.

Niemeyer, H. G., ed. 1982. *Phönizier im Westen: Die Beiträge des Internationalen Symposiums über "Die phönizische Expansion im westlichen Mittelmeerraum" in Köln vom 24 bis 27 April 1979*. Madrider Beiträge 8. Mainz am Rhein.

———. 1984. Die Phönizier und die Mittelmeerwelt im Zeitalter Homers. *Jahrbuch der Museum Mainz* 31: 1–94.

———. 1990. The Phoenicians in the Mediterranean: A non-Greek model for expansion and settlement in antiquity. In Descoeudres 1990, 469–89.

Nilsson, M. P. 1909. *Studien zur Geschichte des alten Epeiros*. Lund: H. Olssons Buchdr.

———. 1972 (1951). *Cults, myth, oracles, and politics in ancient Greece*. New York: Cooper Square.

Notopoulos, J. A. 1964. Studies in early Greek poetry. *HSPh* 68: 11–77.

Nouvelle contribution à l'étude de la société et de la colonisation eubéenne. 1981. Cahiers du Centre Jean Bérard 6. Naples: Centre Jean Bérard.

Oberhummer, E. 1887. *Akarnanien, Ambrakia, Amphilochien, Leukas im Altertum*. Munich: T. Ackermann.

Ong, W. 1982. *Orality and literacy*. London: Methuen.

Orsi, P. 1932. Templum Apollonis Alaei ad Crimissa promontorium. *Atti e Memorie della Società Magna Grecia* 5: 7–182.

Page, D. 1955. *The Homeric* Odyssey. Oxford: Clarendon Press.

Pallottino, M. 1974. *The Etruscans*. London: Penguin.

———. 1991. *A history of earliest Italy*. London: Routledge.

Palm, J. 1952. Veian tomb groups in the Museo Preistorico, Rome. *Opuscula Archaeologica* 7: 50–86.

Papadopoulos, T. 1990. Settlement types in prehistoric Epirus. In *L'habitat égéen préhistorique*, ed. P. Darcque and R. Treuil, 359–67. BCH suppl. 10. Paris.

———. 1996. Euboians in Macedonia? A closer look. *OJA* 15:151–81.

Papadopoulou-Belmehdi, I. 1994. *Le chant de Pénelope*. Paris: Belin.

Pariente, A. 1992. Le monument argien des "Sept contre Thèbes." In Piérart 1992, 195–230.

Parke, H. W. 1967. *The oracles of Zeus: Dodona, Olympia, Ammon*. Oxford: Blackwell.

Parke, H. W., and D. E. W. Wormell. 1956. *The Delphic oracle*. 2 vols. Oxford: Blackwell.

Parker, R. 1996. *Athenian religion: A history*. Oxford: Oxford University Press.

Parlangèli, O. 1960. *Studi Messapici*. Milan: Istituto Lombardo di Scienze e Lettere.

Parry, A. 1979 (1966). Have we Homer's *Iliad*? In *Homer: Tradition und Neuerung*, ed. J. Latacz, 428–66. Darmstadt. (Also in *YClS* 20: 177–216.)

A passion for antiquities: Ancient art from the collection of Barbara and Lawrence Fleischman. 1994. Malibu: J. Paul Getty Museum.

Payne, H. G. G. 1925–26. On the Thermon metopes. *BSA* 27: 124–32.

Pearson, L. 1939. *The early Ionian historians*. Oxford: Clarendon Press.

———. 1975. Myth and archaiologia in Italy and Sicily: Timaeus and his predecessors. *YClS* 24: 171–95.

———. 1987. *The Greek historians of the West: Timaeus and his predecessors*. Atlanta: Scholars Press.

Pedley, J. G. 1990. *Paestum: Greeks and Romans in southern Italy*. London: Thames and Hudson.

Peradotto, J. 1990. *Man in the middle voice: Name and narration in the* Odyssey. Princeton: Princeton University Press.

Peretti, A. 1979. *Il periplo di Scilace*. Pisa: Giardini.

Peroni, R. 1983. Presenze Micenee e forme socio-economiche nell'Italia protostorica. In *La Magna Grecia e il mondo miceneo: Atti del ventiduesimo convegno di studi sulla Magna Grecia*, 211–83. Naples: Istituto per la Storia e l'Archeologia della Magna Grecia.

———. 1988. Communità e insediamento in Italia fra Età del Bronzo e prima Età del Ferro. In *Storia di Roma*, vol. 1, 7–38. Torino.

Perret, J. 1941. *Siris: Recherches critiques sur l'histoire de la Siritide avant 433/2*. Paris: Les Belles Lettres.

———. 1942. *Les origines de la légende troyenne de Rome (281–31)*. Paris: Belle Lettres.

Peserico, A. 1995. Griechische trinkgefässe im mitteltyrrhenischen Italien. *AA* 1995 (3): 425–39.

Pestalozza, U. 1957. Motivi matriarcali divini e umani in Etolia e in Epiro. *RIL* 91: 583–622.

Peterson, R. M. 1919. *The cults of Campania*. Rome: American Academy in Rome.

Pfeiffer, R. 1968. *A history of Classical scholarship: From the beginnings to the end of the Hellenistic Age*. Oxford: Oxford University Press.

Pfister, F. 1909–12. *Der Reliquienkult im Altertum*. RGVV 1 (2). Giessen: Amsterdam.

Philipp, H. 1994. Olympia, die Peloponnes und die Westgriechen. *JDAI* 109: 77–92.

Phillips, E. D. 1953. Odysseus in Italy. *JHS* 73: 53–67.

Piérart, M., ed. 1992. *Polydipsion Argos*. BCH suppl. 22. Athens and Freiburg: De Boccard.

Pipili, M. 1987. *Laconian iconography of the sixth century B.C.* Oxford: Oxford University Committee for Archaeology.

Polignac, F. de. 1991. Convergence et compétition: Aux origines des sanctuaires de souveraineté territoriale dans le monde grec. In *Les sanctuaires celtiques et leurs rapports avec le monde méditerranéen: Actes du colloque de St-Riquer (8 au 11 novembre 1990)*, ed. J.-L. Brunaux, 97–105. Paris: L'Errance/Archéologie Nouvelle.

———. 1994. Mediation, competition, and sovereignty: The evolution of rural sanctuaries in Geometric Greece. In Alcock and Osborne 1994, 3–18.

———. 1995. *Cults, territory, and the origins of the Greek city-state.* Chicago: University of Chicago Press.

———. 1996. Offrandes, mémoire et compétition ritualisée dans les sanctuaires grecs à l'époque géometrique. In *Power and religion in ancient Greece: Proceedings of the Uppsala Symposion 1993*, 59–66. Boreas 24.

Pollard, J. 1977. *Birds in Greek life and myth.* London: Methuen.

Pontrandolfo, A. 1989. Greci e indigeni. In *Un secolo di richerche 1989*, 329–50.

———. 1995. Simposio e elites sociali nel mondo Etrusco e Italico. In Murray and Tecuşan 1995, 176–95.

Popham, M. R. 1994. Precolonization: Early Greek contact with the East. In Tsetskhladze and De Angelis 1994, 11–34.

Popham, M. R., P. G. Calligas, and L. H. Sackett. 1993. *Lefkandi II.2. The Protogeometric building at Toumba: The excavation, architecture, and finds.* London.

Popham, M. R., P. G. Themelis, and L. H. Sackett. 1980. *Lefkandi I: The Iron Age.* BSA suppl. 11. London.

Popham, M. R., E. Touloupa, and L. H. Sackett. 1982. The hero of Lefkandi. *Antiquity* 56: 169–74.

Poucet, J. 1978. Le Latium protohistorique et archaïque à la lumière des découvertes archéologiques récentes. *AC* 47: 566–601.

———. 1979. Le Latium protohistorique et archaïque à la lumière des découvertes archéologiques récentes. Pt. 2. *AC* 48: 177–220.

———. 1983. Enée et Lavinium. *RBPh* 61: 144–59.

———. 1985. *Origines de Rome: Traditions et histoire.* Brussels: Facultés universitaires St. Louis.

———. 1989. La diffusion de la légende d'Énée en Italie centrale et ses rapports avec celle de Romulus. *LEC* 57: 227–54.

Powell, B. B. 1988. The Dipylon oinochoe inscription and the spread of literacy in eighth-century Athens. *Kadmos* 27: 65–86.

———. 1991a. *Homer and the origin of the Greek alphabet.* Cambridge: Cambridge University Press.

———. 1991b. The origins of alphabetic literacy among the Greeks. In Baurain, Bonnet, and Krings 1991, 357–70.

Pratt, L. H. 1993. *Lying and poetry from Homer to Pindar: Falsehood and deception in Archaic Greek poetics.* Ann Arbor: University of Michigan Press.

La presenza etrusca nella Campania meridionale: Atti delle giornate di studio Salerno-Pontecagnano, 16–18 novembre 1990. 1994. Florence: L. S. Olschki.

Prinz, F. 1979. *Gründungsmythen und Sagenchronologie.* Zetemata 72. Munich.

Prontera, F. 1986. Imagines Italiae: Sulle più antiche visualizzazioni e rappresentazioni geographiche dell'Italia. *Athenaeum* 64: 295–320.

————. ed. 1991. *Geografia storica della Grecia antica*. Rome and Bari: Laterza.

————. 1992. Antioco di Siracusa e la preistoria dell'idea etnico-geografica di Italia. *Geographia Antiqua* 1: 109–35.

Pugliese Carratelli, G. 1952. Sul culto delle Sirene nel golfo di Napoli. *PP* 7: 420–26.

————. 1956. Minos e Cocalos. *Kokalos* 2: 89–103.

————. 1962a. Achei nell'Etruria e nel Lazio? *PP* 17: 5–25.

————. 1962b. Santuari estramurani in Magna Grecia. *PP* 17: 241–46.

————. 1971. Dalle *Odysseiai* alle *apoikiai*. *PP* 26: 393–417.

————. 1979. Per la storia dei culti delle colonie euboiche d'Italia. In *Gli Eubei in Occidente* 1979, 221–29.

————, ed. 1983. *Megale Hellas: Storia e civiltà della Magna Grecia*. Milan: Libri Scheiwiller.

————, ed. 1988. *Italia omnium terrarum alumna*. Milan.

Pulgram, E. 1958. *The tongues of Italy*. Cambridge: Cambridge University Press.

Qviller, B. 1981. The dynamics of Homeric society. *Symbolae Osloenses* 56: 109–55.

Raaflaub, K. 1991. Homer und die Geschichte des 8. Jh. v. Chr. In Latacz 1991, 205–56.

Radlov, V. V. 1885. *Proben der Volkslitteratur der nördlischen türkischen Stämme*. vol. 5. St. Petersburg.

Radt, S. L. 1958. *Pindars zweiter und sechster* Paian. Amsterdam: A. M. Hakkert.

Rathje, A. 1979. Oriental imports in Etruria in the eighth and seventh centuries B.C.: Their origins and implications. in Ridgway and Ridgway 1979, 145–83.

————. 1990. The adoption of the Homeric banquet in central Italy in the Orientalizing period. In Murray 1990, 279–88.

————. 1995. Il banchetto in Italia centrale: Quale stile e vita? In Murray and Tecuşan 1995, 167–75.

Raubitschek, A. 1992. The tripods of Odysseus. In *Studia egea et balcanica in honorem Ludovicae Press*, 99–102. Constanza.

Raviola, F. 1990. La tradizione letteraria su Parthenope. *Hesperia* 1: 19–60.

————. 1991. La tradizione letteraria sulla fondazione di Napoli. *Hesperia* 2: 19–40.

Reece, S. 1993. *The stranger's welcome: Oral theory and the aesthetics of the Homeric hospitality scene*. Ann Arbor: University of Michigan Press.

Redfield, J. M. 1994 (1975). *Nature and culture in the* Iliad: *The tragedy of Hector*. 2d ed. Durham: Duke University Press.

Renan, E. 1882. What is a nation? Translated by M. Thom. In Bhabha 1990, 8–22.

Rendič-Miločevič, D. I greci in Dalmazia e il loro rapporti col mondo illirico. In *Modes des contacts* 1983, 187–202.

Renfrew, C., and J. F. Cherry, eds. 1986. *Peer polity interaction and socio-political change*. Cambridge: Cambridge University Press.

Restelli, G. 1972. *Arcana Epiri: Contributo linguistico-storico sulle origini della civiltà ellenica*. Florence: L. S. Olschki.

Rich, J., and A. Wallace-Hadrill, eds. 1991. *City and country in the ancient world*. London: Routledge.

Richardson, E. H. 1964. *The Etruscans: Their art and their civilization*. Chicago: University of Chicago Press.

Ridgway, D. 1988a. The Etruscans. *CAH*² 4: 634–75.

————. 1988b. The Pithekoussai shipwreck. *Studies in honour of T. B. L. Webster II,* 97–107. Bristol: Bristol Classical Press.

————. 1990. The first western Greeks and their neighbours 1935–1985, in Descoeudres 1990, 61–72.

————. 1992. *The first western Greeks.* Cambridge: Cambridge University Press.

————. 1994a. Phoenicians and Greeks in the west: A view from Pithekoussai. In Tsetskhladze and De Angelis 1994, 35–46.

————. 1994b. La presenza Etrusca nella Campania meridionale. In *La presenza etrusca* 1994, 513–16.

Ridgway, D., F. Boitani, and A. Deriu. 1985. Provenance and firing techniques of Geometric pottery from Veii: A Mossbauer investigation. *BSA* 80: 139–50.

Ridgway, D., and F. Ridgway, eds. 1979. *Italy before the Romans: The Iron Age, Orientalizing, and Etruscan periods.* London, New York, and San Francisco: Academic Press.

Ridgway, F., and R. Serra, 1990. Etruscans, Greeks, Carthaginians: The sanctuary at Pyrgi. In Descoeudres 1990, 511–30.

Robb, K. 1994. *Literacy and paideia in ancient Greece.* New York and Oxford: Oxford University Press.

Robert, F. 1953. Le sanctuaire de l'archégète Anios à Delos. *RA* 41: 8–40.

Robertson, M. 1948. Excavations at Ithaca 5. *BSA* 43: 1–124.

Roesch, P. 1987. Y eut-il des rapports entre les Béotiens, les Épirotes et les Illyriens? In *Actes du colloque international sur l'Illyrie méridionale et l'Épire dans l'antiquité, Clermont-Ferrand [October 22–25, 1984],* 179–83. Clermont-Ferrand: Adossa.

Rolley, C. 1977. *Les trépieds à cuve clouée.* Fouilles de Delphes 5(3). Paris: Boccard.

————. 1983. *Les bronzes grecs.* Fribourg: Office du Livre.

————. 1991. Bronzes en Messapie. In *I Messapi* 1991, 185–207.

————. 1992. Argos, Corinthe, Athènes: Identité culturelle et modes de développement (ixe–viiie s.). In Piérart 1992, 37–54.

————. 1995. Intervento. In *Magna Grecia e Corinto: Atti dei trentaquattresimo convegno di studi sulla Magna Grecia, Taranto 7–11 ottobre 1994.*

Rölling, W. 1989. Über die Anfänge unseres Alphabets. *Das Altertum* 31: 83–91.

Rölling, W., ed. 1978. *Neues Handbuch des Literaturwissenschaften.* Vol. 1. *Altorientalische Literaturen.* Wiesbaden: Athenaion.

Romanucci-Ross, L., and G. de Vos, eds. 1995. *Ethnic identity: Creation, conflict, and accommodation.* 3d ed. Walnut Creek, Calif.: Alta Mira Press.

Ronconi, L. 1974–75. Sulle origini mitiche di Siri. *AIV* 133: 41–64.

————. 1975–76. Sulle origini storiche di Siri. *AIV* 134: 155–78.

Roosen, E. E. 1989. *Creating ethnicity: The process of ethnogenesis.* Newbury Park, Calif., London, and New Delhi: Sage.

Rose, P. W. 1992 (1975). Class ambivalence in the *Odyssey.* In Emlyn-Jones, Hardwick, and Purkis 1992, 193–209 (= *Historia* 24 [1975]: 129–49).

Rose, V. 1966 (1886). *Aristotelis qui ferebantur librorum fragmenta.* Leipzig.

Rosen, R. M. 1990. Poetry and sailing in Hesiod's *Works and Days. Classical Antiquity* 9(1): 99–113.

Rouse, W. H. D. 1902. *Greek votive offerings.* Cambridge: Cambridge University Press.

Roux, G. 1984. Trésors, temples, tholos. In *Temples et sanctuaires,* ed. G. Roux, 153–71. Travaux de la Maison l'Orient 7.

Ruijgh, C. J. 1995. D'Homère aux origines proto-mycéniennes de la tradition épique:

Analyse dialectologique du langue homérique, avec un *excursus* sur la création de l'alphabet grec. In Crielaard 1995a, 1–98.

Russo, J., M. Fernandez-Galiano, and A. Heubeck. 1992. *A commentary on Homer's Odyssey*. Vol. 3. *Books 17–24*. Oxford: Clarendon Press.

Rutherford, R. B., ed. 1992. *Homer: Odyssey books 19 and 20*. Cambridge: Cambridge University Press.

Sadurska, A. 1964. *Les tables iliaques*. Warsaw: Naukowe.

Saggs, H. W. F. 1963. The Nimrud letters. *Iraq* 25: 70–80.

Saïd, S. 1984. Grecs et Barbares dans les tragédies d'Euripide: La fin des différences? *Ktema* 9: 27–53.

Sakellarakis, J. A. 1988. Some Geometric and Archaic votives from the Idaean Cave. In Hägg, Marinatos, and Nordquist 1988, 173–93.

Sakellariou, M. 1958. *La migration grecque en Ionie*. Paris and Athens.

———. 1980. *Les Proto-Grecs*. Athens: Ekdotike Athenon.

Salmon, E. T. 1967. *Samnium and the Samnites*. Cambridge: Cambridge University Press.

Salmon, J. B. 1984. *Wealthy Corinth: A history of the city to 338 B.C.* Oxford: Clarendon Press.

Sass, B. 1988. *The genesis of the alphabet and its development in the second millennium B.C.* Wiesbaden: O. Harrasowitz.

———. 1990. *Studia alphabetica: On the origins and early history of the Northwest Semitic, South Semitic, and Greek alphabets*. Orbis Biblicus et Orientalis 102. Freiburg.

Schachter, A. 1986. *Cults of Boiotia 2: Heracles to Poseidon*. BICS suppl. London.

Schauenberg, K. 1960. Aeneas und Rom. *Gymnasium* 67: 176–91.

Schefold, K. 1966. *Myth and legend in early Greek art*. London: Thames and Hudson.

Scheid, J., and J. Svenbro. 1994. *Le métier de Zeus: Mythe du tissage et du tissu dans le monde greco-romain*. Paris: La Découverte.

Schilardi, D. U. 1975. Paros II: The 1973 campaign. *JFA* 2: 83–96.

———. 1976. Anaskaphai Parou. *Praktika*, 287–94.

Schliemann, H. 1963 (1869). *Ithaka, der Peloponnes und Troia: Archäologische Forschungen*. Darmstadt.

Schmid, B. 1947. Studien zu griechischen Ktisissagen. Ph.D. diss., Freiburg.

Schmitt Pantel, P. 1992. *La cité au banquet*. Paris: De Boccard.

Schoder, R. V. 1963. Ancient Cumae: History, topography, and monuments. *Scientific American* 209: 109–18.

Schoeck, G. 1961. Iliad *und* Aethiopis: *Kykliche Motive in homerischer Brechung*. Zurich.

Schur, W. 1921. Griechische Traditionen von der Gründung Roms. *Klio* 17: 137–52.

Schwabl, H. 1962. Das Bild des fremden Welt bei den frühen Griechen. In *Grecs et barbares*, 3–23. Entretiens Hardt. 8.

Schwartz, S. B. 1994. *Implicit understandings: Observing, reporting, and reflecting on the encounters between European and other peoples in the early modern era*. Cambridge: Cambridge University Press.

Scullard, H. H. 1966. Two Halicarnassians and a Lydian: A note on Etruscan origins. In *Ancient society and institutions: Studies presented to Victor Ehrenberg on his seventy-fifth birthday*, 225–31. Oxford: Blackwell.

Scully, S. 1990. *Homer and the sacred city*. Ithaca: Cornell University Press.

Seaford, R. 1994. *Reciprocity and ritual: Homer and tragedy in the developing city-state.* Oxford: Clarendon Press.

Sealy, R. 1957. From Phemios to Ion. *REG* 70: 312–51.

Un secolo di ricerche in Magna Grecia: Atti del ventottesimo convegno di studi sulla Magna Grecia, Taranto, 7–12 ottobre 1988. 1989. Taranto: Istituto per la Storia e l'Archeologia della Magna Grecia.

Segal, C. 1962. The Phaeaceans and the symbolism of Odysseus' return. *Arion* 1(4): 17–63.

———. 1994. *Singers, heroes, and gods in the* Odyssey. Ithaca: Cornell University Press.

Segert, S. 1963. Altaramäische Schrift und die Anfänge des griechischen Alphabets. *Klio* 41: 38–57.

Semple, E. C. 1971 (1932). *The geography of the Mediterranean region: Its relation to ancient history.* New York: Arno.

Severin, T. 1987. *The Ulysses voyage: Sea search for the* Odyssey. New York: Dutton.

Severyns, A. 1928. *Le cycle épique dans l'école d'Aristarque.* Liège: H. Vaillant.

Shapiro, H. A. 1993. Hipparchos and the Rhapsodes. In Dougherty and Kurke 1993, 92–107.

———. 1994. *Myth into art: Poet and painter in Classical Greece.* London: Routledge.

Shefton, B. B. 1994. Massalia and colonization in the north-western Mediterranean. In Tsetskhladze and De Angelis 1994, 61–86.

Sherrat, E. S. 1990. "Reading the text": Archaeology and the Homeric question. *Antiquity* 64: 807–24.

Shils, E. 1957. Primordial, personal, sacred, and civil ties. *British Journal of Sociology* 8: 130–45.

Sieberber, E. 1990. Zur Lokalisation des homerischen Ithaka. *Thyche* 5: 149–64.

Silk, M. S. 1987. *Homer: The* Iliad. Cambridge: Cambridge University Press.

Sjöberg, A. W. 1975. The Old Babylonian Eduba. In *Sumerological studies in honor of Thorkild Jacobsen on his seventieth birthday, June 7, 1974,* 159–79. Assyriological Studies 20. Chicago.

Skoda, F. 1981. Histoire du mot *barbaros* jusqu'au début de l'ère chrétienne. In *Actes du colloque franco-polonais d'histoire: Les relations économiques et culturelles entre l'Occident et l'Orient,* 111–26. Nice.

Slater, W. J. 1990. Sympotic ethics in the *Odyssey.* In Murray 1990, 213–20.

———, ed. 1991. *Dining in a Classical context.* Ann Arbor: University of Michigan Press.

Slatkin, L. M. 1991. *The power of Thetis: Allusion and interpretation in the* Iliad. Berkeley and Los Angeles: University of California Press.

Smith, A. D. 1986. *The ethnic origins of nations.* Oxford: Blackwell.

Smith, C. Delano. 1979. *Western Mediterranean Europe: A historical geography of Italy, Spain, and southern France since the Neolithic.* London and New York: Academic Press.

Smith, J. Z. 1978. *Map is not territory: Studies in the history of religions.* Leiden: Brill.

———. 1987. *To take place: Toward theory in ritual.* Chicago: University of Chicago Press.

Smith, T. 1987. *Mycenaean trade and interaction in the west central Mediterranean 1600–1000 B.C.* British Archaeological Reports International Series 371.

Snodgrass, A. M. 1971. *The Dark Age of Greece: An archaeological survey of the eleventh to the eighth centuries.* Edinburgh: Edinburgh University Press.

———. 1974. An historical Homeric society? *JHS* 94: 114–25.

———. 1979. Poet and painter in eighth-century Greece. *PCPS* 25 (205): 118–30.

———. 1980. Towards the interpretation of Geometric figure scenes. *Mitteilungen des Deutschen Archäologisches Institut, Athens* 95: 51–58.

———. 1982. Les origines du culte des héros dans la Grèce antique. In Vernant and Gnoli 1982, 107–19.

———. 1986. Interaction by design: The Greek city-state. in Renfrew and Cherry 1986, 47–58.

———. 1987. *An archaeology of Greece: The present state and future scope of a discipline.* Berkeley and Los Angeles: University of California Press.

———. 1988. The archaeology of the hero. *AION (archeol)* 10: 19–26.

———. 1991. Archaeology and the study of the Greek city. In Rich and Wallace-Hadrill 1991, 1–23.

———. 1994a. The Euboeans in Macedonia: A new precedent for western expansion. In *Apoikia: Studi in onore di G. Buchner,* 87–93. AION (*archeol*) 16.

———. 1994b. The growth and standing of the early western colonies. In Tsetskhladze and De Angelis 1994, 1–10.

Solmsen, F. 1986. Aeneas founded Rome with Odysseus. *HSPh* 90: 93–110.

Sordi, M., ed. 1976. *I canali della propaganda nel mondo antico.* Contributi dell'Istituto di Storia Antica 4. Milan.

———, ed. 1979. *Conoscenze etniche e rapporti di convivenza nell'Antichità.* Contributi dell'Istituto di Storia Antica dell'Università Cattolica di Milano 6. Milan.

Sourvinou-Inwood, C. 1993. Early sanctuaries. In *Greek sanctuaries: New approaches,* ed. N. Marinatos and R. Hägg, 1–17. London: Routledge.

Spadea, R. 1991. Il territorio a sud de Savuto: Ancora su Temesa e Terina. In La Genière 1991c, 117–30.

Spivey, N., and S. Stoddart. 1990. *Etruscan Italy.* London: Batsford.

Stanford, W. B. 1992 (1963). *The Ulysses theme.* Reprint ed. Dallas: Spring Publications.

Stansbury-O'Donnell, M. D. 1995. Reading pictorial narrative: The law court scene on the Shield of Achilles. In Carter and Morris 1995, 315–34.

Stroheker, K. F. 1958. *Dionysios I.* Wiesbaden.

Strøm, I. 1971. *Problems concerning the origins and early development of the Etruscan Orientalizing style.* Odense: Universitetsforlag.

———. 1984. Problemi riguardanti l'influso dei paesi mediterranei sulla formazione delle città etrusche e il ruolo aristocrazie. *Opus* 3(2): 355–65.

———. 1990. Relations between Etruria and Campania around 700 B.C. In Descoeudres 1990, 87–97.

Suárez de la Torre, E. 1997. Neoptolemos at Delphi. *Kernos* 10: 153–76.

Sueref, C. 1987. Presupposti della colonizzazione lungo le coste Epirote. In Cabanes 1987b. 29–46.

———. 1989. Presenza micenea in Albania e in Epiro. *Iliria* 19 (2): 65–78.

———. 1991. Comments. In *I Messapi* 1991, 211–12.

Susini, G. 1962. *Fonti per la storia Greca e Romana de Salento.* Bologna: Accademia delle Scienze dell'Istituto di Bologna.

Svenbro, J. 1988. *Phrasikleia: An anthropology of reading in ancient Greece.* Translated by J. Lloyd. Ithaca and London: Cornell University Press.

Symeonoglou, S. 1984. Ἡ ομηρική γεωγραφία της Ιθάκης, in ΙΛΙΑΔΑ ΚΑΙ ΟΔΥΣΣΕΙΑ: ΜΥΘΟΣ ΚΑΙ ΙΣΤΟΡΙΑ, Από τα Πρακτικά του Ζ΄ Συνεδρίου για την Οδύσσεια [September 9–15, 1984], 91–109. Ithaca.

———. 1984–90. Ανασκαφη Ιθακης. *Praktika* 1984, 109–121; 1985, 201–15; 1986, 234–40; 1989, 292–95; 1990, 271–78.

Taplin, O. 1986. Homer's use of Achilles' earlier campaigns in the *Iliad*. In Boardman and Vaphopoulou-Richardson 1986, 15–19.

———. 1992. *Homeric soundings*. Oxford: Clarendon Press.

Taylour, W. 1958. *Mycenaean pottery in Italy and adjacent places*. Cambridge: Cambridge University Press.

Terrosi Zanco, O. 1965. Diomede "Greco" e Diomede italico. *Rend. Linc.* 8: 270–82.

Thalmann, W. 1984. *Conventions of form and thought in early Greek poetry*. Baltimore and London: Johns Hopkins University Press.

Thibau, R. 1964. Italia-Aetolia. *RBPh* 41: 98–102.

Thiersch, H. 1928. Äginetische Studien I. In *Nachrichten von der Gesellschaft der Wissenschaft zu Göttingen* 135–66. Berlin: Weidmann.

Thollard, P. 1987. *Barbarie et civilisation chez Strabon: Etude critique des livres III et IV de la* Géographie. Paris: Les Belles Lettres.

Thom, M. 1990. Tribes within nations: The ancient Germans and the history of modern France. In Bhabha 1990, 23–43.

Thomas, C. G. 1993. *Myth becomes history: Pre-Classical Greece*. Publications of the Association of Ancient Historians 4. Claremont.

Thomas, R. 1992. *Literacy and orality in ancient Greece*. Cambridge: Cambridge University Press.

Todorov, T. 1984. *The conquest of America: The question of the other*. Translated by R. Howard. New York: Harper and Row.

Toms, J. 1986. The relative chronology of the Villanovan cemetery of Quattro Fontanili at Veii. *AION (archeol)* 8: 41–97.

Tonkin, E., M. McDonald, and M. Chapman, eds. 1989. *History and ethnicity*. New York and London: Routledge.

Torelli, M. 1971. Testi e monumenti: Il santuario di Hera a Gravisca. *PP* 136: 44–67.

———. 1977. Il santuario greco di Gravisca. *PP* 177: 398–458.

———. 1984. *Lavinio e Roma*. Rome: Quasar.

———. 1987. *La società etrusca: L'età arcaica, l'età classica*. Rome: La Nuova Italia Scientifica.

———. 1988. Le populazione dell'Italia antica: Società e forme del potere. In *Storia di Roma, vol. 1, Roma in Italia*, 53–74. Turin.

———. 1990a. Gravisca viii. In *Bibliografia topografica della colonizzazaione greca in Italia e nelle isole tirreniche*, ed. G. Nenci and G. Vallet, vol. 8, 172–76. Pisa and Rome: Scuola Normale Superiore di Pisa.

———, ed. 1990b. *Italici in Magna Grecia: Lingua, insediamenti e strutture*. Venosa: Osanna.

Touchefeu-Meynier, O. 1968. *Thèmes odysséens dans l'art antique*. Paris: De Boccard.

Traill, D. A. 1993. *Excavating Schliemann: Collected papers on Schliemann*. Illinois Classical Studies suppl. 4. Atlanta: Scholars Press.

Trump, D. 1966. *Central and southern Italy before Rome*. London: Thames and Hudson.

Tsetskhladze, G. R., and F. De Angelis, eds. 1994. *The archaeology of Greek colonization: Essays dedicated to Sir John Boardman*. Oxford: Oxbow Books.

Turato, F. 1979. *La crisi della città e l'ideologia del selvaggio nell'Atene del V secolo a.C.* Rome: Edizioni dell'Ateneo/Bizzarri.

Uguzzoni, A., and F. Ghinatti. 1968. *Le tavole greche di Eraclea*. Rome: L'Erma di Bretschneider.

Ulf, C. 1990. *Die homerische Gesellschaft: Materialien zur analytischen Beschreibung und historischen Lokalisierung*. Vestigia 43. Munich.

Vagnetti, L., ed. 1982a. *Magna Graecia e mondo miceneo: Nuovi documenti*. Taranto.

———. 1982b. Quindici anni di studi e ricerce sulle relazioni tra il mondo egeo e l'Italia protostorica. In Vagnetti 1982a, 9–40.

———. 1991. L'encadrement chronologique et les formes de la présence égéenne en Italie. In La Genière 1991c, 9–20.

Valenza Mele, N. 1979. Eracle euboico a Cuma: La Gigantomachia e la Via Heraclea. In *Recherches sur les cultes grecs et l'Occident*, ed. E. Lepore and R. Martin, vol. 1, 19–51. Cahiers du Centre Jean Bérard 5. Naples.

Van Compernolle, R. 1989. Il Salento greco nell'epoca arcaica alla luce dei nuovi scavi e delle vechie fonti. In Moscati 1989, 137–56.

———. 1991. Reflexions d'un historien sceptique. In La Genière 1991c, 138–46.

Van Compernolle, T. 1988. Les relations entre Grecs et indigènes d'Apulie à l'Âge du Bronze. *Studi di Antichità* 5: 79–127.

Van der Ploeg, J. 1947. Le role de la tradition orale dans la transmission du texte de l'Ancien Testament. *RBi* 54: 7–41.

Vanotti, G. 1994. Ellanico e l'occidente: Considerazioni sul tema. *Hesperia* 4: 123–34.

———. 1995. *L'altro Enea*. Rome: l' "Erma" di Bretschneider.

Vanschoowinkel, J. 1991. *L'Egée et la Méditerranée orientale à la fin du IIe millénaire: Témoinages archéologiques et sources écrits*. Louvain-la-Neuve and Providence, R.I.: Art and Archaeology Publications/Collège Érasme, Louvain-la-Neuve.

Vansina, J. 1985. *Oral tradition as history*. Madison: University of Wisconsin Press.

Vanstiphout, H. L. J. 1992. Repetition and structure in the Aratta cycle: Their relevance for the orality debate. In Vogelzang and Vanstiphout 1992, 247–64.

Van Wees, H. 1992. *Status warriors: War, violence, and society in Homer and history*. Amsterdam: J. C. Gieben.

———. 1994. The Homeric way of war: The *Iliad* and the Hoplite phalanx. *GR* 41: 131–55.

Vellay, C. 1957. *Les légendes du cycle troyen*. 2 vols. Monaco: Imprimérie Nationale.

Vernant, J-P., and G. Gnoli, eds. 1982. *La mort, les morts dans les sociétés anciennes*. Cambridge and Paris: Cambridge University Press.

Vian, F. 1987. Poésie et géographie: Les retours des Argonautes. *CRAI* 87: 248–66.

Vian, F., and E. Delage. 1981. *Apollonius de Rhodes Argonautiques*. Paris.

Vidal-Naquet, P. 1986. Land and sacrifice in the *Odyssey*: A study of religious and mythical meanings. In *The black hunter: Forms of thought and forms of society in the Greek world*, 15–38. Baltimore: Johns Hopkins University Press.

Vogelzang, M. E., and H. L. J. Vanstiphout, eds. 1992. *Mesopotamian epic literature: Oral or aural?* Lewiston: Edwin Mellen Press.

Vokotopoulou, I. 1984. Η ῎Ηπειρος στόν 8ο και 7ο αἰῶνα π.X. In *Grecia, Italia e Sicilia* 1984, 77–100.

————. 1986. *Vitsa: The cemeteries of a Molossian settlement* (in Greek). 3 vols. Athens.

————. n.d. Greek colonization in the littoral of Chalkidike and Lower Macedonia. In Malkin n.d. Forthcoming.

Vollgraff, W. 1905. Fouilles d'Ithaque. *BCH* 29: 145–68.

Von Bothmer, D. 1994. The Greeks and the sea as reflected in vase painting. In Vryonis 1994, 23–58.

Von Fritz, K. 1940. *Pythagorean politics in southern Italy.* New York: Columbia University Press.

Vryonis, S., ed. 1994. *The Greeks and the sea.* New Rochelle, N.Y.: Aristide D. Caratzas.

Wace, A. J. B., and F. H. Stubbings. 1962. *A companion to Homer.* London: Macmillan.

Wachter, R. 1989. Zur Vorgeschichte des griechischen Alphabets. *Kadmos* 28: 19–78.

Wade-Gery, H. 1952. *The poet of the* Iliad. Cambridge: Cambridge University Press.

Walbank, F. W. 1957–79. *A historical commentary on Polybius.* Oxford: Clarendon Press.

Walcot, P. 1992 (1977). Odysseus and the art of lying. In Emlyn-Jones, Hardwick, and Purkis 1992, 49–62.

Walker, H. J. 1995. *Theseus and Athens.* New York: Oxford University Press.

Warden, P. 1980a. Review of *Die Geometrischen Dreifusse von Olympia,* by M. Maass. *AJA* 84: 385.

————. 1980b. Review of *Les trépieds à cuve clouée,* by C. Rolley. *AJA* 84: 102–3.

Waterhouse, H. 1996. From Ithaca to the *Odyssey. BSA* 91: 301–17.

Wathelet, P. 1988. *Dictionnaire des Troyens de l'Iliade.* Liège.

Watkins, C. 1995. *How to kill a dragon: Aspects of Indo-European poetics.* New York: Oxford University Press.

Webster, T. B. L. 1955. Homer and Geometric vases. *BSA* 50: 38–50.

Wehrli, F. 1953. *Die Schule des Aristoteles: Herakleides Ponticus.* Basel: Schwabe.

Weiler, L. 1968. The Greek and non-Greek world in the Archaic period. *GRBS* 9: 21–29.

Weinstock, S. 1959. Review of *Die trojanischen Urahnen der Römer,* by A. Alföldi. *JRS* 49: 170–71.

Wernicke, I. 1989. *Die Kelten in Italien.* Palingenesia 33. Stuttgart: Franz Steiner.

West, M. L. 1966. *Hesiod:* Theogony. Oxford: Clarendon Press.

————. 1971. *Iambi et elegi graeci.* Oxford: Clarendon Press.

————. 1978. *Hesiod:* Works and days. Oxford: Clarendon Press.

————. 1985. *The Hesiodic* Catalogue of Women. Oxford: Clarendon Press.

————. 1988. The rise of the Greek epic. *JHS* 108: 151–72.

————. 1995. The date of the *Iliad. MH* 52: 203–19.

West, S. R. 1984. Lycophron italicised? *JHS* 104: 127–51.

White, R. 1991. *The middle ground: Indians, empires, and republics in the Great Lakes region, 1650–1815.* Cambridge: Cambridge University Press.

Whitehouse, R. D., and J. B. Wilkins. 1989. Greeks and natives in south-east Italy: Approaches to the archaeological evidence. In *Centre and periphery: Comparative studies in archaeology,* ed. T. C. Champion, 102–26. London: Unwin Hyman.

Whitley, J. 1988. Early states and hero-cults: A re-appraisal. *JHS* 108: 173–82.

————. 1991. *Style and society in Dark-Age Greece.* Cambridge: Cambridge University Press.

Wikén, E. 1937. *Die Kunde der Hellenen von dem Lande und den Volken der Appeninenhalbinsel bis 300 v. Chr.* Lund: H. Ohlssons Buchdr.

Wilamowitz-Möllendorf, U. von. 1899. Lesefrüchte. *Hermes* 34: 601–39.

Wilkes, G. 1994. *Barbarian Asia and the Greek experience.* Baltimore: Johns Hopkins University Press.

Will, E. 1955. *Korinthiaka: Recherches sur l'histoire et la civilisation de Corinthe des origines aux guerres médiques.* Paris: Boccard.

Williams, C. K. 1982. The early urbanization of Corinth. *ASAA* 60: 9–19.

———. 1997. Archaic and Classical Corinth. In *Magna Grecia e Corinto: Atti del trentaquattresimo convegno di studi sulla Magna Grecia, Taranto, 7–11 ottobre 1994,* 31–45. Taranto: Istituto per la Storia e l'Archeologia della Magna Grecia.

Williams, D. 1986. Greek potters and their descendants in Campania and southern Etruria, c. 720–630 B.C. In *Italian Iron Age artefacts in the British Museum,* ed. J. Schwaddling, 295–304. London: British Museum.

———. 1989. Night Rider: The Pilot bronze. *AA:* 529–53.

Winter, F. E. 1971. *Greek fortifications.* London: Routledge and Kegan Paul.

Winter, I. 1995. Homer's Phoenicians: History, ethnography, or literary trope? In Carter and Morris 1995, 247–71.

Wiseman, T. P. 1989. Roman legend and oral tradition. *JRS* 79: 129–37.

———. 1995. *Remus: A Roman myth.* Cambridge: Cambridge University Press.

Wolf, H.-H., and A. Wolf. 1968. *Der Weg des Odysseus: Tunis-Malta-Italien in den Augen Homers.* Tübingen.

Wuilleumier, P. 1968 (1939). *Tarente: Des origines à la conquête romaine.* Paris: Boccard.

Xella, P. 1991. Tradition orale et tradition écrite au Proche-Orient ancien: Le cas des textes mythologiques d'Ugarit. In Baurain, Bonnet, and Krings 1991, 69–89.

Yardeni, A. 1994. Maritime trade and royal accountancy in an erased customs account from 475 BCE on the Ahiqar Scroll from Elephantine. *BASO* 293: 67–78.

Yavetz, Z. 1976. Why Rome? *Zeitgeist* and ancient historians in the early 19th-century Germany. *AJP* 97: 276–96.

Yntema, D. 1982a. Notes on Greek influence on Iron Age Salento. *Studi di Antichità* 3: 83–131.

———. 1982b. Some notes on Iapygian pottery from the Otranto excavation: A preliminary report. *Studi di Antichità* 3: 63–82.

———. 1991. Le ceramiche e l'artigianato del Salento tra l'Età del Ferro e la romanizzazione. In *I Messapi* 1991, 139–84.

Zancani, P. 1974–75. La leggenda di Epeio. *Atti e Memorie della Società Magna Grecia* 15–16: 93–106.

Zancani Montuoro, P., M. W. Stoop, and M. Maaskant Klebrink. 1972. Francavilla Marittima: Varia. *ASMG* 11–12: 9–82.

Zerner, C., ed. 1993. *Wace and Blegen: Pottery as evidence for trade in the Aegean Bronze Age.* Amsterdam: J. C. Gieben.

Zimmerman, J.-L. 1989. *Les chevaux de bronze dans l'art géometrique grec.* Paris: Meyence.

INDEX

Designer:	Ina Clausen
Compositor:	G & S Typesetters, Inc.
Printer:	Thomson-Shore, Inc.
Binder:	Thomson-Shore, Inc.
Text:	10/12 Baskerville
Display:	Baskerville